White Music

THE BARRY WHITE STORY

The Myrtle Press
London

TOM RUBYTHON

White
Music

THE BARRY WHITE STORY

also by Tom Rubython

Life of O'Reilly
- the biography of Tony O'Reilly

The Rich 500
- the 500 Richest people in Britain

The Life of Senna
- the biography of Ayrton Senna

Dog Story - An Anthology
- the life and death of our best friends

Shunt
- the biography of James Hunt

And God Created Burton
- the biography of Richard Burton

In the Name of Glory
- the greatest ever sporting duel

Boy Plunger
- the biography of Jesse Livermore

Fatal Weekend
- the weekend that rocked Formula One

To Larry Nunes
without whose extraordinary foresight
there would have been no Barry White

To Gene Page
without whose genius for arranging music
there would have been no Barry White

To Jack Perry
without whose unqualified support and friendship
there would have been no Barry White

To Glodean White
without whose extraordinary love and devotion
there would have been no Barry White

First published in Great Britain in 2017 and
in the United States of America in 2018
by The Myrtle Press

1 3 5 7 9 10 8 6 4 2

ISBN: 978-0-9934731-7-3
USA ISBN: 978-0-9906199-2-5

Cover image by: Janette Beckman/Getty Images
Typeset in Sabon by: Recursive Music & Media
Cover repro by: Swan Press, Northampton

Printed and bound in England by
CPI Group (UK) Ltd, Croydon
CR0 4YY
United Kingdom

Published by:
The Myrtle Press
Billing Wharf
Cogenhoe
Northamptonshire
NN7 1NH
England
Tel: +44 (0)1604 890208

www.themyrtlepress.com

"I've made my own mark and I've created my own history and as long as music is being played, then so is Barry White."

Barry White
August 2001

Contents

Contents

Contents

Contents

Contents

PART FIVE
FOUR YEARS OF PHYSICAL DECLINE AND DEATH

POSTSCRIPT
THE LEGACY OF MUSIC TO MAKE LOVE TO

Appendices

Acknowledgements

By Tom Rubython

Many individuals in London, New York and Los Angeles have assisted me with the writing and researching of this book. Many sought anonymity and some even preferred to communicate through third parties – such is the nature of writing non-fiction biographies, even of people who are long departed. They simply prefer it that way to avoid unnecessary upset to family or friends. Not every life, or even any life, is all pretty.

The White family, by and large, preferred not to assist in this book. Why? They are probably preparing their own version of Barry White's life to come out at some time in the future. When that might be I do not know. It could be a long time, as inevitably family-approved, ghost-written biographies are notoriously difficult and painful to put together and often not worth the effort as they become so compromised and fail to satisfy anybody. Individual family members, almost inevitably, tend to fall out with the ghost writer they unanimously chose so enthusiastically just a few months before. I don't know if that is the case with the White family but I would bet that it was the reason they chose generally not to assist.

But that lack of co-operation proved not to be the impediment I first feared it would be. The four family members I did manage to interview told me wildly different versions of the same events. Many of the different versions of the same story were also at odds with what I knew to be the truth so, in the end, I resisted having too much contact with any family members to avoid confusing myself and readers of this book. For those few who did assist, you have my sincere thanks and I hope that breaking ranks, albeit anonymously, has caused you no lasting problems.

Notwithstanding, I would like to mention personally: Tom Springfield, Gerry Lincoln, Kennedy Jopling, Maria Lewis, Jeffrey Knight, Sandra Sullivan and Don Goodman for their invaluable first-hand insight into Barry White's life.

ACKNOWLEDGEMENTS

I would also like to thank Clive Davis for looking over certain chapters that concerned him, and also Elliot Goldman for second-guessing his old boss. Unfortunately neither Clive nor Elliot could recall the events that came first-hand from Barry White himself – but it was more than 40 years ago. It was interesting that Clive expressed great regret that he was never able to work with Barry White – what might have been?

Once again the best source of stories proved to be working journalists who had interviewed Barry White when he was alive. And there proved to be a great many of them. It seemed that Barry White never turned down an interview or ignored a journalistic request for a sit-down conversation. It is clear that he loved getting comfortable for an interview and talking about himself. As long as he wasn't asked about individual songs he was happy to talk and nothing was ever off the record. Some of those reporters had retained old tape recordings, or full transcripts of the original interviews, and some of these tapes were made available to me.

Many, many times Barry was far too frank with a writer and it was clear over the years that he had been saved from himself by reporters who chose not to write what they had heard. Many times I chose to ignore some injudicious words, however genuinely expressed. It became very clear to me that Barry White was not made for the politically correct world we live in today. I thank all the people, too numerous to list individually, who made the valuable material available to me. I would also like to single out the website called 'Rock's Backpages' (www.rocksbackpages.com). This extraordinary site, which justifiably calls itself 'the ultimate library of music writing', proved to be just that. It contained just about every article ever written about Barry White in the past 50 years, as well as thousands of other musicians. The $300 it costs to subscribe annually is well worth it. Also I must mention Discogs, a pretty amazing website set up by Kevin Lewandowski in 2000 and owned by Oregon-based Zink Media Inc. It describes itself, accurately, as the largest online database of recorded music, and it truly is. It says that it lists more than eight million separate releases by nearly 4.9 million artists, across more than a million recording labels. By my reckoning that is no exaggeration.

Not only does it extensively list every version of very piece of recorded music in existence, together with detailed information, but it also includes

ACKNOWLEDGEMENTS

multiple photographs of album covers, front and back, sleeve, labels and artists. It is also an online marketplace to buy probably everything that it lists, including some of the most obscure vinyl music recordings you could mention. I picked up a few rare Barry White recordings via its service. The database is also very accessible and largely free to its users. This book would be much the poorer without Discogs, that is for sure.

Michelle Edgson was very helpful in going through public records in Galveston and Los Angeles and digging into the early history of the Carter and White families. It is truly amazing how many Carters there were in Galveston in the early part of the century, and finding out which one was which took a lot of digging around. Equally, Melvin White's family life was far from straightforward, but Michelle got there in the end.

I naturally also leaned heavily on Barry White's own autobiography published in 1999, co-written with Marc Eliot. Unfortunately, many of the stories described in that book were at odds with how other people remembered them. But I think I managed to sort that out and it proved to be a valuable source of insight. Marc Eliot did a great job in what were probably quite difficult circumstances.

I must also acknowledge the late Larry Nunes. It's unusual to thank someone for their help who has been dead for nearly 40 years but without Nunes there would have been no Barry White and no book. In 1972, Nunes gave Barry White the modern-day equivalent of a quarter of a million dollars to record his first album. White was unknown and unproven and it was a leap of faith for Nunes – no one else would have done it. So thank you Larry, wherever you are, for giving the world Barry White.

Also thank you to Janette Beckman for the beautiful cover photograph.

On page 580, the very last page in this book, I have selected my own favourite Barry White ballads, instrumentals and pop songs, 30 of his songs in all. I thought you might like to know but please excuse the indulgence.

Lastly I would like to thank personally my close colleagues, David Peett, Kiran Toor, Eddie Broughton, Mary Hynes and Will Adams for their input over the past 12 months; the efforts of all were unstinting, although in the words that follow any errors or omissions are naturally my responsibility alone.

Tom Rubython

Preface

By Tom Rubython

When the Barry White phenomenon happened in 1973, it seemingly came out of nowhere. I was 17 years old and had just passed my driving test – which was significant only because cassette tape players had just started to be installed in cars. This revolutionised listening to recorded music, which had previously been impossible in a car, unless you owned an expensive and unwieldy 8-track player. So the first thing I did was install a cassette player in the old blue Fiat 600 that was my much-loved first car. And the first cassette I listened to in that car was, inevitably, Barry White.

Stone Gon' is the first Barry White album I can really remember; the music was just so memorable.

Back then, like most people in England, I had little idea who Barry White was. I loved his music but didn't think too much about him. And everyone around me seemed to be listening to him as well. If you were born between 1950 and 1960 that was your fate, and I suspect that my personal experiences would have been absolutely typical of the time.

For people born in those years, Barry White was the soundtrack to our teenage years – of that there is no doubt.

It truly was a different kind of music – listening to it now I just wonder where he got the melody and the lyrics for *Girl It's True Yes I'll Always Love You*. Back then the combination of his magical compositions, his extraordinary lyrics and his totally unique-sounding voice had never been heard before. Listening to *Stone Gon'* on my iPhone, it sounds just as good today as it did on cassette tape back in the day. Gene Page's arrangements have proved to be so far ahead of their time. I think it's true to say that if Barry White came along today and recorded exactly the same music, the same success would happen all over again – how many artists can you say that about?

So I bought *Stone Gon'*, then his first album, *I've Got So Much to Give*, followed by *Can't Get Enough* (the really big one). Then of course came *Just Another Way To Say I Love You* the following year.

It was an absolutely magical time, and back then we couldn't wait for the next album to appear in the record shops. In between his solo albums we were buying the Love Unlimited albums and those of the Love Unlimited Orchestra as well. As his music took hold, I remember continually thinking, who is this man Barry White and will he continue making this music for ever? We couldn't quite believe it.

Barry White was successful because he was good at all the requisites of good music. He could compose powerful melodies, write strong lyrics, and sing those songs beautifully.

His voice ranks in the top ten male singers of all time; he is up there alongside Sinatra, Crosby and Pavarotti. But none of those artists also wrote their own melodies and lyrics, and that is what made him different. If you want to hear the true power of White's voice, listen to him sing one of his songs in a foreign language; the true power of his vocal sound is unleashed and it is revelatory. I didn't understand that power until I listened to *She's Everything To Me* sung in Spanish as *Ella Es Todo Para Mi*.

In the first ten years there were 23 brilliant albums, and I bought them all on cassette; then when CDs arrived I bought them all again. And when the iPod came, I bought them all over again, this time in electronic format. My guess is that, over the years, I have spent well over £2,000 ($2,500) buying his albums in vinyl, cassette, CD and electronic format, and I am sure there are millions of people out there just like me. His heirs will certainly never need to work again, and neither will their children and grandchildren.

And so fast forward 35 years.

One thing I am certain about is that I wouldn't have attempted to write this book unless I had been around to experience the moment, first hand, when Barry White burst onto the scene in 1973. I just wouldn't have been qualified.

But fortunately I was.

Where did the idea come from to write this book? I don't know –

somehow it just happened. It seemed like it was meant to happen, but who really knows? All I know is that somehow I just started writing it and, a year later, here I am writing the Preface – with the manuscript about to go off to the fact-checkers, sense-checkers, sub-editors and every other sort of production expert who gets involved at this stage of a book's life.

But I am truly glad the task has fallen to me, as Barry White was a great man in so many ways, despite the many flaws in his character that you will read about in this book. The good outweighed the bad, many times over, as I was gradually to discover.

Writing books is never easy. No one who does it for a living embarks upon writing any sort of book lightly. I am used to writing about racing drivers, businessmen and actors. This is my first biography of a musician, and I decided right away that it should be primarily about the music. I have become really frustrated in the past, reading musicians' biographies that don't provide much focus on the music, and that, to me, seems to be the point. In truth, when all is said and done, a musician is his music and little else.

To make good on this, where possible, I decided that I would devote a whole chapter to each of his 20 solo albums, and a separate chapter to each of the significant Love Unlimited and Love Unlimited Orchestra albums. So this book has been built around his music.

I have listened to Barry White's music all my life but this book required total immersion. So the first task was to reacquaint myself with the 35 albums he recorded in his lifetime: the 20 solo albums, the 10 by the Love Unlimited Orchestra and the five by the Love Unlimited girl band. I carefully listened to it all, from 1972 to 1999, some of it, much of it, many times over. From that I think I got a real and full perspective on Barry White's career and its ups and downs.

After that I put together a detailed wall-chart containing every one of his albums in chronological order to provide a sort of road map of his musical life. And when that was done, putting together a chapter list, the heart of any book, was relatively easy.

Overall, looking back, it was relatively simple and if you are already familiar with the Barry White story you will know it had five distinct parts: 1) his childhood and youth, 2) his 12-year struggle to make it, 3) the 10 years at the very top of his game 4) the 17 years of slow and gradual decline, and lastly 5) the four years of physical decline and his death.

But I must admit it took me a long time to distil it down to that.

He was born in 1944 and had a troubled youth up until 1960 when he finally saw the light. His epiphany led into a 12-year struggle to succeed, culminating in 1972. He finally broke through at the age of 28, first with Love Unlimited's debut single, *Walking In The Rain*, then his own debut album *I've Got So Much To Give*.

The success between 1972 and 1981 was unprecedented, as was his decline from 1982 to 1999. Ill health effectively then marked the end of his mainstream recording career, and he died in 2003 at the age of 58.

No one could ever say that Barry White's life was not interesting. His childhood and youth were punctuated by parental problems, crime sprees, gang membership and a spell in prison. His struggle to succeed was punctuated by marriage and the birth of no fewer than four children before he was 20 years old, combined with endless career knockbacks. The ten years of success were as golden as they could be, this time happily punctuated by marriage and the uniting of his disparate family under one roof. The run of success started with the single *Walking In the Rain With the One I Love* in 1972 and ended with his 12th solo album, a duet with his wife, fittingly entitled *Barry & Glodean*, released in 1981.

The decline, and the release of 11 more albums, was almost continually painful, albeit now softened by money. It was exacerbated by, among other things, a marriage split and the domestic upheaval when the family home and the house of his dreams collapsed after an earthquake. The end was marked by five years of poor health and a struggle to survive, during which he somehow managed to carry on touring.

But it is for those ten years between 1972 and 1981 that he will be remembered, for as long as music is listened to. During that period Barry White was so prolific. He produced music on a conveyor belt, literally churning it out. He always claimed that once an album was signed off, he would never listen to it again. Whether or not that was true is debatable, but it was a nice neat answer to any journalist who wanted to question him about an individual album or a particular song – subjects he quickly tired of discussing. He didn't mind discussing his music as a whole, but individual songs – never. I suspect that the reasons were very personal.

Looking back now, 40 years later, it would have been nice to know exactly where *Girl It's True, Yes I'll Always Love You* came from. I think I know, but not with anywhere near enough certainty to be able write it down with any authority. It would have been guesswork and I tried to avoid that. But it would have been nice to know.

Some pieces of Barry White's music are so exquisite that it is surprising that they have not become classics, although the reason they haven't is simple enough. The masterpieces became hidden by the sheer mass of his music. And that is a great shame as he deserves to be up there with Mozart and Beethoven as a pure creator of non-vocal sound. Vocally, he also deserves to be up there, as his vocal talents were as good as any artist who ever got up to sing, and that includes Frank Sinatra, Luciano Pavarotti, Karen Carpenter and Barbra Streisand.

It was that combination of talents, the writing, the composing and the singing that made him so great. It was also what let him down.

Barry White boasted about his profligacy. But the truth is that there was simply too much of his music in too short a space of time, and it demeaned the individual pieces. If only someone had told him to slow down, life could have turned out very differently for him and he might even be alive today.

Russ Regan, who headed 20th Century Records, and released White's music during the glory years, may not have had good ears, but he was a very astute handler of artists. He restricted Barry White to releasing no more than three singles a year and rationed his output. After White threw off Regan's shackles and took charge of his own career, he doubled that output and the decline began. Regan may have been much criticised for his musical judgement, but his commercial instincts were unquestionable and he was essential to White's early success.

What happened post Regan was very damaging and only served to shorten his career and his life.

Sadly, the *Barry & Glodean* album proved to be the high water mark; after that the Barry White phenomenon ran out of steam and nothing was ever quite the same again.

With the benefit of hindsight we know that Barry lost his way and became confused when each of his albums after 1981 sold fewer than the one before it. He failed to realise that this was the natural way of the world and eventually happened to every artist, whoever they were.

This lack of understanding hastened his decline as he tried to change his musical style to meet the challenge, when he should have just carried on doing what he did.

At some point in the mid-eighties it appeared that he stopped reading from his own script and started reading from somebody else's. And like most of his original fans of the mid-seventies, I grew tired and exasperated with the direction that Barry White's music took.

So over the next 18 years his music slowly and inexorably deteriorated. Very little of what he did after 1981 was as good, and many critics believe that he should have stopped at that point. But had he done so, we would have been denied such great songs as *Whatever We Had We Had*, and songs like *Beware* would never have been written. The *Beware* album in 1981 proved to be the turning point. It was definitely the last album that satisfied Barry White fans.

Beware marked the start of the decline – only three of the ten tracks were good enough to be called Barry White songs. On *Change,* a year later, there were only two. Likewise *Dedicated* in 1983.

For the next four years there were no Barry White albums, but time healed nothing and when he returned in 1987 with *The Right Night & Barry White* it contained nothing that his fans wanted to hear. Unsurprisingly, sales were disastrous. The next album, *The Man Is Back*, was just as bad – as was *Put Me In Your Mix*. Only with *The Icon Is Love* did a sort of recovery begin and sales took off again. But it was a very brief respite as his final album, *Staying Power*, was arguably his worst, in my opinion. Ironically it gained him a couple of Grammys, the first of his career, proving that the entertainment awards system is diabolically creatively corrupt.

PREFACE

So why did it go so horribly wrong? During the writing of this book I had plenty of time to think about that, and I have tried to analyse what happened to throw Barry White so terribly off-course at the relatively young age of 37.

The major influence on the decline appears to have been his misguided attempts to modernise his music. It was wrong, wrong, wrong. What he should have done was defy the trend and go back and keep on doing what he had been doing since 1972. He should also have dug deep into soul's extensive treasure trove of music to find songs to cover.

The few songs he did cover in his career proved to be sensational. Almost everyone agrees that his cover version of Billy Joel's *Just The Way You Are* was far better than the original. Likewise he turned the Four Tops hit, *Standing in the Shadows of Love*, into a classical masterpiece. Equally, there was never a better version of *Volare* than on his album *Put Me In Your Mix*. No one has performed any of these three songs better, before or since.

But they were literally the only mainstream songs that Barry White covered. And that, for me, is the tragedy of his career. If, instead of focusing on trying to reinvent himself as a hip-hop star, he had devoted himself to creating new versions of old songs, then anything would have been possible for the second half of his life. Many classic soul songs cried out to be given the Barry White treatment. Every day, while I was writing this book, I thought about the great songs he could have covered and the music that we lost because he went off in the wrong direction.

It pains me to think about it now.

For instance, Frank Loesser's old classic, *Baby It's Cold Outside,* covered by so many but only mastered by Petula Clark and Rod McKuen, would have been truly sensational sung as a duet by Barry and Glodean White. There were many others destined never to be.

Likewise he missed out on many great opportunities for duets. The few he did, with Tina Turner, Lisa Stansfield and Luciano Pavarotti, were magical moments for his army of fans.

It occurs to me that things could have been very different if he had signed up with the legendary Clive Davis of Columbia and later the Arista label instead of Russ Regan's 20th Century Records. Davis had the best 'ears' in the business, and Regan arguably the worst. Undoubtedly Davis would have steered White towards performing other artists' material. In his own excellent autobiography, 'The Soundtrack of my Life', Davis explains how Barry Manilow only wanted to record his own compositions but how Davis persuaded him that was not good for his career – likewise with Aretha Franklin and many others. Barry White needed that kind of advice, and if his last 18 years had been spent covering other people's music, a huge treasure trove of wonderful songs could have been left behind for posterity. As it was, they were 18 years wasted.

With the benefit of hindsight and the passing of many years, I am very clear that it was Barry White who changed and not the musical taste of his fans. We would have continued buying his music for ever if he had kept delivering it. There was a sort of special contract between him and his fans. But he took advice from people who should have known what they were talking about, but in the end never really understood what Barry White and his music was. As I said at the beginning, you had to be born at a certain time and with a certain mindset to really understand what White's music was about.

It was much the same story with his touring and live performances. He started off brilliantly with a three-part act that stunned and delighted audiences. But ever so gradually his live performances began to decline. Love Unlimited broke up and was replaced by talented but nondescript backing singers. Likewise the Love Unlimited Orchestra slowly dissolved and lost its identity to the point where it didn't really exist anymore. It was replaced by some excellent session musicians, but sadly they could never be the real thing.

So his concerts became just him and a supporting cast, which never made as much sense. But, having said that, no one who went to a Barry White concert ever complained of a bad experience – they simply loved it, even at the open-air Villa Park soccer ground in 1975 when the heavens fell in, or in Sydney in 2000 when everything electrical that could go wrong did go wrong. People forgave Barry White anything because they loved him and they knew he loved them back.

PREFACE

When it all hit the buffers in the mid-eighties, we never saw Barry White at his best again. There were smatterings of the old brilliance in the 12 years that followed, but they were very sparse.

You will have gathered from the above that this book is not a hagiography, but neither is it a hatchet job. I hope I have done his life justice and told it exactly as it was. I've tried very hard not only to record what happened but also to understand why it happened, both good and bad. I believe I have explained and chronicled his life and his music as well as any biographer could. I am certain that Barry White will look down from heaven and like this book and say to himself, "Yeah, that is what happened".

For the most part his life was an open book. He was always open and honest and I found only some parts impenetrable. For instance, no one has ever explained what happened to cause the split with Glodean, a woman he clearly loved deeply until the end of his life. The few people who know have never shared that knowledge and it will probably remain a secret for ever. When asked, Glodean just smiles – it is a secret they will both take to their graves.

What Barry White achieved between 1972 and 1981 was nothing short of extraordinary, but the rest of his life was a continuing struggle to find his way professionally and privately. In many ways the struggle was the negative reward of success.

His final years were not pleasant ones. And what transpired on his deathbed was truly upsetting, to say the least. As Barry White Jnr so poignantly puts it in the last words of this book: "My father during his career was about love and made love for the world through his music, but at the end he was denied love for himself."

So true and so sad.

Tom Rubython
Olney Park
Buckinghamshire
8th September 2017

xxviii

CHAPTER 1

The End Came

Death of a maestro

2003

At just after 10 o'clock on the morning of Friday 4th July 2003 Glodean White picked up the telephone by her husband's bedside at Cedars-Sinai Medical Center. She dialled the number of Michael Jackson's ranch 100 miles up the coast in Santa Barbara where staff were preparing celebrations for Independence Day. A maid answered and quickly put the call through to her boss. When she heard Jackson say hello, Glodean whispered into the receiver: "Barry's gone." Jackson reportedly dropped the receiver and slumped down in a chair, unable to take in the news, as the maid, who had quietly come into the room, took over the call. The maid asked for her number and told the newly-widowed Glodean that Michael would "have to call her back."

Jackson was the first to know of White's death outside the family and it would be almost a day later when the rest of the world found out. He should not have been surprised at the news, as two days before Glodean had called and told him the end was near. But Jackson simply hadn't believed it and was apparently quite unable to comprehend a world without Barry White.

Half an hour later Michael Jackson called Glodean back and said: "Let me know when you are burying him. I want to be there." Glodean told him it was her husband's wish to be buried at sea off the coast of Santa Monica. Jackson paused and didn't speak for 10 seconds. Then he told her she should charter a motor yacht called 'Mojo' for the ceremony. He paused again and told her to "leave it to me." Glodean whispered into the receiver: "Make it next Saturday."

Sure enough at midday on Saturday 12th July, the 100-foot yacht was waiting alongside the quay at Santa Monica to take aboard the funeral party.

Jackson's affection for Barry White should have been no surprise – the two men were the best of friends and often found themselves in each other's company discussing the delicate intricacies of making music. Jackson used to say that Barry White was one of the few men who truly understood him and that White had made a huge impact on his music. He told friends that he would often provide a solution to a tricky musical problem. Jackson and White understood music intimately and were totally 'in synch' with each other's taste. Jackson could spend hours going through in detail how White had arranged the French horns on one of his album tracks. The affection was mutual, and sometimes White would be in the studio when Jackson was recording, helping to arrange the music, often with his friend Gene Page alongside him. He told anyone who wanted to listen that there was "no one kinder, no one more understanding, no one wiser and no one more generous" than his friend Barry. He added: "The maestro is gone but his music and melodic melodies will linger on forever. He was my friend and will be sorely missed."

Michael Jackson's shocked reaction to the maestro's death would be played out by millions of people across America the following day. When the baby boomers woke up from their Independence Day hangovers and turned on the radio and opened their newspapers that Saturday morning, they heard the news that the songmeister of almost two generations of Americans was gone at 58 years old. By the time they heard, White had already been dead for 24 hours. But the exact date and time of his death was uncertain. He had apparently died on Thursday evening but had somehow been kept alive on a machine after appearing to survive two Code Blue emergency interventions during the Thursday night.

What was strange was the fact that The New York Times knew he was dead long before any other news outlet. It carried the news of his demise first, on its newswire service, before midnight on 3rd July. It seems that its Los Angeles bureau had been tipped off by one of its sources at Cedars-Sinai that White had died. But the source had got it slightly wrong as he was still alive but had no chance of surviving. It was only the skill of the doctors and a heart/lung machine that was technically keeping him alive.

The New York Times had clearly been kept up to date about White's condition by hospital staffers – but it had jumped the gun. All the major newspapers had paid contacts at Cedars-Sinai, but The New York Times paid the most and therefore got to know the most, the quickest. The hospital turned a blind eye to the paper, which was always first with the news when a celebrity died there. The hospital's management had long ago tried and failed to put an end to the practice of leaking private medical information to journalists and finally accepted it for what it was.

The headline on its obituary was 'Disco-era crooner dies at 58', which instantly kicked off a firestorm. The newspaper's switchboard was jammed for hours afterwards and no one appeared happy with the description of Barry White as a 'crooner'. To his millions of fans around the world, White was much more than a 'disco-era crooner'. To them, he was 'the man' and would remain 'the man' to eternity. In fact, White's fans were highly insulted by the word 'crooner' to describe a man whose music they had grown up with.

It was not all they were insulted about. The writer of the obituary went on to call White "as rough as his songs were smooth" and accused him of creating "fantasy worlds of opulence and desire." It was not what the maestro's fans wanted to read, and people across America were very cross with their newspaper that day, especially as many of them had spent the previous day with their children celebrating the Fourth of July. Many of those children were no fantasy and had been created in the mid-seventies to the sound of the music of Barry White.

The delay in announcing his death was caused by disagreements between family and non-family members of White's entourage. The family were bitter over the way the last few months of White's life had been controlled by his long-time partner and live-in girlfriend Katherine Denton and his business manager Abby Schroeder.

Ever since he had entered Cedars-Sinai the previous October, Denton and Schroeder had controlled the situation. They were in a position of power because White had previously signed over a power of attorney to Schroeder's husband Aaron, his business manager for 30 years. But the 77-year-old Schroeder himself had been sidelined by a rare form of dementia and confined to a nursing home. The power of attorney was actually granted to Schroeder's company, A. Schroeder International Inc, and Abby, as co-director, was given authority over Barry White's affairs. More importantly, in the absence of her husband, Abby Schroeder controlled and had sole signing powers over all of

White's bank accounts and his money. Schroeder paid all the hospital bills.

Abby Schroeder had to decide where her loyalties lay and who in the family she should take orders from. It was by no means clear whether she should answer to White's estranged wife, Glodean, or Katherine Denton. She took the view that she was responsible to the latter rather than his wife or his children.

The conflicts were endless; most of White's children were older than Denton, in their late thirties, and Shaherah, probably closest to her father, was only five years younger. They all felt that they had a bigger connection with their father and certainly felt very little in common with her. Whereas Glodean had become a mother figure to all eight of Barry White's children, Denton had connected with none of them in that way. While White was in good health none of this mattered, but now his dependency created a new situation that no one was familiar with or really knew how to handle. Emotions ran very high and relationships were quickly shattered.

That was less of a problem to Glodean White, who had split up from her husband 15 years before, than it was to his children. Glodean respected her husband's new life and naturally took a back seat. But in taking Denton's side, Schroeder had deeply upset Barry White's children.

Worse, having obtained Schroeder's loyalty, Denton seemingly set out to deliberately alienate his eight children and sought total control over her boyfriend's medical attention. Whenever challenged, she argued that she was effectively his wife, although they had never married.

Glodean kept her distance and remained neutral, but the children, headed by his eldest son Barry Jnr (by his first wife) and Shaherah, his eldest daughter by Glodean, believed that they should be involved in any decisions about their father. Denton didn't see it that way.

The children took the view that Denton was less interested in keeping their father alive than what would happen afterwards. But she couldn't have known that White had not made a new will for 20 years, ensuring that control of his estate would go to Glodean after his death.

White's death at the age of 58 wasn't a surprise. Everyone in the music business knew that he had suffered from high blood pressure for most of his adult life, which had only been diagnosed at the age of 50. Doctors described the condition as 'chronic' and the late diagnosis meant that a lot of damage had been done to his organs. It had eventually put pressure on his kidneys and they had started to fail. His illnesses were compounded by his three-packs-a-day smoking habit. He had got through more than 60 cigarettes a day ever since he had started smoking at 13 years of age, and he was a hopeless nicotine addict. And he continued smoking even after suffering a stroke.

In a last-ditch effort to cure the problem he had been admitted to Cedars-Sinai the previous October and had spent almost 10 months there, intermittently, spending hours every evening hooked up to a dialysis machine, being kept alive. This continued until May 2003, when he was hospitalised permanently as his condition worsened and he lost his mobility.

There was continual hope that a pair of new kidneys would restore his life to something approaching normalcy. But White's children thought that Katherine Denton had not pushed hard enough to get the life-saving kidneys that White desperately needed. Glodean White was more circumspect and said: "His life could have been saved with an organ transplant."

But the maestro was not helped by being hospitalised in California, which was obsessive about applying the 'first come, first served' principle, which meant that no one, no matter how famous or how rich, could skip the queue for new organs. Glodean said: "One common misconception is that rich people are moved to the top of the recipient list faster than poor people. The fact is that the only things that determine how long a patient must wait to receive a transplant are blood type and the length of time a patient has been on the waiting list and the severity of the patient's illness."

The hope had always been that White could survive long enough to get to the top of the queue. But those hopes were dashed in May 2003 when he suffered a stroke that severely weakened him and made it unlikely that he could survive an operation to replace his kidneys. His right side had become almost completely paralysed, exacerbating his condition. After that happened there was little hope that the medical board of the National Kidney Registry would sanction releasing two precious kidneys to a man in his condition. When that happened death was inevitable, although his children refused to give up hope.

When the news of White's death filtered out around the hospital, the nurses who had looked after him on three separate shifts were devastated and there were lots of tears. They had got used to having him around and being entertained by his distinctive voice. Sometimes he would even sing to them, and some had spent long hours sitting on his bed listening to his stories, even seeking his advice about their own inevitably complicated love lives. In that respect, Barry White had an answer to everything.

After White's death, it was left to Ned Shankman, his long-standing personal manager, to issue a press release announcing the news on Friday evening. Shankman's release said that White had died of kidney failure caused by high blood pressure at 9:30am on the morning of 4th July. The coroner's report would later cite the cause as 'acute renal failure'.

Shankman was economical with the truth and told reporters that the end had come suddenly and unexpectedly on Friday morning. He said that White had died in his private room at Cedars-Sinai surrounded by doctors who were attempting to revive him after his heart stopped. Shankman said: "It was just a series of things brought on by his high blood pressure, which triggered kidney failure and a mild stroke and ongoing low-grade infections that they just couldn't get on top of."

The New York Daily News and most of America's newspapers didn't have the story until a full 24 hours after The New York Times newswire had first reported it. They had held back from running it until official confirmation had come. Consequently, the New York Daily News's obituary was more reflective. The paper had used the extra time well and had more detail and a better perspective. It precisely caught the mood of America, writing that White had a "velvet purr and seductive lyrics which put millions in the mood" and that "his buttery baritone was musical Viagra." The word 'crooner' had been expunged and he was described as a 'soul singer' – which was much more to the liking of his fans.

Most of the obituaries on 5th July were celebratory, and Ned Shankman appeared on all the American network television channels talking about Barry White. Notably he told CNN: "He had a most unique voice, a most unique appearance. He was just a very unique guy."

The news of his death did not reach Europe until Saturday lunchtime, when it led all the bulletins after midday. White had been very popular in Britain and his English fans were stunned, having had no inkling that he was ill.

When they heard the news, tributes poured in from his friends and fellow musicians. Stevie Wonder said: "Barry always talked about love and loving someone and his love for a woman. Every song was a celebration about love, which to me is a great legacy to leave behind." Dionne Warwick said: "He always called me 'Lady D' and I liked that. I used to open my show with *Never, Never, Gonna Give You Up*. He was always cognisant of ladies being ladies and I love him." Aretha Franklin said: "Barry was one of my favourite artists and it was miraculous what he did with his music. Gene Page would talk about Barry all the time. He was definitely the maestro."

Meanwhile, as the day wore on back at Cedars-Sinai it became apparent that White had left no current will. When that became clear, Glodean and the children seized control and virtually threw out Schroeder and Denton.

The lack of an updated will was not good news for Denton, and there was more to come. It was also quickly revealed that White had never divorced Glodean. It became clear that a shocked Denton had not known that White was not divorced, and she had believed herself to be his fiancée.

Observers concluded that the lack of an up-to-date will must have been deliberate. It was thought to be his way of ensuring that his natural children and Glodean would control his estate after he died. Despite their estrangement, Glodean was the love of his life and he trusted her totally.

When she learned the truth, Denton realised that she was in a very difficult position. Her source of money was cut off and she was left living in White's house but with no income. She said that White had assured her that she would be taken care of, together with their soon to be born daughter, Barriana.

However, there was some doubt whether Barriana was actually White's daughter. Glodean considered that her husband had been too ill to have fathered a child in the last year of his life, and so did a lot of other people. When a DNA test was finally carried out, it revealed that White was not the father of Barriana. Not surprisingly, Glodean sought to write Katherine Denton out of her husband's life story and legal action would follow that would rumble on for years afterwards over the division of the estate.

Barry White's body was quickly cremated and Michael Jackson, true to his word, chartered the yacht 'Mojo' exclusively for the family to use on the afternoon of Saturday 12th July. White had long expressed a desire to be buried at sea: "I want to return to the place where all of life once came. I want to be wrapped in a simple shroud and placed within the great natural underwater peace that engulfs so much of this troubled and turbulent planet." State regulations prevented his body being tipped into the sea as he had instructed, so Glodean made the decision to cremate him and scatter his ashes together with one of his famous silk handkerchiefs. She thought that would fulfil his wishes.

It was a bizarre occasion. The 1969-built 'Mojo' was usually chartered for weddings, and this was the first time it had hosted a funeral. It had previously been used by Brad Pitt, Jennifer Aniston and Ben Stiller. It had also featured in episodes of Colombo and Baywatch. The most famous charters had involved former President Richard Nixon, who used it to go for cruises with world leaders after he left the White House.

So, eight days after his death, more than 40 people boarded the yacht to witness the scattering of Barry White's ashes. Most of the party were family and Jackson made sure that he stayed close to Glodean. Wearing sunglasses, he was shielded from the strong sunlight by an aide with an umbrella.

The assembled press and media watching from the shore and in small boats were very surprised to see Jackson there. They were, like most people, unaware of the close 25-year bond that had existed between the two men.

That relationship had started in the late seventies when Michael had wanted to leave the Jackson Five to go solo. His record company, CBS, and his own family were strongly against him going off on his own.

Barry White had known his elder brother, Jermaine, for several years, having met and bonded with him at a music convention in 1975. When 20-year-old Michael announced that he would record a new album, *Off the Wall*, on his own, White became the unofficial mediator, a man both sides fully trusted. As White recalled in his own memoirs written in 1999: "Michael felt I was one of the few people he could trust because he knew that no matter what, I would be honest with him. He loved the fact that I was afraid of nothing and nobody, that I was my own man, something he aspired to be."

The desire for a solo career had created a serious crisis for the whole Jackson family and, as it came to a head, Michael had gone to White's house at

Sherman Oaks for counsel, as White recalled: "I was the one he called when he got into trouble at his label. He came over and that night we talked for five and a half hours about the situation. He cried throughout, because, he said, they'd hurt his feelings so badly. All he wanted was a fair shot at a solo career. And I decided to try and help him get it."

White told Jackson that his first responsibility was to himself and his own music. He effectively told him that he had a duty to split from his family and go solo: "I told him he had to work to get the album he wanted made, no matter what. I told him he'd never know if he could be a hit as a solo artist unless he went ahead and gave it his best shot."

White's feelings about the situation chimed exactly with Jackson's, but what should be done about the family and CBS? "I told him not to listen to anyone or anything but his own calling."

Jackson also told White that he wanted Quincy Jones to produce and arrange his first solo album. White simply told him to be "ruthless" and "go out and get him", regardless of what anyone else thought or felt.

It's no secret that Jackson wanted to take on White to be his personal manager. But that was a step too far for Barry White, as he knew that would be alienating the Jackson family, one of the most powerful in show business, as well as CBS, the most powerful record company in the world.

White told Jackson that he would be his mentor and unofficial adviser for free as long as it remained a secret between them. Jackson started to visit Sherman Oaks every day during the crisis. As White remembered: "He wanted to know the secret of how I'd gotten to control my own music and publishing, the production of my own records and therefore my own destiny. I tried to educate him so that he could understand how the music world operated, to be a little more of a businessman and a little less the temperamental artist."

The advice and the strategy recommended by White worked like a dream, and Jackson got his way and recorded *Off the Wall* with Quincy Jones as his producer. White secretly helped with the arrangements and many of them were used in the final cut of the album. As White said: "It was a good feeling and I only took that as a compliment." *Off the Wall* eventually sold 20 million copies worldwide and went platinum eight times over. Quincy Jones subsequently produced the *Thriller* album, which made him a very rich man.

Quincy Jones never forgot Barry White's recommendation and his contribution to his career. He wrote a song called *The Secret Garden* especially for his friend, and said of him: "Barry had more fibre than any singer/speaker I've ever worked with. I like to think of that as a metaphor for his character and his appeal; he was truly an original and there will never be another."

With White's help, Michael Jackson went on to become one of the savviest pop stars ever, using financial leverage in a way never seen before in the music industry to buy the ABC music publishing company, which included the Beatles catalogue. He took complete control over his own music, which enabled him to become the world's first posthumous billionaire. He used White's financial blueprint to achieve it, which is why he was alongside the family that day in July 2003, and why he had got the first phone call from Glodean to tell him of Barry White's death.

When they were a mile out to sea, Jackson and White's children gathered on the stern deck and the bathing platform to watch the urn being opened and the ashes spread over the sea, together with the silk handkerchief. The waves lapped over and the people on the platform, including Michael Jackson, got their feet wet.

Afterwards, as the guests toasted White, emotions ran high on the yacht. Jackson was overcome as he remembered his friend and his music and all those evenings they had spent together at Sherman Oaks 25 years before. The tears flowed as the yacht's crew pulled up the anchor and the yacht returned to Santa Monica, where everyone disembarked and went their separate ways.

In the media, Barry White quickly faded from view and was soon the forgotten man, until the fight over his legacy began. He may not have left a huge financial legacy, but everyone knew that his song-writing royalties and copyright fees were running at more than $1.2 million a year. That figure was helped by the sales of his albums, which suddenly took off all over the world. Pressing plants were hastily commissioned to re-start the manufacture of almost every one of his timeless albums. By the following Wednesday record shops across America and the world all had fresh supplies.

In the following weeks the world rediscovered Barry White, and his original fans, now in their middle fifties, dusted off their albums and played them continuously in their cars and living rooms. And doubtless, for his new fans, the cycle of love and procreation began all over again.

Six months later, in December 2003, Barriana White was born quietly and privately. By then Glodean and her children had gained full control of Barry White's estate.

Katherine Denton was still living in White's 8,000-square-foot house in Los Angeles, which was valued at $2 million. Glodean had refused to evict her because of her pregnancy and out of sheer decency. She took a cue from her husband and knew that it was what he would have wanted, despite the way Denton had treated her children during her husband's stay in Cedars-Sinai.

Immediately after the baby was born, Denton filed a lawsuit to protect her interests, saying that she wanted ownership of the house in Los Angeles and $2 million in trust for her newly born daughter. But Glodean wasn't ready to make any promises or settlements, and called the lawsuit 'premature'. Denton's lawyers were clear that they wanted a quick settlement and said: "This suit is nothing more than a process of fulfilling Barry's expressed intentions and promises."

In her lawsuit Denton said that White had promised that she could continue to live the lifestyle to which she had become accustomed and that he had told her she would have enough money to live on for the rest of her life in their house in Los Angeles. The lawsuit also continued to call Denton 'White's fiancée', although clearly this could not be true.

Denton stated that White had promised that she could keep the expensive gifts she said he had given her, and she listed them as including a Chow dog, a Rolex watch and a Lexus car. The list of assets that had been given as gifts was important as they were included in White's estate and would revert to Glodean if Denton could not prove ownership.

Everyone knew that the suit was an opening shot and most agreed that, whether Barriana was White's child or not, Denton's financial demands were far from excessive. But that fact and the urge for a quick settlement made them suspicious. Denton was clearly hoping that Glodean would want to settle the suit quickly, and hopefully before a DNA test could be carried out.

But the family were shocked when Abby Schroeder and Katherine Denton appeared together in a television programme put out by the BBC in London. Shaherah White remembers: "Katherine went on a BBC television show showing the baby and Abby was on there and they were talking about this child that was my father's supposedly."

On the programme, Denton showed Barriana to the cameras and said: "Look at this child – she looks just like her father." And no one watching had any reason to disbelieve her.

Glodean stood firm and demanded that a DNA test be carried out. It showed, as Denton must have known it would, that Barry White wasn't the father of Barriana. As Shaherah White said: "It came out it was not his child. No way possible it was his child."

Barry White Jnr was disgusted: "She went as far as naming the baby Barriana. To pretend the baby is his on his deathbed. That's another level of wickedness."

The story of the last days of Barry White concludes in Chapter 67 starting on page 519.

Part 1
Childhood and youth

CHAPTER 2

The Errant Father

The beginning of Barry White

1944 to 1949

Barry White always considered himself a native Angeleno, but by a quirk of fate was actually born a Texan. Fate decreed that in August 1944 his mother, in her ninth month of pregnancy, would suddenly decide to visit her Texas family in her home town of Galveston.

Sadie Mae Carter was no ordinary woman. Born in Galveston, she had grown into a brilliant musician and dancer, talents that were completely underappreciated in her home town as she drifted from one dead-end job to another. With a population of just 60,000, Galveston was one of the oldest habitations in the southwest of America and famous for its cotton. It was a charming town, but a place of no hope for anyone with big ambitions.

Eventually Sadie realised that she would have to leave Texas to have any chance of fulfilling her dreams. She was not alone, and during World War II tens of thousands of African-American migrants left the southern states of Louisiana, Mississippi, Arkansas and Texas in search of opportunity and a new life in California. Sadie knew where she wanted to be and that was Hollywood, where she knew she could shine. However, Hollywood was unattainable, so she sought the next best thing.

So in 1929, at the age of 16, with her life passing her by, Sadie Carter decided to join the migrants. Some of her cousins had already moved to a small town in South Los Angeles called Watts, and that was her opportunity. She saved up as much money as she could from working in clubs and bars, and one day packed herself a single suitcase and got on a train to Watts. She received a very warm welcome from her cousins, who were delighted to see her and share their meagre accommodation. She shared a small bedroom with one of them until she found work and could afford her own small apartment.

When Sadie arrived in Watts she thought it was paradise, and in many ways it was. At that time only 20,000 people lived there, and the vast majority were aged under 21. It was a balanced community of Europeans, Mexicans and African-Americans, all living together harmoniously and grateful for their lot. But suddenly, shortly after she arrived, things started to change fast, and not for the good.

The town had started off peacefully enough when it was founded in the 1870s by a man named Charles Watts, who bought up thousands of acres of seeming wasteland for next to nothing. But underneath the dust there was rich soil, and Charles Watts and his European cousins split the land into a series of small farms. The biggest parcel of 220 acres was farmed by Watts himself. Gradually a township took shape around the rural farmers and the town became a haven for the Europeans who were then emigrating to southern California. As Charles Watts had suspected all along, his town provided fine grazing land and a prosperous future seemed assured for the community of European farmers that took root in the area. The farmers all grew rich as demand for beef grew across the state.

The prosperity saw the arrival of the railroad in 1904, which was welcomed by the wealthy residents as a giant step into the future. The town's station was financed by Charles Watts, who also donated 10 acres of land for the construction. The railroad was built by Mexicans, many of whom liked the area, staying on afterwards to become good citizens.

While the opening of the station eased access to the town, Watts quickly began to attract people of the wrong kind, and the area stagnated significantly as the population grew. The inevitable happened and the European farmers sold off the rich agricultural land for development, wanting to cash in and retire, which signalled the start of an urban sprawl. Then in 1926 things really started to go wrong when Watts was annexed by Los Angeles; it lost its individual identity, and marked the beginning of the end for Watts as a pleasant place to live.

The problems were caused by the city council, which was very liberal in its outlook. Every other region of Los Angeles had imposed racially restrictive covenants that ensured a balanced community and prevented too many black people from settling. Because of Watts's liberality, racial covenants were unthinkable and as a result more or less every black African-American emigre arriving in Los Angeles headed for the town.

The population exploded from 20,000 to 200,000 in a few years, and by 1935 Watts had become a very unbalanced community, which led to plenty of trouble. African-Americans pushed out the Mexicans and the remaining Europeans. While the city fathers had meant well, their policies now meant that Watts very quickly became a 100 per cent black community.

To cope with the population explosion, Watts Towers, a complex of 17 tower blocks of apartments, were built. The towers interconnected with each other, the tallest being 30 metres high. The average family size grew, and half of all parents were unmarried. Watts became a shadow city within a city that most white people simply ignored and pretended didn't exist.

None of this seemed to bother Sadie Carter as she travelled on the bus to Hollywood every day and queued up for any auditions she could find. She could play all manner of musical instruments, which, coupled with a fine singing voice, put her in demand for the musicals that were all the rage at the time.

Her particular talent was song and dance, and her routine was said to be spectacularly good. She also possessed striking looks, and quickly found work in minor roles. Her first big success came when she was just 18 in 1931, appearing in a film called 'Trader Horn' directed by W. S. Van Dyke II. It told the story of an adventurer called Alfred Horn on safari, and was nominated for an Oscar. Sadie was well paid and got to meet all the giants of the film industry including Darryl Zanuck and Louis B. Mayer, both of whom knew her by her first name. By the time she turned 28 she had appeared in good roles in three feature films, one for MGM and two for 20th Century Fox.

She was also a big success in her local community, and every Sunday her singing was a treat for the congregation at the Greater Tabernacle Baptist Church of Los Angeles, where she performed gospel songs for the congregation.

At that stage in her young life Sadie Carter had it all, a sparkling 10-year acting career, good looks and a personality that endeared her to everyone; she was dedicated to her craft and had no time for any boyfriends.

Everything was going fine in her life until the day she met a man called Melvin White. Thirty-three years old, he was the man of her dreams and she didn't need asking twice when she met him on the street and he asked her out. She was a very innocent woman and, despite his obvious intentions, she didn't sleep with him on that first date. But she did on the second, by which time she was already madly in love and couldn't believe her luck. Indeed, the hunky Melvin and beautiful Sadie spent too much time in bed, and the inevitable happened. She quickly fell pregnant and before she had time to realise what had happened to her she was four months gone.

Pregnancy brought her promising career in films to a sudden stop, and she thought long and hard about having an abortion. But for all sorts of reasons that was never really an option. So Sadie Mae Carter took a deep breath and, against her better judgement, decided to throw in her lot with Melvin White, for better or for worse. In her future she looked forward to what she expected would be a happy married life with the man of her dreams. But the dream was to last barely a few months.

One April Saturday morning in 1944, as Sadie pressed him to name the day, Melvin finally confessed to her that he was a married man with a wife, 32-year-old Essilene, and they lived on the other side of Los Angeles. Sadie was devastated and her world fell apart. Not for one minute had she suspected that Melvin White was married – if she had done she would never have even talked to him, as Sadie Carter was not that sort of girl. But even that was not the whole story, and Melvin chose to leave out a few vital facts that Sadie would eventually discover.

That day the sun shone brightly outside, but it turned into the worst day of Sadie's life. She realised that she had been conned, and now had to face the consequences of what had happened as best she could. She came within an hour of making the decision to go to a back-street abortionist, but somehow didn't and chose life for her son, the son who would eventually become Barry White, a global icon.

Sadie clung to the hope that Melvin would leave his wife and marry her as soon as he could – certainly before the baby was born. When he assured her that he would, and that it was only a matter of arranging a divorce, she was fool enough to believe him and began dreaming again.

He continually promised that he would divorce his wife and they would be a happy family. The promises continued week after week, but they were all empty. Through it all Sadie never stopped loving Melvin, even though she realised that he was not the man of her dreams she had thought he was.

Every promise and subsequent promise was just another lie. Moreover, Melvin had forgotten to tell Sadie one key fact – that he was already the father of two young children by his wife. But that revelation was for the future.

As Sadie put on weight she was forced to give up performing and settled into a difficult pregnancy living off her savings and the tiny bit of money Melvin gave her. All the time she kept her spirits up in the belief that Melvin would leave his wife and come to her.

Her life had taken a further step backwards on 28th March when her mother, Katie Brown, had died. But she hardly had time to mourn as Melvin kept making grander and grander promises of how he would look after her. However, the promises meant little and he was constantly making new and even better ones, continually frightened that Sadie would find out about his two children and do something stupid.

The truth was that Melvin White was a snake and a pretty despicable character. When lovemaking became impossible, in the final months of Sadie's confinement, she was increasingly left alone as he stopped visiting. Years later, Barry White defended his father's actions and sought to try and rationalise them: "He was a complicated man trapped in an economic and social world that severely limited his opportunities. He was a decent man and had tried to live his life the best way he could."

Few would have agreed with that assessment in 1944.

So heavily pregnant, in the late summer of that year Sadie was all alone. She felt extremely isolated, and one day had the crazy notion of visiting her family in Texas. She was bored being at home all day on her own and desperately needed some company, so she took herself off to Galveston almost on a whim, planning to spend a few days there before returning for the birth. The town she had shunned 10 years before suddenly had some attractions.

But it turned out not to be the greatest decision she ever made when it became clear that the baby would arrive earlier than planned. On 12th September 1944 she gave birth to her first child in the bedroom of her cousin, Beth. The midwife was called but never turned up. Luckily the birth went off without a hitch and Beth successfully cut the umbilical cord and brought a new life into the world at around 3 o'clock in the morning. He was named Barry Eugene Carter after two of his uncles.

Sadie registered the birth in Galveston and the birth certificate duly recorded him as being born Barry Carter; this was simply because his mother and father were not married, and Sadie had no idea if she would ever see Melvin again. She had no way of contacting him and Melvin had no idea that he had a new son.

Sadie's cousins wrapped her and the new baby in love and she was grateful for that. Barry Eugene was well cared for in the first six months of his life.

When Sadie Mae finally returned to Los Angeles, one of her first visitors was Melvin, who, according to the neighbours, had apparently been calling every day to find out what had happened. When he belatedly learned that he had a son, his first instinct was to ask to see the birth certificate. He had always had doubts about whether he was the father, but went into a rage when he saw that his son had been registered under Sadie's surname as 'Carter', and no father was listed. The name 'Carter' didn't last long; Melvin simply scrubbed out the word on the birth certificate and wrote his own in its place. He told Sadie that henceforth his son was Barry Eugene White. It had no legal meaning, but from then on Barry Carter most definitely became the man the whole world would someday get to know as Barry White.

Melvin White may not have had too much time for his son, but he desperately wanted him to carry his name. As Barry himself remembered: "It was when my father saw my birth certificate for the first time and noticed my mother's surname on it. Well, he just scribbled out 'Carter' and wrote in his own 'White'."

Then apparently Melvin started to question Sadie as to why she had registered him as Carter and wondered aloud whether he was the father after all, although he must have known that he was. Unsurprisingly Sadie was very angry at this suggestion, and would have been even more so if she had known about his own two children that he was keeping secret from her.

Once again Melvin promised Sadie that he would leave his wife and join her shortly. But that was never going to happen. Melvin was a machinist and worked in a factory, and although he was a skilled man and a relatively high earner, his weekly income was nowhere near enough to support two families. As Barry White recalled: "You see he had this other family and there was just so much bread to go around."

Melvin visited his new son infrequently, and only when sex became available again did his visits become more regular. Unfortunately Sadie was not worldly enough to see through him.

Belatedly Melvin had begun to consider his options. He enjoyed going to bed with Sadie but that was all. He had been attracted to her because she was an actress, was very good looking and led a seemingly glamorous life. He was flattered that he could be attractive to such a woman. When she became pregnant and lost her career, suddenly she seemed that much less attractive, especially when she put on a lot of weight and, in his eyes, lost much of her appeal. At the same time Sadie realised that she had fallen for Melvin for all the wrong reasons, now that he was showing his true colours.

But she had to face up to the fact that he was the father of her child and nothing was going to change that. She had no choice but to stick with the little she had. The truth was that Melvin was a simple man who had made his way in life based on his own hunky looks and physique, attractions that Sadie had found hard to resist. But when they started sleeping together again, he treated her like a prostitute.

Many years later, Barry White recalled how, when Melvin arrived, he barely acknowledged his son and he and his mother would go into the bedroom and close the door. They would emerge 20 minutes later. "He'd come in and throw some money down, make love to Sadie and leave." Unsurprisingly, with all this sexual activity a second child, Darryl, was born 16 months later, and money became even tighter. Christened Darryl Lionel White, he was named after Darryl F. Zanuck, for whom Sadie had worked at 20th Century Fox during her acting days. She had adored Zanuck, who had been indirectly responsible for her first break.

It was clear from the beginning that Barry took after his mother and Darryl his father, as White recalled: "Darryl had the tough cynicism of the old man while I had my mother's tender spirit and soul."

As the children got older Melvin started to show more interest in them, but his desire to see them was still lacklustre at best: "My father came around every now and then, although he was never there as much as any of us would have liked."

The two parents clashed over their children's upbringing. Sadie was soft, kind, loving and very generous, whereas Melvin was hard and mean. White remembered: "My mother was everything to me. She taught me through her generous love and understanding what it meant to take care of others. She taught me not to be afraid to engage with my feminine side, which she believed all men possessed."

But most of all, White credits his mother with teaching him about the essence of love at a very early stage in his life: "She taught me that the nature of true love was unqualified, all-encompassing and filled with endless amounts of spiritual passion." His mother said to him one day: "In life you have a choice to be happy or angry – please be happy as a gift to yourself."

But Sadie wasn't happy when she finally realised that Melvin had no intention of divorcing his wife and that they would never marry. She started rationing the sex in an attempt to force him to make a decision, but this had no effect and eventually Melvin stopped calling round altogether. Sadie guessed he must have found another woman to satisfy his lust.

Sadie was left high and dry to bring up Barry and his younger sibling Darryl all on her own with no money besides the meagre welfare payments she received from the state. But she was not inclined to let Melvin off the hook completely, reasoning that he had responsibilities. When she hadn't seen or heard of him for four whole months she went round to the address he had given her, 927 East 28th Street.

She quickly discovered that Melvin and Essilene White had lodged there with two sisters, Jeannette Norman and Lizzie Foate, who owned the house, together with Lizzie's husband Bill, their nephew, Robert, and two other lodgers – but they had moved out suddenly without leaving a forwarding address.

As she spoke to Jeannette and Lizzie in the sunshine, one of them started talking about two children. Sadie quickly realised that she must be referring to Melvin and Essiline's children, as their names were not Barry and Darryl. This was too much for her, and she fainted on the spot, fortunately landing on grass, which cushioned her fall. Lizzie Foate rushed into the house and returned with a glass of water. As Sadie came round and sat up, she asked them what they knew and the whole story of Melvin White's double life tumbled out.

Jeannette Norman told her that Melvin and Essilene had two sons, six-year-old Melvin Jnr and four-year-old Raymond, who had both been born in the house. Sadie immediately realised that her two sons had two half-brothers they didn't know anything about.

That day proved to be the end of Melvin White in the lives of Sadie and her two sons for the next 20 years. She realised that she had been well and truly fooled and he was not the man she had believed him to be. In just a few minutes, Sadie Carter grew up 20 years.

Surprisingly, as she rode the bus home she only had positive thoughts. From now on her focus would solely be on Barry and Darryl, and it was a new woman who walked through the front door of the family apartment that night.

Two days later she told her sons that Daddy was not coming home again and now it was Sadie and Barry and Darryl who had to fend for themselves, and that there may be some difficult days ahead. Barry recalled that he was not at all surprised at the news: "I had learned very early on not to depend on my father for certain things because he was never going to be there all the time for me."

The lack of a father figure invoked self-sufficiency in the whole family. Money was a constant problem, and when Melvin stopped giving her any she examined all the options. She had some arthritis in her knee, exacerbated by the two pregnancies, which prevented her from getting any more film work and ended her dancing career. So she was forced into relying totally on welfare. Being a black single mother with two young children was not easy in Los Angeles in 1949, and the welfare payments were minimal. But Sadie Carter was no ordinary woman. She was immensely proud and vowed to come off welfare as quickly as she could.

CHAPTER 3

Musical Awakening
Talent shows through at an early age
1949 to 1956

S adie Mae Carter pondered the future. Freed of any illusions, she was able to plan for a future, but couldn't help the sense of real despair that flooded her emotions.

A few years before she had been an actress with the world at her feet. Now she was nothing – a single black mother, just a statistic with no future except through her children. The Carter/White family situation wasn't helped by the continuing rapid deterioration of the Watts area of Los Angeles where they lived in their small apartment.

But her talent remained – a talent that, she kept reminding herself, had seen her perform in three feature films and become the musical mainstay of her local Baptist church.

Even though she could no longer perform, Sadie decided that she would use her musical talents to somehow try and make a living. Scrimping and saving, a quarter (25 cents) at a time, she saved what she could from her small welfare checks. After a year she had saved up $50, enough to buy a second-hand upright piano.

The arrival of the piano delighted her eldest son, who until that day hadn't even realised his mother could play. As he said: "My mother had never even told me she could play, but when I walked in the front door and heard her playing Beethoven, it was the most amazing thing, to this day, that I have ever experienced. It was so emotional that I knew I had to learn to play that piano too."

But Sadie hadn't bought the piano for her son. She advertised herself locally as a piano teacher and, against all expectations, quickly started to get bookings. The piano lessons turned into a successful business and she was booked up every week from dawn until dusk. It seemed that even the impoverished people of Los Angeles were willing to pay for their children to learn to play the piano.

Soon Sadie was earning a very good living. The family became self-sufficient financially for the first time and she was able to come off welfare. The people of Watts may have been poor, but they were anxious to better themselves and piano lessons were seen by parents as a stepping stone to better things.

Barry sat in the next room listening intently, and the constant tinkling of the piano awakened latent instincts. He remembered: "It was so beautiful watching that Taurus Queen play that piano and when I was four years old I started getting interested in music through her playing. She was into classical music playing Beethoven and Mozart and all the great masters plus a little jazz and it must have turned a light on in me. I was so proud of my mother and I immediately wanted to play our piano to please her. I didn't want to read or write; I just wanted to play and I started plucking around." Soon Sadie realised that Barry had inherited her gifts, even if he didn't know it yet.

But the effort to please his mother turned into something deadly serious, and every spare moment of this time was spent sitting by her as she played the piano. "She could read and write music fluently and she would sit there at that piano and I wouldn't go outside and play – I'd sit right there and listen. I knew I wanted to know that lady called music. It was not easy as there were not a lot of kids in South Los Angeles who played the piano." It was the start of his musical education and he learned quickly. "My friends never saw me anymore and for the next seven or eight months I just came home and practised. Mama knew how to compose music and taught me to harmonise when I was just five years old."

To further his interest Sadie bought a record player, then known as a phonograph. Sadie had owned one previously, bought from her earnings as an actress, but had sold it when she had given birth to her first son. But she had never sold her collection of 78rpm records and kept buying more, even when she couldn't play them. She had hundreds of records, and not many people in South LA owned a phonograph.

Whenever Sadie put on a record, Barry was never far away from it, as he recalled: "I stayed glued to the phonograph when Mama played her records – symphonies, sonatas, melodies were soaring through me. Nobody's mother had a record collection like hers; she had stacks of 78s and knew every song."

By his sixth birthday he was sitting on a small stool beside his mother harmonising with her on *Silent Night* and *White Christmas*. "Mama was singing Silent Night and I sang the counter line; that's when music came into focus. I found I was fine-tuned. I was always a little boy who loved music." He remembered a magical moment when his mother first played Beethoven's Moonlight Sonata to him: "That blew my mind and I will never forget that day."

Inevitably the young Barry wanted to move on from listening to doing and, although her son was very young and despite her own misgivings, Sadie made the decision that she would give him formal piano lessons.

But young Barry hated it almost immediately and rejected conventional teaching. As he said: "I went crazy for two weeks trying to memorise the scales." Sadie tried her best to teach her son to read music but he never did learn and finally she said to him: "That's all right – you play any way you want." This different approach paid off as he picked up playing incredibly quickly. "My mother tried to teach me the scales, but I told her I wanted to learn it *my* way."

By the age of seven he was playing the piano like a maestro, even though he couldn't read a note of music. He said: "One of the greatest gifts she gave me was when she said okay. She let me do it my way and I discovered I could make the piano sing by figuring out with my fingers which chords pleased my ears."

White quickly discovered that music to him was something he 'felt' rather than 'learned'. He explained: "I had to feel rather than be taught. I'd sit in front of the radio and hear a song and after a couple of tries I could figure it out. By the time I was eight years old I could sing and play any song on the piano – it just came to me." It was a remarkable gift and his mother was astounded by her son's ability to hear something and play it perfectly almost immediately.

To him it was easy: "I never did it for sheer pleasure – it was just an instrument I found I could use to put what was in my heart out there by way of those black and white keys."

His talent became apparent to everybody else when he was at a children's party and someone asked him to play: "I sat down and did a couple of songs including *In the Still of the Night*."

When he had finished there was total silence in the room for a few seconds, then the raucous cheering and clapping that followed became a memory that lived with him until the day he died: "That's when I first learned that you could become a hero in the ghetto another way – not by fighting but by making music."

Around this time Sadie Mac realised that her eldest son was something special. She could see he was gifted musically – that was clear – but as he turned eight years old it was also clear that he had other qualities. One day, after they had played a duet on the piano together, she looked at him and said: "Baby, you're going to end up the leader of many people. You may find a vehicle to take you another way to get into it, but you're going to end up in it." Whatever those words meant exactly, Barry White filed them away in his head and never forgot them

Musically he was almost a prodigy. His early grasp of the piano was crucial as it enabled him later to quickly pick up and play anything in the rhythm section of an orchestra – the piano, the organ, the harpsichord, bass and drums, all came easily.

He said: "Darryl loved fighting but I loved violins. I was drawn to the mystery of sound. Even though Mama taught piano, I never learnt to read or write music. Learning scales was boring for me. It did nothing for me. For me, to know music is to feel music. I didn't read music but I can tell you when someone plays a wrong note on a song. I just felt music."

White never did learn to read or write music and instead became what he called a "multi-instrumentalist who could simultaneously create and arrange music in his head." It gave him a tremendous feel for his craft that no amount of formal education ever could.

It was to be the making of him.

CHAPTER 4

Growing up in South LA
Youth
1956 to 1958

Barry White lived in a tiny apartment in Watts with his mother and brother until he was 11 years old. At times the family was so poor that all they ate for six weeks were eggs. But his mother was the rock that kept him on the straight and narrow, and meant that he always remembered his childhood with a real glow: "We never had money; I never went to summer camp when I was a kid. And I didn't get new clothes every year. But the love we had, oh the love we had."

Sadie established a ritual that every Easter she would buy each of her sons a pair of blue suede shoes. Blue suede shoes were all the rage and ownership implied a certain style and status. She sought to further their education whenever she could, as her son said: "My mother used to read to us a lot. We used to go to church together. Maybe we weren't like other folks – but we loved each other."

But Watts was all that young Barry knew in his formative years and he never left its boundaries, as he recalled: "It was a very heavy place to live. It was rough and tough and you had to learn very quickly how to survive. There weren't a lot of kids in southeast Los Angeles who were into music." His years in Watts undoubtedly shaped his outlook to life and were the main factor that caused him to end up in juvenile jail.

The atmosphere in Watts, the most prominent borough in South Los Angeles, fostered resentment because of discriminatory treatment by police and wholly inadequate public services, especially schools and hospitals.

Sadie did her best to overcome this and bring her sons up as good citizens, but was fighting a losing battle, as Barry White recalled: "I was brought up in the mean streets where the edge of danger and defiance carried an adolescent lure like an advertisement for macho. It made me want to be part of something big and tough. It gave me false courage and allowed me to think I could get away with anything."

Every night Sadie would read to Barry and Darryl from the Bible. She instilled in them a strong sense of Baptist upbringing. But the Bible reading rebounded on her. White was proving to be a very intelligent child and doing really well at school. He listened and absorbed every word his mother read to him from the Bible and took it literally.

As part of the growing-up process she attempted to instil responsibility in her eldest son. When he was just eight years old she effectively made him head of the family. She passed him an envelope with all the family's insurance policies in it, telling him: "If something happens to Mama I want you to know where everything is." It was all part of Sadie's efforts to shield her sons from all the troubles and imbue them with a real sense of decency. Both sons attended the Greater Tabernacle Baptist Church every Sunday, where at the age of eight Barry White was first exposed to gospel singing. He pestered his mother to let him join the Sunday choir and eventually she agreed. He joined the junior choir, which held its rehearsals on Saturday mornings, and was soon recruited into the senior choir, which rehearsed on Sundays.

As the only boy in both choirs, it was his first taste of musical success: "I moved to the senior choir and just about blew the roof off the church. The first time I sung a song, a woman started shouting and that scared me. From then on I noticed a murmur whenever it was my turn to sing." It was the first indication that Barry White's voice was out of the ordinary.

His mother looked on in wonder as he held his own with people some of whom were four or five times his own age. The lessons he learned singing with the choir were invaluable, as he explained: "They taught me about five-part harmonies, octaves, unison, and many, many things. It gave me a range of knowledge of harmonies. And ways to play with a melody line – what you can do with it and still reach the audience out there."

He enjoyed the singing but asked his mother to keep his piano-playing a secret. Singing was cool but playing wasn't: "My friends didn't know I could play but I didn't tell nobody."

A year later White took over management of the choir. Eventually they learned that he could play keyboards and persuaded him to take over the organ playing. For the next six years he ran the choir and attendance at church increased dramatically, until it became standing room only.

But it wasn't to last, as eventually he was worn down by the frustrations of running a choir with a transient congregation. He found that he was having to reinvent the make-up of the choir every year as people continually moved on. No one, except himself, stayed and he calculated that he had to train hundreds of different people to sing in the choir over six years. Eventually it got too much: "I was building choirs and I got really tired of doing that and cut it loose."

But he never regretted the time and effort he put in during those six years: "The experience you get from being exposed to gospel music is incredible when you get to know how to use it. Gospel music is a great music. It gets you involved in everything physically and spiritually. It shows you how to take a melody, any melody, and do it any kind of way you want to do it. It puts you in command of the song."

When he turned 16 he also began to get disillusioned with religion itself. He studied the Bible and examined what it was saying in detail. He took literal meanings and was not the first to find it was completely contradictory. He also found the teaching of the priests did not match what was going on outside the church walls, and couldn't reconcile the two: "I began to understand that my faith was going to have to come from within. I started questioning everything I was taught about the Bible."

When he tried to match up the words of the Bible to the real world he found it impossible, as he explained years later: "I had a hard time believing them. They sounded to me like man-made morality tales meant to give hope to the hopeless, which so many people at our church really were."

White knew that many of their neighbours who piously went to church on Sunday and prayed were in fact gang members and hardened criminals from Monday to Saturday: "Who were all these people calling up and singing to God and Jesus every Sunday and for the other six days bloodying up the streets?"

The difference between the church and the neighbourhood couldn't have been starker, yet Barry White could only see the same people. The neighbourhood was plagued by gangs of black youths who made it their battleground, so much so that when Hollywood was making films of a violent nature the film crews always headed for Watts, as they knew they would not have to construct any sets to get the right effect. The well-known British movie director Michael Winner used the area frequently for his films.

Sadie's eldest son continually questioned her on why the people he observed praying on Sunday were causing bedlam on the street from Monday to Saturday. He said later: "Mama said going to church was the right thing to do." But he admitted he only went to make her happy. If there was a battle going on in White's head between good and evil at that stage of his life, evil appeared to be winning. He admits that he was leading the same double life that he criticised in others. On Sundays he would dress up and enjoy singing in the choir and on the other six days he would be doing something entirely alien to that.

Unsurprisingly Barry and Darryl White were subsumed into this violet gang culture, mainly because they didn't know any different. Darryl was sent to Juvenile Hall for the first time at the age of eight. From then on he was inside prison more than he was out. Barry pursued a life of petty crime, but was cleverer than his brother and never got caught: "As a young boy with no father to act as a role model and set me straight, I couldn't help but get sucked into the street life. I really wasn't a bad kid at heart, I just didn't know any better."

White's descent into the gutter started when he became involved with a gang called 'The Businessmen', which translated as meaning 'taking care of business', and no one was in any doubt what the 'business' was. At that time South Los Angeles had five main gangs and the west side of the city was even more gang-infested, with 12 active ones, as White recalled: "The first gang I was in was called The Roaming Twenties, then I joined the hottest gang around, The Businessmen." The Businessmen were the most famous gang in the whole of Los Angeles; as White described them, they were "the oldest, baddest and most envied gang in South Central." It was the gang that every teenage black boy wanted to be a member of.

The leaders of The Businessmen were old-established and it had become almost a job. The oldest were more than 50 years old and had been members as their full-time occupation for a whole lifetime.

By the age of 10, White was involved with what he called 'gang banging', and he had learned how to fight and more importantly how to defend himself from the attentions of the other kids in the neighbourhood: "I was a dedicated member of my gang. I did everything teenagers do when they are in that environment and at that age. I burglarised, I stole cars and I was in gang fights." Gang banging had nothing to do with sex – it was boys, mostly teenagers, fighting other boys in battles directed by old men.

White had also started smoking regularly and was on his way to the three-pack-a-day habit that he was never able to shake off.

Being a junior member of The Businessmen meant that he was 'protected', as he recalled: "Our leaders knew all the coldest street ways. They were men who had never grown out of joy riding and gang banging. Everything I learned came from them. Those dudes didn't kid around. And no matter what was happening they did it for keeps. When we fought it was for real – these warriors were willing to protect us with their own lives."

Years later White admitted that he had been close to death three times in that period: "I was nearly killed three times. One time a guy dropped on me from behind and tried to stab me, another time they had a shotgun on me and another time it was a .45 pistol. I was lucky in all cases."

Inevitably, eventually the elder leaders of The Businessmen became the father figures that Barry White had never known in his life: "They were all our missing fathers and the streets became the only living rooms we ever felt comfortable calling home. We were The Businessmen, which meant we was in the business of taking care of business."

White recalled the mood: "The gang bangers were like family to each other. And in some cases closer than families. People didn't understand young people's frustration. The greatest thing ever to happen to young people was rap music, because it was an outlet for that frustration. It got it out of them."

White's membership of The Businessmen endured from the ages of 10 to 16. He and his brother were involved in many gang battles, where they and as many as 30 or 40 youths would battle each other for supremacy: "When we dealt with other gangs we could reason with them or we could fight them." But the reasoning didn't happen very often, as he explained: "Most of the time we fought, or we'd be marked as easy victims."

People died in these pitched battles, and although Barry White never said whether he killed anyone, the general perception and the implication is that he most likely did.

Sadie was devastated by her two sons' nocturnal activities and their gang membership, as White remembered: "My mother wanted us to quit. She was convinced that wc were going to kill somebody or somebody was going to kill us." If his mother asked, White denied that he was a gang member: "I told her we went to dances and sometimes fought, but I didn't tell her about the crime stuff."

In 1956 he performed at his first ever recording session. Sadie was invited to play the piano at a recording session for Modern Records for a new Jesse Belvin album. Belvin, in his early 20s, was a singer/songwriter who was rapidly making his name. He had had his first hit in 1953 with a song called *Dream Girl*.

Belvin was a family friend of the Carters, born in Texas and spending his early youth there, where he had got to know the Carter cousins and recommended Sadie for the job. The lead song on the album was called *Goodnight My Love*, which had been specially written by George Motola and John Marascalco for Belvin to record. Sadie arranged for her son to play the piano chords for that song, and 11-year-old Barry took over the piano. He was ecstatic to be in the same room as Jesse Belvin, let alone be playing for him. His favourite song was *Earth Angel* by the Penguins, which Belvin had co-written and had become a huge hit in 1954.

Goodnight My Love proved to be a hit for Belvin, and later White would adopt it for himself, performing his own version many times in the 1980s. He and his mother were reputedly paid $55 for his piano playing on the recording, a sizeable sum of money at the time.

Surprisingly, White attached no significance to his first visit to a recording studio, and soon forgot about it altogether; only those who were there remembered his musical debut with Jesse Belvin, who tragically was to die in a car accident four years later.

Shortly afterwards, with Barry having turned 11, Sadie Carter made the decision to get out of Watts. It was fast becoming a war zone, where gang warfare was constantly raging. Homicides were running at 10 a week, fuelled by the uncontrolled sale of drugs. It was getting worse rather than better, and the Los Angeles Police Department had virtually withdrawn from the town.

Sadie put together the fee from the Belvin recording and the money she had put away from giving piano lessons and found a small house to rent to the west on 42nd Place and Hoover. It was a real step up from the small apartment in Watts.

But most of all she hoped it would get her young sons away from the lure of The Businessmen, which was corroding their childhood almost to the extent where she was losing control of them. Her move away from Watts came in a period when lots of the more prosperous African-Americans were getting out, and Sadie was right to leave when she did.

Watts was a tinderbox waiting to explode, which it finally did in August 1965. It was started by the arrest of a black youth by the California Highway Patrol on drunk-driving charges. Mob rule took over and left Watts in a turmoil that lasted for years.

Barry White, although by then a reformed character, was drawn in by the looting and rampage and freely admitted stealing two televisions during the riots: "I didn't only hear about the 1965 riot, I was in it. I understand the disappointment, the anger that people have. I had the same feelings. They know I've been to jail. I've never hid my past, and I never will. I don't want no young person to think he's stuck in that misery."

The gang warfare went on for more than 25 years and only ended finally in 1992 as neighbourhood leaders began a strategy to overcome Watts's reputation as a violence-prone and impoverished area. That happened as the community became more balanced as Hispanic immigrants from Mexico and Central America, as well as Ethiopians and Indians, moved in.

As for the White brothers, they had long gone their own way. Yet Barry found it hard to make the break from The Businessmen, although at least they were no longer on his doorstep every day. It turned out that being a member of Los Angeles's most notorious gang had actually protected Barry White from his most serious excesses. Once separated from the gang he became a serious criminal in his own gang, a newly created one with just two members – the White brothers.

Barry became severely disillusioned with his fellow man and came to disappoint himself in this period: "I plainly saw that people in everyday life could and would disappoint you and you would disappoint others and ultimately yourself." But he never suffered from any sort of racial prejudice: "Nobody white ever did anything wrong to me. I'm sorry, they just didn't! Not even the police. I was always a well-mannered child and I never got hit or talked to badly. If you know the difference between right and wrong and you try to do right, you're gonna come out on top 99% of the time, believe me."

But by 1959 Barry White was a less than perfect teenager and had been subsumed into the gang culture after years of living in Watts, as he freely admitted: "I was fifteen years old and a very bad boy."

By then they were living in the tiny house on South Hoover Street, but the shadow of Watts remained and White returned to the area whenever he could, culminating in his being arrested and thrown into Juvenile Hall for stealing $30,000 worth of wheels and tyres from a Chevrolet dealership.

CHAPTER 5

The Voice Emerges

All change at 14

1958

Barry White didn't always have the distinctive voice that made him famous. Up to the age of 14 he sounded pretty much like any other adolescent young black boy living in Los Angeles. He was a high-pitched Michael Jackson sound-alike, exactly the same as thousands of other black boys in the neighbourhood. He called it "the high treble of a typical teenager".

But then suddenly and without warning one morning his voice broke, and it was as if a miracle had occurred. That fateful morning his mother Sadie whooped with joy at the new sound emanating from her son's mouth – straight away she knew it was very special.

As White described it himself: "When adolescence hit me, my sound didn't go down to a tenor the way most boys do and stay there. Mine went down twice, first to a tenor and then to a bass singer – the second one was like a drop off the Empire State Building."

According to White, the change came suddenly, overnight: "One morning I woke up with my new voice and hair all over my face. My mother called me over and examined my cheeks and chin closely with her eyes and fingertips." Sadie looked at him and said: "My God, my baby has become a man." White says: "Once my voice dropped there was no escaping its power. Everywhere I went I could see the immediate effect it had on people. There really was nothing else quite like it."

Twenty years on, White remembered the conversation with his mother as though it was yesterday: "I was 14 and I woke up and spoke to my mother like I usually did every morning and it was amazing. My chest just rattled, and I mean vibrations. My mother was staring at me and I was staring at her. She was stunned, I was stunned. She was scared to speak and I was scared and we stood there looking at each other and too scared to say anything. The next thing I knew her straight face broke into a beautiful smile and suddenly tears started rolling down our faces and she said, 'My son's a man now.' That was the day I started shaving and hair started growing on my face. It was unbelievable – my voice had changed to a low bass, unlike any other man I had heard."

Forty-two years later, two years before he died, White described the experience in an interview with writer Lulu Le Vay: "You go to sleep one night, sounding like you have done for the last 14 years. The next day you wake up and wish your mother, 'Good morning,' and woooah." (At this point Barry took hold of Lulu's hand and placed it on his chest). "When I talk you can feel my chest vibrate, can't you? You bet, feels scary. Well it scared the hell out of me and my mother."

At first even White himself was taken by surprise when he started talking: "It always took me by surprise and would continue to do so for many years, especially after I left the neighbourhood. I'd be in an elevator and someone would call for the floor and I'd say, 'Top please,' and everyone's head would turn around to see where that voice was coming from."

From then on he found that he had particular difficulty on the telephone. It was never possible to make what he called a "normal phone call". He said in 1990, explaining the effect: "I'd pick up the phone to make a long-distance call and ask the operator for assistance and hear back, 'My, but you have a beautiful voice.' This happened to me wherever I went. I was uneasy about it at the time but eventually grew used to it."

In the neighbourhood his voice became famous and one Christmas he was invited by the rector of a local Baptist church to recite the classic poem Twas the Night Before Christmas. He delivered a flawless performance, knowing the verses off by heart and not missing a beat before a congregation in silent rapture. Afterwards the rector told him: "Your memory is tremendous."

As he approached the end of his teenage years, White also began to notice that girls were attracted to his deep voice. They found it extremely sexy and he found that he wound up in many a young girl's bed purely as a result of the strength and appeal of his voice.

Someone told him that a deep voice signalled higher testosterone levels and a "higher male quality". He said it became clear to him that women preferred men with deeper voices and that a deep voice meant more sex.

And it wasn't just a theory as, years later, academics at the University of Aberdeen discovered that a low masculine voice is important to the accuracy of a woman's memory of a potential partner and will stick in her mind when she makes a choice of mate. The study found that, based on the pitch of a man's voice, women assess genetic quality and behavioural traits when looking for a long-term partner. They rely on their memories to provide information quickly about the attributes and behaviour of their suitor. Dr David Smith, the lead researcher, said: "Our findings demonstrate that women's memory is enhanced by lower-pitch male voices, compared with the less attractive raised-pitch male voices."

Dr Kevin Allan, who supervised the research, said: "We think this is evidence that evolution has shaped women's ability to remember information associated with desirable men. Good memory for specific encounters with desirable men allows women to compare and evaluate men according to how they might behave in different relationship contexts, for example a long-term committed relationship versus a short-term uncommitted relationship. This would help women to pick a suitable partner."

There was also some evidence that men with deep voices were more fertile. The Aberdeen University report was the first to link voice pitch to reproductive success. And it could explain why men generally have lower voices than women.

There was support for Aberdeen's research from Harvard University. Academics there had been studying the Hadza, an African tribe. They numbered around 1,000 people and lived in Tanzania. Women in the tribe gather fruits while men collect honey and hunt down animals for food. The Hadza do not use birth control, which, according to the academics at Harvard, meant that the effects of the environment or human choices would feed through into more or fewer children being born.

Harvard academics asked 49 Hadza men to say the word "hujambo", a greeting, into a tape recorder. They then asked all 49 about their families, particularly how many children they had and how many of them were still alive.

Harvard found that men with lower voices tended to have more children, but that childhood mortality was not linked to voice pitch. The researchers reckoned that the reproductive advantage of a deeper voice must be due to female preference.

The quality of Barry White's voice and the advantages it gave him were things that he took a long time to catch onto. It took 15 years for him to finally start to perform his own music. And it took another 20 years, after he became successful, for him to finally acknowledge publicly that he had a particularly distinctive voice. Before that he had constantly rejected most of the descriptions of his voice, saying: "I'm a baritone bass singer and it's as low as it goes." In 1992 reviewer Caroline Sullivan doubted whether it was a 'voice' at all when she wrote: "Whether Barry White's can be described as a 'voice' at all is debatable; it is more a low-register reverberation that is sensed rather than heard." This summed it up perfectly, and in later life the voice improved every year he was alive. It just got better and better.

He was very proud of his voice, and when someone suggested that Isaac Hayes was lower, White growled back at them, "I'm lower." He added: "I'm about as low as you can get. I've compared Marvin Franklin of the Temptations' lowest note by singing along with him and his lowest note is like a high note to me."

His voice became a cause of great fascination to magazine writers. When asked about it he always used to thank his mother for the elocution lessons she gave him when he was only five years old: "She was such an intelligent woman, and when I was only four or five years old she taught me to speak clearly and people were always complimenting me on my diction." His mother was in no doubt about the appeal of his voice. She said to him: "Barry, when you grow up you are going to be one of the most dynamic speakers the world has ever heard."

And he always denied he was a singer: "No, I'm not. Barry White is a carrier. He has a sound. But, no, he isn't a singer. Maybe he is a phrase? He can take a melody and a message and deliver it. Instead of a voice, he has a way of delivering."

In his youth Barry used his unusually deep voice to help others woo girls, especially his brother Darryl. He often said that Darryl had the looks but no charm. Many times Darryl would hand the telephone receiver to his brother and say: "Barry, talk to this girl for me in that way you have." Sometimes Darryl got his brother to pretend to be him to ask a girl out over the phone, and it never failed to work.

It even worked with Darryl's regular girlfriend, who once told Barry, thinking she was speaking to Darryl: "That's such a beautiful side of you, Darryl. I've never heard you say anything like that before," having no idea that she was talking to his brother.

Shaherah White was mesmerised by her father's voice: "My first memory of my father was as a small child and I would just lay on his chest and he would be talking and I would listen to the rumble of his voice and I was as happy as could be lying on my Daddy's chest."

Ray Parker Junior, the guitarist who appeared on White's first seven albums, said the voice was all part of his sex appeal: "At 19 my ego was huge and I thought I was quite handsome, but there were girls who would leave me to go and talk to him. He used to say, 'Hey, baby, what's going on?' and that was it. His voice was like thunder – women just loved his voice."

Nathan East, who engineered those early albums, agreed: "His voice was very sexy to women – they would hear that rumble and just melt. He vibrated the room and I think he enjoyed the fact that women admired him and wanted to be with him."

White said of his own voice: "I've been singing since I was a very, very small boy in churches and I have a very unusual voice. And when you take that voice and put it with music, you can get a combination of strange things if the person knows how to work that voice. Especially if the person who owns the voice and the person who makes the music for the voice happens to be the same person."

He always described his own voice as being "unnaturally low" and different from the average voice, but added: "I am sure there are people who don't like Barry White's voice." Years later David Letterman told him, when he first appeared on his show: "Your voice is an amazing instrument and I can feel it as I sit here." Barry was amused by the reaction and said: "I am not the only man on this planet with a low voice. But to have words with that voice and to have wisdom with that voice – that's another mind of voice."

It kind of summed Barry White up.

CHAPTER 6

Guided by Destiny

A love affair begins with astrology

1958

In 1958, Barry White was an undistinguished black teenager, living a double life. By day he was a 14-year-old schoolboy, doing very well and impressing his teachers, but by night he was roaming the streets of South Los Angeles, looking for trouble and trying every car door he passed in an effort to find one unlocked that he could steal.

Then something extraordinary happened that was to affect everything else he did in his life from that point on.

Coming back from a trip to the supermarket for his mother, he was walking to Vermont Square and approaching the busy intersection of Hoover and 42nd Place just before his house. As he waited for the lights to turn green to cross the busy junction, his hood pulled up tight around his head, he was as usual lost in his own thoughts. His mother had warned him many times about getting run over when his mind, as she called it, "was a million miles away."

Suddenly the walk sign flashed and he stepped onto the crossing. He thought he was on his own, with only the waiting drivers for company but, when he was half way across, from nowhere an elderly, shabbily dressed lady wearing a brown trench coat suddenly appeared right in front of him. As they drew level she stopped and stared right into his eyes. Simultaneously her mouth widened and a huge smile appeared across her face.

White was halted in his tracks by this unexpected intrusion into his life. He was forced to stop, returned her stare and smiled, while wondering what was coming next. Because she was smiling he sensed no sign of any hostility. After a few seconds she suddenly said, "You're a Virgo child," in what White described as a "soft cherry voice", which took him by surprise as the voice did not match the person standing in front of him. He described it as "very reassuring", but years later he claimed that he had no idea what the woman was talking about and assumed that she had got him mixed up with someone else.

He answered, "I'm Sadie's child," completely misunderstanding what the woman had meant. "My mother had always taught me to be respectful to our elders so I just shook my head and said 'um-hmm' as we stood looking at each other."

Then the woman asked him the date of his birthday and he replied, "12th September." She nodded: "Yes, as I said, a Virgo child."

White still had no idea what she meant as no one had ever told him about the signs of the zodiac and what they meant. But before he could respond she said: "You're going to be a great, great man one day."

A clueless White asked her what she meant by 'Virgo child'. She replied: "It means you are destined for greatness," adding, "and remember, Barry, always appreciate and take your opportunities first and worry about everything else later."

With that she walked away, leaving White in the middle of the road with the waiting cars honking their horns for him to get out of their way. He quickly ran on and reached the other side. He looked back but the woman was gone.

He stood on the sidewalk for a full five minutes and wondered whether he had fallen asleep on his feet and had dreamed the whole thing. As soon as he realised he hadn't, he ran home and told his mother what had happened. Sadie smiled and carried on with the washing-up. As her son sat down at the table he grabbed a Coca-Cola from the cool box and hardly said another word. She sorted out the groceries and was starting to put them away in the cupboard when her son asked her: "What's a Virgo child?" Sadie had no idea what he was talking about; like her son, she was unfamiliar with the signs of the zodiac.

White went to his room but couldn't stop thinking about the old woman and what she had said to him. He resolved to find out what a Virgo child was: "I had to know what she meant. I started asking everyone what a Virgo child was, but no one knew. At first I thought it might have to do only with my birthday, until I learned a couple of weeks before and after, which sparked an even greater level of curiosity in me."

Eventually White was drawn into a whole world that was strange to him – that of the horoscope and the art of predicting the future by the date and time of someone's birth. He learned about the meaning of the 12 signs of the zodiac. He recalled later that he had not realised before that there were 12 signs, nor apparently did his close family and friends. He said: "I was amazed how much people behaved like their signs described."

It became an obsession and he could not stop talking about it to his friends and anyone who wanted to listen. Eventually Barry White got a reputation as a sage and became known as something of a relationship expert, so much so that his friends used to approach him regularly for advice. White called these friends his "students of love"and started providing counselling services. Sometimes it all got rather formal, as one day when a boy 10 years older asked him to help solve some relationship issues he was having with his girlfriend. They both came over to White's mother's house and sat on the sofa for an hour while White gave them advice: "All I was really doing was talking common sense. I told him he should listen to what his woman was saying and that he should examine all the circumstances and see if there were answers he was missing. I told him to look to himself for resolutions before looking to others for blame. The next time White saw his friend he said to him: "Man it's amazing – everything you say is right."

He counselled another friend who was having problems and couldn't understand why he wasn't getting along with his girlfriend: "The first place you have to look for your mistakes is within yourself, not in her. She is reacting to whatever you are doing."

White believed fundamentally that men didn't understand women: "We're always the aggressors and we are born with a fierce anger and brute strength we have to learn to control."

Word started to spread around the neighbourhood about young Barry White's remarkable ability to reunite couples and solve their relationship problems. They told him it was the way he gave the advice that made the difference, not necessarily the advice itself. Although he never asked for money, people started paying him by leaving money on the hat stand.

It almost became a full-time job, and his mother used to come home from work to find much older strangers in her living room having earnest conversations with her 14-year-old son.

By the time he was 15 White had 22 what he called "client couples" coming to see him regularly. He took it all in his stride and said: "I talked about things in a common sense way in such a fashion that both women and men could hear themselves through me." Years later he wrote a song called *Practice What You Preach*, which reflected on his time as a counsellor.

Many songs later came out of that period, and his counselling activities were only ended by his arrest.

In 1978 he took his talents one stage further when he devoured a new book called 'Love Signs' by Linda Goodman. The book was regarded by many as the definitive book on the subject, and was described as a guide to love and compatibility based on the 12 signs, exploring in depth all the possible combinations. It covered how compatible the readers were with their lovers, friends and even colleagues. White became enthralled by it and his copy rarely left his side.

He recalled: "I practically memorised it. I couldn't believe how much there was in there about me. It was a book that I could relate to that talked to me about me." White became something of an expert and he admits that he almost became that woman who had stopped him at the road junction: "It got to a point where I could talk to someone for a little while and make a pretty good call as to what their sign was. More often than not I was right on the money."

The shabbily dressed lady was not Barry White's only brush with destiny in 1959. A few weeks later he was walking home from school when he passed a backyard with the radio blaring out a song by a new group called The Flamingos. The sound of that song stopped Barry White dead in his tracks. It was to change his life.

The song was *I Only Have Eyes For You*, originally written by Henry Warren and Al Dubin for a musical called 'Dames' in 1934. Ben Selvin made it a hit that same year and it became a favourite accompaniment to the foxtrot in the thirties.

Twenty-five years later it was rediscovered by Terry Johnson, an unrecognised musical genius, who, with his Flamingos bandmates Jake Carey, Tommy Hunt, Paul Wilson and Nate Nelson, recorded it for the group's first album.

The Flamingos, like Barry White, had honed their singing skills in a church choir at the Church of God and Saints of Christ in Philadelphia, where there were no musical instruments, just voices. Phil Hurtt, the producer, recalled: "One of the things that separated them from a lot of the doo-wop groups was their sound. It was a smoother, accurate harmony. Their blend was awesome."

Terry Johnson had no idea what to do with *I Only Have Eyes For You* and pondered for days before the answer came to him in a dream: "I was laying down in my room with the guitar on my chest, playing around with the chords, but no matter what I tried it just didn't fit. Finally, it was about 12 or one in the morning, and I fell asleep. In my dream I heard *I Only Have Eyes For You* just the way it came out on our record. I heard the 'doo-bop sh-bop' backing vocals, I heard the way the harmony would sound so clear, and the structure of the chords. As soon as I woke up, I grabbed the guitar off my chest and it was like God put my fingers just where they were supposed to be. I played those chords and I heard the harmonies, and so I called the guys. I woke them all up and I said, 'Come over to my room right now – I've got *I Only Have Eyes For You.*' They were like, 'Are you crazy? It's almost four o'clock,' and I said, 'I need you all now, otherwise I may not be able to remember. So they came to my room, all of them grumbling, and when they heard me do it they looked at me like, 'What the hell is this?' They laughed at me: 'What's doo-bop sh-bop?' You see, although in my dream it was doo-bop sh-bop, I had everybody doing a different thing, changing things around to make sure no one could really pick out what we were saying."

When they had recorded the song it almost didn't get released at all, as George Goldner, the producer, didn't think it was commercial enough to be a single, so they recorded a cover of Russ Columbo's *Goodnight Sweetheart*. But the disc jockeys of Los Angeles ignored it and started playing *I Only Have Eyes For You* non-stop. Goldner realised his mistake and rushed it out as a single.

And that was how Barry White got to hear it: "To this day I've never seen the reaction in women to a song the way I did then. That song did more for us boys trying to get next to our girlfriends than anything else we tried. It also taught me a lesson I've never forgotten – how women react to a musical sound they really like, and these are the things I have tried to take into the studio." White went straight out and bought the single, which he quickly wore out playing on his mother's gramophone. He recalled many years later in his memoirs: "In my opinion The Flamingos' recording of *I Only Have Eyes For You* is the greatest love song of all time." 'Rolling Stone' magazine agreed and named it one of the best 500 individual songs of all time.

CHAPTER 7

A Criminal Goes to Jail

Barry White goes out of control

1960

By the time he was 15 Barry White was finished with gangs, and for him membership of The Businessmen was no longer 'cool'. But the fact that he was no longer a member of a gang didn't change the way he behaved, not at all. In fact, his character became very unpleasant when he turned 15 and got worse rather than better, as he readily admitted in his 1999 memoir: "My bad behaviour became something of an addiction."

Barry White spiralled totally out of control. It was early 1960 and by his own admission he was a "very bad boy". He was already a veteran of a life of petty crime, for which there seemed no end. It was only a matter of time before he got into serious trouble.

He was living in the tiny house on 42nd Place and Hoover in West Los Angeles with his mother and brother, and Sadie had little idea what he was getting up to. He had become schizophrenic: inside his house he was a loving son and butter wouldn't melt, but as soon as he stepped outside the front door he changed into something else entirely.

Stealing was a way of life for him. Everything from a chocolate bar to a Cadillac was in his range. He was, as he admitted, "addicted to badness". He even used to steal cars just for fun, and often after a joyride round Los Angeles he would return the vehicle to the exact spot that he had picked it up. As he said: "I was exposed to so much that I was in danger of becoming desensitised." He admitted many years later that he had been involved in the theft of more than 200 cars: "For a year I couldn't go to sleep without having stolen a car. I must have stolen between 150 and 300 cars."

And it was this that eventually led him to prison, as he committed one crime too many.

On the first Friday of February he and some friends set out to steal some tyres from a local Chevrolet dealership called Fletcher Jones. The particular tyres they were after were expensive specials. White had always worked on his own in the past when he had gone, as he put it, "burglarizing houses, fighting, drinking and stealing cars," and had been clever enough always to avoid capture.

But on Friday 5th February 1960 he went too far: "The boys said we could make a lot of bread with these tires so I reluctantly agreed to go along." The actual theft went perfectly and they got away, each carting off a supply of the expensive items. But the crime was too big to be ignored and the tyres too traceable. By Saturday afternoon a determined effort by the LAPD had picked up two of the robbers, together with some of the loot. One of them ratted on Barry White and the police surrounded his house and took him off in handcuffs on the Sunday afternoon. As White recalled: "My poor mother did not know what was happening and it broke her heart because my young brother Darryl, only 14, was also in jail for something he'd done."

White was full of remorse and he never let his mother visit him for the whole of the time he was locked up. It was the worst moment of his life when he heard the gates clang behind him at Juvenile Hall: "It was the loudest clang I ever heard in my life. I'd never been locked up like this before. I'd been busted for little things before, but my mother would always come and somehow get me out."

It turned out that the tyres were worth thousands of dollars, much more than White had realised. The police had thrown him into Juvenile Hall and there was no question of bail before his trial, which would be two months away at least. He said: "Well, I knew my mother wasn't coming this time."

Barry White hated being confined in Juvenile Hall: "I didn't like people telling me what to do, when to get up, when to go to bed, what to eat, when not to eat, when to use the toilet and when not to use the toilet." He was frightened about leaving his mother to fend for herself: "She didn't deserve having two sons behind bars."

And for the first time Barry White began to consider what the future might hold for him: "I began to analyse some things in my life. My partners were getting shot or beat up hanging out with gangs. And I started thinking and I started looking at what rewards you get from that. I looked at some friends of mine who were alcoholics. They worked hard at being alcoholics and their reward was sitting around deteriorating. Being a criminal, the reward is usually jail. The harder you work at crime, the more time you get. So I looked at the only thing I could do best, that I could benefit by, and that would be the most valuable to me. And that was music."

After a few weeks White knew that he had to change – something had to give. But the truth was that he was so riven with badness that he couldn't see any light at the end of the tunnel. So he began a mental struggle with himself, to find himself, and he didn't know which way it would come out. But he did know that his whole future depended on it: "When I was in jail my ultimate goal was to change my life because my freedom had been taken and I had to get over that hurdle. You ask yourself, 'You are in jail but how did you get here?' I concluded that it was nothing but Barry that put me here." White knew that the next step was the penitentiary, but he knew no way out. He said to himself: "How are you going to get out of here? Well, it's Barry that's put you in here, and it's Barry that's gonna get you out of here."

And so it proved.

CHAPTER 8

Epiphany

Release from juvenile prison

1960

Barry White claims that his awakening from his bad ways and his eventual calling to the music business occurred on the evening of Wednesday 10th August 1960. He was a month off his 16th birthday and lying on his bunk in Los Angeles's Juvenile Hall. Life was as low as it could get and he had been there for more than six months.

He had already done much soul-searching as to why and how he had ended up there. He had a strong desire to change his life but couldn't work out how, as he explained: "My freedom had been taken and I asked myself how did I get here? I realised it wasn't anyone but me who had put me here and that it was up to me to get myself out."

White realised that his life could go three ways: he could return to jail and be there for the rest of his life, get himself killed, or sort himself out. He knew option three would be the hardest, because he knew himself. He wasn't a bad boy but he was worldly wise enough to know that he had always favoured the easy option and had been too easily influenced by people he looked up to. He said: "I decided there and then that music would be my saviour."

White had just gone to bed and sunk into the lower bunk of his shared room when along the corridor someone turned on a transistor radio and out of it came Elvis Presley singing the chart-topping ballad *It's Now or Never*. White had heard it countless times before as it had spent the last few weeks of July and nearly all of August at the top of the singles chart. But as he was closing his eyes to go off to sleep suddenly the words of Elvis Presley sparked something off in his head: "I had heard it before but it was like hearing it for the first time. Just for me."

It's Now or Never was not just another song – it was the biggest-selling record of Presley's career to date. The lyrics not only turned White's head that night, but also those of a whole generation of young people who found resonance in them. The song proved so significant to Americans that it is worth recounting its history. *It's Now or Never* was not a new song, but a reworking of an old Italian melody composed by Neapolitan songwriter Eduardo di Capua at the start of the century. Presley had heard it while he was serving in the US Army in Germany, and it had been first recorded by Tony Martin as *There's No Tomorrow* in 1949. Presley had immediately liked the melody and knew that, with some new lyrics, it could be a hit for him. It so happened that Presley was being visited at his army barracks by Freddy Bienstock, a music publisher who ran Presley's own publishing company, Gladys Music Inc. Presley asked Bienstock to investigate and see if he could find some writers to put new words to the old tune. Bienstock promised to get on to it as soon as he got home to New York.

Gladys Music Inc had been formed by Presley and his manager, Tom Parker, in 1956 and was named after Presley's late mother Gladys. It was based at the Brill Building in New York, which rented out suites of offices to people primarily involved in the music business. Bienstock soon discovered that the song was out of copyright in the US and on his first day back in the office he searched the Brill Building for some lyricists to put new words to the tune.

It so happened that the only two lyricists in the building that day were Aaron Schroeder and Wally Gold, so they got the job by default. Schroeder had very successfully composed some songs for Presley before, and they were hired to rework it into a new song for him. The two men liked the tune and attacked the project with gusto, so much so that they reputedly wrote the brand-new lyrics in half an hour.

It was all ready for when Presley returned from Germany in March 1960, and he recorded it at the RCA studios in Nashville on 3rd April. It was released as a single on 5th July and went to No 1 in almost every country, becoming one of the most successful vinyl singles of all time. The release was delayed in the UK because the copyright of the original composition had not run out in every country. However, the delay just heightened expectations and when it was released it was the first record ever to go straight to No 1, remaining there for eight solid weeks.

It certainly was to prove significant for Barry White, and he actually believed that Presley was delivering a personal message straight to him that night.

He immediately thought to himself: "It was like he was telling me, 'Change your life, Barry, you're thinking about going another way. It's now or never.' I understood that."

White sat bolt upright in his bunk and swore that he would change his life from that moment: "I have to change my ways because if I don't I'm going to end up in jail for the rest of my life." He swore from that moment that he would turn his fortunes around.

White claims in his own memoirs that on the next morning, 11th August, "Everything around me looked and felt just a little bit different."

Three weeks later, when his court hearing was scheduled, he was in a completely different frame of mind from when he had entered the correctional facility. Whereas earlier he would have seen a prison sentence as a badge of honour, now he was desperate to avoid that outcome. He had turned 16 and knew he was old enough to be sent to a proper jail. It was a crucial moment in his life, and if he had been sent to jail the odds are he would never have shaken off the stigma.

On Friday 26th August 1960 he was sitting in a holding room with his fellow juveniles. Each one was called and returned with sentences ranging from probation to jail sentences of up to two years. He had never been so frightened in his life and wondered what was in store for him. He was certain he was going to jail for at least a year, and that would mean Soledad State Prison, a correctional training facility with nearly 6,000 inmates.

White was up in front of Judge Hamilton, who had a history of handing out tough sentences and showing little mercy to juveniles who had got themselves into trouble with the law. He had previously sentenced his brother Darryl to jail time and knew he was dealing with his older sibling. When his name was called, White remembered how he felt: "My stomach flip-flopped and turned upside down and sideways."

But something seemed to touch Judge Hamilton that day. Maybe it was the fact that he knew that the effect of having two brothers in prison would be catastrophic for the White family and their mother. Or maybe he just saw something redeemable in young Barry.

It was immediately clear that Judge Hamilton had done his homework, had studied White's school record and had been surprised at what he had found. The boy's school history was excellent and that made Hamilton angry: "You're not doing anything but conning your mother," he said, "and now you're trying to con me because we both know you know how to do the right thing." The Judge laid into him and gave him a serious lecture on how he was wasting his young life and destroying his future before it had even started. White just stood there with his head bowed as tears came into his eyes. He knew that every word uttered by the Judge was true and he was genuinely ashamed of himself. The Judge's monologue, which went on for more than eight minutes, made a huge impression on him.

At the end of it White heard the magic word 'probation', then the Judge leaned over and whispered in his ear: "I'm going to let you go home, boy." The words didn't sink in at first and White thought he was talking about somebody else, as he didn't believe there had been the slightest possibility that he would be going home that day.

But the leniency came with a strong warning – Hamilton told White that this was his very last chance. He told him that any future misdemeanours and subsequent hearings would be reserved to him and that prison would be the automatic result, with 22 months the minimum sentence if he broke the terms of his 12-month probation. Hamilton had handed down what was effectively a suspended sentence.

When the Judge banged down his gavel and shouted, "Next case!" it was a mightily relieved Barry White who scampered out of the court to be transported back to Juvenile Hall and begin the process of obtaining his release after nearly seven months inside.

Over the next two days the juvenile officers prepared him for release. He retrieved his personal possessions and signed the forms that would give him his freedom. The following Sunday morning he walked free. Nearly 40 years later he remembered the big smile on his face as he walked out of Juvenile Hall and heard the gates slam behind him: "I came to grips with owning up to my mistakes and made up my mind to never hand my freedom over to anyone else again in my life. I knew I was never going back in and the life I had known up to then was all history."

During his and his brother's absence, their mother Sadie had taken positive action of her own and found a new home. She had moved house to 48th on

Avalon Boulevard in South Los Angeles, putting as much distance as she could between her sons and the gang culture.

It was an emotional homecoming for Sadie, who hugged and hugged her son to welcome him home. White remembered: "It was a new day and a new ball game. In fact it was a whole new song. I was going to change everything."

CHAPTER 9

Meeting Mary

Sex, children and an emotional meltdown

1957 to 1963

Whilst all this turmoil had been going on in his life, Barry White had met a girl and fallen deeply in love. He first met Mary Smith at school when he was in the eighth grade and she was in the seventh. He was just 13 years old and she was barely 12, but almost straight away they were two people in love. She was a typical pretty neighbourhood girl next door and they were genuine childhood sweethearts, as Barry White said in his 1999 memoir: "We were crazy about each other in that special private universe way only kids can be."

They quickly formed a close bond and White later admitted that his early relationship with Mary was the first time he had experienced what he called "true, true love." He recalled: "I deeply fell in love with this young girl, not understanding the philosophy of love. I learned what it is when you fall in love and lose contact with reality. You are slowly giving the power of your will and mind to something else."

Mary's real name was Elizabet (Betty) Smith, but for some reason she started going as Mary, which was the name by which Barry White always knew her.

For the first three years it was a platonic relationship overseen by their parents. According to White, they never even kissed. He claimed later that he was not much interested in sex before then: "She was my girlfriend but I wasn't interested in making love and screwing in the back of cars when I was young. I was interested in music, gang banging and church. I had a lot of other things on my mind."

The relationship was only consummated when they both suddenly discovered sex as he turned 15 and she was approaching her 14th birthday. White remembered that it happened unexpectedly at the Los Angeles Exposition Park in the daytime. And once they discovered sex they found they couldn't stop themselves despite their relative youth.

A lack of sex education meant that as soon as they started having sex regularly they ran the everyday risk of Mary becoming pregnant. As White remembered: "When we finally consummated our love we practised the rhythm method," but, he admitted, "You've really got to know what you are doing and I had no idea what I was doing." Only youth prevented Mary getting pregnant then.

They were rescued from that fate when their lovemaking was interrupted by his arrest and seven-month incarceration in Juvenile Hall. When he came out it started up again. Everything was all right for two months until, as White remembered, "For one of the very few times in my life I lost the beat."

The news when it came was desperate for both of them. Announcing it to their respective families was the most difficult thing either of them ever had to do.

News of the pregnancy naturally hit both sets of parents hard. The couple were not out of school, were not living together and had no income. In fact, both Barry and Mary were living at home with their respective parents. Despite all that, they decided to keep the baby, confident that their love for each other would make everything right. But it didn't.

Almost as soon as Mary realised she was pregnant the ardour started to cool. Something changed as they both faced up to the realities of the situation. Mary and her parents clearly expected Barry White to leave school, get a job and make an honest woman of their daughter. But he didn't.

Even so, Barry and Mary remained a devoted couple and it was proud, if young, parents that found themselves with a baby boy on 29th June 1961, naming him Barry jnr. The father was 16 and the mother 15. They continued to live with their respective parents and carried on much as before except that there was a third person in the relationship.

10 months later, incredibly, Mary was pregnant again, and this really began to expose the strains in the relationship, made worse by Barry's infidelity. He was hardly the most faithful of boyfriends and, once he discovered the joys of sexual intercourse, he certainly didn't practise monogamy in any shape or form. He was a good-looking teenager standing 6 feet 3 inches tall. Girls loved him and by all accounts he loved them back. As he said: "I've never not got a woman I wanted."

But despite his frequent wanderings, like many men of that era he expected absolute fidelity from his partner.

One day White called on his girlfriend by surprise and found her with a friend of his called Clifton. They were just friends and there was absolutely nothing going on, but White saw red and there was a scene. As far as he was concerned they were having too good a time together and he found that he strongly resented it. A huge wave of uncontrollable jealously came over him: "It's where possessiveness and jealousy comes from. Out of all the emotions we get, jealousy is the worst of the negatives."

Despite that intensity, Barry and Mary gradually grew apart. White tried to describe his feelings in his 1999 memoir: "It messed me up and I felt betrayed as if Mary had cheated on me behind my back. I was so hung up in my definition of purity that I didn't want to see Mary even talk to another boy. To me she was one of the most beautiful women I'd ever seen, with a soulful slightly square elegance I'd found in no one else except my mother."

In truth, they were far too young to have a young child and another on the way while still at school, and it was an untenable situation for both of them. The relationship was effectively over, but it took many years and a marriage before it would finally end: "It was enough for me to take her off the pedestal I had put her on. That's how pure her image was to me. I guess I'd had my mother all to myself and I wanted Mary the same way."

There were of course parallels with his own mother's situation when she had become pregnant twice in quick succession with a man she would never marry. But Barry White never saw these similarities, although his own mother fretted with the usual 'like father, like son' worries and often wondered if they would turn out to be true.

The relationship gradually stopped being benign and turned fractious. It was not helped by continual money worries. They depended totally on Mary's parents and this was not a recipe for a successful relationship with a proud partner like Barry White. Mary's mother always took her side and it wore White down; the permanent presence of his mother-in-law became intolerable.

But White carried on loving Mary despite it all, as he admitted: "I knew I would never fall in love again with any other woman in that same pure way. I would love again of course but not fall in love. And as far as my feelings for

Mary were concerned I didn't realise I was the one who had changed."

And as White grew older he realised that his feelings were complicated by his feelings for other women, and a schism developed between him and the mother of his children that hurt him and affected him badly. He felt trapped and started drinking heavily: "The confusion messed me up so bad that for the next six months I became an alcoholic." He drank from early morning to late at night until he could no longer stand.

Something had to give.

MEETING MARY

CHAPTER 10

A Murdering Brother

Childhood marred

1964 to 1965

Barry White's brother, Darryl, went to Juvenile Hall for the first time when he was only eight years old, and it set the scene for the rest of his life. As his mother Sadie said: "I can't remember a single Christmas when Darryl was not locked up." As Barry readily admitted: "Darryl White was truly unredeemable."

The problem was that Barry was a mummy's boy and Darryl was a daddy's boy, and they followed those respective personality traits. Sadie was a truly honest person with an extremely good heart, which was basically what Barry was. Melvin had been the opposite, a thoroughly deceitful man who usually preferred to tell a lie, even when the truth would have sufficed. Darryl followed in his footsteps, only ten times worse, as Barry said: "Darryl chose not to listen to my mother. He chose to listen to his father who was wrong till the day he died."

Although Barry White blamed his father for how Darryl turned out, he didn't hold him responsible: "My father wasn't in the house taking care of us, he had another family. I've forgiven him as I know that in his time, as a black man, things were a lot different. Men corrupt more easily than women, lying, deceiving – it's part of being a man."

And Darryl White carried another burden around with him that was totally down to his father – the way he looked. He was extremely good-looking and had the hunky physique directly inherited from Melvin White. This meant that Darryl didn't really have to try with the opposite sex – it all came to him. As his brother remembered: "Darryl had a million different ladies."

Arguably Darryl White was a more talented musician than his older brother Barry. He had an excellent 'ear' and a feel for a rhythm. But what he had in raw talent, he lacked in motivation. And when he fell in love with crime and out of love with music the pattern of his life was set forever.

At the root of Darryl's talent was radio. He listened to the Los Angeles radio stations all day. His ear was so good that he was the first in the city to spot a new musical trend almost before the disc jockeys themselves detected it. Barry remembered many years later: "Every day he would come home and ask if I had heard this new song or that one."

Almost always Barry hadn't, and was alerted to new music and new artists time and time again by a brother whose musical taste eerily matched his own. He said: "I firmly believe that if he hadn't fallen in love with crime as deeply as I fell out of love with it, he would have gone on to become a great musician in his own right."

The brothers used to harmonise together whenever they could: "We could harmonise like you wouldn't believe ... the White brothers, oh, what they could have been."

But it didn't take long for Barry to realise that Darryl didn't have the focus to succeed. To Barry, music was a passion, but to Darryl it was just something to do, as he said resignedly: "Unfortunately we didn't and it couldn't. Darryl had the ability but not the desire and you have to have both to succeed in anything as difficult and demanding as show business."

A life of crime robbed Darryl White of the fame and fortune that eventually fell to his older brother, as Barry himself admitted: "Crime robbed Darryl of a side of himself that could have made him a very successful person."

Darryl's main problem was the huge chip on his shoulder that he carried from the age of eight. He always believed that anyone he met was trying to do him down. And he loved his life as a hard man too much, as his brother recalled: "Darryl craved the action of violence and could never get enough. We'd be somewhere, and he always liked to fight. He taught me how to fight. His idea of harmony was confusion, people screaming and hollering; he loved that shit. He told me, 'Once they see you're a fighter, you don't have to worry.'" By the time he was 14 Darryl White was well over 6 feet tall and his day was full of trouble, as Barry remembered: "Everywhere we went he'd start trouble. He was bad, he really was."

Sadie was powerless to prevent her youngest son from sinking into a life of crime: "My mother knew what he was up to and it affected her deeply. Whenever he was out at night she had trouble sleeping and when she did get to sleep she dreamed terrible dreams about her son. One night she begged him not to go out and her fears proved all too true."

One black day those bad dreams turned into reality as Darryl came in the front door holding the side of his face with blood everywhere. He had been slashed with a razor from his ear to the base of his neck. He rushed to the bathroom and locked himself in. His brother broke the door down and held him in a bear hug as his mother inspected the wound. She saw he was going to die if he kept losing blood at that rate: "I'd never seen that much blood in my life," said Barry. "I threw my arms around him and tears filled my eyes." Sadie wrapped Darryl's whole head tightly in a towel and a neighbour drove them all to the emergency room. Darryl was panicking and his brother kept whispering in his ear that it was going to be all right. The doctors at ER stabilised him, then stitched him up just in time – but it had been a close-run thing. Only his mother's quick thinking with the tightly coiled towel had saved him – another five minutes and he would have been dead.

This was just one of many incidents. One of Darryl's favourite occupations was to walk the streets of LA and gratuitously punch someone in the face. He and his friends would have a competition about who could punch the biggest person and lay them out cold. Barry said: "He lived a cold brutal life and only those who have a real taste for blood can survive that way for very long."

Barry was also later shocked by his brother's conduct towards Al Samuels, a toy store owner who, as we shall learn later, had not treated the White family very well. Samuels had fired Barry as manager of the store, which was now managed by Sadie. As a result Darryl went to the store, grabbed a fireman's axe, placed Samuels's head on a table and raised the blade. Sadie rushed and put herself between Samuels's head and the axe, then grabbed the telephone receiver to call her eldest son: "Barry, you've got to come down here right now. Your brother is here and he's going to kill Al!"

Barry rushed over to the store and managed to defuse the situation. He told Darryl: "This guy isn't worth killing. All he did was cheat me out of a few dollars. It isn't worth it." But Darryl replied: "I was going to bring his head to you." He seemed determined to chop off Samuels's head as he shouted: "No, this motherfucker has to go! There can't be no white motherfucker come into our family and do this, man!" Realising the absolute seriousness of the situation and the drastic effect it could have on the whole family, Barry walked slowly around the back of his brother, put his arms around his chest and lifted him off the ground. He physically removed him from the shop and carried him four blocks down the street. It was a giant man carrying another giant man, and it was only the oral authority of an older brother that gave Barry White the edge over his younger sibling. Finally he talked him down from the edge.

That day the situation had been defused, but Darryl White carried on, fuelled by drugs, wreaking his mayhem. The assault charges piled up, meaning that he was more or less permanently confined to Juvenile Hall. Barry shied away from any form of violence after watching his brother in action: "Seeing it so close to me and what it did to him was one of the strongest reasons I resisted a life of senseless street violence."

Things went from bad to worse for his brother until it got to the point where Sadie was happier when he was in jail. Another terrible incident occurred when Darryl was in a gang that robbed a bank; they kidnapped a woman as a live hostage and when the police gave chase they threw her out of the moving getaway car onto the highway in front of the police car. Somehow Darryl avoided capture, but boasted to everybody that it was he who had thrown the woman out of the car. After that Barry sensed that his younger brother was a cold-blooded killer and Al Samuels would probably not have been his first murder.

Darryl White's luck finally ran out and he was sentenced to 50 years in prison, which in California at the time was an indefinite sentence. Sadie believed it was a life sentence and that Darryl would never be released. And that was what 50 years meant in the mid-sixties.

In truth he was better off inside, and the Carter-White family could get on with their lives without the shadow of a murderous son and brother hanging over them. But that reality didn't make it any easier to bear the loss, as Barry recalled: "I felt a part of myself had been taken away and it made my mother and me very sad and I didn't know what to do to make it better for us."

Barry White witnessed his brother's eventual demise with a sinking feeling as he realised that it could so easily have been him but for that night of epiphany in September 1960. One day a dark chill ran down his spine as he contemplated seeing his brother in jail again: "I knew that if I didn't keep absolutely on top of things in my life I could easily be watching my own future being played out before me. I needed to anchor myself in a way that would, if nothing else, impose a sense of responsibility that would keep my mind on my music."

But before that happened, there was an incident that directly impacted on Barry White, and one that he was very lucky to walk away from.

CHAPTER 11

Seconds from Oblivion

A narrow escape from the law

1965

Barry White found himself a whisker way from his own life sentence soon after his brother had been locked away for 50 years. Although he had resolved to behave himself, focus on his music and keep out of trouble at all costs, it seemed that trouble followed him around.

It all started when he dropped in, unannounced, at a party. He had long given up the gang lifestyle, but almost by accident he and two of his cousins ended up at a house party with many of his former gang members. White recalled: "I'd been off the street for some time and a lot of my brothers wanted to say hello. There were so many familiar brothers and sisters there and the action spilled out on to the street. It was all good-natured and a typical hot Saturday night party. There seemed to be no danger."

Everything went well and White and his cousins enjoyed a magical evening catching up with old friends in a spirit of bonhomie. Just before midnight White began to make moves to leave the party, but leaving took at least half an hour as there were so many people to say goodbye to.

Then, just as they got to their car, some members of a gang called The Roman Twenties turned up. The Roman Twenties were the second most feared gang in Los Angeles after The Businessmen, and Barry and Darryl White had been members of both. The Romans had been founded in the 1920s by some Italian-Americans and diversified from petty gang violence into high-level crime; they had subsequently been subsumed by African-Americans and the Italian heritage virtually forgotten.

This was clearly a party where members of The Businessmen were welcome but not others, and the appearance of 20 or so members of The Roman Twenties was bound to lead to trouble. Sensing this, White jumped out of his car and made an effort to cool the situation. He was trying to defuse a possible confrontation and walked up to the apparent leader of The Roman Twenties,

Michael McGarry. White knew McGarry well from the old days and told him: "Go home man, get out of here." Naturally McGarry wanted to know why. He respected Barry White and stopped to listen. White suggested that it wasn't a good idea to go to a party he wasn't invited to. Surprisingly McGarry, the de facto leader that night, took his advice and withdrew. They slapped each other on the back, bumped fists and left together, laughing as they went into the night. White knew that a major confrontation had been avoided and he was mightily relieved.

After White and McGarry had left with White's cousins, the gang split up and went their separate ways. But an hour later some of the more hot-headed younger members came back and there was the inevitable confrontation. One member, believed to be Milton Harris, was shot in the affray. The gun was fired at close range and it was thought likely that Milton would not survive as he was taken away in an ambulance. The Los Angeles Police Department regularly ignored gang woundings, but they could not ignore a possible murder. They immediately swung into action, setting up an incident unit across the street. It was a crime too far, one that they were determined to solve, and huge numbers of officers turned up. They sealed off the street and started interviewing everyone at the party – arrests were made immediately of anyone suspected of being involved in the shooting.

As White drove home later that night and pulled up in front of his mother's house, he found the neighbourhood surrounded by police. Wondering what was going on, he innocently got out of his car and wandered up to the police officers. He was immediately thrown to the ground by police and handcuffed, together with both of his cousins, before being bundled into the back of a police van.

They were taken to an interrogation room at police headquarters and left alone, doubtless being observed and recorded. After half an hour a police sergeant came in and said: "Who the hell is Barry White?" When White put up his hand, the sergeant said to him: "So you are the bad boy?" White feigned ignorance and indifference. But he sensed that he was in serious trouble and began to shout at the sergeant that he had done nothing wrong.

It was a week before Christmas and eventually the cousins were all put in separate cells to cool off. White remembered: "I feared I was about to be locked up through Christmas and I was worried about my kids and what this would do to my mother."

The following day White and his cousins were kept in the interrogation rooms and were subjected to long individual grillings. Officers accused White of taking a gun to the party and shooting Milton Harris. White told them that he hadn't been there and he didn't even know who Harris was, and that it was all news to him. By then he had calmed down and resolved to answer the questions as honestly as he could. Luckily his two cousins repeated his version of the story word for word.

But the police wanted the names of the rival gang members who had turned up at the party, and White refused to answer those questions, insisting that he was no squealer. He said: "The police got no names from me and never would, even if they threatened to lock me up for the rest of my life."

The police interrogators eventually told him that neighbours had put him in the frame for the shooting and said that everyone was shouting his name when it happened. From that moment White knew that the evidence was all hypothetical and that the police had nothing to link him directly to the shooting. But he also knew that they could charge him and keep him locked up for a long time until it came to trial. Milton was in a coma and police detectives were waiting to interview him if he came round. As the fifth night of incarceration passed, White became more and more despondent, praying and praying that Milton would not die.

Milton did eventually regain consciousness and told his questioners that Barry White had nothing to do with the shooting and hadn't even been there. Milton's belated testimony was enough to clear White's name.

So on Christmas Eve White walked free and swore he would never put himself in that position again. It had been a truly frightening five days and he decided that the first steps to redemption would be making an honest woman of the mother of his children.

CHAPTER 12

Break Out

First chance in the music business

1960

Meanwhile with all this personal turmoil going on in his life, Barry White was having more luck with his ambitions to break into music. Those three days in September 1960, when he was released from prison, proved to be some of the happiest of his life. He spent virtually the whole time in the bosom of his mother, Sadie, learning again how to live on the outside after close to seven months of incarceration. He kept remembering the Elvis Presley song, repeating the lyrics to himself and feeling an odd reassurance that everything was going to be all right: "I had very little education, no trade, no nothing – just an idea and a belief in myself."

But to his intense surprise the resolutions he had made inside took more living up to than he had imagined. He found himself itching to get back "on the scene" and re-join his old friends in the gangs. And that he might have done were it not for a surprise knock on the door. At first he thought it was his old pals and remembered making a grab for his coat. But it turned out to be three old school friends who had a proposition for him.

The three faces at the door were Theo Reed, Leroy Saunders and Earl Harris, with whom he had messed about in break times in the schoolyard, people he had long forgotten about. But they hadn't forgotten him or the make-believe jamming they used to do together in their breaks.

It turned out that the three friends had formed a pop group called The Upfronts with a fourth boy. But the fourth boy was unreliable and didn't pull his weight. Suddenly he stopped turning up for rehearsals and they decided to replace him. They wanted someone to sing bass and they thought, "Who better than Barry White?"

White was naturally interested and said to them: "Just show me where I'm supposed to go and tell me what you want me to do." They told him he had to be approved by their manager first – but that, they thought, would be a formality.

When the door closed behind them and Reed, Saunders and Harris left, White couldn't believe what had just happened. He had always loved music but had never considered it as a career. As he said: "When The Upfronts came knocking at my door, they truly changed the direction of my life. Music was the only thing I had to hang onto."

The three men had unwittingly given Barry White a lifeline and a future, as he readily admitted: "I came into it not knowing what I had to offer – all I had was the will and the love for music."

The next day, as promised, the three boys arrived at his house and took him to meet their manager, Lummie Fowler. Fowler, a former postman, ran a management company called Lummtone. He was a multi-talented executive who managed, produced and wrote songs for music hopefuls like The Upfronts. Among the other groups he managed were the Colognes, the Elgins, George Powell and the Troopers, and the Five Ramblers.

Fowler's house doubled as Lummtone's offices and he had converted his garage into a makeshift studio. The three boys didn't take any chances and White was introduced to Fowler as The Upfronts' new bass singer. Fowler was having none of it and his demeanour made it instantly clear that it was his decision whether Barry White was accepted into the group. Fowler looked him up and down and said: "We'll see." Then the three went right into the garage and started rehearsing with their prospective new bass singer. After a few minutes Fowler had heard enough and nodded approval, saying to White: "Welcome to The Upfronts."

The following day Fowler took his protégés, including an astonished Barry White, to the TGG recording studio on Highland Boulevard to 'lay down' some songs. Barely a week after gaining his freedom, White couldn't believe what was happening to him: "I was blown away and I instantly fell in love with the music industry."

In those days the record industry was very different and you could record a hot record on Tuesday night and have it on the streets and being played on the radio by the following Wednesday. So The Upfronts and their newest member entered the studio full of hope and equally full of trepidation.

Barry White had never set foot into a recording studio before and admitted he had never seen a set of drums in real life, or really any other instrument other than the piano. He was immediately fascinated, like the proverbial boy in a sweet shop: "When I walked into that room where that big mixing board was with those knobs and meters and the tape recorder, I just stood against the wall and knew that was where I wanted to be."

He was transfixed by the mixing board, not that he knew what it was. As he said: "It looked to me like a giant robot lurking in the middle of the room." He pointed to a man standing behind it and asked who he was. It was the engineer. He was surprised that The Upfronts were going to record with people he called 'real musicians'. He certainly didn't consider himself, or any of his friends, to be real musicians – far from it. But White immediately felt a connection with all the instruments lying around the recording studio. He immediately felt an urge to play them all and believed he could: "To see all these instruments and equipment together was amazing. The instruments were like people – they had living souls to me."

White compared his situation in the studio that day to the jail where he had languished for months and where he had been only the previous week: "I'd never felt anything like this before. I knew I'd walked into something, this little room cluttered with men, instruments and machinery. They called it a studio but I called it freedom."

It was a true 'life breakout' as White called it, but he had no idea that it was a place where he would spend much of the rest of his working life, turning himself into a global icon in the process. "It was the first time I went to a recording studio and I knew I didn't know a damn thing about it and I had to learn." Before long The Upfronts had recorded their first song, which somehow Lummie Fowler persuaded a record company to release. The song, called *Little Girl*, was quite good but it had no chance of being a hit. The Upfronts were just one group among hundreds of hopefuls in Los Angeles in the early sixties with dreams of stardom. And Barry White was one of tens of thousands of pop wannabees. He later discovered that he wasn't even a named member of the group – he was just the unpaid bass backing singer. However, he didn't seem to mind and he was just glad to be a part of the scene. As he said: "We all knew we were working 'on the come' and would get paid if the record became a hit."

He added: "It didn't matter to me as somehow my life's true journey had begun."

But despite that, White nearly blew his career off before it had properly begun. It was all down to his hot temper, the same one that had led him astray in his youth. The Upfronts were in the studio one night working with a well-known sound engineer, one who didn't suffer fools gladly. Suddenly the engineer turned around to White and said: "Hey, what the fuck are you doing?"

Behind the glass of the sound room, White made some derogatory comments about the engineer. But he was unaware the microphone was open and his words were picked up by the engineer, who proceeded to berate White and ordered him out of 'his' studio for daring to answer back to him.

A red mist descended, White threw down his headphones and stormed through the soundproofed door to where the engineer was sitting behind the control board. He grabbed the startled man by the throat. But before he could do any damage, Lummie Fowler stepped in and tapped him on the shoulder. He waved him outside, saying, "Can we talk for a minute?" White thought about it, took his hands down and followed Fowler outside.

Fowler looked White up and down and said: "You are a very talented fellow so let me share something with you that I've learned being in this business as many years as I have. Don't ever talk to people like that in the music business as long as you live or everything you have worked for will disappear like it never existed. If you get that kind of reputation you will never be seen as anything but one more hostile black musician and it will all end for you."

By now White had calmed down, his temper had subsided and he had returned to reality. He promised Fowler there and then that he would take the advice and never forget it. Fowler advised White to go back into the studio and carry on playing as if nothing had happened. He said the engineer would be as sorry as he was now and everyone would want to forget that it had ever happened. But Fowler also warned White that there would be no second chances.

Barry White learned the lesson well. "From that night on," he said, "my vile temper evaporated and the name Barry White gradually came to be associated with a musician who was soft spoken, polite and, beyond that, musically talented. I knew I didn't know how to behave and I never came into the studio again with an ego – ever in my life."

White realised that he had, in modern parlance, an 'attitude problem'. He remembered: "It was a valuable reminder that what works on the street may not work on the inside and confidence does not always mean muscle and ability isn't always enough."

White had quickly discovered the differences between the street and the studio and that people got ahead in the music business because of ability and attitude and not what he called 'menace'.

White never knew what might have happened to his career had Fowler not been there that evening, and admits that it could all have turned out very differently. He realised he had learned a valuable lesson and promised to himself that he would never forget it. He went out of his way from then on to make himself useful at the studio, brewing endless cups of coffee and filling in on any instrument that was required, while never demanding a cent in payment for any extra work or effort. It was another 'epiphany moment' in his life. White recalls that period: "I went to the studio every day and eventually got the chance to play a little keyboard. Now I became the person who could sing and play, one of the few of my age who could do both."

His willingness to do anything endeared him to all the musicians and engineers and he gradually became one of the most popular people in the building – nothing was too much trouble for Barry White. The engineers, producers and arrangers suddenly loved him. He took out their dry cleaning, did their shopping and minded their children. He did anything they wanted, as he recalled: "I was the boy with the flapping shoes, I was the one who was not embarrassed to walk up to you with my flapping shoes and ask, 'Do you have anything for me to do?'"

His willingness brought all sorts of benefits for which he did get paid. He picked up musical odd jobs as it became clear that he could play virtually any instrument as well as sing. White recalled: "Other musicians kept telling me I was good and my name started getting around in studio circles. People began talking about me. 'Hey, have you seen this new guy Barry White? He has this certain style of playing.' I was a rhythm pianist who also took care of the rhythm of life. That became my thing and I began to become known for it among other musicians."

The reputation he began to build for himself by the time he turned 17 was remarkable. A well-known group called The Atlantics adopted him as a backing singer and so did The Majestics. He started to help out the engineers and producers and sat in on sessions, offering his ideas, which, to his surprise, were often taken up.

All this was going on while he was still in his last year at school in the 12th grade. But the pull of the music business finally took hold and with four months to go before he graduated, White suddenly quit John Adams Junior High School on the morning of his 18th birthday, which also coincided with the expiry of his probation period. It was a bold move, as he explained: "I never really liked school all that much anyway and the morning my probation ended, as soon as I opened my eyes, I knew I wasn't going back."

That decision took some explaining to his mother. When he told her she burst into tears and sobbed uncontrollably as if her world was ending. When she regained control she said to him: "Why Barry, why, when you are so close to finishing?" He answered simply: "Because Mama, I am going to Hollywood."

And so he was.

Part 2

12-year struggle to make it

CHAPTER 13

Going to Hollywood

A paid job at last

1962

It was the summer of 1962 and Barry White was only a few weeks shy of turning 18. But in August he had an awakening, as he explained: "One day I woke up and said to myself, 'Man, you have got to go to Hollywood.' I just knew it was time to make my own way in this world and to do so I knew I had to learn what went on in Hollywood. I knew that Hollywood was where the big boys in the music industry were and I wanted to see it for myself."

What he meant by going to Hollywood was literally going there every day, walking the pavements and seeing what turned up. He had no plan – he would walk and walk until he bumped into something, or rather someone, who could give him some work.

But he had put this notion out of his head until it reappeared on the evening of 11th September 1962. It was the day before his birthday and this time he decided that he was going to go and do it and make an attempt to break into the music industry properly.

He remembered: "I laid my clothes out the night before school started on September 12th, which happened to hit this year on my birthday, my 18th birthday, and I was going to graduate. But when I got up the next morning I said to myself I wasn't going to school today, I'm going to Hollywood today."

But that decision was easier said than done, and he had to get past his mother, as he recalled: "I was standing there combing my hair in the mirror and I shouted out, 'Mum, I'm not going to school today,' and she went crazy and said, 'Baby, you got to go to school – it's your last semester, you're gonna graduate.' I said to her, 'I gotta go to Hollywood today.'"

Sadie screamed out loud and cried her eyes out when he told her, as he remembered: "It was one of the deepest cries I have ever heard from a woman's mouth."

When she had recovered from the initial shock, she shouted at him: "What are you going to Hollywood for? You don't know nobody and nobody knows you. You don't have nothing, you have no money ... there's loads of white people out there and you're a young black boy going out into the grown-up white world. Barry, I'm telling you, you're going to get killed out there."

White told her: "You're right. I don't know anybody and I'm black. Everything and everybody that could possibly be against me is except for one person ... me." He added: "I've got determination, Mama, my love for my music and my love for myself, and that's why I got to go to Hollywood."

With that he grabbed his haversack and started walking. He did just what he said he would and took himself to Hollywood to walk the fabled streets. He explained years later: "My mother begged me not to go to Hollywood. She knew I didn't know no one and I had no clothes. But I knew I didn't need those things she worried about." Jack Perry, his closest colleague, recalled much later: "To make the walk from South Central Los Angeles you have to be a very determined person because that's a 15-mile walk and Barry did that."

What he didn't realise was that he was not the only young boy with the idea. It was clear that there were hundreds like him just walking the streets hoping they were paved with gold. But he was unperturbed by the discovery and resolved to rise above the rest. In reality it just made him more determined to succeed. As soon as he arrived that first time he remembered being on the corner of Vine Street and Hollywood Boulevard: "I stood on that corner facing Capitol for four hours. Capitol Records always represented Hollywood to me. I didn't speak to nobody. I smiled at people and they smiled back."

White was very surprised at how different Hollywood was from his own neighbourhood in South Los Angeles: "I didn't see nobody fighting, calling nobody bad names. I didn't see raggedy cars, I saw people with nice shiny cars. I saw people going about their business, people with briefcases. It really inspired me and I knew that this was it – man, this is where you are going to be."

The next day he again walked straight to the famous round Capitol Records skyscraper. Capitol was owned by the British EMI company and was arguably the most famous record label in the world. It was the first record company to set up in Hollywood in 1956.

White walked around and round, gazing up at the 13-storey building where he knew that on the 13th floor legendary music executives worked, including Alan Wendell Livingston, later famous for turning down the Beatles and being rescued when they were signed by one of his employees, George Martin.

As he stood there, he forlornly hoped someone might come out, recognise him and invite him in to the studios where Frank Sinatra had recorded his most successful albums.

After more than 30 laps of the building he moved onto the equally famous Wallich's Music City. Then he walked the streets, taking in the office buildings of all the record companies he knew. On the first day nothing happened, and neither did it on the second day. Nor the third or the 30th day. He walked and walked every day with no particular daily purpose. The only benefit seemed to be his shrinking waistline from all the exercise, and he lost nearly three stones.

Finally, on his 31st day of pounding the pavements he got a break and bumped into an old friend who invited him to observe a recording session at the Leon Rene studio. White didn't need asking twice, as Leon Rene was a famous producer, songwriter and performer, known for R&B and rock and roll music. With his brother Otis, Rene had founded Excelsior Records in the forties, which, although initially successful, had foundered when the record format changed from 78rpm to 45rpm and the label was slow to make the change.

When Excelsior failed, Rene set up a new record label called Class Records in 1951 with his son Rafael. It had broken many new acts and had a few hit records. He added a second label called Rendezvous in 1958. Eugene Church and Bobby Day were the label's stars. Bobby Day in particular had a huge hit with *Rockin Robin*.

Getting invited to the studio was just the break that White had been looking for, and he resolved to make the most of it. As soon as he got there he sought out Leon Rene. He shook his hand, but that was as far as he got, and he hardly registered with him.

The session was an unknown girl group who were recording a song called *Tossin Ice Cubes*.

As he sat in on the session he noticed that he knew the keyboard player, whom he didn't particularly rate. White knew that he could play a lot better, but also knew that he wouldn't get the chance. In any case, he realised that the song they were recording was pretty poor.

Then halfway through the session Leon Rene decided to add a syncopation hand clap to the track. After trying out three people, he couldn't find anyone who could do it properly. White remembered: "It was the rhythm thing again, which was so deceptively hard for most people."

White knew he could do it, but didn't dare speak up and offer his services. But when Rene was about to give up, White whispered: "I can do that."

Rene turned round and said: "Who said that?" He looked at White and shouted: "Who are you?" When White told him, he asked: "And you say you can clap your hands to this rhythm?"

White nodded, went into the sound room and managed to do the hand clap perfectly in one take. Rene was floored and took a hundred dollar bill from his pocket, rolled it up and pushed it into White's grateful palm.

It was by far the most money he had ever been paid to do anything, and he couldn't believe it when he unfurled his hand afterwards. Rene said: "Barry White, you are a very gifted man. You nailed it, son. I don't know who you are and I have never heard of you, but you're a real talent." Those words meant much more than the money, and White skipped off into the street. To be told that by Leon Rene meant something, and to be given money as well was more than he could have dreamed of.

When he got outside White examined the hundred dollar bill closely, as he had never handled one before. He knew the union scale for what he had done was only $25, and he couldn't believe Rene's generosity.: "I had earned real money without having to look over my shoulder for the police while doing it. A hundred dollars free and clear."

It was also significant to White as the first money he had earned in Hollywood. He couldn't have been more pleased with himself. He spent a dollar on a hot dog and years later remembered the look the vendor gave him when he handed over the bill. He decided to walk all the way home, rather than catch the bus, which he could now afford, so he could hand over the other $99 straight to his mother when he got back. He said: "I wanted to give it all to my mother. I wanted to prove to her I had been right that I could do something worthwhile by going to Hollywood."

It took him three and a half hours and two sore feet to walk all the way home to South LA. But there was one significant difference in his walk home, at least to him. When he had journeyed to Hollywood that morning he had just been, as he called himself, "One more dreamer pounding the pavement." He believed, as he walked home that same evening, that he was now a working musician. "I was walking on air."

CHAPTER 14

Two-Year Funk

Ups and downs of life

1962 to 1963

As he turned 18 in 1962, word of Barry White's performance at the Leon Rene studio was getting around. Jobs started appearing and as every week passed it seemed that White got himself further established in Hollywood's music industry. He even had some business cards printed. Recalling that period much later, he said: "Word had gotten around about me being this dude with a good sense of rhythm." He added: "It seemed that rhythm and melody spoke to me."

He was offered all sorts of good jobs in various studios around Los Angeles and he soaked everything up like a sponge: "I was accumulating all this key information. I was different and I wanted to learn everything I could about the process from anywhere and anyone."

His mother started taking more and more phone calls for him at home, enquiring about his availability for sessions, and after a few weeks it dawned on White that it was possible that he could have a future in the music business: "I began to realise that if I tried really hard I just might be able to make a pretty good living at this music thing."

He was also very ambitious, and all through his life he claimed that, at certain crucial times, he could hear a voice in his head that guided his actions. It was just such a time now, and the inner voice whispered to him: "You know, Barry, you could probably write, arrange and produce a record all on your own."

But just as he heard the voice, so his new-found career seemed to spin off the rails. The phone calls stopped coming just as quickly as they had started, and so did the job offers. The sudden dearth of work left him bemused and he failed to realise that this was one of the vagaries of the music business.

The cyclical nature of the work was nothing to do with him, or his talent, or his abilities, but it caused him to go into a funk and he blamed himself for his perceived failure. As time went on and no work appeared, he believed he had done something wrong and began to seriously question his own musical abilities. It was a miserable time as the Christmas holidays approached.

As 1963 dawned Barry White was ready to exit the music business altogether. At 18 years of age he thought his career in music was already over. As he said: "Although I had music in my heart, I began to have serious doubts."

To try and get over it he resolved, for the first time, to write some of his own songs. He had always thought himself capable of writing good songs but had never knuckled down to it. It was as if he had held that talent in reserve for when he would need it. Now he had time, he gave it a try, genuinely expecting to be successful.

But he was very surprised to find that the songs he wrote were not very good. The music was passable but he realised that the lyrics were very poor. He wrote too many words and he rhymed everything. He quickly realised that he was far better at composing music than writing lyrics, and that it was the words that were letting him down. Proof of this was his very first composition, which he grandly called *Love's Theme* – but the words he put with it were rubbish. It was, however, destined to be a hit, albeit ten years after he wrote it. He admitted: "That kind of success was a long time coming."

His ego was severely bruised and it was another wake-up call: "I discovered my talents weren't as fully developed as I'd hoped."

The drying-up of work and the discovery of the limitations of his songwriting ability had severely shaken his confidence. He was no longer certain of ultimate success. He eventually managed to find some occasional work as a jobbing musician, but it paid him very little and he stopped going to Hollywood every day.

He resolved to try and get a regular job that paid a regular wage to resolve his domestic problems, as he now had four young mouths to feed and a domineering mother-in-law to please.

White was multi-talented and there were many other things he could turn his hand to. He was forced into a succession of menial jobs paying the minimum wage, which was very difficult for a proud man to endure. All he could take from it was that he was experiencing every facet of life and how the world really worked. He had an advanced realisation of life and an innate ability to pull off many tricks. In quick succession he washed cars, worked as a hairdresser and even took up painting and decorating. He worked as a janitor at a hospital at weekends. He did anything he could to put bread on the table for his young family. Once he even worked in a mortuary, even though he hated dealing with dead bodies. But he found he could turn his hand to most things. "I had music in my head but nothing in my pockets so I sold newspapers, fried burgers, worked in construction to keep my babies fed."

He also worked on the building of the new sports stadium in Los Angeles, the Memorial Sports Arena, for less than $20 a day. Little did he know that 20 years later he would be booked to appear there in front of 20,000 fans and be paid $100,000 for one night's work by the owners.

But there was one thing that all the different jobs he took had in common: they were all very poorly paid. And all the money he did earn was passed to Mary to clothe and feed his children and to pay the rent. There was nothing left for him; he had no money in his pocket and often went hungry at the end of the day. Things got so bad that he remembers going to a supermarket, filling his trolley, then picking a ready-cooked chicken from the deli counter. As he walked up the aisles he ate the chicken as quickly as he could, then left the trolley at the store entrance and walked out. He said later it was the only way he could survive: "Some might call it stealing. I called it survival."

Then one morning there was an unexpected knock on the door. It was a man called Al Samuels, who had a most unusual proposal that was to take Barry White's life off in a very unexpected direction.

Al Samuels told White that he was opening a toy shop in the South Los Angeles area and wanted him to manage it. He told him that when he had enquired in the local neighbourhood shops for staff, everyone had recommended him. White was taken aback and thought to himself: "Sell toys – that's about as far away from music as you can get." But he was intrigued and knew instinctively that he would enjoy being in the toy business. In fact, second to music, he couldn't think of anything else more enjoyable. He was up for it.

Then Samuels, sensing his enthusiasm, said: "I can't pay you a regular salary but I will give you some money to get by on every now and then." They were fateful words – basically Samuels was offering Barry White a partnership and if he worked for virtually nothing now he could end up with a slice of the business later. It was a vague promise and a deal anyone else would have found easy to turn down. But the truth was that White would have gladly paid for the chance to work in a toyshop, especially as it would be just a few minutes' walk away on the Santa Barbara Boulevard.

White was bemused, suspicious and intrigued all at the same time, and admitted that he had never had an offer like it in his life. However, he thought: "What do I have to lose as the record business isn't doing anything for me at the moment and at least this gig keeps me close to home."

Samuels showed White the proposed shop premises and for the next few weeks taught him as much as he could about selling toys. He took him on buying trips to toy wholesalers. In return White started working 18-hour days to get the venture going. "I made a commitment and it was total. Standing in the warehouse I fell in love with the whole idea of selling toys."

White found himself in the warehouse every Tuesday and Friday morning buying stock, and the rest of the time in the shop selling it, as he took to toy retailing like a duck to water. Samuels was delighted and told him after a few weeks: "Children really like you – they think you're so cool. They talk about you and can't wait to get out of school so they can come to the store."

White studied the art of toy retailing, then applied his own recipe. After the shop closed each night he completely rearranged the displays so when the children returned the next day it all looked new and different. As he explained: "I moved the toys around so not one item of merchandise was ever in the same place. Nobody told me to do this but I knew that every day the kids came in it would look like a brand new store to them and it made them come back."

And they did come back, often with their parents, day after day. The shop was a success and before long the only competing shop in the area was forced to close. Soon Al Samuels was out scouting for a bigger location.

But as successful as the shop was, Samuels did not reward White with a regular salary. He brought him bags of food and other household goods so his family could survive, but never any hard cash. One day he decided to reward White by outfitting his modest house with some new furniture. White should have been suspicious but he wasn't, and naively went along with the suggestion.

Samuels took Barry White down to Golds Furniture Store and told him to choose everything he wanted. He ordered enough furniture and new electrical appliances for the whole house. Two days later a big Golds van appeared outside White's house and unloaded the new gear. Mary was delighted and gave all their old furniture and kitchen appliances to neighbours.

But two days later White got the shock of his life when the Golds van reappeared and the removal men reloaded all the furniture and took it back to the store. When White asked why, the Golds driver told him to ring the store manager. When he finally got the manager on the phone he told him that Al Samuels's check had bounced.

White was devastated and the family were left sitting on the bare floorboards. As he had given away all his old furniture he was worse off than before. After a few hours he became very angry, especially when he couldn't find Al Samuels or get him on the telephone. The following morning he resolved to tell Samuels what he thought of him and resign his position.

But Barry White had made a serious mistake – he had fallen in love with his job and it had become his whole life. So he calmed down and said nothing as neighbours lent them their old furniture so they had something to sit on.

The following Monday, when Samuels came by the shop, White initially acted as though nothing had happened, as did Samuels. Then, at an appropriate moment, White gingerly told him that the furniture had been taken back. Samuels acted shocked and claimed that he knew nothing about it, that it must have been a mistake and that he would look into it for him. Then he gave him $75 to buy some second-hand furniture, but the new stuff never reappeared. White bought some more furniture and the incident was all but forgotten.

Then Samuels moved the shop to new, bigger premises. But there were clearly financial problems brewing about which White knew nothing. One morning he arrived to open up the new shop and found that it had been emptied overnight. At first he thought they had been robbed, but then realised that Samuels had been during the night and cleaned it out.

The toy dream was over and White was devastated. By his own admission he stood in the middle of the shop and cried his eyes out. He remembered: "It hurt me more than anything had before in my life." He went home and once again started doing odd jobs to earn money.

Samuels eventually resurfaced and opened another toy shop in the area. To White's amazement he cheekily asked Sadie Carter if she would manage it. To his greater amazement, his mother agreed.

White was forced to return to doing any work he could get to support the family, and he went into a downward funk that last until 1963, when he turned 19 years of age.

Gradually he began to re-establish himself in the music business, albeit at the bottom of the ladder. He found that he was being called upon to give advice to young artists and it made him realise that he could have a future as an arranger of music, the person with the biggest influence on how a record actually sounds. As he said of that time: "I always felt I had the special kind of talent it takes to become an arranger of music."

And he wasn't wrong, as he was about to meet the man who would change his life forever, Gene Page.

CHAPTER 15

Marriage to Mary

A proper family and four children

1962

Barry White never enjoyed a conventional youth. At the age of 16 he first became a father and by the time he had turned 17 another child was on the way. At 18, he was the father of a boy called Barry Jnr and a baby girl called Lanese.

But he was estranged from their mother, Mary, and living at home with his own mother, while Mary remained living at her home with her mother. They literally never saw each other and White had walked away from her after he confessed openly that he didn't love her anymore.

The truth was that during all this activity and the birth of Barry Jnr, his childhood love affair with Mary had turned sour.

But despite his absence, White was under great pressure to regularise his affairs and underneath everything he craved respectability. So he found himself thinking long and hard about making an honest woman of the mother of his child and child to be, even though he no longer loved her or wanted to spend time with her. As he explained: "When I turned 17, I welcomed more responsibilities as a way to prove I was a decent honest guy."

But getting married was an inexplicable decision, as White was actually going out with another woman he had met after leaving jail. He hadn't seen Mary, or his child, for almost eight months – since he had told her he had fallen out of love with her. There was also another complication. This second woman, who Barry White never named, had fallen pregnant herself.

If ever there was a mess, this was one.

But despite all this, Barry White struggled with his conscience. He had thought by not seeing the pregnant Mary he would wipe her from his past along with, it seemed, Barry Jnr. It was not a period of his life he was proud of at all, and he wrestled with it every single night he was apart from his child.

Then fate intervened, as it often did in Barry White's life. He and Mary separately and unknowingly went to the same party at a friend's house. The two started talking and decided on the spot to get back together. There was renewed pressure from Mary, Sadie and his prospective mother-in-law to get married. The latter put him under enormous pressure, as he remembered: "Mary and her mother pushed me hard to get married. She kicked my ass as hard as she could until we made our relationship legal and our children legitimate." White promised to think about it and admitted: "I was a different person from the one who'd gone a little crazy and spent time in jail, and I had stopped drinking."

To complicate matters even further, in 1962 White's daughter by the unnamed woman was born, and named Denice. The mother was later revealed to be a woman called Gurtha Allen. Luckily Gurtha's family exerted no pressure, and Denice's existence was unknown to anyone but them. Also fortunately for White, Denice's mother quickly met someone else, who became Denice's de facto father. Denice's mother took the pragmatic decision to bring up her daughter with her new partner and White agreed to give up any rights to his latest child. She took her stepfather's surname as her own and was known from the start of her life as Denice Donnell.

White said later: "No one but the two of us knew we had a daughter. Denice was our secret love child." It was a lucky break and it enabled White to concentrate on Mary. But even then White was overwhelmed. At 17 he was simply too young to be the father of a young child, let alone a second with a different mother.

He was saved by the two mothers, who rushed in to support Mary with help and money. White agreed to let them get on with it: "I figured there was no way I could handle fatherhood." But there was a price to pay, and that was marriage.

He finally buckled and married the heavily pregnant Mary on 18th November 1962: "After avoiding it for as long as I could I did what I thought was the right thing and walked down the aisle in front of the proverbial shotgun."

Mary's name on the marriage register was Betty Smith and her age was recorded as 16.

There was no honeymoon and obviously no immediate consummation of the marriage. As soon as the reception was over White went back to his mother's house and Mary returned to her mother's house. He felt embarrassed about being married. It was not what he had planned at the age of 18 and not what he had wanted.

From his point of view it had merely been a tidying-up exercise. As he said: "I had serious doubts about the wisdom of the move, besides the fact that my feelings for Mary had changed." The 18-year-old readily admitted it had all gone wrong in his life: "I felt too young and incapable of being the man of my own house. In spite of my size and streetwise sensibilities I was still much a baby myself."

Sadie was deeply embarrassed that her eldest son had returned to her instead of setting up a marital home, or at least going to live with his wife. When he walked through the door she told him firmly: "She's your wife now and she belongs with you."

But the wayward son wasn't much interested in listening. White told his mother that he was never going to live with Mary and said: "I don't really like her that much any more."

Even though he had rationalised it in his head, White quickly realised that he had miscalculated and made the mistake of his life. While marriage had legitimised his child, he found the downside outweighed the upside. He had not particularly cared for his mother-in-law before the marriage, and now that it was official he found her attitude to him intolerable: "It had taken the fun out of everything for me and I really had no idea what I had gotten myself into."

But things got worse and Sadie had no sympathy for him at all. His mother and mother-in-law joined forces in an attempt to tame him. Finally they won and forced White to find a small apartment in which to make his family whole and finally move in his wife and be a proper father.

On 12th December 1962 Lanese Melva White was born and mother and two grandmothers were delighted. Not so the father who was forced to take any sort of work he could to support them. It made him have serious doubts about whether he would ever break loose and have any future in the music business at all: "My number one problem was trying to figure out how to make money more consistently, as I was stony broke. There was pressure on me from all quarters to find a regular job." But with a regular job came regular hours and

White realised that was not for him: "There was one thing I hated to do and it was to get up early to go to work. Not that I couldn't do it. When I had to and when we needed bread, I was willing to do all sorts of jobs."

Now they were married and living together other problems emerged. Mary and her mother believed they should be able to control every aspect of Barry White's life and make all his decisions for him. His wife's priority was that he should provide for her and her children. She told him that "nothing else mattered" and that he should "put his crazy and unrealistic ambitions firmly aside and concentrate on a proper and regular job."

He struggled and struggled with it, but was determined: "I was a family man with no job and no money but I was determined to keep my family together."

White had big ambitions and nothing, including his domineering mother-in-law, would deflect him from that. However, fate tried very hard and a familiar pattern emerged as Mary got pregnant again, and before they knew it a third child was born on 19th May 1964, a girl they named Nina. Both Sadie and Mary's parents were aghast at this latest turn of events, unable to believe what had happened. But that was nothing when four months after the birth of Nina, Mary announced she was pregnant again and a year after Nina was born came a son, a fourth child they named Darryl arrived on 20th June 1965. In four years, Mary had given birth to four children.

So by the time he was 19 Barry White was the father of five children altogether – Barry Jnr, Lanese, Nina and Darryl, plus Denice, who no one knew about. He liked the fact he had two boys and two girls but that was all he liked. His mother, his wife and mother-in-law drove him crazy and he spent as little time at home as he could get away with.

When he got his first regular job with Mustang Bronco Records in 1965 life got much easier, punctuated by the happy sound of children running around. In that period there was more money to spread around, but it did not make for a happier atmosphere.

He remembered: "It's very tough if you were a young kid who has four children. I struggled mightily to take care of my family and to protect and provide for them."

CHAPTER 16

Meeting Gene Page

The first game changer

1963 to 1965

In the summer of 1963 Barry White was to get together with a man called Gene Page, who would be the catalyst for all the success he would eventually enjoy. It's not an exaggeration to say that, without Gene Page, there would have been no Barry White.

They weren't complete strangers, as they had first gotten to know each other when White was still at school and hanging around the doors of recording studios. As Gene Page recalled: "I had known Barry right at the beginning of my career when he was still at school, and we'd always been good friends."

But fate intervened and they first started to work together when White took a phone call from an old friend called Earl Nelson. He had met Nelson in 1961 when he had first gone to Hollywood, but the two men had lost touch, and in the intervening period 35-year-old Earl had teamed up with Bobby Day to form a new duo called Bob & Earl. It was their second time together as they had both been members of a group called the Hollywood Flames in the late fifties.

But the duo floundered after failing to produce any hit records, and amidst some acrimony Bobby Day resumed his solo career. However, Earl Nelson was not a man to give up on what he fundamentally thought was a good idea. His excuse for the failure, as he told everyone, was that he had chosen the wrong 'Bob'. His innovative solution was to find a new 'Bob' to keep the duo going. In 1962 he found his new 'Bob', a man called Bobby Relf. And that was Barry White's luck, as he knew Relf very well, having met him when he was a member of The Upfronts.

When Nelson and Relf started recording together they both happened to mention the same name independently of each other – Barry White. They told each other how much they both admired his talents, so much so that they decided to invite him into their team for their first recording session together.

On that team were also Gene Page and Fred Sledge Smith, who worked for the Mirwood record company. Thirty-year-old Smith was scheduled to produce and 24-year-old Page was to arrange the session to record some songs for Bob & Earl.

White and Page embraced each other warmly as they walked into the studio. Page told White: "Well, Barry, it's a very small world, my friend – what have you been doing?" Page smiled as White told him what had happened since they had last met, especially when he told him about his tangled personal life and the five children he had fathered.

But it was soon down to work and White observed Page and Smith going about their business. Nelson and Relf had written a novelty disco song called *Harlem Shuffle*, which they believed had potential. The song featured lyrics that would eventually became known the world over: "You move it to the left and you go for yourself, You move it to the right yeah if it takes all night, Now take it kinda slow with a whole lot of soul. Let's do the Harlem Shuffle."

Smith, Page and White cut it to disc and it was released as a single in 1963. Initially sales were slow but respectable, although it was a popular song in discotheques. But the slow take-up in sales led to the quick demise of the second duo of Bob & Earl.

But the true significance in pop history was the beginning of the great partnership between Gene Page and Barry White. Page would go on to arrange most of White's music, including all of his hits.

The 24-year-old Gene Page was already a success in the music business when he met White, but the two men enjoyed working together and Page valued White's input on the *Harlem Shuffle* recording. Page was highly regarded at Motown and everywhere else as a multi-purpose conductor, composer, arranger and producer. There was nothing he couldn't do in a studio and it was Barry White's incredibly good fortune to have linked up with him right at the start of his career.

Page had been born in Los Angeles, four years before Barry White in 1940. But almost immediately the family had moved east and his childhood was spent in New York. The Pages were a musical family: his father composed and his mother sung his songs beautifully. His brother Billy was also an extremely talented musician. Music wafted through the family home continually, as Page recalled: "My father was very much into composing serious music." Page was taught to play the piano by his father and he became a child prodigy, winning a scholarship to the Brooklyn Conservatory of Music.

When Page was 17 the family returned to Los Angeles and all hopes his father had that his son would become a concert pianist would soon disappear. Page embraced Los Angeles and despite his upbringing described himself as a 'West Coast baby'. He admits that he had expected to do as his father wanted, but the move back to Los Angeles had derailed that: "Initially, I wanted to go for being a concert pianist but, you know, the pressure in something like that is really too intense. So after attending college I started to write and make demos for my brother Billy, for the American Music Company. At that time folks like Glen Campbell and Johnny Rivers were doing demos of Billy's songs and I'd arrange them. It was from this work that I met up with Jimmy Bowen, who later produced people like Frank Sinatra and Sammy Davis Jr."

His father's hopes were finally dashed when his son's musical talent was recognised before he had turned 20 years old. He was hired by Reprise Records as a full-time music arranger for the label's artists. It was a huge break and gave him the chance to work with some of America's biggest stars, as he recalled: "I stayed there a couple of years working on their acts – Frank, Dean Martin and so on – until I went independent."

That move to become an independent producer at only 21 was very brave. But he didn't have to wait long and his big break came when he was 'discovered' by Phil Spector. Spector was the most famous record producer in America and the man behind an emerging pop phenomenon called The Ronettes. In the late summer of 1964 Spector's usual arranger, Jack Nitzsche, was on a long vacation and Spector, overrun with work, was desperate, so he gave Page a chance with The Righteous Brothers, then consisting of Bill Medley and Bobby Hatfield.

Barry Mann and Cynthia Weil, the famous husband-and-wife songwriting team, had written *You've Lost That Loving Feeling* for Spector and he was desperate to cut a tape with the Brothers before anyone else took the song. Page admitted later that Spector had only turned to him 'in desperation'.

The rest was history. Page's arrangement practically invented the famous Spector 'Wall of Sound'. Page recorded the melody first and the lyrics were sung by Bill Medley and Bobby Hatfield, with the melody overdubbed afterwards. It ran to 3 minutes and 45 seconds and no one thought it had a chance of being a hit record at that length. But they were wrong, and *You've Lost That Loving Feeling* went on to become part of Spector's signature sound, in the process propelling The Righteous Brothers to a huge debut hit.

Robert Palmer, the writer and composer, described the effect of Page's technique as creating a sound that was "deliberately blurry and atmospheric". He called it "Wagnerian rock 'n' roll with all the trimmings."

Page had greatly enhanced the recording of this epic track, which topped the charts on both sides of the Atlantic, but he received no credit for his work. Phil Spector took all of the credit for the record's success, but those who had been in the studio knew that it had mostly been down to Page.

Word gradually got round and Page attracted the attention of Berry Gordy at Motown. He was soon working regularly for groups like The Drifters and The Mamas and the Papas, and was arranging hit record after hit record as Motown's brand of music took the pop world by storm.

But once again Page failed to get any of the credit, and it was only during his last year with Motown that Berry Gordy began to publicly credit his arrangements.

Inevitably the lack of recognition meant that Page started looking beyond Motown, although he never forgot that period in his life. He recalled it later in an interview with British writer David Nathan: "It was a fantastic experience working with such an incredible amount of talent. It would seem that you'd only just finish with one and start working with another great artist. What would happen is that the company would present me with a demo of the song, explain the kind of feeling they'd want and I'd maybe meet with the artist ahead of time to establish their vocal range and what key to do the song in. But I wasn't always there when the artists put their vocals on – only if the song was particularly difficult, which happened sometimes. There were times when I'd have to sing the song for the artist myself – but believe me, I can't sing, so they always erased it pretty quickly – as soon as the artist had gotten the song right."

If Berry Gordy had treated him better, Page would have probably stayed at Motown for the rest of his career. As it was, he returned to Los Angeles and the life of an independent producer, immediately working with up-and-coming stars like Barbra Streisand.

By the mid-sixties Gene Page was already established as the go-to-guy for any pop artists needing lush arrangements of strings to heighten the sound of a ballad. Nobody, it seemed, could put together violins, cellos and French horns like Gene Page. He was known for his unique craftsmanship and some extraordinary string arrangements with intricate horn patterns.

Barry White recalled that first studio session: "Of course I had no way of knowing that one day Gene Page would be the arranger for so many of my records." He added: "He was a great talent and in my opinion was one of the most educated black men in music. He would become a very close friend of mine."

White was mesmerised by Page's flamboyant style in the studio. Page expressed his passion for music by putting a lot of physical movement into conducting, which Phil Spector called 'swelling and swirling'.

The arrangements for all the songs that day had been meticulously planned by Page during the week before, and White had never seen better advance preparation for a recording session. It seemed that nothing was left to chance and before the session started Page went through exactly what he wanted with all the musicians and the annotated music, even down to the amount of passion with which each individual piece of music should be played.

His conducting was in the style of Leonard Bernstein; he closed his eyes and lived the moment. He was not afraid to interrupt any recording if he felt it wasn't right. Smith and White watched in admiration, making suggestions they thought relevant, but in the main they left it to Page. There were at least four or five interruptions before a complete run-through of most of the songs that day. But it was all done with very good humour, which was not always easy with prima donna musicians, many of whom thought an arranger was an unwanted and unnecessary luxury.

White was mightily impressed with what he saw that day in the studio, and arguably getting back together with Gene Page was the most important event of his life.

In time Page/White became a special combination. Because White couldn't read music, the options open to him for collaboration with an arranger were very limited. But Page got it immediately, as White explained: "Gene was my unofficial transcriber. I could always say to him I want this kind of sound, sing it for him, and he'd be able to put it down as part of the musical arrangement."

When the two men said their goodbyes at the end of the day, neither quite realised what a seismic impact their reunion would have. But from that day on they remained very close, speaking together most days. But more significantly, Page was the first to seriously recognise Barry White's talents and sought to nurture him where he could. And that included financial support from time to time. Although still in his mid-twenties, Page was earning very good money and could command up to $500 a day in the studio on big projects. He had already amassed more than $50,000 in his bank account. At first White wouldn't accept handouts, but Page insisted, telling the younger man that he had plenty and it was burning a hole in his pocket. The money helped support White's family at a time when times were very hard, as White recalled: "Gene Page used to feed my family, pay my rent and give me gas money, food money for my children. I never had to pay him back. I tried many times but he'd never take it."

As that partnership was getting established White got another opportunity with Earl Nelson. Shorn of both of his 'Bobs', Nelson had decided to relaunch his solo career with a new name – Jackie Lee. What was wrong with his real name, Earl Nelson, no one knew, but he felt it was too country and western and that it would hurt his pop music career.

The name Jackie Lee came from his wife's first name and his own middle name, and it mightily confused his friends and everyone who knew him in the music business. White didn't entirely agree with the decision, but recalled: "Earl changed his professional name, which was something a lot of guys did in those days when they didn't make it or they wanted to start over."

Nelson's first move was to approach Barry White and suggest a collaboration. White was again all ears, as Earl Nelson told him: "Let's cut something for ourselves."

Together they wrote an A-side called *Ooh Honey Baby*, which was standard pop fare. But more interesting was the B-side, which Nelson wrote on his own as a sort of joke. It was called *The Duck* and as soon as Barry White heard it he sensed it might become a hit: "*The Duck* had hit written all over it. I listened to it once and I knew it was going to be a smash."

White was right, and *The Duck* was a Christmas hit in December 1965, reaching No 9 in the Billboard singles chart. In those days getting in the Top 10 was a very big deal indeed, and one record could turn an artist into a star. White told Nelson that he needed to milk the success as quickly as he could and get out on tour to exploit the song's success. Nelson agreed and offered Barry White a fee of $400 for a three-month tour assignment; he also appointed him his road manager. White was overjoyed and didn't try and hide it: "$400 to me sounded like a million dollars and I accepted it in a heartbeat."

The nationwide success of *The Duck* meant that bookings flooded in, including a week's run at the famous Apollo Theatre in New York.

But that was the easy bit and the truth was that Barry White was not a man of the world. It suddenly dawned on him that, save for his birth, he had never travelled outside the Los Angeles city limits. Moreover, he had never been away from his mother, except when he was in prison. He also had to explain to his wife Mary that he was going away for three months, and he knew she would not be pleased. But that was typical of America at the time – fewer than 20 per cent of Californians had ever been outside the state, and only eight per cent of Americans had flown in an aircraft. Even fewer had passports.

White told Earl Nelson that he would need an advance to settle his affairs before he left. Nelson immediately took a roll of cash from his back pocket and reeled off $100. "As good as done," he said.

A few days later they were on the road in Nelson's car heading for New York City. White felt tangible excitement as he left the confines of Los Angeles. The two men took it in turns to drive almost non-stop, and it took three days before they hit the Lincoln Tunnel into Manhattan. White couldn't cope with driving in the narrow confines of New York and handed the wheel over to Nelson, as he remembered: "The traffic was so crazed and I couldn't handle it."

They checked into a small hotel and drove over to the renowned Apollo Theatre, where they had been booked to appear for a week with seven other acts. To save money Earl Nelson decided to use the theatre house band as backing for his performance. At rehearsals White had to show the house drummer how to perform the roll-type rhythm that was particularly important on *The Duck*. But it was hopeless, as White said: "He couldn't play the groove."

When White took the sticks to show him how it was done it caused a startled Earl Nelson to say: "I didn't know you could play the drums like that. Why don't you just do it yourself in the show?" What Nelson didn't know was that White had never played the drums before in his life. He just had a natural feel, as he explained: "I had never had any formal training on the drums. But I knew how to play them without actually having played them."

White was a sensation and no one believed it was his first time playing. The other acts performing at the Apollo that week also asked him to accompany them, and the house drummer was given the sack. White picked up an extra $200 and said: "Although I was only originally there as a road manager, I suddenly found myself on stage in the spotlight playing in front of an audience and they loved it. I jumped in and I developed my playing of the drums as the week went on."

The bands played nine shows in eight days and White was exhausted at the end with his dual roles as performer and road manager. But he took his duties very seriously. As he said: "I was successful as a road manager because I did not go out partying or with women." He added: "Jackie [Earl] may have been on a tour but I was on a mission."

The week at the Apollo was a big success, playing to surprisingly full houses. At the end of the week, the Apollo manager gratefully gave Earl Nelson a fat white envelope stuffed with mixed notes. White guessed that there might be a thousand dollars inside. Nelson reeled off $100 and give it to his road manager as a grateful bonus.

But there the good times abruptly ended.

On the following Sunday they drove out of New York and headed for Florida, driving through the Deep South where they had managed to squeeze in some extra bookings in Georgia. But neither man had any experience of the ways of the south. In truth it would have been better had they not accepted any bookings there, as the area was still riven with racial tension not seen in California.

But both Earl and White were clueless, as White admitted: "I was from Los Angeles and I didn't know about separate black and white restaurants and rest rooms."

The trouble started when they drove into a small town called Hattiesburg in Mississippi, which had a population of fewer than 50,000 people. White and Nelson quickly got into an altercation with some local rednecks at a bar. They came off worse and were arrested when the police arrived. The police asked no questions and they spent the night in jail before being released the following morning.

Next they stopped in the coastal port of Mobile in Alabama, and White innocently went to a phone booth to call home. He made the mistake of calling the operator 'Baby', and while he was waiting to be connected police cars arrived and surrounded the booth. They accused him of using profanity on the phone, as the operator had reported him calling her 'Baby'. The police threatened him with jail if it happened again.

They then drove to Louisiana, where they had the misfortune to book into a hotel where members of the Klu Klux Klan were staying. They found themselves surrounded in the hotel car park by members of the Klan. A beating looked likely, but White bravely faced them off and the Klan members thought better of it and withdrew.

Driving on to New Orleans, they had a booking at a club in the French quarter, where they witnessed a murder first hand as a woman stabbed a man to death in front of them.

By then Barry White had had enough, and told Earl Nelson that he was returning to Los Angeles immediately, saying that he would never leave the city again. "I told Earl I was going home and I didn't like this and I didn't like that and I preferred the studio to the road." Nelson begged him to stay, but White had seen enough of America outside California.

Despite the fact that he had never flown in an aircraft, he called Delta Airlines and booked a flight home the next morning. And that was that as far as Barry White was concerned. As the plane touched down at Los Angeles, he vowed he would never leave state lines again.

Returning home early proved to be a good decision, as the offers of work suddenly started to flood in. A few days after his return White ran straight into Gene Page. After exchanging pleasantries, Page asked him if he would like to attend a Holland, Dozier & Holland recording session with Diana Ross and the Supremes at Motown's studios. White didn't need asking twice.

Page warned him that he would only be there to observe and must stay in the background, but told him he would be able to experience a top-line recording session at first hand.

In the meantime he resolved to try himself out in the market. He had some money in his back pocket and he hired Downey Productions to press a single he had written and recorded called *Man Ain't Nothin*, with *I Don't Need It* on the B-side. It was his first ever record to be pressed. But he was so embarrassed that he recorded it under the name 'Lee Barry', listing himself as the writer/composer. It was unmistakably Barry White but the record was dreary and uninspiring. Predictably it went nowhere, but he was proud to at last see a piece of black vinyl with his name on.

A few weeks later Gene Page proved to be as good as his word when Barry White was officially invited along to the Motown studios where Eddie and Brian Holland and Lamont Dozier were laying down the tracks for a new Supremes album. White remembered: "Gene lied and said I was a back-up singer." For the first time White was able to observe a top team in action. And what a team it was. Lamont Dozier wrote the music, Eddie Holland the lyrics and Brian Holland produced and arranged the recordings. White remembered: "It was a great moment for me, breathing in the same air as my lifelong idols. They wrote songs that took my head in another direction of music. Holland, Dozier & Holland were who I wanted to be."

More importantly, when he got home White realised that, for the first time, he had heard the sound he himself was trying to create in the studio, but so far without success. As he explained: "When the music started I knew instantly that that was the sound still so elusive to the heart, ears, mind and soul of everyone I'd yet had the chance to work with in rock and roll."

The session had taken White a step closer to finding the secret ingredient that would make him a really successful musician, as he explained: "I could hear it in my head but had not yet found a way to really get it down on a record. But that day in the studio I felt I'd taken a giant step closer to my goal."

Those few hours had truly unlocked something in his psyche, the last barrier preventing him from making the great music he knew he was capable of: "The session taught me I could do anything my imagination allowed. Their use of horns, bass lines, the sweep of their strings, their harmonies – they opened the door and left it open for me or anyone else to walk through."

The time was getting closer and there would be many great moments to come for Barry White. But the next important step was meeting another man who would become very important in his life.

CHAPTER 17

The Mustang Bronco Years

Bob Keane leads to Larry Nunes

1966 to 1968

In early 1966 Paul Politi got on the telephone to Barry White, who was recovering at home after his distressing time on tour with Earl Nelson.

Politi was an old friend of White's from his days bumming around studios in Hollywood looking for work. In the intervening period Politi had landed on his feet and was working as an executive at Mustang Bronco Records, an independent record label.

Politi told White that they were looking for a new A&R man and he said that the president of the company wanted to interview him the following day. But when White asked Politi what an A&R man was, he said he didn't know and Politi said: "We'll figure it out after you get the job."

Mustang Bronco was an interesting place to be in the mid-sixties. It was run by Bob Keane, a 43-year-old veteran music producer who, having started at 16, had made his name as America's best-known clarinet player. But his career faded early after being interrupted by the draft, and for ten years after that he drifted around Los Angeles making a living playing in clubs.

Eventually he grew tired of performing and at the age of 32 started his own record label, Keen Records, in partnership with businessman John Siamas. Keane proved to have very good 'ears' and quickly discovered a promising soul singer called Sam Cooke. Under Keane's supervision, Cooke promptly recorded two hit records that quickly earned the new label $1 million. But Siamas proved to be a serial swindler and had pulled the old trick of registering the company solely in his own name. When Keane found out there was a huge row and Siamas sacked him, leaving Siamas with all the money and Sam Cooke's contract under his sole ownership. There were plenty of precedents in the music business for how Siamas had behaved. In the early days of the Rolling Stones, Bob Easton had pulled a similar trick on Andrew Loog Oldham in Britain, and it was a common swindle in the record industry for unsuspecting and trusting newcomers.

Keane dusted himself off and set up again, this time with backing from another man who had also been swindled by John Siamas and wanted revenge. The newly formed Del-Fi label had another quick success with an artist called Henri Rose, and this time Keane used the profits to buy out his partner. In 1958 there was even more quick success when Keane discovered Ritchie Valens, who had two giant hit records straight out of the box. But bad luck struck Keane again when Valens was killed in an air crash with Buddy Holly 18 months later.

With the discovery of Cooke and Valens, Keane had built quite a reputation in a very short space of time and even more success followed.

But Keane had been very lucky and inevitably the success went to his head and he started believing his own press cuttings. He was spending money like water and Del-Fi Records got into financial trouble. At the same time he lost his mojo and hit a streak of bad luck, signing up a lot of artists who failed to break through. Simultaneously he started to build a state-of-the-art eight-track recording studio at the Del-Fi offices. Costs suddenly rocketed as new technology emerged in the shape of multi-track mixing boards, which Keane was forced to install at huge cost. Bankruptcy loomed and Keane started spelling his name differently, as Keene and Keen to help ward off creditors.

Sensing trouble ahead, Keane set up Mustang Bronco Records as a sister label in case the worst happened. It almost did and the company had to be rescued by an entrepreneur called Larry Nunes, who bought out Keane and refinanced the whole business. Keane owed money all over town, and after Nunes had settled all the debts he owned 100 per cent of the equity and Keane effectively became his employee. Nunes invested new cash and finished off the recording studio, leaving Keane to run it under the Mustang Bronco label.

It was then that Barry White arrived on Keane's doorstep. White was lucky, as Keane had already interviewed two candidates for the A&R job and was about to make a choice when he asked Politi for his opinion. Politi told them that neither was as talented as Barry White. Keane said: "Who's Barry White?"

Politi told him: "Barry doesn't have a track record but he has more talent than both of these guys put together. He's raw and undeveloped but I think he is a diamond in the rough."

Keane was intrigued and agreed to meet White at nine o'clock the following morning. Straight away Keane was impressed with White's musical ability when he sat down to play the piano in his office, as he remembered: "I immediately recognised he was something special." But Keane also realised that White had very strong opinions and the two men didn't quite hit it off. White was also less than impressed with Keane. The dislike seemed mutual, so much so that Keane told Politi he would not offer White the job after all. But Politi wasn't happy with that and told Keane that he was making a big mistake. Keane subsequently changed his mind and offered White $60 a week to start.

But that was not the end of it. Sensing that he was not first choice, White pondered whether he should take the job. Politi urged him not to be so stupid and told him how many people in Los Angeles would jump at this chance to get into the music business.

But White was his own man, would not go where he felt he wasn't wanted, and worked out the solution in his own head. He surprised Keane by saying that he would work for $40 a week until he proved himself. Keane was taken aback but nonetheless agreed, and White said he would start the following Monday (when he had found out what an A&R man was). White was pleased with the outcome and was clear that he had not compromised his principles: "I sure wasn't about the money, but the opportunity. I just needed some dollars to get back and forth on the bus. The rest of it I would earn."

The bus ride to work proved daunting, as White remembered: "I was catching the bus to work every day from 48th and Avalon to Selma and Vine, and that was quite a few buses."

He quickly discovered what an A&R man did. It stood for 'Artists and Repertoire', which meant in essence 'finding, developing and producing artists and finding material for them to record'. He could handle that, and thought to himself: "As long as they don't ask me to make the coffee."

He attacked the job with a gusto and performed well, quickly pleasing his new boss. He also formed a smooth partnership with Politi and they worked together trying to find new artists to develop. White was excited about having a studio attached to the offices, and said: "I couldn't wait to get to work." Soon he found that he was addicted to the recording studio: "I never grew tired of the millions of lights and keys in the control box."

It also proved to be a great job for making high-level contacts in the industry. His first was Hal Davis, who ran the Los Angeles office of Motown Records. A big presence in every way, Davis was visiting the Bronco offices to meet with Bob Keane. White bumped into him in the corridor and, looking him up and down, couldn't help complimenting him on his dress style. A flattered and surprised Davis introduced himself and asked White what his role was.

After they had exchanged pleasantries, Davis looked him up and down in turn and offered some sartorial advice of his own, which was basically to smarten himself up. Davis explained that personal image was everything in the music industry, where style was often as important as substance. He told White that he changed his own wardrobe every three months and that he had a lot of nearly new clothes he could let him have. The two men were virtually the same size and White couldn't wait. Davis was as good as his word and a week later he delivered six bags full of clothes to Bronco's offices.

The bags contained a complete wardrobe of clothes that were as good as new, and would have cost nearly a thousand dollars to buy in the stores. White was delighted and said: "The threads were the coolest I had ever seen. Beautiful shirts, slacks, jackets and everything I didn't have."

White started wearing his new clothes to the office and quickly realised that Davis was correct about how vital it was to look the part as well as be the part, so much so that within a few months White was promoted to vice president of the company in charge of the whole A&R department, leapfrogging more senior colleagues including Paul Politi.

White loved his new job and started taking his full salary of $60 a week. He worked closely with Politi, spending every night out in clubs looking for new acts. Over a few months they saw hundreds of new acts and eventually found a singer they believed had real talent, called Viola Lyons. A beautiful and vibrant 25-year-old Californian, she was a remarkable woman who already had six children and was on her second husband when White and Politi found her singing in a run-down club.

Bob Keane didn't like her name and renamed her Viola Wills, telling White to search for some songs for her. White decided to write his own and together with Ronnie Goree, who also worked at the label, they wrote two songs.

Politi remembered: "Barry said to Bob, 'What's my budget?' and Bob said $50 – but he said it kiddingly. But Barry went and produced a record for $50 for Viola. And it was a hit."

That first record was called *I Got Love* on the A-side and *Lost Without the Love of My Guy* on the B-side. It landed just outside the Billboard Top 100 and sold well enough to make money on the small investment of $50. Wills went on to become a moderately successful solo artist and her records also sold well in Europe.

But White and Politi had made a huge, almost schoolboy, mistake with their first artist. The B-side, *Lost Without the Love of My Guy*, proved a lot more popular with DJs at radio stations than the A-side, and this wrecked any chance of real success in the Billboard singles chart. White vowed never to make that mistake again.

Two more singles followed and all of them sold moderately well, enough to make a good career for Viola Wills. Many years later she remembered her association with the young A&R man: "I was very lucky to come across Barry White."

In his memoirs, Keane recalled that he had given White the budget of $50 for this first single only as a joke, not thinking that he would take it seriously. He didn't believe that anyone could cut a record with so little money. But White decided to play all the instruments himself and spent the $50 on hiring a bass player, as the guitar was the only instrument he didn't play. He explained: "I took Bob very seriously and for $50 I wrote and produced a hit record and that gave me my first understanding of the business."

Next White and Politi signed a young male singer called Johnny Wyatt, who again enjoyed moderate success from a single that White wrote and produced for him. The record, called *This Thing Called Love* with *To Whom It May Concern* on the B-Side, was produced on a very tight budget and made good profits for the record label.

Despite the lack of a really big hit record, Keane was pleased and saw that White was an excellent producer and was making money for the studio. Keane increased his salary as the profits rose and soon White was making more than $200 a week. For the first time in his life he had spare money in his pocket and his family had food on the table and nice clothes to wear.

As Keane's trust in him grew he handed White more and more artists. White started producing the label's prized acts such as Jackie De Shannon and the Bobby Fuller Four, and money started flowing into the studio's coffers. Bobby Fuller and White got on like a house on fire. The two of them cut a new album in less than two weeks and Fuller called White 'the most outrageous arranger' he had ever come across. White took it as a big compliment and the album sold very well.

In an effort to find new talent, White took out an advert in 'Soul' magazine, which was owned by Larry Nunes and distributed around Los Angeles. White wrote the copy, which read 'Move over Motown, Bronco's bustin' in'. The advert announced that Mustang Bronco was a home for new talent, exactly the message that White and Keane wanted to put across. Keane remembered: "Soul magazine brought a lot of people to our door and Barry hustled up some action." Keane and White started to become close, having got over their mutual antipathy. They lunched together every day at a local hang-out called the Brown Derby restaurant, which was famous as the 'in' venue for every wannabe in Hollywood. White also started to stay over at Keane's house and became 'Uncle Barry' to his children. White later acknowledged that he learned much of what he knew from Keane. Keane remembered: "Barry did some terrific work" and White returned the compliment by saying of Keane and Mustang Bronco: "That's where I went to school as a producer."

Fresh from the early successes, Keane asked White to find him an artist that sounded like Diana Ross. Ross had become the biggest female solo artist in the world, emerging from Berry Gordy's Motown record label. Keane felt that there was plenty of mileage for Ross look-a-likes and sound-a-likes to succeed.

Keane kept the pressure up on White, but finding a new Diana Ross was not as easy an assignment as it looked. She had a deceptively good voice, which was hard to replicate. There were plenty of girls who looked like her, but none who sounded anywhere near as good as she did.

In early 1967, after months of scouring the clubs, White and Politi had a breakthrough. They found an 18-year-old girl called Floraine Taylor, who fitted the brief precisely. She was managed by her husband, a 5-foot-tall former rocker called Johnny Taylor. She had already recorded an unsuccessful single for Valiant Records, and with her sisters Darlene and Norma had formed a group called The Sweets. Despite the early failures, Barry White believed that she could be a huge talent. Bob Keane quickly changed her first name from Floraine to Felice and dumped The Sweets.

After a few weeks of rehearsing and coaching, White marched into Keane's office and said: "She's ready."

But there was one problem. Felice Taylor was basically a nice person, but had a very unpleasant streak in her personality that surfaced from time to time. She was also known to like a drink, and her bad behaviour tended to coincide with her drinking. With all the attention Barry White and Paul Politi showered on her, she believed she was a star before she became one, and started to act the part. The occasional unpleasantness gradually became the norm, as Keane remembered: "Felice was ungracious, stuck up and had delusions of grandeur – no one liked the woman after meeting her."

At one early live performance she had apparently gone on stage drunk and started insulting the audience, who responded badly and started throwing empty beer bottles at the stage. Luckily White and Politi were standing in the wings when this started and Taylor had to be rescued from what had become a baying mob out to get at her.

Despite that, White and Politi set about writing some songs especially for Taylor and quickly hit a rich seam. In quick succession they wrote *It May Be Winter Outside*, *Under the Influence of Love* and *I Feel Love Coming On*. The songs, which had seemingly come from nowhere, sounded really good to both men and they dived into the studio to record Taylor singing them. They worked for four days and nights straight without leaving the Mustang Bronco building. Liking what he was hearing, Bob Keane agreed to spend some more money, and White hired Gene Page to join them to help with the arrangements. The combination worked brilliantly.

They were all great songs, but inexplicably none of them were a particular success for Taylor in the US, just breaking into the Top 100 on the Billboard charts. But they all sold well enough to make the label a good profit on another relatively small investment.

But it was a different story overseas, and the label made plenty of money when the songs caught on rather better in Europe, especially Britain and Germany. In September 1967 the British Broadcasting Corporation (BBC), the state-owned broadcaster, had just launched a new pop station called Radio One to compete with all the illegal pop stations operating from ships in the English North Sea. Taylor's *I Feel Love Coming On* became its late-night anthem and the relentless playing propelled it to No 11 in the British charts in November of that year. The other two songs, *It May Be Winter Outside* and *Under the Influence of Love*, went into the charts on the back of it.

Felice Taylor's success in Britain alone, with Barry White's three songs, earned Mustang Bronco more than $150,000 in royalties, and a delighted Keane gave White a rise to $450 a week. This time he felt he had earned it and was happy to take his money. As he said: "England was my first friend."

But White couldn't understand why the songs hadn't been big hits in the US, and began to realise that there was some secret ingredient in making and recording hit records that he had not yet managed to discover. He had no idea what it was and it would be another eight years before he found out. When he did he would turn those same three songs into huge US hits for himself.

Bob Keane recognised the potential and, far from being discouraged, told White to keep on going and eventually he would have a big American chart hit. He was very impressed that White and Politi had written all three songs and gave White permission to record more songs he had written when there was downtime in the studio. He told him to sing them himself to see if there were any that could be recorded successfully by Mustang's growing list of artists. Keane's only proviso was that they couldn't spend any money on musicians.

So White got his friends in at evenings and weekends to play casually while he sang the lyrics. Eventually they amassed a library of ten songs including *All in the Run of a Day, I've Got The World To Hold Me Up, Fragile – Handle With Care, Out Of The Shadows, Where Can I Turn To, Under The Influence Of Love, Your Heart And Soul, Long Black Veil, Come On In Love* and *I Owe It All To You*.

Bob Keane listened to them all but deemed them 'non-commercial'. White didn't agree with this judgement but did not consider himself as a performer – as far as he was concerned he was just the demo singer. A master tape containing all the songs was put on a shelf and forgotten, and nothing was done with them.

Then a year later in 1967, under pressure from White, Keane relented and against his better judgement agreed to release one song from those sessions called *All in the Run of a Day* as a single. On the B-side was a Ronnie Goree song called *Don't Take Your Love From Me*. It was the first recorded music from Barry White under his own name but, as Keane had foreseen, the single went nowhere. He remembered: "I had never thought of Barry as a performing artist – and remember, for a long time, neither had he."

Despite his disappointment, Barry White loved working at Mustang Bronco, and found he was learning all the time, even though his respect for Bob Keane had gradually begun to falter after he rejected all his songs. By this time he was effectively running the day-to-day operations of the record label and having the time of his life.

His opinion of Keane dipped further when a letter from Motown arrived saying that *It May Be Winter Outside* was too close in sound to a record that had been released by The Supremes under the Motown label. White thought that was rubbish but was horrified when Keane sided with Motown. Keane said: "After listening to the Motown song and playing it against ours I believed it did sound like Barry had written the melody very close to their song." And then he added: "To put it mildly."

From that moment White's once warm relationship with Keane became considerably cooler, and he realised that Keane was not the man he had been at the start of his career. Although still well under 50 years old, it seemed to White that Keane had lost his musical mojo.

This was confirmed when White tried to sign a group called The Remarkables, fronted by Frank Wilson, who worked as a writer at Mustang Bronco Records. The group consisted of Frank, his three brothers and one sister. White believed them very talented, but Keane vetoed it, leading to another fracture in the relationship.

One Monday morning a few months later, Keane called Barry White into his office and told him that his partner, Larry Nunes, was visiting the offices later that week. White's reaction was, "What partner?" It was the first he had heard of Keane having a partner. And it turned out that Nunes was not a partner but the owner of the business. Keane said: "He's the money man, kid. He is the guy who writes the checks."

As soon as White left Keane's office, he ordered the staff to carry out a complete clean-up, buying some paint and repainting the corridors himself. Keane just laughed when he saw what he was doing, but White instinctively knew that Nunes was a man they had to impress.

Bob Keane had first met Larry Nunes when he did a deal to sell him Del-Fi's excess stock of records and returns, and the relationship had developed from there. Nunes was a major force in the record business and a very wealthy man. Still only 36, he was of European descent and had started life as a long-distance truck driver. His initial success in the record business had come as a distributor of record returns, known as cut-outs; they were the records that shops returned as unsold. No royalties were ever paid on cut-outs, and Nunes and his partner, Monroe Goodman, had made a fortune as they gradually cornered the market.

Next they formed a company called Tip-Top, which started putting record racks stacked with cut-outs in small convenience stores. In the process, Nunes invented 'rack jobbing', the system of distribution that saw reps deliver the music directly to the stores rather than via the traditional wholesaler method. Nunes and Goodman consolidated all their interests into one company, which they called Record Service Inc (RSI), with its headquarters in Los Angeles. RSI quickly established 13 sales offices across the United States. Nunes expanded the company into regular record distribution with a company called Privilege Records, which ended up distributing records for every major record label in the United States, thereby creating a near monopoly in non-record-shop distribution. Nunes profited mightily when the line between regular merchandise and the cut-outs became blurred, especially since on cut-outs no royalties were payable to anybody. How much money Nunes made out of this blurring no one knows, but it was a lot. Some of that money was invested in a chain of record retail stores.

Nunes had always had ambitions to own a record label and this had originally attracted him to Del-Fi. Nunes insisted that his rescue of Del-Fi and Mustang Bronco be kept secret, and that Keane would continue to run the labels as before.

But there was a problem. Nunes was a close associate of Mo Levy, the record industry entrepreneur, who was widely thought to be involved with organised crime and the Mafia. Outwardly Levy was a respectable businessman who owned more than 90 companies employing more than 1,000 people with interests in recording, artist management, music retailing, clubs, disc pressing, and tape duplication. Although Keane was grateful for Nunes's money, he later told friends: "I wondered if I had made a deal with the devil."

As Mustang Bronco became more successful, it turned out that Larry Nunes was keen to meet Barry White, the man who had made it happen, and that was the reason for his visit.

Larry Nunes arrived at the Mustang Bronco offices the following Thursday. He was preceded by three sturdy bodyguards and followed by two pretty secretaries. He had the look of Elvis Presley and was dressed all in black – jacket, shirt, trousers, socks and shoes. White later described him as looking like a movie star: "He had an air of mystery about him. I loved his walk and I loved his talk and he had great style and personality." White immediately christened him 'The Man'.

When Bob Keane introduced him, White felt an immediate chemistry: "He said to me, 'How are you doing, Barr?' It was a term of endearment I came to love and I called him 'Larr' in return."

It turned out that Nunes already had a very favourable impression of Barry White. He had particularly liked the single he had produced for Viola Wills, and was keen to meet the man responsible.

After he left, the two men kept in contact and Nunes made a second visit to the offices a fortnight later. This time there was a more frank conversation without Bob Keane present. It gradually emerged that Nunes was not happy with his investment in Mustang Bronco and was eager to know what was wrong. White remembered: "Larry took me aside and asked me what I thought was wrong with the records we were making at Mustang."

White told Nunes that the company had had many near misses but no break-out hits and told him straight that Bob Keane had 'lost it'. Nunes said that there was little he could do about Keane for now, and asked White to 'crack on' and do what he could to keep the label healthy.

But then Barry White witnessed something proving that not only was Bob Keane a poor producer, but that he had lost his ability to judge new talent. White loved it when artists walked in off the street without an appointment.

Most of the people who arrived were no-hopers, but some had talent. White had good instincts and could usually sort the wheat from the chaff. In June 1967 an unknown singer/songwriter called Jimmy Ford entered the building holding hands with a girl called Bobbie Gentry, who White presumed was his girlfriend. He recalled: "A kid called Jimmy Ford walked into our office with this shabby looking country girl at his side. I could tell in a minute he was a strong songwriter, the real thing, gifted, with a song that he unfortunately couldn't sing because there was too much of a southern twang to his voice, which is why he wanted the girl to record it for him."

Ford wanted to sell the song and asked for $50. White recalled: "I took the song to Bob and he listened to it. I told Bob we should buy it. But he said it was awful and didn't think the girl had anything." Despite pleadings from White, Bob Keane rejected it out of hand. It was a colossal misjudgement, as White recalled: "I went back to Bob once more and I tried to convince him. At the time Jimmy Ford was so desperate for money just to pay his rent he was willing to sell the rights to the song outright for $50." But Keane was having none of it and really upset White when he turned his back on him.

White had to tell Jimmy Ford, who was sitting in reception, that there was no deal. Ford shrugged his shoulders, grabbed Gentry's hand, and walked off up the street to the Capitol Records building, where he was given the $50 he wanted.

Five weeks later at the end of July the song, then called *Ode to Billie Jo*, was released, sung by Bobbie Gentry, and it immediately knocked The Beatles off the No 1 spot in the American singles chart and stayed there for four weeks.

It is believed that when Ford sold the song to Capitol they decided to credit Gentry as the writer. No one had any idea how successful it would be and it led to a dispute over who really had written it, which raged for years. It would have been Mustang Bronco's crowning moment but for Keane's stinginess over $50.

But White himself was not immune to the odd mistake, and it was around this time that he made an expensive error of judgement. Keane had signed a group called The Versatiles, and White recorded some songs in the studio for them. But for some reason he didn't rate the songs or the group, and Keane released them from their contract on his advice. More crucially he also gave them back their rights to the songs and ownership of the master tapes.

Soon afterwards The Versatiles changed their name to The Fifth Dimension and had a string of hits for Soul City Records with the songs they had originally recorded at Mustang Bronco and which Bob Keane had paid for. It was Barry White's turn to look stupid, and he realised that his 'ears' were also liable to the odd mistake.

The Gentry/Fifth Dimension rejections were colossal mistakes. The loss of both proved to be part of a run of severe bad luck that never seemed to end, and in his heart White knew that it would only be a matter of time before Mustang Bronco was shuttered. Earlier, in 1966, Bobby Fuller, leader of the Bobby Fuller Four, had been found suffocated in his car outside his Los Angeles apartment. Bob Keane's bad luck had started many years before when his teenage discovery Ritchie Valens, who had recorded two huge hits for Keane, had been killed in the 1959 air crash that had also claimed the life of Buddy Holly. Then Keane's protégé soul singer Sam Cooke was murdered in a Los Angeles motel. Bobby Fuller's death and that of Cooke were later linked by journalists, and neither was ever fully explained.

After that Keane started acting strangely. The eight-track recording studio was a huge asset and the income from renting it out could have saved the company. White said: "We had an incredible eight-track studio which was a very big deal back then." He realised just how big a deal when he was approached by the managers of Holland Dozier & Holland, who wanted to book 600 hours of studio time for a large up-front payment. But White recalled: "Bob wouldn't rent it out."

The company struggled on until the end of 1967, when the death of Bobby Fuller and the loss of Bobbie Gentry and The Fifth Dimension together proved to be the last straw for Larry Nunes, who finally realised that Bob Keane, by then 45 years old, couldn't cut it any more.

One day in July 1968 Larry Nunes suddenly arrived at the Mustang Bronco offices unannounced. He marched into Keane's office with four security men and told him: "Since Bobby's death nothing much has been happening here so I have decided to pull the plug and close shop."

Nunes paid off the staff and told them it was all over, leaving a devastated Barry White high and dry – Mustang Bronco had become his whole life. The company's back catalogue was absorbed into Nunes's other music companies and all the artists released. He put the state-of-the art studio up for sale. White was angry with Keane, but he was also angry with Nunes. He would not have been surprised if Nunes had fired Keane, but he never expected the shuttering of the whole label. He had embraced hopes of replacing Keane himself.

White was as angry and upset as he had been when Al Samuels closed down his toyshop. He said: "The pain cut so deep I made a promise to myself I would not work for another company as long as I lived. The demise of Mustang Bronco broke my heart. I'd put everything I had into that daily grind trying to make something work and then suddenly there was no more company. I never wanted to be hurt like that again."

After Mustang Bronco closed, Keane started a new company called Robert Keane Enterprises Inc. He tried to help White and gave him some independent producing work developing a new singer he had discovered called Danny Wagner. Keane asked White to produce Wagner's new album called *The Kindred Soul of Danny Wagner*. White did all the work and put together 12 tracks for the album, including three he had written himself called *Out of the Shadows, This Thing Called Love* and *I Lost a True Love*. But when the album was released on the Imperial label, Keane got the producing credit and White's contribution was forgotten.

Predictably Danny Wagner did not break through; *I Lost a True Love* was deemed good enough to be released as a single, but it went nowhere. Wagner never made another record and Keane's new venture was over as quickly as it had started.

Nunes had been right in his assessment of Bob Keane and, after a few more attempts, Keane left the music business and started selling Westinghouse burglar alarm systems to celebrities around Beverly Hills. He became their number one salesman, earning $60,000 a year in commissions.

Ten years later he had a revival in the music business when he guided his two sons, Tom and John, to musical success as the Keane Brothers, but he was never a mainstream player again.

But the Mustang Bronco years had been good for Barry White. Everyone now recognised his talents and he would never go hungry again. From that moment on there was a steady demand for his services and he was now only a couple of years away from the start of a period that would turn him into a global superstar.

CHAPTER 18

Split from Mary

The final schism

1966 to 1969

Seven years after Barry and Mary had married and after two more children had been born, making four in all, his friends urged him to draw a veil over his marriage. It was not working and clearly making him very unhappy. Home was almost like a war zone.

His friends had long suggested that he would find it far easier to make it in the music business without a wife in tow. They said it would give him freedom to take jobs anywhere in the country to further his career. But he was adamant that he would never leave his children. As he said: "I was not going to let those little ones pay for my wanting to be in music. I'd brought them into this world and I was going to care for them even if it meant me never playing another note for the rest of my life."

He adored his children, Barry Jnr, born in 1961, Lanese, who had arrived on 12th December 1962, Nina, who was born 19th May 1964, and finally Darryl, another boy, born on 20th June 1965.

He had seen them through years of struggle until 1966, when his pay had gone from $40 a week to $200 a week overnight. There had followed two years of prosperity with his weekly wage eventually topping out at $400 a week. But the abrupt and sudden closure of Mustang Bronco in the middle of 1968 put an abrupt end to the good times. After two years of financial stability the closure had a serious negative effect on the family.

And Barry White had no savings to fall back on.

But it was not quite back to the days of living hand to mouth. He had brief moments of prosperity such as when he was asked to write some music by Hanna-Barbera, via a friend who recommended him. It was for an hour-long cartoon show called *The Banana Splits*. The show aired on NBC for two seasons between September 1968 and September 1970. As he recalled: "I was starving to death when a friend of mine asked me to speculatively submit some songs. I liked cartoon shows and I needed the money. I submitted two songs and they took them both." They paid White $1,000, which provided a brief respite from penury for the family.

Also in 1970 he wrote a song called *Your Sweetness Is My Weakness* and Earl Nelson picked it up. Nelson recorded it under his pseudonym of Jackie Lee, with his old partner Bob Relf. Barry White did the arrangement and it was released as a single with another Nelson/Relf song, *You Were Searching for Love*, on the B-side. It was virtually unrecognisable from the version White later recorded in 1978 but at the time earned him a much-needed $500.

Some of the money he earned was spent on another single he released himself privately on a label he called Original Sound Records. It was called *Little Girl* with a cover of the Elvis Presley hit, *In the Ghetto*, on the B-side. This time he went under the pseudonym of Gene West. Despite his efforts to interest Los Angeles radio stations to play it, only a few hundred discs were pressed and most went to White's friends. White had so little confidence in his own abilities that at the last minute he switched the official A-side to *In The Ghetto*, which negated the whole reason for doing it in the first place. But the record was beautifully produced and arranged and demonstrated beyond doubt that Barry White had a great voice.

Money was continually short, putting pressure on the family and the marriage. It was made worse by the fact that the family had got used to a much better way of life. No longer would they eat eggs for supper two nights running. Now they wanted more and Barry White had to find it. Throughout this period Gene Page was lending the family money, but it was never enough.

The money problems exacerbated the problems in the marriage. It was a marriage he had never wanted, but he had got himself entwined in it over a long period as Mary became pregnant time and time again. Because of the four young children there was no easy way out – he was poor and he was stuck. He would not get out until his hand was eventually forced.

And that was not all he had to contend with at home. By this time his natural father, Melvin White, had come back into his life, his own marriage having run into difficulties. As his young children had grown up he was around more and more and able to acknowledge publicly the existence of his second family.

Melvin was also older and wiser than he had been as a young man, and had plenty of regrets. He seemed more interested in his grandchildren than his own two sons, who he had written off as failures. He was not particularly proud of either of them; as he saw it one of them was in prison and the other was a star-struck musical wannabe who could not hold down a regular job. Sadly, at the time both observations were true.

Melvin liked Mary a lot and formed a bond with her. He believed she was the star of the family and a perfect mother to her children. He also adored his four grandchildren and did all he could to make Mary's life easier. He went shopping for her and gave her money when he could. He was also a regular babysitter and spent many hours happily chatting to Mary's mother as they cared for the children.

At first Barry White was pleased to see his father, but that feeling soon faded as he formed an alliance with Mary's mother, which White called 'the alliance of the in-laws'. He recalled: "Now Mary had my father as well as her mother on her side."

In almost everything Melvin took Mary's side, but what really annoyed White was when Melvin stated to interfere in his own life. He started dropping hints about the futility of the music business and how difficult it was to make a success of a career in it. He said that his son might be better pursuing an alternative career. White listened to his father and agreed to disagree with him. As politely as he could he told him it was nothing to do with him: "Dad, I am not quite ready to give up my dream." But his father made it clear that he believed it was a forlorn dream and that his son was wasting his time.

Melvin's views on the subject emboldened Mary, who had completely changed her mind about the family's future. She had previously been very supportive of her husband's career ambitions to make it in music. But she suddenly turned against him and joined the chorus, as White described: "She was suddenly singing a different tune and insisting I get a 'real job'." White knew where it was all coming from and blamed his father. Mary denied it and said she was her own woman and had changed her mind and lost faith. White's attitude was that she had got what she wanted when they married and would have to live with the consequences. He was unapologetic about following his dream, as he said to her: "You got what you wanted – why shouldn't I get what I want. I have to do my thing."

White thought his father's presence was very demotivating and considered carefully whether he should ask him to stop visiting. But it was something he knew he could never do, as he explained: "He was my father, the man from whose seed I had sprung, and I wanted him to know that to me family was everything and he was as much a part of my family as anyone else."

This was sorely tested in the weeks and months ahead as his father interfered more and more and started coming over most weekends when, more often than not, he stayed over on Saturday night.

White's patience was really tested when one weekend Melvin sat in a corner huddled with Mary and her mother for most of the day, whispering among themselves while White played with his children. White asked Sadie what he should do and she recommended throwing Melvin out of the house, but that was something White could not do: "To turn him out now would be to show proof that I had inherited the wrong legacy from his soul. I wanted him to know that I was bigger than that and would be there for him for the rest of his life."

With all the whispering and secret conversations, White knew that something was up, but shrugged his shoulders, safe in the knowledge that nothing they could say would alter his course. Mary's mother became more vociferous and White made sure he was out working every day, taking any job he could.

Then one weekend Melvin took him to one side and asked for a talk. He said what he believed to be some profound words: "Barry, you are never going to make it in music. You've been trying for so long to make it in this business and you still ain't done shit. One day you are going to look around and the world is going to hit you like a brick in the face."

White didn't like the menacing look on his father's face as he delivered his monologue. He finished by saying: "You better think about doing something more constructive."

White realised that this was the start of a battle between him and his family about his future. It was about whether they would own him or whether he would continue to be his own man. But he had no immediate answer as he knew there was a strong possibility that his father was right and he was wrong, as he admitted to himself: "They could be right."

But he quickly pulled himself together and vowed: "What they think just don't mean shit to me. It wasn't what they thought about me – it was what I thought about me that counted."

White also thought that his father was unwise to lecture his son about his lifestyle after what he had done to his mother 20 years before. He also thought his father had failed to appreciate how everyone had forgotten his reprehensible conduct back in 1946 when he had effectively abandoned Sadie and her two young children.

Underneath, White was seething about how his own father had taken his wife's side against him. But he said nothing and his respect for both his parents, whatever they said or did to him, never wavered. "I could have built a pretty good case for cutting him out of my life. But I wasn't about to do that. I had a lot of compassion for my father." He also felt very sorry for him: "I believe he had never been truly happy in anything he did or anyone he loved. There's an expression that goes 'the son is the father to the man' and this was my chance to show what I was made of, to demonstrate my compassion and my humanity and I wasn't going to blow it."

At Easter in 1969 it all appeared to come to a head. White was between music jobs again and doing some work in a restaurant kitchen to earn money. Easter Sunday paid treble time and White was eager to do the shift, as keeping enough money coming in to support his wife and children was not an easy task. The never-ending visits of parents and in-laws made his life a misery and Eastertime was no different. Instead of praising him for working at Easter, they carried on scolding him for his lack of success in life. White thought it so unfair but still would not hear a word said against any member of his family.

Then he got the shock of his life when his wife delivered the hammer blow as he returned from work on Easter Sunday: "It was about six in the evening and I found Mary in the kitchen. She gave me a kiss and asked if I would take a walk with her."

It was an unusual request and White was tired out from a hard day's work doing something he did not particularly like. But he agreed and they went outside and walked down the street. After five minutes Mary turned quietly towards him and whispered the words he had never expected to hear: "I want a divorce." It was a huge surprise and he was shocked.

Yet, just as he had never expected to hear the words, they were what he had waited a long time for. He had been trying to find a way out of the marriage for two years and now it was being presented to him on a plate. Naturally he asked her reasons – not that he needed the answer, which he knew already. She readily admitted that her mother and his own father had been whispering in her ear for some time that a divorce was inevitable, and she had finally listened to them.

Then she told him something that cut to his core: "You're the only person, besides your mother, who likes your music."

It was a stunningly wrong-headed thing to say, especially in the light of what was to follow just three years later. But they were also hurtful and very distressing words for her husband to have to hear from his wife.

Nevertheless, it was what she thought, and she told him: "You've been at this now for 10 years and nothing's happened. I don't think you're going to make it." Then she added the stinger: "You can't even make enough money to support your own family."

It was not exactly what White wanted to hear after he had spent all day from early in the morning on Easter Sunday working to bring in a bit more money – especially when he knew that his wife, mother and father had spent the day in front of the television watching the Easter parades.

He was poleaxed. He felt queasy inside and experienced pangs of self-sorrow that he didn't feel very often except when he had been emotionally wronged. As he recalled himself very clearly 30 years later in his memoirs: "That little speech messed up my head big time. I didn't argue but inside I felt awful. From the beginning I'd sacrificed everything to give her what she wanted."

White put up no argument. In fact he said very little, which appeared to annoy his wife intensely. If she was looking for a reaction she didn't get it. Later he learned that she had hoped he would cave in and agree to give up his music, but if she thought that was a possibility then she had misread the situation completely.

However, she had made the move and there was no going back on it – and White would not let her go back on it. The insult she delivered to him that evening was so hurtful and so final that there could be no way back for the marriage. From that day they never slept in the same bed again. And they never kissed again, such was the schism that suddenly opened up.

They agreed to stay living together for the sake of the children, but all normal 'married couple' activity ceased. The truth was that they could not afford to physically separate at that moment, as White admitted: "Neither one of us could afford to move out."

But now there was no mistaking that the marriage was well and truly over and that there would be no going back: "I knew it in my mind, in my heart, in my soul and in my being."

White also knew that it was a watershed moment in his life, a moment when he put old ways behind him and made a grab for the future. He said: "I was more than ready to begin my new life."

And what a new life it would turn out to be.

CHAPTER 19

Turning Down Motown

...and meeting Aaron and Abby Schroeder

1968 to 1969

In the summer of 1968, as he walked out of the door of Mustang Bronco's Los Angeles office for the last time, from that moment on Barry White resolved that he would always be his own man: "I swore I would never work for anyone else again."

This promise to himself was tested very early on when he received a telephone call from Hal Davis, of Motown Records, then the hottest label and possibly the most coveted, especially for black artists. Davis and White knew each other well from his time at Mustang Bronco and Davis wanted to sign him up.

Motown Records had been started by Berry Gordy in Detroit in 1959 and had just celebrated its 10th anniversary. Those first 10 years had been momentous and the label had scored 79 hits in that time, unprecedented for a small start-up label. The name came from the city's nickname, an abbreviated form of 'Motor Town', and it was the first African-American-owned record label. Davis wanted to sign Barry White very badly indeed, having sold him hard to Berry Gordy. Gordy had already recognised his talent based on a recording White had done in 1966 called *All in the Run of a Day* for Robert Staunton.

White attended a meeting with Davis and Frank Wilson, who was a freelance Motown A&R man and a very close friend of White's. Wilson was so keen for the meeting to take place that he offered to collect White in his car. During the journey Wilson said to his friend: "Barry, don't blow this. They are very keen for you to come and work for them and they are talking telephone numbers." White listened to his friend but was nonplussed and knew in his own mind that he was not going to work for anybody ever again.

But he was flattered by the approach and very surprised at how strongly Davis came on when they sat down. Hal Davis was no ordinary executive and when he spoke people listened – even Berry Gordy often deferred to him. Davis laid out a plan that was designed to develop White's career and turn him into a star. In the light of what was to happen it was incredibly prescient and a good indication of why Motown had become so successful at spotting talent. White remembered: "I had caught the eye of the boys at Motown and they thought I had a good voice and they wanted to put me on their very impressive roster of writers, producers and artists."

White was very surprised that he was being treated as an artist, as he had done nothing to justify himself as a performer at that point, and didn't himself think that he had a future at that end of the business. He said: "They offered me a heavy salary, expense account, use of a company credit card and all of that." Hal Davis slid an envelope across the table; when White opened it and saw the salary offer he let out a loud whistle. Davis smiled. It was the response he wanted.

Barry White was beyond flattered and as he read the offer letter it gradually dawned on him that the label was offering him a very well-paid job. However, he had sworn that he would never be an employee again: "They told me everything I could possibly want to hear and it made me very proud."

If White was minded to go and work for a company again, his first choice would have been Motown Records. He owned every single that Motown had ever released and his respect for the company couldn't have been greater. Likewise Hal Davis. But he was true to himself and told them that he couldn't bear the disappointment if it all went wrong. So he turned Motown down, as he explained in his memoirs: "In spite of everything, after listening to what they had to say I politely but firmly turned them down."

Frank Wilson, who was sitting at the other end of the conference table, couldn't believe his ears and interjected: "Barry, don't you want to discuss this first and at least think about it?" White just shook his head. Hal Davis stood up and closed his file as the meeting broke up. He said to White: "Barry, the offer's on the table." There was nothing more left to be said.

When they got outside Wilson flipped and told his friend he was "out of his mind". Wilson hadn't seen the salary offer but when White showed him the number in the envelope he also let out a whistle. Wilson told him: "Barry, you have four kids and no money coming in. You should take that offer." The offer was $1,000 a week – $50,000 a year – plus bonuses, and Wilson thought it extraordinary, and even more extraordinary that White could possibly turn it down. White told him: "I just don't want to go that way – there's too much chance of big time heartbreak there and I've had enough of that."

White felt badly about saying no to Davis, who had been a great friend to him for the previous three years. He was also passing up the chance to work closely with him. Although Berry Gordy had discovered them, Hal Davis was the driving force behind the Jackson Five and Diana Ross and the Supremes.

Turning down Motown was arguably the lowest point in Barry White's life. He was virtually down and out and surviving on hand-outs, as he acknowledged many years later: "I was struggling and hustling and getting nowhere. Sometimes I thought those rough days would never end. But I kept pushing and pushing and I had the one little thing that was most important, a belief in myself."

White wasn't completely crazy, and told Frank Wilson that he did have another iron in the fire. The previous week he had been approached by a freelance TV composer called David Mook. Mook was acting on behalf of Aaron and Abby Schroeder, a husband and wife songwriting team who had just set up a music publishing company in Los Angeles, having moved their headquarters to the west coast from New York.

White admired Mook, who became famous for composing the *Scooby Doo* theme tune. Mook told him that he had signed up with the Schroeders and had got a much better deal than he might have done from a traditional music publisher, most of which were notorious for ripping off writers and composers, especially new ones.

Unbeknown to White, Aaron Schroeder was a very accomplished lyricist who had written 17 hit songs for Elvis Presley in the sixties and seventies and more than 1,500 songs in his whole career from 1945 to 1969, when he had turned to publishing.

The following day White walked to the shiny new offices of A. Schroeder International Inc on Sunset Boulevard. Schroeder had taken space in the glass and steel 9000 building, where many companies in the music business had leased offices. At 60 metres high and 16 storeys, it was the second tallest building in West Hollywood. White felt very proud to be walking through the stainless steel entry doors and into the impressive modern lobby. It seemed that the whole of the music industry was constantly passing through, as he remembered: "It felt magical to me."

When he got upstairs, White found both Aaron and Abby to be very warm people. They told him that they had signed Randy Newman as the first big client on their books and also a very promising newcomer called Jimi Hendrix. Then they told him that they really wanted him to come on board. Schroeder asked him what artists inspired him, and he immediately replied "Ray Charles." He told Schroeder that Charles had been his "inspiration" even though his music was entirely different.

White had no idea why the Schroeders were so keen to hire him, as he had no personal connection. He could see that it was a friendly family business and just the sort of place he would like to work if he was looking for a job, which he wasn't.

The Schroeders came right out and offered him a job as a staff writer, with a starting salary of $400 a week as an advance against writing royalties. It was another huge offer straight off the bat. White was very flattered and sorely tempted. He felt that the Schroeders were honourable people who would not let him down.

He recalled: "I surely needed the money but in the end I felt I had to say no. I explained to them how I couldn't be anyone's hired gun again."

Aaron Schroeder wasn't about to take no for an answer and shot straight back: "OK, give us an alternative you can live with." White thought about it for a moment and asked if it would be possible for them to set up a joint publishing business together, a company that would own all the rights to his songs. Aaron Schroeder didn't say a word, but stood up and walked around the big table. He proffered his hand, White took it and the deal was done. The company, called Savette Publishing, was registered the same day. They gave him a small office and an advance of $2,000, and he signed a five-year exclusive contract. He had no idea why the Schroeders had offered him such a great deal, but said: "They were quite confident I was going to write some very big hits."

These two serious offers had given White a big lift the week after leaving Mustang Bronco. As he said: "My wounds were still fresh from Mustang Bronco but I guess the upside was that all these people wanted me to come and work for them and I began to feel that somehow I must belong in this business."

The deal with Aaron Schroeder was White's first introduction to music publishing and would prove very important to his future earnings. Not only did he get the writer's royalty but he now owned half of all the income his songs generated externally. He said: "If you're lucky enough to be a composer and a publisher then you're in a fine position. And you get a lot of benefits from it through BMI and ASCAP's collection societies. Publishing to me is a kind of science. It's the thing people should take under most consideration when they start. It's a science. It's just like pressing records. It's a science and a business."

To help him finalise the deal White needed a lawyer, and the Schroeders recommended a young man called Ned Shankman. Aaron scribbled his address on a scrap of paper and White walked straight round to his office. From that day the two men started a relationship that would only get closer and closer as the years passed. As Shankman remembered: "Barry had all the talent and intelligence, but he was pulling himself out of the ghetto."

It was only after he signed the deal that White discovered that Aaron Schroeder was a very famous and accomplished lyricist. When he found out that he had written the words for the 1960 Elvis Presley hit *It's Now or Never*, he was blown away. That was the record and particularly the lyrics that had set Barry White on the path he was on today.

The following day White told Schroeder the whole story of his being in prison and hearing the song and vowing to change his life. "It sent a genuine icicle down my spine when I found out that Aaron Schroeder had written *It's Now or Never*. He had sent out a time-beam to me with that song, years before we were obviously destined to meet. When I found this out I couldn't believe it. I was both stunned and thrilled and sensed I had finally found my true cosmic and creative family." Then White asked Schroeder what his birth sign was, and the answer came back 'Virgo'. Barry White cried his eyes out in front of them. He really had come home.

And so it proved, as for the next 36 years until his death Aaron then Abby Schroeder looked after the publishing interests of the man who was to become one of the world's great composers and songwriters. Abby also effectively became his administrative manager, handling all his contracts and detail negotiations. White said: "From that day she made sure I was always well protected." White was full of praise for the husband and wife team in his 1999 memoirs: "Abby and Aaron are truly amazing people. They are honest and sincere, the rarest of breeds in the music business. They understand loyalty like few people I have ever met in any walk of life. Most publishers live by one sacred rule: 'Get the songs and ditch the writer.' Abby and Aaron's way of doing business was to me radically different. They sought to protect the writer in the belief that doing so would help make better songs come from him."

In 1994, when the contract expired and White had become a global sensation, earning more than $1 million a year just from his publishing, Abby Schroeder told him that they didn't need a new contract and that they would continue working together, but White could walk away any time he liked. She said: "We love you and as long as you love us back we can continue to work together." She added: "Imagine us as a bow – as long as we're together we're tight. When you want to leave just let the string go and you are free."

White never had any reason to let the string go, although he could have made a lot more money in 1974 by doing so, as he said: "There are truly some things money can't buy, the kind that Aaron and Abby showed me, and I showed them it is always going to be top of my list."

CHAPTER 20

The Love is Unlimited

Meeting the three girls

1969

His wife, his father and his mother-in-law had given up on Barry White. They believed that after 10 years of trying to succeed in the music business, he was all washed up and was not going anywhere. Not so the man himself. Barry White knew how close he was to succeeding; he could smell it, taste it, and for him it was now just a matter of time.

And just at that moment of maximum pessimism, fate played its hand.

Fate had always played a huge role in Barry White's life and his ultimate success would rely on a series of coincidences and chance meetings that came together, just in time, to turn away failure and ensure eventual success. Barry White always knew that someone was up there looking out for him, and so it was to prove.

Now fate played its hand again and he met the three girls who would eventually become the group called Love Unlimited and give him his first taste of real success. Coincidentally on that very same day he also met the man who would become his closest confidant and best friend for the rest of his life, Jack Perry.

The final phase of his struggle began in July of 1969. He was a free agent with a publishing deal but otherwise no particular prospects. He had set up his own label called Mo Soul Productions, but that was really just him, Earl Nelson and a few friends looking for opportunities to record. Even this wasn't plain sailing, as there was already a record label called Mo Soul, which caused confusion in the record trade, as White admitted: "We didn't even know of its existence until we had registered our name." But he didn't think of changing it.

White had turned down a $1,000-a-week offer from Motown Records and spent most of his time pondering whether that had been a mistake. On many mornings he came to the irrefutable conclusion that it had been. He got by any way he could and luckily some work always seemed to be around the corner, as he remembered: "I had a wife and four kids to feed and I knew the only way to make it work was to build my own niche. So for about three years from 1968 to 1971 that's what I did."

Then by chance, almost at his lowest ebb, Barry White met a young girl called Andrea 'Trixie' Robertson, who was a singer/songwriter with a very powerful voice.

White was immediately impressed and described her rather indelicately as "someone who could plain sing her arse off as well as write." When he heard her sing, he thought she had something special and for a moment he got very excited, so much so that he told her he would do his best to raise some money to make a record.

Making good on his promise he did the rounds of the independent record labels in Los Angeles to try and raise money to pay for a recording session. The trudge round Hollywood was dispiriting, especially as White was looking for just a few thousand dollars for a session. After a dozen or so rejections he was ready to give up until he came across Danny Kessler, an A&R man at Sidewalk Records. Kessler took a chance and gave White enough money to rent some studio time and produce a demo tape for Robertson.

White didn't realise at the time that Sidewalk was owned by Transcontinental Investing Corporation Inc, better known as Transcon in the music industry. Transcon had bought Sidewalk from its founder, Mike Curb, a few months before. Larry Nunes was Transcon's major shareholder, which White found out by accident when Kessler dropped it into the conversation. Ordinarily, if he had had a choice White would have turned down the money once he had learned of its origin – but he didn't have that luxury.

Andrea Robertson suggested to him that he hire some backing singers and a band for the recording. White told her that he couldn't afford it, but Robertson told him they were friends of hers and would work for nothing. Robertson was very manipulative and got everybody to work for free.

The three girls she wanted to use played in a band together called The Croonettes, and were friends from her high school days in San Pedro. Since they came very cheap, White voiced no objections and they duly turned up for the recording session at Continental Studios on Hollywood Boulevard on a very hot August day in 1969.

The three backing singers were two sisters, 24-year-old Glodean James and 23-year-old Linda, and their friend Dede Taylor, who was also 23. Dede had been born in Buffalo, New York, but the family had moved to San Pedro when she was a baby. The James family were San Pedro natives. All three came from very respectable families and had first formed The Croonettes ten years before to earn some pocket money performing for friends and family. Dede was happily married with three young daughters and Glodean was a single mother with two young children who were looked after by her mother and father. Linda was single and unattached.

The Croonettes had grown up to become well known around San Pedro and they played gigs every week. They performed in small clubs and at high school dances, mostly in the Long Beach area, and earned good money from it – but not enough to give up their day jobs. Glodean worked at the California Board of Education, Linda at the Bank of America, and Dede was a temp secretary.

The band Andrea suggested was one that her cousin played in and was led by a young man called Jack Perry, who remembered: "Trixie was the cousin of a bass player in the band I was with and she wanted the band to do an audition, with her, for someone called Barry White. Nobody wanted to do it because it was a free audition. But we did it anyway."

White was so taken with the three girls that he didn't particularly remember meeting Jack Perry that day, but he did remember that first meeting with the girls: "I met the trio. They were all thin, pretty, black and well turned out." He wasn't expecting much and thought they were "typical music wannabes".

But that thought only stayed in his head until they opened their mouths and started to sing. He recalled: "They knocked me out and Andrea had been right about these good-looking young ladies. I was very impressed with their attitude towards what I was doing and their own part in it. They were very talented and like every other black girl group in the sixties they had grown up with dreams of being the next Supremes." White knew that they were a long way away from that, and it would take a huge effort to knock them into shape, but he believed the raw material was there in abundance: "Their look and their attitude was so positive." The girls sung a number called *Are You Sure?*, which they had written themselves.

He believed that lead singer Glodean in particular was talented and he also found her very attractive, as he remembered: "She was playful and easy to get to know. She had a very funny sharp sense of humour, a wonderful way of saying exactly what was on her mind, which always put a smile on my face." Glodean was distinctive because of her fingernails, which were four inches long and perfectly manicured.

The truth was that Barry White was smitten, and Glodean James had made an instant impact on him. She remembered: "Trixie needed help and she called me and I called the other girls and we said we would do it and that was our first encounter with Barry and he seemed like a nice guy." Linda James vividly recalled that first meeting: "Trixie had really built Barry up and told us his background. He had a kind of glimmer in his eye when he looked at Glodean. I could see the look."

Trixie Robertson encouraged the relationship and by all accounts White had fallen hard for Glodean, although initially it was not reciprocated. Glodean recalled: "Trixie came to me one evening and let it be known that Barry was interested in me. I said that was nice but I was not into having a relationship at this time."

Barry White was surprised at the rejection. He was not used to chasing girls, more the other way around, so he also played it cool, keeping his feelings to himself. But later he admitted: "I fell in love. I just knew I was in love." He also realised that other girls he thought he had loved were infatuations and not the real thing: "It was the way she was, the things she said, her intelligence. Most pretty women are dumb and I found a woman who was bright, smart, and intelligent."

White admitted later that he was surprised that Glodean did not succumb to his charms straight away. But he knew how attractive he was to women and bided his time: "There was the charm and all that stuff and I was a young man who was trying to start his own business. But it had no effect on her." He knew he had to earn her respect. He told her: "A woman should have a man who loves her, who will acknowledge her mental ability, who considers her beautiful." She appeared unmoved.

But he did not let it put him off the group. He just loved their perceived innocence, and the sweetness of all three girls won him over. He liked how that came over when they sang: "I loved their manner, their awareness and their open way of dealing with me. The look of them and the attitude of them was so positive." He was also impressed that they had good jobs and were grounded.

White took them to one side and told them he was very impressed with what he had heard. He said if they worked hard they could have a real future in the music business and strongly implied that he was interested in helping them. But surprisingly he found that, like Glodean, they appeared not to be interested and thought he was on the make. They told him firmly that they were there to help their friend Trixie and asked him to keep his focus on her. Linda explained: "A lot of people had tried to sign us up but we were always sceptical. We were in no hurry. We'd decided not to jump into it with anyone but wait until the right time and the right person came along." It was a surprisingly mature approach.

White was surprised and delighted all at the same time and thought to himself: "These girls know exactly what they are at." It was an understatement to say that he was impressed as he said: "These honeys were nobody's fools."

Almost as important that day was the arrival of Jack Perry in his life. If Glodean was the female love of his life, then Perry was arguably the male equivalent, and fate played its hand again when they met for the first time.

Jack Perry was a talented musician who, like Gene Page, came from a very talented musical family. He had started playing keyboards at the age of four. His father and his uncle were exceptional players of the piano and organ, and music was a continual presence in the family home, so much so that by the time he was nine Perry was able to play the piano by ear. He also learned about electronic music when he started playing in night clubs. He found lugging around an acoustic piano too difficult, so he bought a Wurlitzer electronic piano and a Hammond B3 organ.

Whilst White was busy making eyes at Glodean, he also had time to notice how good Jack Perry was. Unlike Glodean, Perry did not play hard to get, and from that day he was rarely away from Barry White's side.

It turned out to be an amazing day. White, the three girls and Perry's band produced what White called 'two terrific demo tapes' for Robertson. The next day he started hawking the tape around to record companies. But as good as the demos were, it was hard work. For some reason Robertson's sound did not resonate with record label executives.

Then White got a lucky break when Robertson mentioned to him two producers at the ABC-Dunhill label. They had apparently shown interest in signing her up in the past after hearing her perform in a club. White figured he had nothing to lose and schlepped over to ABC's office.

To his surprise he found both producers were gushing about Trixie's talent and were keen to listen to the tape. So White played it and to his even greater surprise the two execs said yes on the spot.

A jubilant White called round to Andrea Robertson's house on his way home to tell her the good news. However, it appeared that she already knew as the ABC execs had called her on the telephone. But they had also said to her: "What do you need that guy for?" There was a strong suggestion that she 'lose' him.

It was typical of what happened in the music industry when promising talent appeared. After White told her the good news, she said she had some news for him. She told him coldly that she would be dispensing with his services as her producer for 'financial reasons'.

It was a shock and White realised that he had been used. But he just shrugged his shoulders. It was yet another disappointment, but he knew that she wanted creative control of her own output with no interference from him. He immediately cut her loose as she requested and wished her well.

That was a mistake, as Andrea 'Trixie' Robertson was never heard from again.

Much more disappointing was the fact that White had also seemingly lost touch with the three backing singers in whom he had seen so much promise. He therefore considered that the whole exercise had been a waste of his time and told Jack Perry what had happened. Perry was more optimistic and was sure the girls would get in contact with him.

But weeks passed and they didn't call. Then out of the blue, three months after the first session, Glodean James called him up at his office at Schroeders and asked if they could meet.

It turned out that the three girls had been waiting for their own phone call for more recording sessions with Trixie Robertson. They did get the call but were told that Barry White was no longer part of the deal and they would also have to work for free again. When they got to the studio Jack Perry told them the story of what had happened to White and they realised that they too were being used and walked out, leaving Robertson to it.

Shorn of their loyalty to Robertson, they resolved to approach Barry White to ask him to be their producer. White asked them to meet him for lunch at Kabuki, the sushi bar in Crenshaw district.

As soon as they walked in and saw him sitting at the table, the girls realised that they were nervous at meeting him again.

After a lot of small talk, during which nobody was coming to the point, Linda James finally broke the ice and said: "You don't love us do you, Uncle Barry?" White was taken aback by the directness and the 'Uncle Barry' bit and told them: "I'm only 25 and no one's uncle." With that they all burst out laughing and suddenly the ice was broken. From that day all three girls called him 'Uncle Barry', despite his protestations. As he admitted: "I think it helped forge a special link between us. I came to love it when they used it but I made them understand that they were the only ones allowed to call me that."

The girls wanted to know what had happened and why he had not followed up his initial interest. White told them that he had not approached them again because they had made it clear they belonged to Andrea at the first session and that he had a policy of not poaching artists. Now it was the turn of the three girls to make it clear that they were free agents and wanted Barry White to produce them. They told him that they believed Andrea had made a big mistake in going it alone without him.

White realised that the girls were very raw and a million miles from professional standard. He decided not to beat around the bush and told them straight – that they were talented but raw and would require months of work, that it would be a long haul and that there would be no overnight success. They would need a lot of rehearsals and had to be prepared to work every evening practising and rehearsing probably for the whole of the next year, before they were ready to go into the studio. The girls nodded in unison. It was tough talk but they knew it was the medicine they needed.

The girls insisted on paying for lunch, but he wouldn't hear of it. "We invited you," they chortled. He told them to be on their way and when they were gone he picked up the tab, although in truth he barely had enough cash to cover it.

But as he left the restaurant he felt really good. He thought to himself that the timing couldn't have been more perfect. He thought the girls' voices were perfectly tailored to the sort of songs he knew he was going to write and believed that they had a very special sound that he could develop, as he recalled years later in his memoirs: "There was something about the way they sang, as undeveloped as it was, that spoke directly to me."

As he walked down the street he started musing and whistling to himself. Finding them was the first step to finding himself, as he admitted: "I still hadn't found the right sound but I sensed I was about to make the leap to a place where I could create a more perfect world of love and romance with my music." He called the music he intended to create "the perfect backdrop for the amorous adventures of all our lives".

Somehow something magical had happened, and Barry White was finally on his way.

CHAPTER 21

Making it Happen
Creating Love Unlimited
1969 to 1971

When Glodean, Linda and Dede met again, Barry White had been busy. He had got together a plan, a programme with the ultimate aim of producing an album. But he again warned the girls about what he called "the realities of the music business" and not to raise their expectations too high. But the truth was that expectations were high on all sides.

His plan to produce a whole album for a new act was almost unknown and the girls couldn't be anything else but very excited. In truth, White had little choice but to go for an album as he had no confidence that he could find the girls a song good enough to be released as a single, let alone become a hit. The years of trying for a breakout single and failing had severely knocked his confidence.

He told them that an album would cost at least $15,000 to produce and there was no guarantee he could raise the money. In fact, he told them that the odds were against them as no new act had ever made an album first time out that was produced by an unknown producer, which he confessed to them he was.

However, he said he believed that he could do it, but that he required "total commitment" from them. He wanted them to know that if they wavered he would dump them immediately. He also said it may take as long as five years to break though and get some success. But the girls believed in him. They were undaunted and put their lives in his hands.

True to their word, they met him every night to rehearse in the garage of Dede Taylor's house. They quickly decided to dump the name The Croonettes and asked White to come up with an alternative. But a suitable name eluded him for a long time.

That is until he and Earl Nelson went into the studio in mid-1971 to record a song White had written called *Oh Love (Well We Finally Made It)*. Gene

Page was co-opted to do the arrangement and the three men quickly realised they needed a female to sing with Nelson. They recruited a girl singer called Tracey Andrews and called the improvised duo Smoke. It was finally released in May 1972 on the new Mo Soul label but it had no distribution and went nowhere, although it was a very good song. Smoke never performed again and it made Barry White realise just how good the three girls had become. The song triggered something in his mind and after the final session with Nelson and Andrews when they had completed the final cut, he was left on his own in the recording studio. Suddenly the janitor, thinking the building was empty, turned off all the lights, leaving him in the dark. As he sat in the darkness thinking about a name it suddenly came to him. He would call them Love Unlimited.

When he told them that night, the three girls were delighted with their new name and Barry White was delighted with them. He really believed in them and he called it "the perfect name for the perfect group". He saw the girls as an extension of himself and his music, the perfect platform for what the Barry White sound would be, as he said: "To me Love Unlimited was the very definition of wonderful, peaceful, sweetness, innocence, flirtatiousness and beauty." He added: "They not only knew how to sing in harmony but they were also the living embodiment of it."

The girls were also ecstatic, as Linda James recalled: "We always had this moody type of music in us but Barry brought it out and exploited its potential."

Gradually the sound White was searching for began to emerge. But it would take another six months to perfect and for White to write enough music for a debut album. By the summer of 1971 he had begun to think about how he would raise the money to get the girls to cut an album in a studio. Then he got lucky.

In August White took a call from Paul Politi, his old colleague from Mustang Bronco. Politi quickly came to the point: "Barry, I'm calling to tell you that Larry Nunes is looking for you." When he asked why, Politi told him that Nunes wanted to finance a new record in partnership with White.

Barry White took a moment to take this all in. "Too good to be true," he thought. There was still some lingering bitterness about how Nunes had abruptly walked in, closed down Mustang Bronco and put White on the street.

Barry White: The Maestro

Above: Barry White at the piano at The Felt Forum in New York during one of his first concerts on 9th March 1974. He was enjoying staggering success after the release of his first two solo albums. But the best was yet to come later in the year when the album *Can't Get Enough* was released, containing his signature song *You're The First, The Last, My Everything*.

Barry White's childhood in Watts, Los Angeles

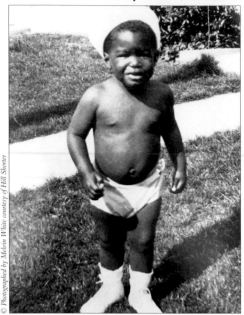

Above: The earliest known photograph of Barry White aged 1½, taken by his father, Melvin White, in Watts, Los Angeles, in 1946.

Above: Barry White, aged three, on his first bicycle, a birthday present from his mother on 12th September 1947.

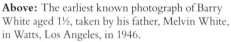

Below: Melvin White photographed in his mid-forties with the inevitable cigarette in his hand. His heavy smoking was eventually to cause his premature death at the age of only 69 in July 1980.

Above: The first known photo of two-year-old Barry White with his mother Sadie Mae Carter in 1946. The young man was registered as Barry Eugene Carter on his birth certificate but his father objected and he became Barry White.

Left: The photograph of Barry White aged three taken by his father, Melvin in 1947 and kept by him in his wallet until his death.

The Mustang Bronco years, 1966–1968

Above: Felice Taylor was the second singer that Barry White produced and arranged during his time at Mustang Bronco. He scored his first real success as a producer with her music.

Below The first-ever recorded single by Barry White was *Man Ain't Nothin'*, released and paid for by White privately on the Downey Productions label in 1966.

Above: Viola Wills was discovered by Barry White and Paul Politi in 1967 at Mustang Bronco Records, and they produced a hit single called *I Got Love* for only $50.

Above centre: Barry White released his first solo record under his own name in 1967 on the Mustang Bronco label. But the record, called *All in the Run of a Day*, went nowhere.

Above right: *I Got Love* by Viola Wills was the first mainstream record produced by Barry White at Mustang Bronco Records in 1967. It was the single recorded for only $50.

Left: Richie Valens and Bob Keane during their heyday in the sixties. Bob Keane gave Barry White his first real break when he hired him as an A&R man in 1966 at Mustang Bronco Records.

Breakout; real success comes in 1972

Above: Glodean James, Barry White, Linda James and Dede Taylor photographed in Los Angeles in 1974.

Left: Russ Regan, president of 20th Century Records photographed in the seventies. Regan signed Barry White in 1973 after learning that Elton John, who Regan mentored in the United States, liked his music.

Above: The very first mainstream single released as a solo performer was *I'm Gonna Love You Just A Little Bit More Baby*. It reached No 3 in the Billboard singles chart.

Above: Larry Nunes was the man who discovered Barry White and financed his early career to the modern-day equivalent of a quarter of a million dollars. Without him there would be no Barry White.

Above: Ray Parker jnr was regarded as one of the best guitar players in the United States. He was a key member of Barry White's team in the 1970s.

Above: Barry White at work at Whitney Studios, Glendale, in 1973 after experiencing his first success with the Love Unlimited girl band. He was recording his first solo album, *I've Got So Much to Give*, financed by 20th Century Records.

Above: Gene Page, the genius producer, photographed in 1976. Page arranged all of Barry White's recordings from the very start of his career. Without Gene Page there would have been no Barry White.

Above: Dede Taylor, the third member of Love Unlimited, photographed before going on stage in New York on 9th March 1974. She was a very heavy smoker, which eventually claimed her life prematurely. Ten years after this photo was taken she was diagnosed with lung cancer and died three months later on 29th November 1985 at the age of 38.

Above: Linda James, sister of Glodean James, photographed before going on stage to perform in 1974. She was the most laid-back member of Love Unlimited and got to enjoy the group's success. When she realised her career was over she met and married a Swiss doctor and moved to Berne, Switzerland, in 1980.

Above: Barry White conducts the Love Unlimited Orchestra at the Royal Albert Hall in London on 13th May 1975. The hall did not particularly suit his style and it was not quite the success he had enjoyed on the continent of Europe.

The enduring friendship between Barry White and the Jackson family

Above: Barry White at the piano at White's house at Sherman Oaks, California, sorting out a problem on an album in 1978. Barry White became a mentor and musical advisor to the Jackson family, especially Michael Jackson, advising him on setting himself up as a solo artist and eventually splitting away from the Jackson Five. Jermaine Jackson was for many years his best friend.

Above: Glodean White in 1976 with her only child by Barry White, Shaherah, who was born on 6th November 1975.

Above: Barry White and Glodean James photographed during Love Unlimited and Barry White's European tour in May 1975. They had married the year before on Independence Day, 4th July 1974.

Above: Barry White and Glodean James step out together backstage before a concert at the legendary Felt Forum in New York City on 9th March 1974. They became an item shortly after they met but had to wait for the divorce from his first wife, Mary, to be finalised to marry themselves.

Above: A sign of the power of Barry White and his music came in 1977, when he was at the height of his success. He was featured on the cover of *Jet* magazine twice, in the first issue of the year and the last. *Jet* sold over one million copies and was the leading magazine in America for the African American community.

Barry and Glodean: The love story of the seventies

Above: In May 1975, almost a year after their marriage in Las Vegas, Barry and Glodean White came to England for the first time as man and wife. They undertook a nationwide tour of the UK along with Love Unlimited and the Love Unlimited Orchestra. They are photographed together at a press conference during the tour on 11th May 1975.

Above: Barry White lays the law down at a press conference in London, England, in 1977. Five years after his initial success it had all gone to his head and for a short time he lost his way.

Above: Muhammad Ali and Barry White were very close friends, and Ali was a frequent visitor to White's home in Sherman Oaks. On 16th May 1975 Ali invited White to be a guest on the television show he hosted on the ABC network.

Above: Barry White sits in front of the giant swimming pool at his Sherman Oaks mansion in Los Angeles, California.

Above: Barry White with his wife Glodean relax in the blue-themed bedroom at their home in Sherman Oaks, California, in 1987.

The albums of Barry White, Love Unlimited and the Love Unlimited Orchestra

Barry White recorded 35 albums during his career, for himself, Love Unlimited and the Love Unlimited Orchestra. They were recorded over a period of 27 years between 1972 and 1999. He also produced eight albums for third party artists at various labels. All in all Barry White went into the studio and emerged with 43 albums, writing at least half of the songs himself.

The very first solo album
I've Got So Much To Give was Barry White's first solo album, released in 1973. It was fought over between Columbia and 20th Century Records and eventually won by 20th. White was born as a solo artist.

Another uncommercial album
Stone Gon' was Barry White's second album and contained just five tracks of music deemed 'uncommercial' by Russ Regan of 20th Century. But even he recognised that it would probably sell millions of copies.

The breakout album
Can't Get Enough confirmed Barry White as a global superstar in 1974. It contained the iconic *You're the First, the Last, My Everything,* which became his enduring signature song and meant he would become an icon.

Musical overload apparent
Just Another Way to Say I Love You was the first Barry White album that disappointed. It was good, but not as good. It still sold millions of copies and was revered by his now growing band of fans who bought anything he recorded.

The quality fades
Barry White produced 12 albums in just two years and his own work suffered as a result. *Let the Music Play* was still great music but just not as great as before. The world was suffering the first signs of Barry White overload.

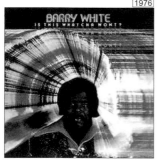

Is this what they want
Two solo albums a year was just one too many, and this was the second of 1976. *Is This Whatcha Wont?* was overload. It was also poor value at just five tracks when everyone else had more, much more.

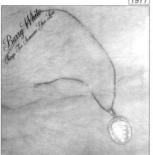

Sales deteriorate but not the music
Barry White Sings for Someone You Love was the only solo album of 1977, but the damage had been done and now each album was selling fewer than the one before. He was very disappointed.

Just the way he was
The Man was released in 1978 and featured Barry White's first hit cover of someone else's music. *Just the Way You Are* was as big a hit for him as it had been for its originator, Billy Joel. His version was simply sublime.

© CBS Records

The fans still loved Barry White

I Love to Sing the Songs I Sing reflected everything that fans loved about Barry White. Sales had now plateaued and the album featured seven great songs that would endure for ever.

The message is poor

The Message Is Love marked the start of Barry White's deal with CBS Records and was released under the Unlimited Gold label. It also marked the beginning of his decline, as the album was poor by his standards.

More of the same

Sheet Music released in 1980 was more of the same and the album was mediocre music with no chart success and no outstanding individual tunes. The extraordinary talent seemed to have deserted Barry White.

© CBS Records

The only duets album

Barry & Glodean was the only duets album Barry White ever made. It was a real treat and marked a return to form duetting with his wife in 1981. But his fans had begun to forget the maestro and the sales reflected that.

Beware of decline

The *Beware* album in 1981 marked the serious decline of Barry White and his music. Although the title track was business as usual, the rest of the album most certainly was not. It also marked the decline of the album cover designs.

Change for the worst

Mediocre is the only word that can describe the *Change* album, and CBS only reluctantly released a few singles from it. For 1982 he had tried to modernise his musical output but had upset his traditional fans in the process.

© A&M Records

Step back to go forward

Dedicated in 1993 marked a return to more traditional White music. Although much improved, it was nothing like the sound of the past and sales were again very poor. The long decline continued. CBS walked away when its contract expired.

A four-year rest

It was four long years since Barry White had recorded an album. He finally found a new label called A&M Records. John McClain took over guiding his career. *The Right Night & Barry White* was a disaster and quickly forgotten by everybody.

The man wasn't back

The Man Is Back was no innocent title but was supposed to mark a resurgence of Barry White's career and a realisation of past mistakes made. That was the message from A&M anyway. Unfortunately it fell on deaf ears.

1991

1994

1999

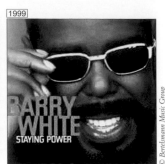

No good mix here

Put Me in Your Mix was two years in the making and none the better for it. Aside from two tracks, Barry White fans would never have recognised the music. One highlight was his cover version of *Volare* – a real treat.

An iconic performance

After two poor years Barry White finally picked it up and produced an album worthy of his name. *The Icon Is Love* sold millions of copies round the world. The last track, *Whatever We Had We Had*, about his split from Glodean, was a classic.

A couple of Grammys

A&M declined to renew the contract and five years passed before *Staying Power* emerged, arguably the worst album Barry White ever made and certainly the last. But it won him two Grammys, the first of his career.

1972

1973

1974

A wing and a prayer

The album that started it all was *From a Girl's Point of View,* thanks to one song called *Walking In the Rain With the One I Love*. The rest of the album was pretty mediocre, but that one song from the album took off and the rest was history.

Second album hits the spot

The second album from Love Unlimited called *Under the Influence of Love*, hit the mark completely with eight great songs; *It May Be Winter Outside* was the best track and reached No 11 in the British singles chart.

Third album is superb

Barry White really hit the spot again with his third album for the three girls of Love Unlimited, *In Heat*. Sales were disappointing but it was nothing to do with the music – there was simply Barry White overload in the marketplace.

1977

1979

1974

Difficult times for the girls

Four years separated Love Unlimited's third and fourth albums, and the group went out of fashion as 20th Century refused to release any more records. Barry White financed *He's All I've Got* himself, but the writing was on the wall.

The final throw of the dice

Another two years and the first album on the CBS deal, *Love is Back*, did nothing to increase sales despite being the best album from the group, with some superb music tracks on it. Their fans didn't want to know any more and it was all over for the three girls.

Rhapsody in genius

Rhapsody in White is one of the best music albums Barry White was ever involved with – eight beautiful tracks of modern classical music. *Love's Theme*, the final track, did the impossible and became an instrumental No 1 on the Billboard singles chart.

1974

1974

1975

Waste of time

Barry White was flattered into doing the music for the terrible 'Together Brothers' movie and came up with 21 terrible pieces of music to suit the film. Best forgotten – and it has been. But it did terrible damage to his reputation.

Beautiful music

White Gold, the second proper album from the Love Unlimited Orchestra, followed on from the good work of the first. It was simply beautiful instrumental music mostly composed by a man at the very top of his game.

More of the same

Music Maestro Please was a title that summed up Barry White at the time. It just tumbled out of him and the Love Unlimited Orchestra and its music was hugely popular particularly in the United States of America.

1976

1978

1979

A sweet summer

It seemed that Barry White could conjure up music to suit every occasion, and *My Sweet Summer Suite* was no exception. It was simply a collection of brilliant instrumental music much appreciated by his army of fans across the world.

The gradual decline

Two years passed before *My Musical Bouquet* came along, and Barry White was running out of ideas for new instrumental tunes. But this album was still as good as it got, although sales had started to decline sharply.

Super nothing tunes

Super Movie Themes was arguably the very worst album of Barry White's career. It was the last album he owed to 20th Century Records and it seemed that the maestro took revenge and gave them an absolute stinker of an album.

1981

1981

1983

Almost over

The first album for the Love Unlimited Orchestra on the new deal with CBS, *Let 'Em Dance*, produced very few sales. The American love affair with the orchestra was over and they had enough instrumentals to dance to for a lifetime.

Lovely music and a lovely man

Barry White collaborated with bandleader Webster Lewis to put out *Welcome Aboard*, under the Love Unlimited Orchestra banner. Two of the tracks are simply sublime music from this beautiful collaboration of two maestros.

Goodbye to the orchestra

1983 saw the end of the Love Unlimited Orchestra as the world lost interest. The final track on the *Rise* album was appropriately called *Goodnight Concerto*. Hardly any of it was great music and the orchestra had run out of steam.

The smoking habit that eventually killed Barry White

© Laurent Maous/Gamm-Rapho

Above: Barry White smoked cigarettes from the age of 13 to the day he died. His habit was extraordinary and he got through three packets of 20 most days. He smoked everywhere including on stage at his concerts. In the spring of 1975 he came to London and a cigarette hardly ever left his lips.

But Larry Nunes was serious. He had been continually hearing good things about Barry White in the year since the label had closed and was determined to sign him for the same reasons that Motown and the Schroeders had sought to do so. Apparently Nunes had realised that he had made a mistake by throwing the baby out with the bathwater.

After Politi rang off, White called Nunes's office. After speaking to three secretaries, Larry Nunes finally came on the phone. They did some small talk and catching up, then Nunes got to the point: "I want to go into business with you." He told White to get over to his offices to discuss a deal that afternoon. But when Barry White got there he found a queue of people in Nunes's outer office waiting to see him. Nunes was incredibly busy juggling with all the demands of his growing business empire.

White sat down and waited, but it was clear that Nunes had no time in his schedule to see him that day and he rearranged the meeting with a secretary for the following morning. An hour later Nunes asked his secretary where Barry White was. She told him he had gone home after waiting three hours. He berated her: "You should have shown Barry straight in."

The following morning it was a different scene and this time the secretary escorted White straight in to see Nunes. Nunes had cleared the morning of meetings to accommodate him and greeted him with a huge bear hug. It had been more than a year since they had last seen each other and Nunes desperately wanted to strike a deal as he believed White was ready to go places – in fact, he was certain of it.

Nunes told him that he had consolidated all his music interests under the stock-market-quoted conglomerate Transcontinental Investing Corporation and become its major shareholder. The merger meant that he was no longer running the business day-to-day, which left him with time on his hands to manage his own private interests.

White told him about Love Unlimited and how he had been developing them for the past year and that they were now ready to record an album. Straight away Nunes offered to finance the album, and asked: "How much?" White was taken aback, and said he didn't really know. Nunes told him to get busy and come back to him when he did. Then he hit White with a big offer.

He told him that he wanted to buy into White's company, Mo Soul now ready to take Larry Nunes's money and cut the album. He called Nunes and arranged to visit him the following afternoon. Nunes said: "Bring the girls with you."

It was a seminal moment in Barry White's life as all four of them stood together in Transcon's reception. Nunes came out himself to greet them, which was something he never did. He ushered them straight into his office with not a secretary in sight. He had the whole $32,500 ready in crisp $100 notes. He told the girls: "All I am going to ask of you is that you give it your best shot."

It was the defining moment in Barry White's life. And he realised it as he stood in silence, unable to take in what was happening to him. As Larry Nunes chatted to the three girls, he thought to himself: "This is my moment – what I have wanted all of my life and I have to make this work."

When they got up to leave Nunes called out to him: "Make it happen, Barry," then whispered in his ear: "After this day you will want for nothing." White whispered back to himself: "This is the greatest thing that has ever happened to me."

Like Larry Nunes, he sensed the start of something big, but what happened next far exceeded his wildest expectations.

CHAPTER 22

Loving Glodean

Getting it right second time around

1971

In the first few months of 1971 Barry White spent many of his waking hours in close proximity to Dede Taylor and Linda and Glodean James. The four of them became as close as close could be. But it was the chemistry between two of them that really began to sizzle. It was clear even before there had been any physical contact that Barry White and Glodean James were falling in love.

But equally all the girls knew that Barry White was a married man and it was only this realisation that stopped the relationship getting any more serious than it was. Like many women, Glodean had the strictest of rules about going with married men.

White was no longer living at home in the small apartment in south central Los Angeles he had shared with Mary and the children. When he did stay over they were in separate bedrooms and to all intents and purposes he was an occasional lodger. He stayed with his mother most of the time as things were too fraught at home.

White was very careful not to let his children or their grandparents be affected by the problems in the marriage: "Although Mary and I were no longer living as husband and wife, we never wanted to put that burden on our parents so we behaved civilly to each other and did the best we could to make our home environment appear warm and loving for our kids." Sadie filled in for her son at home and relieved the pressure that arose from his frequent absences in the evenings rehearsing with Love Unlimited. She cooked and cleaned and read bedtime stories to the four children. And whenever Mary wanted a rest, Sadie took the children back to her house. White remembered the time: "I worked with the girls every moment I had and I struggled hard to get the bills paid."

Although White had the $32,500 budget to make the album, he didn't take much of the money for himself, treating Larry Nunes's money with great care.

In his memoirs White was circumspect about his early relationship with Glodean. He remembered it differently from others at the time, saying simply: "In the middle of all this hard work we started liking each other." Glodean remembered: "The more I communicated with him the more I found myself enjoying talking to him and seeing the other part of him aside from the producer, the man, and then I kind of got interested."

But it was clear that White had fallen hard for Glodean much earlier, from comments he made at the time. He admitted that it had happened for him when they had first met in 1969. "There were things I was willing to do for her and with her that I couldn't do with any other woman," he said. "Love is not a thing you can play with. Love is truly divine. You can tell the difference between infatuation and love. It's a feeling I got; things I was willing to tolerate to make it work. It's the difference between having 500 dollars and 20,000 dollars. I just knew I was in love."

But it was well over a year before anything happened as they tiptoed around each other, each of them unwilling to make the first move. Inevitably, eventually the love affair finally began. According to White, one day he was over at Glodean's house and looking at her substantial music collection. Suddenly he came across a single that had been recorded by Felice Taylor, one of his artists at Mustang Bronco in 1967. *It May Be Winter Outside* had got to No 42 on the Billboard singles chart, and when he told Glodean that he had written and produced it, she laughed and didn't believe him. She still didn't believe him when he showed her the small print under the title, which read, in upper-case letters, 'B.WHITE'. Even then she wasn't sure it was him.

But when she finally realised it was him she was mightily impressed. She had loved that record and it had given her a lot of inspiration early on in her singing career.

White swears nothing happened that night, and a few weeks later she invited him over for a home-cooked supper. Among her many other talents Glodean was a superb cook. When supper was over and they were listening to the radio, she suddenly said: "Can you dance?"

White replied: "When I was a kid I was the baddest dancer."

She replied: "Show me your moves."

She put a record on the gramophone and he obliged. Then he grabbed her, pulled her towards her and kissed her before she knew anything about it. When she recovered her senses she didn't resist, and that was the end of any further resistance. She had crossed the line and she knew there was no going back.

It was the beginning of a great love affair, and from that moment he and Glodean were virtually inseparable. White opened up to her and shared his innermost thoughts, his hopes, his dreams and his fears. He recalled: "I told her how I was inspired through music to shape my perfect world, a world that now included her." He also explained to her for the first time his complicated personal life and she understood why it had taken so long for them to express their obvious feelings for each other.

The beginning of the affair signalled that it was time for him to make the split from his wife final. It had been two years since they had effectively gone their separate ways and it was time for him to make it permanent, despite the pain of leaving his children behind. "I knew now that I could no longer live under the same roof with Mary and one night I just packed my bags and moved out."

At that time there was no question of White, still a married man, moving in with Glodean. So he moved his things temporarily to Larry Nunes's guest house at his mansion in Sherman Oaks. Nunes was very pleased to see him, as by this time the two men were very close friends and Nunes enjoyed hanging out with White, who he believed would soon make the breakthrough to stardom. For his part, White enjoyed the sheer luxury of the guest house with its swanky all-marble en-suite bathroom, something he was totally unused to.

Despite their closeness, White didn't want to make a nuisance of himself and after a fortnight he moved to the Franklin Arms Hotel in West Hollywood, which specialised in short-term accommodation for singles in the process of divorce. Nunes told the hotel to send the weekly bill to him for settlement.

Within a few weeks Glodean had overcome her inhibitions and any reservations she had, and moved into the hotel with her new boyfriend. On the first night together at the hotel they made love for the first time. White said: "It felt like an eternity since I had been with a woman and it was one of the most amazing moments of my life. I had that feeling one gets very rarely in life when the creative spark ignites the flame of love and your house of passion goes up in one glorious blast of hot flames.

"I never wanted that night or that feeling to end. We made love deep into the night and for both of us it felt like the first time, every time."

White remembered in his memoirs that he was deeply in love with Glodean: "Love became the grand theme of my life. It became my work, my soul and my bliss. Right then and there at that precise moment I knew I had made it. I had become successful in the most profoundly meaningful way possible." It was also the start of a 15-year period of monogamy. White admitted in an interview at the time that, before Glodean, he had enjoyed at least 80 lovers: "I was making love to a lot of women when I met her but since then I've been faithful."

The prose was dramatic but White was happier than he had ever been at any stage of his life. In fact, he realised that he had never been happy in his life and it was a serious wake-up call for the future: "I felt engulfed and liberated all at once."

Glodean also became the spark for his songwriting. Most of his songs were about love and relationships, and he needed that spark: "I loved writing the music that she inspired. Music that in turn brought us closer together and deeper in love and I couldn't get enough."

Glodean had finally rescued him from his failed marriage, a marriage that had sapped all his confidence. His renewed confidence was the most visible sign of his new relationship: "My relationship with Mary had ended so badly, I'd been turned off from the idea of passion and women. Now I had been rescued, resurrected and rejuvenated. I felt as if I had been born into a new world of privilege, a free and open world where love and beauty and feelings and joy were truly boundless."

It was certainly a relationship that looked set to end in marriage, as soon as his divorce from Mary was finalised. "My feelings for Glodean were so different from anything I had known before. This was no ghetto romance born out of frustration and false hopes, but it was a love that was also a union, a creative union in which I had found the physical embodiment that was sweet and caring and feminine within my artistic body and soul."

The first song that was born out of the romance was *Can't Get Enough of Your Love Babe*. Released four years later as a single, it went to No 1 in the

Billboard singles chart in 1974, the golden year of White's life. It was arguably the most successful single of his career, and its words reflected his love for Glodean. White called it his "private love letter". His lyrics read: "My darling, I can't get enough of your love babe, girl I don't know, I don't know why, I can't get enough of your love babe."

Publicly he proclaimed that it was his musical tribute to Glodean and didn't care that the whole world knew. As he said: "I was in an extended state of ecstasy, a result of our physical and emotional union. Here was a woman I could relate to on every level, a woman who not only understood me as a musician but loved me for it. Here was a woman who came as close as anyone to personifying my lady music." On the day he wrote the song he said: "I wanted to give her something that night that came from the deepest and most sincere part of me."

Once they got together both White and Glodean were extremely careful not to show their feelings while they were working. They were more aware than anyone that the new relationship could easily upset the dynamic of the working group. This was during the period when success had been far from assured and they were fighting for their lives. They had the money to cut an album but neither the material nor the ability to record it. That would come in time with hard work. White remembered: "I never let my feelings for Glodean interfere with the special dynamic of the group and in many ways it actually enhanced it. We eventually became this one big crazy family. It was as if Glodean and I had these two terrific daughters. We understood it without having to verbally define it. And we took great joy from our tightness."

Paul Politi said that a big change came over the couple whenever work loomed: "Glodean and Barry had a wonderful relationship. But when we went on the road together, all of a sudden she wasn't Glodean, Barry's wife, she was part of the Love Unlimited trio. It became about business and she would call him Mr White."

So the relationship had no effect on the working dynamic, but it did enhance it. It made the link between the three official, and as a result they worked even harder. As White said: "We were on a mission together and we would succeed or fail as one."

They became a proper family, the family White had never felt he had.

CHAPTER 23

A Moment of Creative Truth

With Love Unlimited in the studio

1971 to 1972

This was huge. Barry White had $32,500 in his pocket and finally all the tools to make an album with genuine chart potential. He had the money and the performers, something that had never happened to him before. This time there were no excuses and it was all up to him.

The first thing he did was to hire Gene Page to arrange the music. Page was expensive at $500 a day, but for White there was never another choice: "When my ship came in, why would I use anyone else?" Page's fee took a big chunk of Larry Nunes's money, but White knew from working with him that he was essential to the process. Page brought in Frank Kejmar as his engineer, and Jack Perry tagged along to help. As well as Kejmar and Perry, he assembled a small orchestra and some backing singers.

Gene Page wasn't expecting much, as he remembered: "We didn't have a record deal but we worked on an album." Nonetheless he attacked the task enthusiastically and hoped for the best.

Barry White chose Whitney Studios in Glendale to record his first album. It was an unusual choice as the studio was used mainly by animators and professional choirs. But he wanted to be different: "I found Whitney, because I wanted a studio that wasn't in Hollywood. I wanted to have privacy and serenity and peace when I cut the album. The only other people there were Hanna-Barbera doing cartoon overdubs and some choirs recording Christmas albums."

The process began in September 1971 and White gave himself two months to get the job done. He wanted to be finished by Thanksgiving on the fourth Thursday of November and have the album in the can by then. It gave him roughly eight weeks and he remembered his thoughts at the time to Marc Eliot, the co-writer of his memoirs, which were published in 1999: "I had to put in everything I had learned in my musical life, from my days as a little boy listening to those 45s alone in my room. Every album, every record, every melody I had ever heard helped serve as the springboard for the making of this album."

The stakes were very high, and this was the make-or-break moment in his career: "I knew it was my first big chance but that it also could have been my last. It was my moment of creative truth – it was now or never."

The first job was for Gene Page to get White's compositions down on paper so the musicians could play the music. Page also chose two songs they would cover, as he realised there was nowhere near enough original material for an album. Inexplicably they forgot about the three songs Barry White had written for Felice Taylor – although they had failed to take off at the time, all three had enjoyed huge airtime in the UK. If they had just taken them out of the cupboard they would have saved themselves a great deal of trouble and transformed the first album's prospects. But they didn't and that made the whole thing very painful.

The creative process was to prove extremely draining to everyone, but Page listened intently to White's ideas and directions, writing out charts for the different instruments and helping him to start to fashion what became his unique, symphonic soul sound.

White was aware of the pain and was feeling it himself. He had a rare and real ability to detach himself from himself and organise the managing process himself. He knew what he had was not good enough and strived to make it better, as he admitted: "Three years had been spent preparing for this day and there were a lot of people in the industry who felt I couldn't produce my own album. What they don't know is that I am more critical than anybody. I'm a double Virgo and a perfectionist. I'm objective with myself and I deal with myself as if I were my artist and I was my producer and songwriter. As a producer I tell the artist I call the shots."

Despite that the music came really slowly, as he remembered: "I had something in mind but it took a long time for the idea to really formulate. I was listening to symphonies and good music, trying to evaluate it in my own mind and to create a feeling within me to come up with something totally different from anything that I've ever done before."

In reality White was trying too hard. Now the moment of creative truth had

178

come around he was thrown completely off balance.

The emotional support he received from Larry Nunes during this period was as crucial as the financial backing. Nunes deliberately kept out of his way and only attended one recording session, which just happened to be the day that White's father, Melvin, made his first trip to the studio. Melvin, who only a year before had told Barry he was talentless and should get out of the music business, was intrigued at his son's newly found success and respectable bank account. When he was introduced to White's father, Nunes told him: "You are very fortunate to be the father of Barry White." When Melvin heard those words his face lit up and suddenly he realised where his son had been heading all those years and how well he was regarded in the music industry.

White watched his father's face and was overcome. He put his giant arms around the shoulders of both his father and Nunes: "Larry infused my spirit and inspired it with his faith. I made myself a promise that I would not let this man, or myself, down."

As he was leaving the studio Melvin went up to his son and whispered: "I'm very proud of you, son." White broke down and hugged his father tight. As he said: "He had given me life and if he was big enough to come and tell me how proud he was of me then I wasn't going to be too big to put my arms round him and give him the hugs and kisses he deserved."

While all this was happening Glodean James stood by watching. By then she had fallen in love with Barry White and although she knew that a proper introduction to his father was not possible, she was overwhelmed with emotion as she watched father and son bond.

Meanwhile it was proving a real struggle to pull that first album together. Things that White would pull off effortlessly just a year later seemed to take ages, and inspiration was thin on the ground.

White decided that the album would be aimed at young women and the difficult subject of love and finding the right man. He called it a 'concept album' as he explained: "It was love strictly from a woman's point of view, grown out of the girls' personalities and life experiences as well as my developing relationship with them."

Day after day he desperately pulled together the songs he had written to try and find the right combination. But recording a whole album for a new group was desperately risky, as Glodean admitted: "We were a brand new group where usually you go with a single and see how it does – throw it at the wall and see if it sticks. But Barry had so much confidence in us as a group now we were going to do a whole album."

But the album's gestation proved doubly difficult and White was still having trouble with what he hoped would be the signature song and the one that would be released as a single if all went well. He had composed the melody but the right lyrics completely eluded him for almost a whole year, as he remembered: "I'd come up with a couple of melodies and some chord changes that went well together but I couldn't find the lyrics to go with them."

He was literally tortured by what he perceived as his own shortcomings: "I know my artists and there's no one I know better than Barry White. I kicked him out of the studio on a couple of nights because he couldn't get his thing together. The producer in me got disgusted and told him, 'We'll pick it up another night.' I am always asking myself, 'Do I believe what the artist is singing and do I believe what he is saying?' Can I close my eyes without looking at this man and say, 'I'm right there with you?'"

Later White blamed his creative block on it being a 'concept album project'. Much later he told journalist John Abbey: "Eventually things started to come together in what I'd have to call an organic manner. The songs I wrote and what the girls were doing with them slowly evolved into an amazingly integrated mould of ideas, attitudes, feelings and mutually satisfying interpretations."

It was a tortured process, but in the end the torture worked.

Barry White had already decided that the title song would take place in the rain. The rain represented a woman's teardrops – an expression of sadness that every woman would identify with. But that was all he knew. He described the process: "Woman meets man, woman loses man, woman meets a new man and moves on to a new life with renewed hope and optimism inspired by her revitalised feelings of love."

In theme with the album White wanted to tell the story from a woman's point of view and he knew exactly what he wanted to portray in the song: "Break-ups are always hard and it is a familiar formula for a love story that both men and women can and do identify with. The truth is that although we often think the end of a love means the end of everything meaningful in our lives, we can and do go on, we find new loves and we try it all over again."

White believed that the teardrops, or the rain, were the cleansing and purification process, which he called "a ritualistic washing away of tears of a love gone bad". It didn't make complete sense, but in his head White knew what he wanted.

But although he had the melody, he just couldn't find the lyrics to make it all happen, and it troubled him for months.

Then in late October he sat up late into the evening talking to Glodean. After she had gone, he went to bed, and as he slept the words he wanted finally came to him in a dream. "I saw the words clearly in front of me. I woke up immediately and wrote them down. I was half asleep but I wrote feverishly so as not to lose any of them."

He finally called the song *Walking In The Rain With The One I Love*. It was significant that the lyrics were finally inspired by that late-night conversation with Glodean James, his lead singer, as he remembered: "They were my conversations with Glodean about her life and what she had experienced."

The previous day it had rained hard on the windows of the recording studio. White could hear it but the girls in the soundproofed room couldn't. So White quickly rigged up a microphone and pressed it against the window where the rain was beating down: "I'd always loved the sound of rain and stuck a little Sony microphone out of the window to see if I could capture it." As it turned out the sound quality was poor, but it made him remember that he already had some good sound of rain falling on glass: "I remembered I had recorded the rainfall when Los Angeles was hit by a freak storm in 1970." He resolved to find that recording, and it was eventually used on the cut.

White decided to make the exchange of words in the song take place in a telephone call, not an easy thing to do with a piece of music. He described it so: "At the end is a man's voice. The man is the woman's saviour, the person who came along and dried the woman's tears and ends the heartbreak." The telephone call was actually recorded by White alone speaking into a receiver to get the effect: "The engineer fixed my phone so that when I picked it up it went directly into the twenty-four track. There was nobody on the other end and I pictured in my mind Glodean saying her part. It went, 'Hello, I'm home, did you get caught in the rain? Oh yes, and it was so beautiful.'"

It was a breakthrough moment, as Jack Perry, his friend, remembered: "He borrowed a Roberts reel-to-reel two-track from me to record it and you can hear him on the phone with Glodean." Gene Page remembered: "Barry did his own thing, which was utterly fantastic."

White recalled: "Glodean couldn't believe what I had done, and when *Walking In The Rain* was finished I knew the album was done as well."

The four minutes and 47 seconds of *Walking In The Rain With The One I Love* became the song that defined Barry White. He described the song as being "Romance inspired as two people meet, go together, and break up and then move on to new loves."

It was a huge risk, as large sections of it were far from conventional, with a long instrumental at the end. It was also way too long to be a hit single, or so he thought. But it turned out to be a masterpiece when sung by Glodean James and backed by Gene Page's orchestra, who recalled: "Love Unlimited bust wide open with *Walking In The Rain*."

With *Walking In The Rain* finished, White put everything together and decided the order of the tracks. The first song was *I Should Have Known*, which he co-wrote with Robert Bell, the founder of Kool and the Gang. The second, *Another Chance*, was co-written with Tom Brocker, a young wannabe soul singer; later renaming himself Tom Brock, he would become a protégé of White's and, as with Jack Perry, they would enjoy a lifelong association.

The third track was the original song written by the girls called *Are You Sure*. The fourth was *Fragile – Handle With Care*, a song he had written earlier at Mustang Bronco and which he completely rearranged. White's favourite song on the album was the fifth track, which he called *Is It Really True Boy – Is It Really Me*. He explained: "I wrote it immediately after I'd broken up with a girl, so it's written with real feeling. It became my favourite track on the whole album." But it was not as good as he thought, and a critic later called it 'tuneless'. The sixth song on the album was *I'll Be Yours For Evermore*, also written by White.

In truth White was desperately short of material, and the seventh song on the album was a cover of a 1967 song called *If This World Were Mine* written by Marvin Gaye and sung in a duet with Tammi Terrell. It had only been a moderate hit for Gaye, but White turned it into a Barry White anthem and a song that reflected the sort of music he wanted to write.

The penultimate song had been composed by legendary songwriters Kenny Gamble and Leon Huff earlier in their careers. It had originally been written for their house band, The Intruders, who had a modest hit with it in 1967. Called *Together*, it was another song that White liked and he thought it would translate from male singers to girls and produce a different sound.

But in truth, the songs were all much of a muchness and lacked anything really distinctive, with one exception – *Walking In The Rain* – the song that saved Barry White's career from an early grave. And White knew it too: "It proved the key. It gave me a theme, a completed cycle of related songs about old and renewed love as seen from a woman's point of view."

The album lacked a name and no one could think of anything suitable, even when the obvious title was staring them in the face. It should have been called *Walking In The Rain*, but when the final deadline came White decided to call it *From a Girl's Pont of View, We Give You … Love Unlimited*. It was hardly the catchiest name, but it was what he wanted.

As soon as the master tape was finished White took it to Larry Nunes's office and the two men sat on his couch and listened to it, all 34 minutes of it. It seemed much longer and both men got caught up with it.

It was good but not great, but crucially it was good enough. At the end Nunes's eyes moistened and he said to White: "Nice job, Barry, well done." White said: "I never forgot that moment."

Nunes kept the master tape and straight away took it to Russ Regan, who was head of A&R at Uni Records, a label owned by MCA, run by Lew Wasserman. Regan had a good reputation for spotting new talent and was coming off a great run, having discovered Elton John, Neil Diamond and Olivia Newton-John in quick succession for the Uni label. Nunes believed he would "get" Love Unlimited and Barry White.

Regan had started his career with Motown, giving the label its first No 1 hit record, and had then moved on to launch The Beach Boys and help Frank Sinatra out of his sixties musical funk. No man in the music industry at that time had a bigger reputation than Regan, although some thought he had been 'lucky' so far in his career.

But he was to prove 'lucky' again. Regan heard the tape once and signed

Love Unlimited to the Uni Records label straight away.

After his struggles of the past, White couldn't quite believe that it had all proved so easy. "The girls and I were ecstatic. I had promised I would see them through to a deal and now Larry Nunes, a man I considered no less than my saviour, had helped make it come true."

White designed the album sleeve himself with help from George Whiteman, a professional album designer, and illustrations from an artist who simply called himself Gomez. Whiteman took a series of photos of the three girls and also hired some models from an agency. He dressed the girls in black outfits with gold necklaces and placed them leaning over a gold cloud coming off a rainbow. On the back cover was a series of five images of men and women shot by Whiteman in a summer scheme that reflected the theme of the album – love. Whiteman also designed a logo that became the band's printed signature.

Walking In The Rain, by far the best song on the album, was immediately scheduled to be released as a single, and no one was in any doubt that it would be a hit. And they weren't wrong, as it climbed as high as No 14 in the Billboard Hot 100. It also reached No 6 on the US soul singles chart.

The album itself struggled to get to No 15 in the LP charts. But in reality it didn't matter, as *Walking In The Rain* carried everything, and the single soon passed the million sales mark.

MCA Records was quick to release the single in the UK and it was an instant hit, selling 12,000 copies in the first two weeks and reaching No 14 in the British singles chart. BBC Radio One DJs Alan Freeman and David Simmons, at different ends of the musical spectrum, were both playing it in advance of its release.

At this stage Barry White was far better known to the British public than he was in America, and everyone seemed to remember him as being the maestro behind Felice Taylor's *It May Be Winter Outside, I'm Under the Influence of Love* and her really big British hit *I Feel Love Comin' On* five years before. White's songs had had a far bigger impact in Europe than anyone realised.

But their enthusiasm wasn't quite matched by sales, and just when it looked set for the Top 10, sales stumbled and No 14 proved to be the peak. Inexplicably the British single was a minute shorter than the USA single and the album version, and this may have been the reason. Disappointingly the album itself didn't sell many copies in Britain and barely registered on the charts.

John Abbey of 'Blues & Soul' magazine was pretty scathing about most of the introduction having been edited out of the British single. He said: "The thing that has appealed to one and all is the brilliant 'rapping' that precedes the song itself and unfortunately the minute that's been docked comes from this section."

It was all part of the vagaries of the music business, and there was nothing that Barry White could do about it, but he vowed he would never let it happen again.

As soon as the single entered the charts White knew instinctively that the girls must get out on tour to capitalise on the success. He told them the time had come to give up their day jobs; Glodean resigned from her job at the Board of Education, Linda waved goodbye to the Bank of America, and Dede decided that there was no more secretarial work for her.

White recalled: "We hit the road for a long cross-country tour." For the girls it was their first time out of Los Angeles and White vowed to show them the United States properly. They were helped by the hype, and *Walking In The Rain* was continually playing on the radio. As White said: "We were sitting on top of this beautiful world which we had idealised in our music. We were stars now and were ready to meet our fans. The excitement in the air was unbelievable."

Larry Nunes put up the front money for the tour and White hired nine musicians – five horns, three strings and a drummer – to back Love Unlimited live.

White also handed the three girls money to buy some stage outfits for the tour. He wanted at least four changes during the 90-minute act, as he remembered: "They were the most beautiful and stylishly entertaining female act that anyone had ever seen."

Putting together the stage act proved easy. They had spent nearly two years in rehearsal and had plenty of well-rehearsed material to use. As White recalled: "I took great pride knowing that I had turned these girls into slick, professional, high-calibre performers, and I worked with them to relentlessly to find a way to channel their energy into an even higher level of onstage greatness."

One of the first engagements was at the Sugar Shack nightclub in Boston for a week, followed by their first trip to New York. The tour, like the album, was held together by *Walking In The Rain*, and the stage routine was opened by White's song *Oh Love (Well We Finally Made It)*, which inexplicably wasn't even on the album. That song had special significance for White as it referred directly to his own experience: "I'd smile and think to myself, 'Yes we did, yes we did.'"

As the tour started sales of the *Walking In The Rain* single took off, although album sales spluttered. In truth the album was very forgettable – and was soon forgotten.

Privately White shuddered to think what might have happened if *Walking In The Rain* had not worked out. As it was, it became the anthem of a generation and was played regularly on American radio stations for the next 40 years. It was a record people never tired of hearing, including the writer himself, as he admitted: "Nothing has ever surpassed that feeling that I felt the first day I heard *Walking In The Rain With The One I Love* on the radio."

He recalled: "We were knocked out with the success of that record. The next thing we knew it was a million-seller and in 1972 we had our first gold record. We couldn't believe it and we were on top of the world."

Music journalists from all over the world clamoured to interview the three girls from Love Unlimited, who had suddenly, without warning, burst onto the music scene. They were also interested in their Svengali.

As it was, Barry White did most of the talking. He told journalists at a press conference: "Love Unlimited and I have become one person even though we're four people. They didn't know anything about the record industry and I've always kept my arms around them so nobody could hurt them. That was my first million seller and their first million seller, a fantastic launch for the girls and my Mo Soul production company."

Roger St Pierre of the British 'New Musical Express', for one, was bemused by Barry White and how he looked. He described him as "sounding like he's stepped straight out of a Cheech and Chong parody." But St Pierre recognised the work White had put in and called him "a respected back room boy of the American record business. White is now receiving the acknowledgement he has long merited."

John Abbey said: "This is a man who works almost exclusively on ideas, atmospheres and feelings. Happily, he has the talent to be able to harness these intangible qualities too and can thus turn them all to his own advantage." Abbey forecast a "big future" for Barry White.

White had plenty of time for reflection: "Of course no one wanted to hear about the eleven years it had taken me to find those couple of minutes of music." He also lavished praise on Gene Page and knew he had been just as much a part of the success as him or the three girls: "When you say Barry White, Love Unlimited, whatever else you say, always mention Gene's name."

For Love Unlimited it was the start of a fabulous period, although they would never scale the singles chart again as they did with *Walking In The Rain*. Other singles released from the album were not successful – *Is It Really True* and *Are You Sure* went nowhere.

But the success of that first single had unleashed unbounded confidence in Barry White, and suddenly his talent as a songwriter exploded. "Necessity put me here," he said, "and my God-given talents clinched it."

Part 3

10 years at the very top of his game

CHAPTER 24

So Much To Give

Enter Barry White, the singer

1972

After the dust had settled on Love Unlimited's first album and live tour, Barry White was full of ideas for the future. Suddenly he felt that there was music bursting out of his veins. He wanted to follow up his success with the three girls by finding an equivalent male act and envisioned his future as being the Svengali of separate male and female acts. He had accomplished one half of that ambition with the three girls, but with only Love Unlimited to perform his songs he believed he was cut off from half of the market. As he explained: "I was intent on finding a male artist who could properly express the other male side of my musical romantic equation."

But there were obstacles in his way. No one else shared that ambition for his future. Russ Regan fundamentally disagreed and told White that the sensible thing was to work on a follow-up album for Love Unlimited and forget about anything else. Tellingly Regan said to him: "Why do you want to fool with success?"

But White was in no mood to listen. The success had already got to him and he felt there was much more to come. As soon as the Love Unlimited tour ended, he quickly wrote three new songs for a male singer. He found that suddenly it all came so easily: "I'd hear songs in my head which I wanted to write. I was able to pick sounds out of the air and find them on the piano."

The songs were titled *I'm Gonna Love You Just a Little Bit More, I Found Someone* and *I've Got So Much to Give*. He said: "Now I had three songs that I had written for a male artist."

With success had come confidence, and White's talent just seemed to explode. And he was clearly better at writing for a male artist than a female one. The new songs were a cut above anything he had written before and, to many, including Gene Page and Jack Perry, it seemed like a completely new sound. As he said: "I looked at it more as scoring sound, like movies. I was trying to tell a story musically in a song. My whole thinking had changed."

In his 1999 memoirs he revealed that those three songs were written for Larry Nunes. Nunes and White had grown very close during this period, and White would often be found at Nunes's house at Sherman Oaks in the San Fernando Valley, staying in the guest house in the grounds.

But this time all his problems were turned around – he had the songs but no artist. So, with the songs finished, Barry White began the difficult task of trying to find someone to sing them.

He tackled it the only way he knew and the way he had always done – by touring clubs with Paul Politi and looking for a male act that fitted the criteria. But every night the two men came home frustrated and exhausted from the search. There was no one out there who even came close to what they wanted. The only artist they could think of who matched the requirements was Lou Rawls. The 38-year-old Rawls, a soul singer with the deep smooth voice, was the closest to what White wanted. In fact, he would have been perfect for Barry White's material. But Rawls was already an established star, and White didn't think he would take kindly to having an unknown 28-year-old telling him what to do. When Rawls had burst onto the music scene in 1966, Frank Sinatra described him as having "the classiest singing and silkiest chops in the singing game."

White was beginning to wonder whether the answer to his problem was nearer home than he thought. Because he could not write music in the traditional way, his technique was to compose on the piano and record the result onto a tape cassette, which he then gave to Gene Page to turn into sheet music that the musicians could play. Then he sang the lyrics over the tape himself and wrote them down as he went.

After the success of Love Unlimited, he had plenty of access to a recording studio and no longer had to worry about the cost. So he went into the studio and recorded his voice over the music on a demo tape to see what it sounded like.

It sounded just fine, and it suddenly dawned on him that Barry White could be the male performer he was looking for. As he remembered: "I went into the studio and I cut a demo, just the piano and me. And while I was sitting at the board, I am listening to this artist, I'm listening to the relationship between what he is singing, the lyrics and him and the marriage of the sound between the melody and him, and then I really get scared because I knew sitting at that board that Barry White was the singer of the three songs."

It should really have come as no surprise, as seven years before he had written and recorded ten of his own songs at Mustang Bronco. But those rough-and-ready recordings, with his friends playing the instruments, had only been meant as demos to show off his own songwriting talents. One song, *All In The Run Of A Day*, was picked out by Bob Keane, who half-heartedly released it as a single. It flopped and he had blamed himself. Amazingly no one, including Bob Keane, had ever thought of Barry White as a singer, even though the man who inside five years would become a global superstar was sitting under their noses the whole time.

Since then, performing his own songs had never occurred to White, but now, suddenly, the idea just grew and grew in his head. As he explained: "One afternoon, a few days later, as I was sitting at the board listening to the playback again, it suddenly hit me – boom – my stomach flipped so bad it scared me when I suddenly realised that there was only one artist I knew who could sing these love songs the way I write them and that his name was Barry White."

It was a revelation that shook White to the core. Prior to that moment he had just never envisaged himself as a professional singer. His ambitions had been limited to being a combination of the ultimate A&R exec/producer/arranger/ songwriter and manager. As he explained: "I didn't want to be known as a singer. I wanted to produce. I wanted to be the creator. Singing was more or less a hobby. Producing, arranging and writing – that's my business, and I was very familiar with it. The way I saw it, in those days, singers carried a stigma, and no one respected them in the industry as artists."

It was true – inside the business in the fifties and sixties the performers were considered cannon fodder to be exploited and manipulated by the people who ran the music industry. That was soon to change, but it was the way it was then. As White said: "I wanted to play to my strengths in the studio and behind the scenes. I wanted to develop and guide other artists rather than be one myself."

There was no denying the power of his voice, as White himself admitted:

"The truth was that all my adult life people had been telling me how good my voice was." One day he had been singing to himself in a studio corridor along with some music coming through the open door of a sound room. A woman passing by had said to him: "What a beautiful sound you have to your voice, young man. Do you sing?"

White's feelings about himself revealed that he suffered from a lack of an inner self-confidence. This had also been the case with his writing, which had improved immeasurably after he had enjoyed some success and gained confidence.

Now he was facing the biggest decision of his life.

Even after he 'discovered' himself, White initially dismissed the thought that he might sing and perform as himself. But suddenly the woman's words came back to haunt him, and he could no longer deny what he heard. As he explained: "It wasn't until I had my producing 'ears' on that I finally heard the voice of Barry White. For the first time I became fully aware of the uniqueness, the powerful romantic pull and the emotional depth and lure of my own voice. That's when I realised that I was the artist, that I should be recording, and that was the voice for the songs. But I didn't want to sing."

The realisation that he could sing initially didn't solve anything. It actually made things worse and just kicked off the deep feelings of insecurity that had always lurked beneath. As he freely admitted: "I could hear for myself the magic that was clearly there, but I didn't think I had the stomach or the temperament to pull it off. The thought of actually being a singer out front had always horrified me."

Larry Nunes kept pressuring him to find a male singer, and White continually fobbed him off. But one day he could fob him off no longer and told Nunes that he had heard a new artist who might be good enough, meaning himself. Nunes immediately asked his name and White suddenly blurted out, for no reason he could think of: "White Heat."

It was a spontaneous reaction and he was certainly not going tell Nunes who White Heat was. And fortunately Nunes didn't ask.

This worked for a while, but after a few weeks Nunes demanded to meet 'White Heat' and hear the demo tape that he knew White must have, by now, recorded. White knew he couldn't fend Nunes off for much longer, as the studio bills were beginning to mount up.

He talked it through with Glodean James and Paul Politi. They both told him that he must tell Nunes who White Heat really was. But that would prove easier said than done, and time and time again White prevaricated when the subject came up.

Staying at Nunes's guest house one weekend, White finally confessed that White Heat was really Barry White: "Larry, I have found someone with a sound that is very unique, and that someone is me. The only thing is that I don't want to be a singer."

White played Nunes the demo tape of himself and asked him what he should do. Nunes was stunned that this talent had been under his nose all along and insisted that White did the obvious thing and started recording the music himself. There followed three days of intense discussions about what to do. At times it got heated, as White continually refused to even consider or discuss it. He told Nunes: "Singing is my last love. I would hate the hot lights and the daily grind of it. And I would hate the fast-paced lifestyle that I would be expected to live." He added: "I don't respect them, they all act like big kids with a lot of money – that's not me."

But White was in a difficult place. He knew that he owed Larry Nunes everything and could not easily turn him down. He suggested he perform under the pseudonym 'White Heat', but Nunes refused, calling it a 'cop-out'.

Then Nunes pressed all the right buttons, telling him: "If you love me, you'll do it for me."

Nunes had said the magic words – the words White could not resist, and to which he finally acquiesced. "He made me use my real name, and behind Larry's confidence and his money I went into the studio and the songs came out of me like firepower from a cannon."

It was a seminal moment and, as he had predicted, a moment that would change Barry White's life forever.

To finance production of the album, Nunes went straight to Russ Regan. By then Regan had left Uni Records and moved to 20th Century Records, the recording division of the film studio 20th Century Fox. Fox's music division had been closed down three years earlier when the studio's chairman, Darryl Zanuck, had been sacked and replaced by Dennis Stanfill. Stanfill belatedly realised that it had been a mistake and hired Regan on a big salary to revive the company's music division.

White was in a very good contractual position for his first album because he was not tied to the contract that Love Unlimited had signed with Uni Records. This was especially important as he wanted to work with Russ Regan again, mainly out of loyalty for his help in launching Love Unlimited.

It became Regan's first decision as president of 20th. Initially he agreed to finance the recording of Barry White's new album and was granted first option to release it. But it was only an option, and White knew this when he went into the studio – nothing was guaranteed.

After the success of Love Unlimited's first album, he had no hesitation in signing this one-sided deal with Regan, who seemed equally pleased to sign up White again. Neither he nor Nunes could conceive of any possibility that Regan would not want to release the album, having financed its production.

Surprisingly it was not until after the deal was signed that Regan asked Nunes who the singer would be, and was shocked when he was told it would be White. He said: "I didn't even know you could sing." As Regan remembered many years later: "Barry said to me, 'I can sing, man,' and I said, 'Well, I'm the president of this company and I can do whatever I want,' and that was that."

White told Regan that the album would be from his own "inner spiritual feelings" and side one would be about the negative side of love – when a man loses out and lives in the past of lost loves. He told Regan that side two would be about a man appreciating what he has got and "how much he has to give and will give".

Russ Regan loved it and sat smiling and nodding vigorously as Barry White explained the album concept to him: "The album will be true of me. It will sum me up, spiritually, mentally and creatively."

What White didn't tell him was that the album would contain only five songs, and some would be more than seven minutes long. If he had told him that, Regan might not have been so keen to hand over the money – in fact, he definitely would not have done so. But that was for later, as White recalled: "Russ gave me $37,000, and I went into the studio and cut that album."

Then fate intervened again.

White had decided separately to do his own arranging on the album as well as producing, and to save money he decided he would not use Gene Page. But when he took on the singing duties, he realised that he could not also produce and arrange himself so he re-hired Page. It was a crucial moment, for without Page much of his later success would probably never have happened. Certainly, the new album would have been much the poorer for it.

So serendipity ensured that Page was hired and, sensing what had happened, he demanded a doubled fee. White had no choice but to agree, and a newly enthused Page threw himself into the project. He decided to hire at a vast daily cost a full orchestra that could do justice to what he knew they were going to create.

White and Page, together with Frank Kejmar, Jack Perry and young guitarist Ray Parker Jnr, assembled at the Whitney Recording Studios in Glendale over the winter of 1972 to record the new album.

White and Page hammered out the songs and the arrangements. Once again, Page was asked to get down on paper what White had in his head as he worked at his piano. Page recalled the process: "Barry dictated, demonstrated and hummed out the parts. It was highly unorthodox, and it was also brilliant. Barry would play with so much energy that the legs of the piano would buckle; his sweat would pour out into the keyboard."

White reciprocated the praise: "Gene was my right arm when it came to the string orchestration. But he couldn't write down the attitude of what I was saying. He could only write down the notes. I had to give the musicians attitude once I got to the studio. And I gave it to all of them: not just guitar, bass, piano and drums. There's violas, cellos, French horns, oboes. What I did was fill in with a feeling. You might move from C to a B-flat chord, but in moving to it there's a little space where I can slip in a beautiful little lick on the harpsichord or piano."

White added five extra guitarists to Page's original orchestra, and Ray Parker coordinated them perfectly. Initially Page thought this crazy and a waste of money, but White told him: "Trust me." Against the sound of the orchestra, the guitarists became lost and Page thought it a waste of time, but eventually he saw that White was right. He gradually came around and said many years later: "Barry was the first to have five guitarists on one song, all playing different parts. The guitarists couldn't hear it. And sometimes I couldn't either.

I'd question it, but suddenly, magically, the parts and counterparts blended to perfection with the harpsichords, French horns, flutes and mandolins. Barry had it all inside his head: licks for tenor solos, accents for horns, complex patterns between drummers and bassists." Ray Parker Jnr said: "Barry put a lot of spirit into his music, and what you hear is very much what he was."

White explained: "Everything I play, write and arrange comes from in my head and my heart. I tell the musicians what to play, but more importantly how to play it. As long as I can communicate with someone who can understand what you mean besides humming it out or playing it out, that will work."

Orchestras are notoriously difficult to put in a studio and produce a good result, as all the different instruments tend to bounce off each other. It needs a bigger area with specially designed acoustics. But Page modified the studio at Whitney so it worked, and he proved to be at his brilliant best with superb arrangements for all the songs. Jack Perry remembers that Page really revved up the orchestra to an absolutely outstanding performance.

But in the end, in spite of all the magic, it was the songs that really mattered and the album's first track was a real surprise – a cover of an old song.

White fulfilled a lifetime's ambition by recording Holland Dozier & Holland's *Standing In The Shadows of Love*. It had originally been a hit for the Four Tops in 1966, but White's version was radically different and unrecognisable from the original, as well as being three times as long. The Four Tops' version was very successful, but Barry White transformed it into an 8-minute anthem of outstanding quality.

It would always be White's all-time favourite of the songs he recorded that had been written by other people. It had deep meaning for him personally, as he described: "The shadow is the supreme place to observe the game of love while being in it. The darkest place to run where there still is just nowhere to go. Why? Because it is the shadow of doubt." Whatever that meant, it resonated for White for the rest of his life. Surprisingly, the original singer, Levi Stubbs, loved White's version of his song. The lead vocalist of the Four Tops took nearly 30 years to tell him, and White was deeply flattered when they evenutally, many years later, appeared on the same stage at a concert in Belgium.

Critics loved it too. Bob Fisher of 'New Musical Express' called it "a slanting rearrangement of the original with a neoclassical introduction resplendent with pizzicato strings," in the process paying a huge compliment to Gene Page's arrangement.

But Fisher wasn't so complimentary about the next track, *Bring Back My Yesterday*, which he called "a plodding, droning, half-spoken, half-intoned ballad". Luckily Fisher was almost alone in his condemnation.

Bring Back My Yesterday had been put together with Bobby Relf at a previous session, and White described both songs on side one as being about the negative side of love for a man: "It really is the negative side of things, with the guy losing out, and the second track deals with a guy living in the past and asking to live yesterday all over again. I particularly like the monologue on this one because it really seems to fit the mood."

Side two opened with a track called *I've Found Someone*, which was really a six-minute musical love letter to his then girlfriend, Glodean James. White said: "It is about a guy who appreciates that what he has – the woman he loves – is not an everyday person and he's really just telling everyone how proud he is of her."

The title track, *I've Got So Much To Give*, was inspired by a movie called 'The Vikings', as Jack Perry recalled: "What people didn't know about Barry was that he was a movie buff. He watched films all the time, and he knew them upside down and inside out." Much later, White said it was one of his favourite songs of all time: "It says everything. It was my favourite song on the album. Anyone could have written this song, and I would have loved it."

Ed Greene, a session drummer, working for White for the first time, said: "It was like this – I've done a lot of sessions, but the feeling of being part of something unique, funky and musically satisfying rarely happens at the same time. It happened when Barry White was in the room." Greene's reaction was typical of how everyone felt about the cut, including the writer himself: "*I've Got So Much To Give* is my personal favourite on the album because it sums me up spiritually, mentally and creatively."

The final track on the album was to prove pivotal. Gene Page literally flipped out and went dancing down the main corridor at Whitney when they had finished recording *I'm Gonna Love You Just a Little Bit More*. Jack Perry recalled the moment nearly 30 years later: "As soon as Barry laid it down,

Gene said to me, 'Let's hear what it sounds like.' I remember immediately the harpsichord came in, Gene ran down the hall yelling, 'Barry White's gonna be a star!' There were no grooves like this one before this groove, and there hasn't really been one like it since."

So much so that White and Perry later recorded a purely instrumental version for their own enjoyment, as Perry revealed: "Even without vocals, without strings, the rhythm is what captivates you. And then you bring in a classical harpsichord and strings. The music is phenomenal, and I don't think anyone has made any music like this since. It's warmth, it's beauty, it's Barry White without anything else. That's the maestro. They are the lines he hummed into a tape, orchestrated, and you heard that. A lot of hip-hop artists took off on this groove."

In fact, the whole team was in rapture over the song, including a young session musician called Nathan East attending his first serious recording: "He would just have a hand-held tape recorder and sing a string part."

White modestly put it down to a grand vision that came together for that one song: "It was a combination of the drum groove, the bass lines, the guitar lines, the horn lines, the string lines, and you put that up with tempos. The tempos were very important: how fast or how slow a song goes." White said about his own song: "I meant what I said about that lady called music. I'm gonna love you a little more than the rest of them."

But it was more than that, and White attempted to describe how he put feeling into his songs, the feeling that made it indisputably the Barry White sound. "It comes from my sensitivity," he explained. "I'm highly sensitive." White always claimed he could look at a man and tell whether he was in love, in the same way that he could tell someone's star sign without being told. As he explained: "I know how a man looks when he's really in love and he's hurt. I know how a woman looks when she's really happy with a man. I can look at it and write about it, exactly what she feels at that moment. It's like an artist seeing a certain setting, and he just paints it. It's a gift."

With only five songs, but 35 minutes of music, White believed that the album was finished, and he put it on a tape for Nunes. It was a genuine masterpiece and Nunes recognised that immediately. But the shortest song was 5½ minutes and the longest eight minutes. It was very different from what anyone in the record business was used to, and Nunes admitted that he thought to himself at the time: "It's not obviously commercial."

But White himself was in no doubt that he had found himself musically, and that the album defined what the Barry White sound was, as he explained: "The Barry White sound is rhythm and melody. I use violins differently – people were used to violins as a swaying, flowing sound, but I used them with rhythm and as a rhythm instrument. That's the Barry White sound."

Next Russ Regan had to hear it.

CHAPTER 25

A Shocking Rejection

Russ Regan says 'no', then 'yes'

1973

Meanwhile, over at 20th Century Records, Russ Regan had been hearing things he didn't like about Barry White's first album. People were whispering in his ear about the length of the songs, especially how White had transformed *Standing In The Shadows Of Love* from a 2½-minute pop tune into an eight-minute ballad. The more Regan heard, the more he worried, especially as almost all of the feedback to him was negative. He became more and more anxious to hear the tape.

It was a very confident Larry Nunes and Barry White who walked into Regan's new office at 20th Century Records in January 1973. They both sat down on his couch and handed him the cassette. His first words were: "Five songs – that's it? That's all we've got? That's never been done before." He walked over, put it in his machine and pressed play.

Gradually the blood drained from their faces as they realised that they were not getting the reaction from Regan they had expected.

Regan grimaced all the way through the 35 minutes of the tape. He read the newspaper and allowed himself to be continually interrupted by phone calls. At the end, he didn't hesitate and told both men that he hated it and could see no potential for "five, long radio-unfriendly songs". He told Larry Nunes he was passing on the opportunity, as the album was "not commercial".

Barry White visibly recoiled in his seat – the two most damning words that a music industry executive could ever utter to an artist were "not commercial". And when the words were spoken, it was generally thought to be all over, especially for a new artist like White. Regan, defending his decision, said: "*Standing In The Shadows Of Love*, I think, went on for 20 minutes or something like that, and that had never been done before."

Larry Nunes was shocked and asked Regan if he could play the tape to Jose Wilson, who was the label's head of promotion for black artists. Regan nodded his head and the two men went downstairs to find Wilson. They went through the same routine. This time Wilson was attentive and said he liked the music but agreed with his boss that it was "not commercial". Nunes had now heard these damning words twice and could scarcely believe it.

The three of them went back upstairs to see Regan, who was pleased that Wilson had confirmed his opinion and was adamant that he would not release the album. To soothe Nunes's feelings, he said that as long as he got his front money back, Nunes and White could pitch the album to other labels.

Barry White was disgusted as they sat in Regan's office and received the final verdict. He turned round to Nunes and said: "Let's go." But Nunes could see that his friend was deeply hurt by the rejection and Regan's apparent 'care not' attitude. In the lobby he sat White down and said: "Don't worry about it. We'll have a deal somewhere else before this day is through." At the time, Nunes was driving a Cadillac Eldorado convertible. He lowered the top in the sunshine, and together they cruised round Hollywood, calling at every record label office they passed.

Suddenly Nunes was enjoying himself – he was in his element, and it reminded him of the time when he had sold records out of the trunk of his car. White remembered Nunes's performance that day: "Larry was fast, he was smart and he was very convincing."

They stopped first at A&M Records. The fact that Larry Nunes was calling in person to pitch an artist made the A&R men pay attention. Chuck Kaye, who had a huge reputation and later became one of the giants of the American music industry, partnered with David Geffen, listened, but he also passed. Then they stopped at Uni Records, where Joe Sutton was now in charge of A&R. But he didn't like it either and asked White when the next Love Unlimited album was coming. The truth was that Kaye and Sutton didn't trust their own ears. The fact that Nunes and White were sitting in front of them meant that they already knew Regan had passed on the album, so they passed too. It was almost contagious.

By now White was losing confidence and wondering whether he could have been this far off. He wasn't really bothered about Russ Regan, as he regarded the man to be a musical philistine, but Chuck Kaye's rejection had hurt and worried him. He said: "I knew a hit record when I heard it and I wondered what was wrong with these guys." The truth was that it was just too different and too new, and both Kaye and Sutton had had the same negative vibes that Regan had and didn't trust their own judgement. Most people needed to hear it a few times to get it, and busy record company execs didn't have time for that.

Larry Nunes had one more label to try: Jack Gold at Columbia. Gold was a close friend who ran Columbia Music's A&R department on the west coast. Nunes said ominously: "If he doesn't like it, then we'll have to rethink everything."

They needn't have worried. As Barry White put it: "Jack flipped out." Gold worked for the legendary Clive Davis, who ran the Columbia label from New York, and he declared: "Clive has got to hear this." Gold dialled Davis's office and said down the phone: "Octavia, can you put me through? It's urgent." Octavia Bennett knew that her boss was on the phone but sensed the urgency in Gold's voice. She wrote "Jack on two – urgent" on a notepad and went in. Davis quickly ended his call and pressed the flashing line two. As soon as he picked up, Gold pressed the play button and Davis heard *Standing In The Shadows Of Love* playing through the handset. He pressed hands-free as he read though a memo and listened to the instrumental introduction. Straightaway he liked the music and found himself tapping his fingers on the top of his desk. He put the memo to one side to fully focus on what he was hearing as the artist built up the instrumental tempo for nearly three minutes until he heard the voices of the backing singers, then Barry White. After five minutes Davis shouted down the phone: "I want that artist!" not having a clue who Barry White was. He added: "I'll be out to the coast on Sunday to sign him."

And that was that.

White and Nunes looked at each other and smiled. Clive Davis was the biggest honcho in the whole of the music industry. If Davis was on your side, no one else really mattered. On the drive home, White thought to himself: "After a crazy see-saw and wild and wonderful day that had seen me flirt with hitting bottom, I had landed on my feet back on top of the world."

White and Nunes had no idea how lucky they had been. Clive Davis had a strict routine for listening to new music, which stacked up higher in his office every day. Before each tape was put in front of him, it was screened several times by his executives so as not to waste his time. Davis said: "There simply weren't enough hours in the day for me to listen to everything."

But Barry White had circumvented the process and landing the approval of Davis was a real coup.

Clive Davis was an oddity for a top music executive. Trained as a lawyer, he had somehow made the move over to A&R and combined both talents. He had a reputation for having, as one producer described it 'an impeccable ear'. One of his favourite sayings was, "Consumers buy records because they like them" and it was a mantra he felt he needed to keep repeating, mostly to his own A&R staff. He told them: "Your judgements are born of the excitement and enthusiasm of good music and they must by necessity be cold and calculating."

Davis had run Columbia since 1967 and had dragged the label kicking and screaming into the rock and pop era. He had discovered Janis Joplin, had star acts such as Simon & Garfunkel and Bob Dylan on his label, and his influence and support had seen 'Rolling Stone' magazine through its launch to overcome its subsequent financial difficulties. In just five short years it was said that he had taken Columbia Music's annual operating revenue from $5 million to $50 million.

Davis was true to his word and flew from New York to Los Angeles on Saturday. Whether it was a regular scheduled visit or a special trip just to sign Barry White, no one knew, but it was on the basis of a few minutes of music he had heard on the telephone.

When Davis arrived he went straight to his regular bungalow at the Beverly Hills Hotel and went to bed. On Sunday he met with Jack Gold to listen to the whole tape and discuss their offer to White. Davis not only liked the songs, but also really liked the music and the arrangements, which were entirely to his taste. He could 'feel' the potential audience for Barry White's sound.

Davis admitted that he did not have any idea where his own talent for finding new stars came from. He couldn't read music and neither did he understand musical structure. He thought his skill came from having a 'sense' about music. As he described it: "I tend to get into melodies instantly. This is something you feel. Something happens in your chemistry, your blood, when you hear a record: a tingling sense of electricity, a sense that an audience will grab a song and take off with it." This is what Davis had felt immediately upon hearing *Standing In The Shadows Of Love* over the telephone – something that Russ Regan could never feel.

The following day, White and Nunes met with Davis in his bungalow, with Jack Gold hovering in the corner. Nunes was unusually nervous, even though he had met Davis a few times in the past at conferences and they had got on well. Nunes knew that Davis, in the wrong mood, could be very dismissive. He had a grand and almost aristocratic style; as one top music producer put it: "If Clive's in the room, it's Clive's room."

But they needn't have worried. Davis greeted them warmly, keen to renew his relationship with Larry Nunes. After greeting him he weighed up Barry White and immediately liked what he saw. He waved them to a couple of comfortable sofas. As usual, Davis had the air-conditioning turned up to full chill and the two men shivered together. Davis questioned White carefully about the album and his vision of himself as an artist in the future. Normally, Davis wouldn't sign new artists without seeing them perform live at least twice. But this was for a one-album deal and he already had the material in front of him on tape. It was unusual for him to be presented with a finished album ready for pressing.

Davis was very impressed with what he heard and White's vision of where he was going and how he saw himself as an artist. Equally, White was impressed with Davis's grasp of the detail of the music business and particularly the intelligent comments about the tape he had listened to. As Davis recalled: "I always tried to give a tape my fullest attention – whether I liked it or not." In this instance, he "really liked it". "There was no need to hide my emotions if I liked what I heard."

After half an hour Davis called the meeting to a halt and said that a contract would be waiting for them to sign by Wednesday evening. As White and Nunes left the hotel they were surprised by the number of music industry people they recognised hanging round outside waiting to see Davis. "This is one important dude," thought White.

By the middle of the following week they had fleshed out a deal and Davis agreed to pay White a $75,000 advance against royalties. That was an astounding sum for a new album from a first-time artist. The album had cost $30,000 to record, so he and Nunes were already in profit from the get-go, even after giving Regan his money back.

Strangely, in the middle of the week, Nunes took calls from both Chuck Kaye at A&M and Joe Sutton at Uni, asking if the deal was still available. He told them both, "no".

They duly signed the deal with Columbia on Friday afternoon, and Davis handed White a cheque for $75,000, which he said he could cash on Monday morning.

That Saturday night the two men threw a party at Nunes's house to celebrate. During the weekend word about the deal that White had signed with Columbia filtered out around Hollywood, and it seemed inevitable that it would soon reach the ears of Russ Regan.

It did, but in the most unlikely way. Regan was hosting a party at his house to celebrate the recent success of the De Franco family pop group. Elton John also attended the event. Elton was one of Regan's top artists, and he had shepherded his career in North America.

Out of the blue, Barry White's name came up in conversation. Elton knew about White, and the new album was mentioned. Elton asked Regan if he had a copy and Regan replied that he had a cassette somewhere. Elton asked if he could listen to it and Regan agreed but warned Elton that it wasn't very good, was "radio unfriendly" and again uttered the most damning words of all – "not commercial".

Elton John just nodded, put on some headphones and sat down in a corner to listen. After half an hour he put the headphones down and asked Regan if he could take the cassette home. Regan agreed, but Elton's request set off alarm bells in his head. He thought that if Elton wanted to take the cassette home, he must have liked it. And that thought frightened him.

Even at this early stage in his career, Elton John had a reputation for knowing what he was about. Unusually for an artist, he was an avid reader of the music industry trade magazines and newsletters. He obtained copies of most music in his genre before or on its release and listened to hundreds of hours of contemporary music from other artists every week. And if he was 'curious' about another artist, he analysed everything about their music that made them a success. And Elton John was clearly curious about Barry White.

For Russ Regan, it was time for some serious soul-searching. He knew he did not have the 'ears' he was reputed to have in the music business and that he relied heavily on other people's opinions. In his heart of hearts, when he was being totally honest with himself, looking in the mirror with the bullshit of the music business stripped away, he knew that a lot of his success had been down to dumb luck. He knew his real talent had been down to asking someone for something when no one else had thought to or wouldn't dare. But what he lacked in musical taste he more than made up for in chutzpah.

Suddenly, Regan realised he had made a big mistake and that, having financed White's album, he would have egg on his face if it was a hit for another label. Later, someone else at the party told him that Clive Davis had bought it and that he had flown specially from New York to LA to close the deal.

Then it was certain. If Clive Davis liked the album it must be good, and Regan must be wrong. He knew he had to strike back fast to have a chance of holding on to Barry White.

In such a situation he was at his best and, as soon as the last of his guests had departed, he swung into action.

At 5.40am, as early as he dared, he picked up the phone and dialled Larry Nunes's home phone number. Nunes had his bedroom window open, as did White in the guest house. White was awoken by the sound of the ringing telephone. No one likes to hear the phone ringing at that time of the morning, and White's first thought was that one of his children must have had an accident and it was Mary calling to tell him the worst. It was the type of phone call he feared and had often thought about receiving ever since his first child had been born.

A sleepy and hung-over Nunes picked up the phone and also expected to hear some bad news, so was surprised to hear Russ Regan on the other end of the line.

Regan bellowed down the phone and asked him why he was selling "his album" to Clive Davis. Nunes told Regan that he had passed on the album and released his option. He told him he would be receiving a cashier's cheque on Monday morning for $30,000, a full refund of the advance. Regan replied that he had done no such thing, and just because he didn't like it didn't mean that he didn't want to release it. He reminded Nunes that White had signed a binding option with him. Nunes told him it was too late and that White had signed a contract with Columbia and had received an advance. Regan asked him if he had cashed the cheque and Nunes replied "No", to which Regan said, "Well it's still mine then."

After a few minutes of argument, Nunes told Regan that he had better speak to White himself, who was in his guest house. He put Regan on hold and buzzed the guest house telephone. When White answered, Nunes simply said, "It's for you," and replaced the receiver.

White was deeply relieved when he realised it was Russ Regan on the phone. His immediate thought was that he wanted his $30,000 back and was ringing about that. But he wasn't ready for what he heard next. Regan said: "Well, I told Larry and I'm telling you – I'm keeping the album for 20th."

White was stunned and speechless. He needed time to think, so he told Regan to hang on while he went to the bathroom. Thinking he might be dreaming, White filled the sink with cold water and splashed his face to wake himself up. He stared at himself in the mirror and thought in disbelief: "He wants to keep the album he doesn't really hear and doesn't really want."

When White realised he wasn't dreaming, he went back to the phone and said: "What are you talking about, Russ? We just made a deal with Clive Davis."

Regan replied: "Well, that's too bad because I'm keeping the album."

White told him: "Russ, you said you didn't like the album."

Regan replied, matter of factly: "Don't matter. I'm keeping it."

White, now angry, said: "Fine. You tell Clive he can't have it."

Regan replied: "I will" and put down the receiver.

A few minutes later Regan was trying to wake up Clive Davis at the Beverly Hills Hotel, but the receptionist wouldn't put him through to Davis's bungalow. When he finally did get through, Davis told him he had a signed a contract and had paid the $75,000. "But," said Regan, "they haven't cashed it."

Davis wondered what on earth difference that made, but he could see that Regan was not in the mood to listen to reason and put the phone down with Regan's words ringing in his ears: "I'll see you in court."

When the dust settled, both Davis and Nunes realised that it would go to court, but that they would probably win. But that would take two years and, in the meantime, the album would languish on the shelf. Davis was very friendly towards talent – it had been the hallmark of his career and he didn't want to treat Barry White any differently. In any case, he realised he was taking a big gamble on a new artist, so he reluctantly released the album back to White and Nunes, who equally reluctantly handed back the $75,000.

It was major blow to both men. It was a dream deal they had signed with Columbia, and they realised that getting into bed with Clive Davis was preferable to a deal with Russ Regan, whose dark side they had seen close up. But Nunes said to White that there was very little they could do: "It is what it is. This is the music business for you." Subsequently the threat of legal action was quietly dropped and it was 20th that released the album.

White decided to call the album *I've Got So Much To Give*, after track number four, and it was released on 27th March 1973. This time, there were no doubts about the quality of any of the tracks. The album went to No 16 on the LP chart and No 1 on the soul chart, but it was the release of two singles that set the world alight. *I'm Going To Love You Just a Little More Baby*, as predicted, was a huge hit. It went to No 3 in the Billboard singles chart and No 1 in the R&B chart. It was the fastest-selling single in the history of 20th Century Records. The title track, *I've Got So Much to Give*, went to No 32.

White recalled: "The album sales were phenomenal and, literally overnight, I had become the label's biggest-selling artist. For the first time I realised the true power of my voice."

White was also suddenly relaxed about singing himself: "I really lived for Love Unlimited but I was happy now that I had made the album. You see, for me, personally, it was my creation and I was proud of it. They were my inner spiritual feelings and once I got a grip on my talents and understood what I was doing, I never doubted myself."

It was suddenly a marvellous time to be Barry White. As Smokey Robinson recalled at the time: "Barry grooved into being the kind of artist he was. At first, he saw himself as a producer but after he saw the response he got from people around the world, I think he grew to like it."

But not all the critics were as optimistic, as White recalled: "People wrote that I was going to have one album and no more. He ain't as bad as Isaac

Hayes, they said."

The critics argued that White's musical style would not endure and one said that it was "overly repetitive" and lacked the "social consciousness that fuelled the work of other similar singers". 'Blues & Soul' magazine's reviewer wrote: "Vocally he won't be rivalling Mario Lanza but he has a certain depth to his voice that wins you over, a warmth that makes his lyrics so convincing."

'Blues & Soul' magazine's reviewers were embarrassed for evermore and the critics were mostly wrong. Nancy Wilson, one of the biggest female singing stars of the time and a multi-Grammy winner, told it how it was: "I will always remember hearing for the first time that unforgettable melodious voice."

Barry White suddenly shot to international stardom and became an immediate sensation around the world, quickly becoming Russ Regan's biggest-selling artist.

Jose Wilson took the album around to radio stations and was very surprised at the reaction to what he believed to be "not commercial" and "radio unfriendly". When he reported back to a cynical Russ Regan, he told him firmly: "You don't know what you have here. There's something about Barry White's voice. Every woman who hears this album falls in love with it and with him."

A SHOCKING REJECTION

CHAPTER 26

Under the Influence

The second Love Unlimited album

1973

B arry White now had a problem. He was with one record company and Love Unlimited was with another. He was also having to deal with a new boss at Uni Records, a man called Mike Maitland, whom he did not particularly like. Uni Records was also in the process of a corporate upheaval. It was being absorbed into MCA Records, which owned it, and was changing out of all recognition. It was certainly not the same label to which he had originally signed Love Unlimited.

Mike Maitland had taken over from Russ Regan, who had moved to 20th Century. At their first meeting Maitland greeted Barry White's arrival in his office with a yawn. That yawn spawned instant dislike and it appeared that the feeling was mutual. White thought Maitland a "dour man with little imagination" so what followed should have been no surprise.

When White told Maitland the news that he had a new album ready for Love Unlimited to record, he got an even bigger yawn. Maitland proceeded to tell White that he hadn't liked the first album and thought the group had got lucky with the single. He believed the girls were a one-hit wonder and he wasn't exactly keen to pay for another album. He clearly wanted out of his contract with Love Unlimited, although he couldn't quite come straight out and say it. White remembered: "Uni was in chaos after Russ's departure and Maitland and I didn't hit it off very well." That was an understatement. But the girls were a hot act and on top of the world and White knew that the material he had written for the second album was much better than the first.

White left Maitland's office shaking his head and amazed at the latter's lack of enthusiasm. Nonchalance very quickly turned to annoyance and annoyance to anger.

That evening White got madder and madder with what he had witnessed, and he had difficulty getting to sleep. By the following morning he was seething, especially when he received a phone call from Maitland while he was having his breakfast at the Franklin Arms Hotel.

When White picked up the phone in the hotel's reception, without any greeting or preamble Maitland told him that Uni's promotional budget for the second album was nil.

White was aghast but not surprised: "It is the oldest and saddest story in the music business – once they have hit artists they move them down the food chain to make way for the next big thing and let the established talent sell on the memory of their previous hits for as long as they can before they fade."

But it wasn't even just that. It was effectively the group's marching orders, although White didn't realise it at the time. He was so wound up that when he put the phone down he resolved to go and have it out with Maitland in person: "I wasn't about to have any of it. I'd put too much time, blood, sweat and tears into my career and Love Unlimited to let some record executive arbitrarily dictate our future."

Straight away he called a cab and headed off to Uni's offices. He brushed past the downstairs receptionist and stormed into Maitland's office, catching him completely by surprise. White demanded that Maitland release the girls from their contract.

But he had to take a step back and catch his breath when Maitland merely looked up from his desk and whispered, "Yes, OK. Fine with me. I don't want the group anyway. I'll give you their immediate release."

With that Maitland passed over a piece of paper with his lawyer's name and phone number and told White to get on with it. He immediately phoned the lawyer and told him to expect a call. While that was going on, White grabbed the other phone on Maitland's desk and dialled Russ Regan. As soon as Regan picked up his direct line, White said: "Russ, Love Unlimited is yours if you want them."

Regan replied: "You can get me Love Unlimited?"

White responded: "I sure can, and I've already got their next album recorded and ready for release – it's called *Under The Influence Of Love*."

Regan spluttered: "Well I want it, I want it."

Then, without really thinking what he was saying, White delivered the punchline: "It's going to cost you $90,000."

Regan shot back: "You have a deal."

For once Barry White was lost for words, whispered back "Deal," and put the phone down.

While this was going on Maitland had finished the call with his lawyer and looked quizzically at White. White deadpanned it. If Maitland had known that Russ Regan had offered $90,000 just like that he might have changed his mind and demanded the album back.

There was one problem, however. White had told Regan a little white lie. There was no album "already recorded". But White had written and rehearsed all the songs and it would take just a few weeks' work in the studio to finish it off.

As soon as he put the phone down Russ Regan got the contracts drawn up and they were ready for signing within 24 hours. Regan still had before him the spectre of Clive Davis and was frightened White would take Love Unlimited to Columbia. But he needn't have worried too much as Davis was about to be fired from his job as president of Columbia in the most dramatic fashion and for the moment would cease to be a thorn in Regan's side.

The following day, White and Larry Nunes, together with Linda, Dede and Glodean, got in a car and went to 20th's offices to sign the contract. White was waiting for any last-minute snags to emerge or for Regan to change his mind. But he didn't, and as soon as the ink on the signatures was dry, Regan handed him a cheque for the full $90,000 they had agreed. White and Nunes looked at each other in sheer disbelief. After all the struggles of the past they found it hard to believe it could be so easy.

Luckily Regan expressed no desire to hear the demo tape or know anything else about the album. He just seemed desperate not to mess things up, as White confirmed: "Russ never even heard the album when he made the deal, that's how much he wanted it."

Gradually White started to realise the extent of his own new 'star power': "It was a whole new ballgame and one in which I was calling all the shots." He loved his new power, but was careful not to abuse it and kept pinching himself just to make sure it was all real. He knew that, with a few wrong moves, it could all be over tomorrow.

This time the studio recordings were a breeze. The whole team knew exactly what to do and Barry White, with his confidence in himself sky high, became the real maestro he was always capable of being. He found the writing came a whole lot easier after the success of his own album, and the songs he wrote were infinitely better than those on Love Unlimited's first album.

White finally remembered the three songs he had written at Mustang Bronco for Felice Taylor, which had been hits in the UK but had done nothing in America. He immediately seized on two of them, *It May Be Winter Outside* and *Under The Influence Of Love*, for the new album and found that they fitted Love Unlimited's sound perfectly. He wondered why he had not included them on the first album, but concluded that it was better late than never.

The album opened with *Love's Theme*, a four-minute instrumental that was another song written eight years before at Mustang Bronco, followed by *Under the Influence of Love*. Then came *Lovin' You, That's All I'm After,* then *Oh Love (Well We Finally Made It)*. This was the song that he had written in 1966, and that Earl Nelson had recorded with female session singer Tracey Andrews under the pseudonym Smoke. White and Nelson had released it privately under the Mo Soul banner and it had gone nowhere, but now the four songs made for a stunning side one.

The two opening tracks of side two were pleasant but undistinguished, albeit still better than anything on the first album. They were *Say It Again* and *Someone Really Cares For You*. The seventh track was the song that made the album, *It May Be Winter Outside*. And lastly came *Yes, We Finally Made It*.

All the eight songs and 33 minutes of music were written by Barry White, with a bit of help from Paul Politi. Gene Page turned in some fabulous arrangements and it was all finished in a week, well under budget.

When it was complete Barry White took the tape to play it to Russ Regan in his office. But when they sat down Regan covered his ears with is hands and said he was not interested in hearing it. He said he could no longer trust his own 'ears', and that was the reason for his reticence.

White had decided to call the album *Under The Influence Of Love*, which he said caught the Barry White mood precisely. Barrymania was happening all over the English-speaking world, and anything connected to him was selling. The new album immediately raced to No 1 in the Canadian album charts and No 3 in the US. It became an underground sensation in gay and black bars and dance clubs.

The reviews were all four stars and upwards. One reviewer, who had called Love Unlimited's first album "disappointing", raved about the second, saying that this time "it succeeded, with room to spare". *Love's Theme* was called "a stupendous mood-setter" by another reviewer. The somewhat flowery review read: "Love Unlimited served up a nonstop diet of heart-felt, if not always heart-stopping, music. A sweetly tempting by-product of its era, Love Unlimited's variations on his trademark waka-waka guitar and lush strings are never less than fascinating, however, and the poignancy of the nostalgia train continues to churn."

According to the reviewers, the standout tracks were *Love's Theme, Under The Influence Of Love, Oh Love (Well We Finally Made It)* and *Yes, We Finally Made It.* Each of them was deemed of superior quality to the very best on Love Unlimited's first album.

When John Abbey of 'Blues & Soul' magazine suggested that White's current music was vastly improved from the album he had produced for Felice Taylor eight years before, White agreed: "Yes, it really is, isn't it? But my whole thinking has changed since those days."

The performance of the three girls had also got better, to the obvious satisfaction of their mentor, who said: "The girls do a super job on the songs and they're my pride and joy."

Despite all the hype, the performance of the three singles chosen to be released from the album was disappointing. They were *It May Be Winter Outside, Oh Love (Well We Finally Made It)* and *Under The Influence Of Love.* The first went to No 83 on the Billboard charts and *Under The Influence Of Love* to No 76. The second bombed out. However, the album sales more than made up for it, doing very well all over the world. It had hit a chord.

The disco scene was taking off across America and Love Unlimited's music was a staple of that changing trend. One reviewer, John Clemente, said enthusiastically: "Love Unlimited's music roused lovers from their seats to end a night of revelry with a slow grind to a sweet love song."

Eventually *Love's Theme* became a phenomenon in itself and straddled two albums, released as a single in late 1973 and spending a week at No 1 on the Billboard 100. The success of this third album really changed things for Barry

White. He was no longer a 'fluke' but a fully-fledged and recognised star.

With three successful albums under his belt, Barry White and the three girls found themselves needing representation, and Russ Regan was able to recommend a pair of excellent managers called Sid Garris and George Greiff, who took over the running of all their business affairs and their burgeoning bank accounts.

1973 had ended extremely well, but 1974 was poised to blow that all out of the water. Barry White was on a very hot streak indeed.

CHAPTER 27

Stone Gon'

Second solo album

October 1973

If Russ Regan thought *I've Got So Much To Give* was non-commercial and un-releasable, then Barry White's second solo album, *Stone Gon'*, consisting of five tracks totalling 35 minutes of music, must have been his worst nightmare. But by now he was past caring. Regan had given up trying to predict what White's next move would be and had decided that it was best to just let him get on with it. So Regan's sole contribution to the second album was to ask him what it would be called as they passed each other in a corridor at 20th's offices. White stopped, thought about it for a moment and just said the words, "*Stone Gon'*." Later he revealed that they just came out of his mouth randomly as he stopped to talk to Russ Regan. But he decided they sounded good and told a bemused Regan: "Just wait until you hear it."

Not everybody at 20th Century Records was a sanguine as the boss. No one at the label could quite believe Barry White's success. 20th's executives believed that he was riding the most incredible wave of luck and that the luck was about to run out.

Barry White quickly picked up the vibes: "Even as I was enjoying my ride atop the charts, I could hear the whispers in the hallways of 20th Century Records about how I was one lucky fellow. They kept wondering with scepticism in their voices what I was going to come up with next."

Although he never showed it publicly, privately it annoyed him that no one had any confidence in his ability to sustain the success. He resented the fact that he was almost treated with contempt by the people in his own record company. So when they asked him what he was coming up with next, as they did continually, his answer came back: "I'm coming up with Barry White."

Many of the executives at 20th believed his early success had gone to his head and that he had become a braggart – but White responded to friends: "I'm really a modest man. I'm not bragging. Barry White doesn't brag."

With all that going on in the background, White wasn't taking any chances with his second solo album. He brought in his now established backroom team of Gene Page and Frank Kejmar to arrange and engineer it, together with Jack Perry playing keyboards. They also had the services of the incredibly talented 19-year-old Ray Parker Jnr on guitar. It was a crack team and as good any working in Hollywood at the time.

They all assembled at Glendale Studios full of confidence. Thirty years later, Jack Perry claimed that Barry White came into the studio to record the album with no preparation at all. But it didn't matter as he and Gene Page just stood there while Barry White played the piano and the melodies and the lyrics flowed out. Perry recalled: "Barry knew exactly what he wanted but he never wrote anything down. He would come to the studio, sit at the piano, fiddle out the chord changes and melodies, then tell the band what to play."

Stone Gon' was certainly simple enough with only five songs. The album opened with the 8½- minute *Girl It's True, Yes I'll Always Love You*. It was a deeply romantic song, going at its own pace, with White asking the question: "There's that look again. You know what I'm talking about. It's in your eyes. The look that says does he really love me and need me as much as he says he does?" Reviewer Stephen McMillian later called it "the perfect wedding song".

The second track, *Honey Please, Can't Ya See*, was a modest five minutes and destined for a single release. In it White sings of his "undying love and affection for his woman". It quickly became a disco favourite and was incredibly pleasant to dance to.

The last track on side one was the classic nine minutes of smooth music entitled *You're My Baby*, considered by many fans to be one of White's finest, although unremarked upon by reviewers at the time.

Side two contained only two songs, *Hard to Believe That I Found You* and *Never, Never Gonna Give Ya Up*, the latter also destined to be released as a single. All the reviewers loved this track, which was edited down for its single release. It began with a long instrumental and some heavy breathing, then burst out of itself.

White was genuinely stunned by his own work on *Never, Never Gonna Give Ya Up* and explained how it actually happened and how the words were written – certainly it was not conventional songwriting. He claimed that he just stood in front of the microphone in the studio, with no prior preparation and the melody playing, and that the words just poured out of him. He explained: "There's no way in hell you can write those kinds of lyrics. You have to turn down the lights and close your eyes and put a woman right there, in front of your eyes, that you feel is the perfect woman and you just start rapping. You're in front of the microphone and you know you have to say something. It's got to make sense; it's got to be sincere. You open your mouth and somebody, somewhere speaks for you."

Jack Perry remembered the process as being "truly magical". He added: "His songs were all in his head and some would come to him in a dream."

Whatever it was, it worked and that song was one of the surprise single successes of the year. The reviewer for 'Allmusic' summed it up perfectly: "His patented mix of love monologues and rich vocal dynamics would come to mark the best songs of the period. White's inventive arrangements of mesmerising backdrops and vocal seduction display unerring sensitivity."

Another critic called White's arrangements "other worldly" and wrote that his "grooves were the soul seduction of high-heeled boys and sequined girls" that would soon "take over discotheques", and so it proved. Another said that his "voice washed onto the shores of romantic pop like hot bubbly bathwater." They called his music "sweaty sexy anthems full of strings that seemed to arrive via moonbeams." The plaudits were endless.

White put a lot of his songwriting success down to his background in gospel music, when he directed the church choir for eight years: "Gospel music is a great music when you get to know how to use it. It shows you how to take a melody, any melody, and do it any kind of way you want to do it. It puts you in command of the song."

He was also, by then, confident that he knew what women wanted and how to translate that into music, as he explained: "My music deals with the relationship between two people and I've always written music that people can play during romantic moments. One thing I do is speak sensitively to women. Most men don't do that. They don't think it's manly to express themselves in a tender manner to women."

Once the music was finished White turned his attention to the album cover.

This one is now considered a classic design, featuring a single photograph of White at his piano with Glodean leaning on it, portrayed out of shot as the hand of a woman with long manicured nails and a half-full glass of wine. Barry and Glodean were photographed in the studio by 34-year-old South African Norman Seeff, who was the go-to photographer for album covers at the time and famous for his work with the Rolling Stones.

The concept for the album cover was down to Craig Braun and Bob Maile, who had also worked on *Sticky Fingers* for the Rolling Stones two years before, albeit with help from Andy Warhol. They came up with a background setting that was effectively a white glacier, supposedly giving the effect that the album contained, as White put it, "music that keeps you warm". Inside the cover included a handwritten card in the shape of a poem, which read: "Nothing can ever change my dear, the way I feel about you because if I didn't have you here, I'd be lost without you and so I take time and place to give this card to you and pray that we will always be together, strong and true." It wasn't the greatest ever composition of words but it summed up the mood of the album.

The release of *Stone Gon'* on 2nd October 1973 came only 10 months after White had leapt to stardom with Love Unlimited. One reviewer called the new album "sensually charged", and it was certainly that.

Any fears that the album would not be a success soon disappeared when it quickly reached No 20 in the Billboard album chart and stayed there for a long time. It was No 1 on the soul album chart, while in Britain, which was quickly proving to be White's best overseas market, it quickly reached No 18.

Never, Never Gonna Give Ya Up was edited right down, released as a single and went to No 6 in the Billboard singles chart. The second single was *Honey Please, Can't Ya See*, on which great hopes were pinned, but which only went to No 44 in the singles chart.

By now even 'Rolling Stone' magazine had started taking notice of Barry White's music, but it was hard to tell whether its review of *Stone Gon'* was praise or not. The magazine called White an "imitation Isaac Hayes", the strong inference being that Hayes was the real thing and White inferior. It stated: "Even if Barry White is imitation Isaac Hayes, who would have thought anyone could match Hayes' pretension for pretension?" To 'Rolling

Stone', Isaac Hayes was a god and White was the imposter.

Soon White was getting tired of the unfavourable comparisons with Hayes and retorted: "He's into his own thing and I'm in mine. I just feel I'm better in mine than he is in his." In hindsight, 'Rolling Stone' got it wrong, as it often did, and Isaac Hayes gradually faded away as Barry White rose to superstardom.

Aside from the comparison with Hayes, 'Rolling Stone' had very little good to say about the album: "White's productions are too excessive to be called 'songs'. They are dreamy, shimmering symphonies whipped up to a light chop for the dance crowd. Perhaps because the five cuts (the shortest, 5:05) always seem on the verge of choking on their violin tracks or being talked to death and their ultimate survival is unexpectedly exhilarating. *Never, Never Gonna Give Ya Up* and *Honey Please, Can't Ya See* work best, but White keeps things well controlled throughout – musically, at least. Now if he'd only stop talking."

But 'Rolling Stone' was soon proved dead wrong. Barry White was singing the type of songs that women wanted to hear – romance and seduction, not lust and rampage. It was also getting noticed that White was writing, producing and performing all of his songs at a time when it was unknown for artists to have that much control over their output. White attempted to explain away his success as he said: "I always dealt with simplicity. Make it so simple that even a fool could understand it with no problem. Everybody can understand simplicity."

But Barry White's music was far from simple and his growing success could no longer be ignored when he won what was arguably the most important recognition in the music industry, being named at the end of the year as Billboard's top new male vocalist for 1973.

CHAPTER 28

A Rhapsody In Genius

Rhapsody in White - sheer orchestral brilliance

January 1974

A s he turned 30 years of age, suddenly creativity burst out of the skin of Barry White. In the three years from 1972 to 1974, he was to write the music and lyrics for no fewer than nine full-length albums. He also produced them and to varying degrees performed on them. It was an unprecedented amount of activity for a pop musician, especially one relatively new to the scene.

To the world at large it appeared that Barry White had come from nowhere and become an overnight star. But only White himself knew that his 'overnight success' had come suddenly after 15 years of sheer frustration, struggle and poverty when the outlook had seemed to be permanently bleak. And he quickly realised that his natural creativity had been strangled by a lack of confidence that had prevented him from doing his best work.

After 15 years he found that he had so much music in his head for both female and male artists. That sudden feeling of confidence in himself unlocked it all. Without that initial success, which had come from the three girls in Love Unlimited and his own first album, it is unlikely that it would ever have emerged at all.

Having achieved initial success with both the male and female version of himself, he believed that there was also a third category in which he could succeed. He wanted to form an orchestra to perform his music without lyrics, which everyone in the music business called instrumentals.

The idea came to him after the growing success of the instrumental *Love's Theme* on the second Love Unlimited album, which had created a minor sensation in discotheques. It suddenly dawned on him that he had a lot more of this type of music in his head: "I recorded Love Unlimited's second album called *Under The Influence Of Love* and I wrote a theme for them called *Love's Theme*. Suddenly deejays from all over the world were calling us about this instrumental. I've always loved symphonies and I've always loved pure music with no singer."

Obviously most instrumentals were deemed "not commercial" by record label executives and there was little enthusiasm for his latest idea at 20th Century Records but, as he said: "I was very successful and I'd got a little clout at the record company."

So he persisted and that persistence was eventually to lead to an album called *Rhapsody in White*, arguably the best pop instrumental album of all time. White described the process as taking a traditional orchestra and making it "funky".

And when he really started thinking about it he found he literally had hundreds of tunes stored in his head, some of which he knew were very good. To enable that music to be unleashed and come out he decided to create a permanent classical orchestra rather than just hire in session musicians. In his own mind there was a bit of him that thought pop, rock 'n' roll and soul music was all a bit down-market, and the mark of true greatness was to be a classical composer. He had a secret longing to be a Beethoven, a Mozart or even a Leonard Bernstein, as he readily admitted to Marc Eliot in his 1999 memoirs: "I've always had a great love for instrumentals, which comes from my mother, who used to play Bach, Beethoven, Brahms and all of the masters for me on her piano. It instilled in me a love of the sound of purely instrumental music."

White realised that it was an expensive flight of fancy to create a new orchestra to record his own compositions, but he used his newfound fame and earning power to somehow get it done and get 20th to pay for it. He also knew it would have to be successful.

All this led eventually to the formation in late 1973 of a new orchestra that he called the 'Love Unlimited Orchestra'.

White remembered: "I knew I still wasn't running at top speed and I wanted to go at top speed so I decided to push my luck and call Russ Regan to tell him about my new plan." With three hit albums under his belt, he thought he was in a good position to try it on with Regan.

Despite that outward confidence, it took three whole days for Barry White to pluck up the courage to make the phone call. After all, he was asking a top music executive to fund a new era of classical music, composed by him, and also to create a new orchestra from scratch (and pay for it as well).

By the end of the third day of failing to pick up the phone, White realised his request was ridiculous, but decided he had to go for it anyway. After all, what was he to do with all this good music he knew was waiting to come out of his head to be recorded?

He finally plucked up the courage on the morning of the fourth day.

When Regan answered, White casually said: "Russ, I've got an idea." Initially Regan sounded positive, thinking that a new album might be ready. White continued: "Hey man, I have this idea to cut an orchestra album."

Any enthusiasm Regan was displaying turned to silence at the other end of the line, and White imagined what Regan must be thinking: "Aw now, come on Barry, you're just taking advantage." But Regan actually said: "An orchestra? We can't sell no orchestra." White chimed back: "You're gonna sell this one and that's what I want, Russ."

Then Regan said it right on cue, just as White had imagined he would: "Barry, you are the hottest producer in the world and you are taking advantage of your record company." There followed a silence, then Regan shouted down the line: "You're crazy! It'll never sell. Nobody wants an instrumental."

Although he was shaking like a leaf at the other end of the phone, White shot back, sounding as confident as he could: "With the album that I'm envisioning I think we can create a whole new market."

After a few more silent seconds he added: "I'm gonna cut an album with a full orchestra and that's the way it's going to be." He thought about adding "so there" at the end, but wisely didn't. But Regan was still having none of it: "You're just taking advantage because you have got some clout now."

But as he was saying the words, Regan realised that it was quite likely that he was wrong and White was right. As White told him: "Russ, you're not going to know what I'm talking about until you hear it on record – and then you might not even get it." And he added the stinger: "It seems to me we've been down this path before – haven't we, Russ?" White was referring to that fateful day in January 1973 when Regan had turned down his first album.

Regan didn't need any reminding of that and just sighed down the telephone, realising that he had been beaten: "OK, I'm not going to say 'no' but just tell me one thing. What do you plan on calling this group?" White laughed to himself when Regan described his 40-piece orchestra as a 'group' and replied, "The Love Unlimited Orchestra," a name that he later said just popped into his head at that very moment.

Regan thought for a second and decided he didn't like it: "The girls already have that name. If anything you should call it the Barry White Orchestra. You see, that's what I mean."

For once Regan was right and White had made a mistake, but the latter explained his thinking, which was hardly rational: "I know, but the three ladies of Love Unlimited are so dear to me that I want to name my orchestra after them."

An exasperated Regan asked: "What's your first single going to be?" White told him it would be *Love's Theme*. Regan thought that White had really gone nuts and whispered down the phone, "Oh my God."

Regan was right and White was wrong. Calling it the Love Unlimited Orchestra was a colossal mistake because it never formed its own identity as a separate act. It also confused the original Love Unlimited girl band in the public's mind. People could just not make the distinction and in the end it lessened both acts and took away much of their potential. The Love Unlimited Orchestra in particular never really got off the ground commercially as it should have done with the incredible music that White composed and the orchestra played. If he had taken Regan's advice and called it the Barry White Orchestra, who knows what might have happened.

But Regan was to be very wrong about the potential for *Love's Theme* as a single, as would be proved a few months later.

So, with Regan's approval, White put together the Love Unlimited Orchestra as a 40-piece string-laden orchestra that would also serve as the regular backing band for himself and Love Unlimited. The cream of Los Angeles's young musicians were recruited, including Ray Parker Jnr, still only 19, and the equally talented 18-year-old Kenny Gorelick on saxophone.

And so began the creation of *Rhapsody in White*, as White and Gene Page got busy in the studio, spending considerable sums of Russ Regan's money. It proved to be a brilliant name for a brilliant album and the debut album of the Love Unlimited Orchestra.

Rhapsody in White featured seven brilliant tracks from its eight compositions.

White wrote all the songs with the exception of *Midnight and You*, which was composed by Gene Page and his younger brother, Billy. Paul Politi was also heavily involved with four of the compositions.

The album opened with a track called *Barry's Theme*, followed by six classic instrumentals arranged brilliantly by Gene Page: *Rhapsody in White, Midnight and You, I Feel Love Coming On, Baby Blues, Don't Take It Away From Me* and *What a Groove*. Only the last-named was to prove disappointing.

All six featured compositions that became Barry White classics with some memorable lyrics mostly used just to set the scene at the beginning of the instrumental beat. It developed into a sensational album and was undoubtedly one of White's very best, with all eight tracks deserving more recognition than they got at the time.

They also had a wonderful time at the Glendale studios cutting the music. Gene Page recalled the routine: "We'd follow basically the same routine with the Love Unlimited Orchestra. He'd lay down a basic piano track, maybe with a chorus or two. Then he'd give me some idea of the general concept he was aiming at. He'd write the melody, put it together, we'd put the rhythm track, then the strings."

Page was amazed how it all happened, and Barry White tried to describe his technique in more detail to Marc Eliot in his memoirs: "When I write a song, I can hear the melody, the special lyrics, and the dynamic arrangement, each distinctively and all at once. I'll hum a melody into a cassette tape, beat out the drum part on my leg, and know immediately if I have the makings of a new Barry White song – that's the first part of the magic. The second is mixing it all together. I don't follow the so-called rules of chorus-verse-chorus because I don't know or care about those rules.

Jack Perry recalled: "Barry hears music backwards because so often he'll write a chorus followed by a verse when it supposed to be the other way around. He does it this way because he can't read music."

White was dismissive of people who criticised him for being unable to read a sheet of music: "You see, reading music is the white man's invention – feeling music, that's my heritage." He added: "I suppose in that sense you could say I have a phonographic memory."

The *Rhapsody In White* album was to be the embodiment of all those principles.

The album's opener, *Barry's Theme*, was a simple instrumental that built up to a terrific beat, followed by the title track, *Rhapsody in White*, featuring a classic Gene Page string arrangement, combined with an almost unbelievable beat of drums.

Track three was Page's own composition, *Midnight and You*. The lyrics were just a few seconds at the start to set the scene: "There is no place than I'd rather be than with midnight and you. Right on, baby, right on." Jack Perry really loved the sound of it straight away and said: "This has the beginnings of smooth jazz and the rhythm is amazing and we were fortunate to find a beautiful flute solo on the master tape."

The introductory lyric of the fourth track, *I Feel Love Coming On*, was exquisitely sung by Barry White: "You know what I feel like doing to you right now? I feel like squeezing you and teasing you and holding you and baby, pleasing you. Baby you know what? I feel love coming on." Even Bob Fisher of 'New Musical Express', who had been a Barry White critic, liked the lead into it: "Barry White introduces it in his best obscene phone call style."

The fifth track, *Baby Blues*, started with White singing: "Certain things turn me on, the way you might say a word, the way you wear your hair. You have a certain smile on your face, or just the way you are standing there right now. You really, really look good to me baby in your baby blue panties, yes love, you look good to me right now in your baby blues. Your baby blues and you." *Baby Blues* was a sensational piece of music in its own right and received extensive airplay on radio stations, although it was never released as a single.

The sixth track, *Don't Take It Away From Me*, carried on the theme and started off with White singing: "Don't deny me of the things I want, the things from you that I need, the things about you that I love. Darling please, angel please, don't take it away from me", then turned into a dance track that one reviewer described as "sounding like hip elevator music with a disco beat". Bob Fisher described it as "A well-worn instrument of pop emotion. The lowly weak man pitted against the high-on-a-pedestal-too-good-for-me-woman."

After all that, the seventh track, *What a Groove*, was a real let-down and very forgettable.

And if all that brilliance wasn't enough, the last track on the album was the classic *Love's Theme*, the break-out single that had a vocal version on Love

Unlimited's second album, *Under The Influence Of Love*. It had originally been written by White in the mid-sixties when he was at Mustang Bronco, but put on the shelf by Bob Keane as being "not commercial". White had written it with a vocal, but after Gene Page arranged the string parts on the track he wanted to make it an instrumental and get rid of the lyrics. White argued strongly against it and for the vocals, but he changed his view after hearing Page's beautiful string arrangement. Scott Edwards, a bass guitarist who worked with both men, witnessed the discussion in the studio: "It was an instrumental and after Gene Page did his string parts, Barry said it was so beautiful, he decided not to put on the vocals and that's how it became *Love's Theme*. Barry realised that Gene's strings were so beautiful, so why mess it up with a vocal?"

Love's Theme was recorded with a full orchestra and ran for just over four minutes. No one expected it to be a hit when it was released as a single in November 1973. Sales built slowly before it went to No 1 on the Billboard charts for one week in January 1974, and reached the Top 10 in 25 countries around the world. White marvelled at the success, but wasn't really surprised, as he explained: "Producing, arranging, and writing – that's my business and I'm very, very familiar with it. People listening to music in a discotheque are listening with a totally different frame of mind than radio. The discos helped me 100 per cent. They are expressing on that dance floor what they feel. They're in it. When you get a smash out of there you usually got a big one."

Love's Theme became one of the best-selling pop instrumentals of all time and reached No 10 in Britain. It earned a gold record for White, and the whole music industry was stunned by the unlikely success. White said: "We had a double smash on the same song."

The success was all the more unlikely as the record was eight years old. It had actually been the first song that White had written properly, in 1965, nine years before it became a hit. As he remembered: "It was incredible, it really was, to have a song like that to be the first song a man writes. Up to then I always thought I had writing potential, but just that, potential. Even when I was writing at Mustang I didn't feel I had real skills yet. I felt that suddenly in 1965."

White couldn't have been more pumped up about *Love's Theme* and he felt there was no limit to what could be achieved in the future on all his musical fronts: "Everything I play, write and arrange comes from in my head and my heart. I tell the musicians what to play but, more importantly, how to play it. As long as I can communicate with someone who can understand what I mean it'll work."

The album's production went remarkably smoothly, although the album cover proved to be problematic, especially the title and the cover lines, because they needed to explain what the album was all about and it needed some skilful writing.

The final version read 'The Love Unlimited Orchestra – *Rhapsody in White* – Arranged and Conducted by Barry White – Featuring *Love's Theme*'. It was a real mouthful and White had realised his mistake in naming the orchestra after Love Unlimited. It was already causing confusion, not least with his own record company's sales team and distributors. But it was too late to change it and they ploughed on, hoping to explain it with one of the longest cover titles in pop history.

The album cover also became a classic, consisting of one picture of White standing in front of an indoor swimming pool with four black models in the background. The back cover was a drawing of White conducting his orchestra, although in reality it had been Gene Page doing all the conducting.

Love's Theme became an enduring classic and for many years ABC Sports used it as the opening music for its golf coverage. It featured in the 2004 Tina Fey comedy 'Mean Girls' and Cathay Pacific Airways used it for its television commercials. And from then until now it has consistently earned Barry White more than $100,000 a year in royalties – more than $6 million to date.

Russ Regan could never really understand it, especially the success of *Love's Theme* as a single. It went against every music industry rule and he said so to White: "Barry, how can you explain this?" White told him: "Russ, when you're dealing with creativity don't try to get intelligent because it doesn't work. Just go with what you feel, man." It was good advice, but not for Russ Regan, as he simply didn't 'feel it'.

Amy Hanson retrospectively reviewed the album for 'Allmusic', saying that it "showcased the sounds that would inspire a generation of producers, arrangers, and performers to start a million mirror balls spinning the world over." It was no exaggeration. Another reviewer called the album "smarmy but a triumph".

Hanson summed up the album's merits: "From the opening bars of *Barry's Theme*, the album unleashes a groove which really keeps it all mellow. And even though we have to listen through three tracks to first hear White's trademarked vocal come-on, *Midnight and You*, it's well worth the wait. He gets a little more vocal on side two, across *Don't Take It All Away* and again at the beginning of *Baby Blues*, which has 'shag rug in front of a fireplace' written all over its arrangement. But the masterful finale, of course, is *Love's Theme*. The song's lush strings and smooth wah-wah guitars not only typified a genre, they also became an aural catchphrase for an entire generation of clubbers."

Stephen McMillian for 'Soul Train' was even more effusive: "*Rhapsody in White* provided some of the most danceable and romantic music ever performed in music history."

It was left to Bob Fisher to throw in the negatives, calling the album "eight hastily-thrown-together backing tracks" and saying that White was the "first easy-listening soul artist taking the camp arrangements of Bert Kaempfert and James Last and boiling up the mixture to make the music hip enough for a rock audience."

Few people agreed with Fisher's appraisal, which was quickly forgotten when the album reached No 8 in the Billboard album chart, an exceptional performance for an instrumental album, and got to No 2 on the soul charts. It quickly went gold and continued to sell well for the following 40 years. Russ Regan was amazed, and so was everyone else in the music industry.

But Barry White would never reach the same instrumental heights again, as nothing could ever follow *Rhapsody in White* for sheer quality.

CHAPTER 29

Feel the Heat

In Heat – the third Love Unlimited album

March 1974

At the end of 1974 things could not have been going better for Barry White. Almost the whole of the staff of 20th Century Records was working on his projects. A new album from one of his three acts was appearing, as regular as clockwork, every one and a half months.

Russ Regan was beside himself as his company's sales had gone up tenfold in a few months. His life was now all about Barry White, an artist who only 12 months before he had casually rejected and told to go someplace else.

But with success came anxiety. Regan was uncertain how much, if any, resentment was festering inside White's head over that rejection in 1973.

Regan was mindful of how coldly he had turned down White's first album, *I've Got So Much To Give*, and had then brutally reclaimed it all in the space of a few days. Since then White had delivered eight albums and contractually was free to go to any label he liked, where doubtless he would be welcomed with open arms and a very big up-front payment. In fact, Barry White and Larry Nunes had spoken to several labels about a contract, but in the end had decided to stay with the 'devil they knew', which is how they frequently referred to Regan.

Both men were aware of Regan's severe shortcomings, but figured that they could use them to their advantage. Besides, he wasn't all bad. His skills as a huckster were unrivalled, and that was a very useful skill in the music business.

Nevertheless Regan constantly felt the shadow of Clive Davis at his shoulder, especially now that Davis had resurfaced with his own new record label, Arista. He thought that if Davis had been willing to fly from New York to Los Angeles to sign White when he was an unknown, what would he be prepared to do now? He wondered what up-front cheque Davis might waggle in front of White, thinking that it would be at least seven figures.

So Russ Regan decided to move first.

He rang 20th Century Fox's chairman and chief executive, Dennis Stanfill, and asked permission to write Barry White a check for $1 million. Stanfill just grunted "yeah" and Regan wondered if he even knew who White was. He needn't have. Stanfill, an accountant by training, was a financial wunderkind who had rescued 20th Century Fox from near bankruptcy and had made it into one of Hollywood's most profitable studios. The 44-year-old knew exactly who Barry White was and how much he was contributing to 20th Century's bottom line. He just wondered why Regan hadn't called earlier.

As soon as the check was signed off, Regan didn't waste any time, and once it was in his hand he started searching for White, sending Paul Politi out to find him.

Politi found White at Glendale and asked if it was OK for Russ Regan to call in. A year earlier, a message like that might have struck fear into White's heart, but not now. White was firmly in charge and Regan just did as he was told. That was how it was.

Regan got the address, called up his car and went straight round. As soon as there was a break in the session, he pulled White into the corridor and said he had something for him. He reached into his pocket and handed White a white envelope continuing the million-dollar check.

White looked at him and the envelope quizzically, and asked: "Is this my dismissal?" Regan laughed nervously. White thought to himself: "Russ is pretty stupid, but not that stupid." But he wasn't sure, so he opened the envelope and took out the check. Regan declared grandly: "Barry, you are the franchise."

White showed no emotion and looked Regan up and down, wondering whether the normally tight-fisted executive had lost the plot. He handed him back the check and said rather dismissively: "Give it to Larry." As he turned to go, White paused, turned his head and shouted down the corridor: "Oh, and thank you."

Regan walked out, got back into his car and drove straight to Larry Nunes's office, where he received a somewhat warmer reception when Nunes opened the envelope. When Regan told him how non-plussed White had been, Nunes told him not to worry – he was always like that when he was working and didn't like any distractions, even for the delivery of a $1 million check.

Regan pumped Nunes for information, trying to get any inkling as to whether White might be speaking to other record labels. Nunes immediately sensed what he was about and quietly teased him, dropping Clive Davis's name a few times. Regan went away none the wiser.

After he had gone, even Larry Nunes was bemused at Barry White's reaction to getting the check. As he gazed at it, he thought to himself: "We have come a long, long way, Barry."

Although he was a wealthy and very successful entrepreneur, Nunes had never seen a check for a million dollars before and wondered whether he would again. He decided to make the most of it and was glad that he had the weekend to savour it before taking it to the bank on Monday morning.

Many years later, White explained his apparent nonchalance: "I was appreciative for sure but I did not want my concentration broken for anything. When I'm recording it doesn't make any difference if someone wants to give me a single red rose or a seven-figure cheque – all my focus is on one thing. The studio is my temple and the music I create is sacred."

There was also no danger of White leaving 20th for Clive Davis or anyone else. He had got used to the ways of Russ Regan and had a thing about loyalty, as he explained: "My philosophy is you have to be loyal to something, you can't be a whore all your life. I think that there's a time when people give their word to each other it has to mean something. I'm a street cat, see, I belonged in gangs and when you had a partner you went down with your partner – whether you won the fight or lost it, you went down together."

Somehow in between albums Barry White managed to embark on his first world tour in 1974. He took everyone with him including the orchestra and the three girls. And they had a marvellous uninhibited time. The tour had limited dates but included a stop-off in the UK. White and most of his party had never been outside America and hardly ever outside California, as he admitted: "What a trip in every sense of the word. For the first time I was able to see with my own eyes a world that had only existed in school books, newspapers and on television."

White was stunned by the reception he got from the Germans, Italians and French, as his songs were not translated into their language. It opened him up to a brand new world: "I went from being a nobody on the streets of

South Central Los Angeles to a face recognised in foreign countries by a whole new audience for my music who couldn't speak my language who I hadn't even realised I had." It would be the first of many world tours that White undertook over the next 25 years.

There was an even bigger impact on Glodean, Linda and Dede. As White described it: "They giggled, shopped, and gawked and carried on like kids on a day trip from school with their favourite teacher to their most wondrous field of dreams."

During the British leg of the tour the three girls went tobogganing in the snow to make a promotional film for their album *Under The Influence Of Love* and particularly the spin-off single *It May Be Winter Outside*, which was to reach No 11 in the UK charts. Tobogganing was all the rage in the UK at the time and snow was thick on the ground that winter for the whole time they were in the country. Given the theme of the song, the tour's British PR people thought it was a great idea.

But tobogganing, especially in the UK, is not without its dangers. When the toboggan was going full speed down a hill with the three girls aboard and the cameras rolling, inevitably it hit a bump and Glodean fell off. The toboggan rolled over several times and she sprained her ankle and wrist. She ended up in a hospital casualty (ER) department and was bandaged up.

Aside from that it was indeed a magical time. White recognised the turnaround in his fortunes and was determined to take nothing for granted: "Life had gotten so much sweeter for me. I was bigger than I ever dreamed I would be. I'd succeeded in lifting myself out of the mean streets. I'd left behind forever the dead-end world of muggers and killers. And I was no longer this big loveable dude whom everybody liked but who hadn't really done anything with his life. Now it was my time to howl and I had turned on the world with the sound of my success."

Now the 15 years of struggle and reality paid off. Most big pop stars of the seventies were pulled into a world of drug-taking, misusing women and every excess available. But White never even came close to anything like that. For him success meant striving for more success and working even harder to sustain it. Once he had it, he was determined to keep hold of it, as he said: "In my world making music was and still is as pure and vital as the pulse that throbs through my heart. The very thought of misusing my gifts was to me the true definition of sin."

Before leaving for the world tour there was one last album to cut for 1973, for early release in 1974. This was to be Love Unlimited's third album, and Barry White was brimming over with new material for it. He called it *In Heat*, which he decided he most definitely was when it came to music. For Barry White fans it was another masterpiece, and many people believe it is Love Unlimited's best work.

The album ran to seven songs and 29 minutes of music. He took his usual team into the studio, consisting of Gene Page and Jack Perry together with engineers Frank Kejmar and Paul Elmore, and the ever-present guitarist, Ray Parker Jnr. Twenty years old, Parker was the secret ingredient of White's work in the seventies, and was later to have a fabulous career as a singer/songwriter. Ironically, in 1978 he was poached away from under Barry White's nose by Clive Davis's Arista label.

White and Page also assembled a brilliant team of back-up musicians for the album. By now every talented player in Los Angeles had heard about Barry White and everyone wanted to work with him, even if it was just for the experience. The team for *In Heat* was like a Hollywood roll-call, and included guitarists Wah-Wah Watson, Lee Ritenour, David Walker, Dean Parks and Don Peake, bassists Nathan East and Wilton Felder of the Crusaders, drummer Ed Greene and percussionist Gary Coleman.

The first track was *Move Me No Mountain*, written by Aaron Schroeder and Jerry Ragovoy and previously performed by Dionne Warwick and Chaka Khan. It was very unusual for Barry White to start an album with a song that he had not been involved in writing, even more so when it had already been recorded by others. But its choice was no surprise – it was a Supremes sound-alike and suited the three girls perfectly. It would be impossible for their fans not to enjoy it.

The second track many consider one of White's best-ever ballads. It was called *Share A Little Love In Your Heart*, and he had written it earlier in the year. It was not really the right material for a single, but was so good that it got released anyway and became a modest hit, climbing to No 21 on the Billboard R&B chart. One reviewer called it a "sumptuous song", and they were not wrong.

The tempo changed with *Oh I Should Say, It's Such a Beautiful Day* written by White as a feel-good 3½-minute song. It was followed by *I Needed Love – You Were There*, which was generally agreed to be the classic White track.

The fifth track had the most interesting history. Glodean suggested that they use the piano introduction from *Lost Without The Love of My Guy* as the base for a new song. Her husband resisted the idea but relented when Glodean pushed hard for it. He reused the piano chord progression and it became *I Belong To You*. It was brilliantly arranged by Gene Page and described by one reviewer as a "majestic ballad". It was issued as a single and briefly went to No 1 in the Billboard R&B charts and No 30 in the main Billboard singles chart. Glodean had been right, and her husband grudgingly acknowledged that his wife had 'good ears'. Reviewer John Clemente described it as "invoking a feeling of sultry seduction and passionate angst."

It was the sort of review Barry White liked.

The sixth track, *I Love You So, Never Gonna Let You Go*, was a nondescript but typical Barry White composition for Love Unlimited, albeit instantly forgettable.

The album ended with a vocal version of *Love's Theme*, the orchestral version of which was to stun America and go to the top of the Billboard singles chart for one week the following year. It was Glodean's idea to do a vocal version and she got Aaron Schroeder to write some lyrics without telling her husband. Surprisingly he agreed to it, although White preferred it without the lyrics. The vocal version of *Love's Theme* had new orchestrations with subtle differences from the original version. Later Julio Iglesias and Andy Williams also recorded it.

The album cover was the least adventurous of any of White's releases of that year and featured a single photograph of the three girls in revealing evening gowns. It was shot by Michael Paladin and designed by Jack Levy and Eddie Douglas.

Despite garnering some excellent reviews, *In Heat* sold relatively modestly and got to No 15 on the Billboard R&B charts. But it was generally regarded as a disappointment sales-wise after such a glittering year. It was possible that, with eight albums released in a year, there was some Barry White overload in the market and *In Heat* suffered because of it.

When the album was finished, White was delighted to be asked to rearrange the musical score of Dino De Laurentiis's remake of the movie 'King Kong'. John Barry had written the main score but for various reasons De Laurentiis wasn't happy with the opening theme and wanted a new version. His 19-year-old son, Federico De Laurentiis, was a serious Barry White fan and suggested to his father that White could possibly be a solution. De Laurentiis was a direct man and told his young son to get on a plane and make it happen.

Federico De Laurentiis flew to Los Angeles with a singular mission, to persuade Barry White to rearrange the score. When he landed at LAX, severely jet-lagged, he went straight to the Glendale studio where he had been told White was working.

There was some confusion, as White was expecting Federico's father to show up. He looked the young boy up and down quizzically and wondered how the fabled Italian producer had managed to stay so young. But when that was sorted out he was immediately won over as Federico kept addressing him as 'Maestro'. White had never heard the title used before and told Federico: "Hey, man, I like that." Federico told him it was an Italian way of addressing the conductor of an orchestra.

White needed no persuading to do the job, and when Federico proffered a $25,000 fee he just said, "Yes." He was absolutely flattered, to his core, to be asked to try and do one better than John Barry, by then the world's foremost cinematic composer and musical arranger.

The two men hit it off and White invited Federico to stay at his home while they spent an enjoyable two days in the studio rearranging the theme. The young man took it back to play for his father, who was in Rome doing pre-production for the film. He and Federico's sister Raffaella loved it.

The De Laurentiis remake of 'King Kong' was a surprise hit in 1976 and the seventh highest grossing movie of the year. It was as though Barry White had sprinkled his stardust on the film – he really could do no wrong between 1972 and 1975.

However, the film had a tragic undertone for Barry White. Six years later, in July 1981, he was sitting in a hotel lobby in New York reading a newspaper when he noticed a short article entitled 'De Laurentiis's son killed'. He couldn't believe what he was reading. The article detailed how Federico had been the only passenger in a small Cessna that had collided with another plane near Anchorage. His pilot and the pilot of the other plane were also killed.

White let out a howl and burst into tears in the hotel lobby. Glodean, sitting next to him, jumped from her seat. His mind immediately went back to those three beautiful, magical days in Los Angeles six years before. He turned to Glodean and said: "He was the most beautiful and most charming young boy I had ever met. Life is so fragile, we must never forget that."

FEEL THE HEAT

CHAPTER 30

Divorce and Remarriage

A proper family at last

1974

The growing chemistry between Barry White and Glodean James was becoming impossible to hide and soon all of Hollywood seemed to know that they were an item. Although White was living somewhere else, it made things potentially very tricky at the family home. Fortunately Mary and her mother were not plugged into the Hollywood zeitgeist and news of the affair escaped their ears.

Simultaneously White's success had brought about a dramatic change of attitude towards him from his wife, her mother and his own father. None of them had believed he could possibly become successful in the music business and had told him so. Now they were stunned at what had transpired. And deep down they were annoyed that they could have been so wrong.

The change in status had happened so quickly. In the middle of 1972 Barry White was a penniless wannabe relying on handouts from people like Gene Page, when a $10 bill in his hand was the difference between eating and starving. But by the middle of 1973 he was an international superstar, earning in excess of $1 million a year and suddenly living in a world where money was simply irrelevant.

The sudden influx of money enabled White to regularise his personal affairs – it gave him enough money to finally divorce Mary and marry Glodean, something he had waited a long time to be able to do.

But it proved to be a complicated union and an almost equally tangled uncoupling. White brought four children to the relationship and Glodean brought two – so they had a family of six before they had even started. White had 11-year-old Barry Jnr, 10-year-old Lanese, nine-year-old Nina and eight-year-old Darryl. Glodean brought nine-year-old Bridget and eight-year-old Kevin. It would have been impossible to pull off without money, but the new riches from Barry and Glodean's musical success enabled it to happen.

White remembers the precise moment they decided to tie the knot. He was recording his third Love Unlimited Orchestra album of 1974 and a track called *Satin Soul* was being cut in the studio. Even though it had no words, something in that music, just as had happened with Elvis Presley's *It's Now or Never* in 1960, triggered a new resolve. As White described it: "That day, after much thought, I decided I felt ready to try it again."

It was a brave decision, as it would mean an inevitable separation from his four children, whom he loved dearly. His relationship with Mary had deteriorated ever since they had separated. And having more money did not improve her in his eyes. He now saw that she was not the woman he had thought she was, either as a wife or a mother.

But Barry White also realised that he himself had changed significantly over the past 15 years: "I was a different Barry White from the little boy who'd married Mary at such a young age. I'd done a lot of growing up. And I was no longer the jealous, insecure, primitive soul who separated himself from true love by false barriers – such as pedestals so high no woman could ever hope to mount them."

But the one true difference between Mary and Glodean was the latter's understanding of the music business and what Barry White was about professionally. Mary had no understanding of it at all, whereas Glodean understood it all perfectly, as White explained: "Mary thought my music was a great waste of time, an interference with the business of my real life. Glodean only knew me as a musician to whom music meant everything."

White began to realise that the appeal of Mary had been as an unattainable fantasy and someone who sent him to what he called the "land of music" in search of inspiration. Whereas he thought Glodean to be the real thing and a woman who inspired him: "In her I had found someone with whom I could truly share the harmonies of love that played through the rhythms of my life. I'm the kind of guy that likes to look at old movies when it took six months to walk a lady to her door, when it took a year and a half just to get a kiss. Those are the kind of people that stay married. You should know something about the people you're involved with."

But before there could be any marriage, White had to obtain a divorce from Mary. That was complicated by the fact that he now had money and someone else he wanted to marry; whereas five years before he could have probably obtained a divorce cheaply and easily, now it was a wholly different scenario.

There was also the matter of custody of the four children, which Barry White thought Mary was determined to use as a negotiating tool to get the financial settlement she wanted and felt she deserved from a husband who was now earning a million dollars a year – White believed that she wanted a piece of that and he believed that she was determined to get it by any means she could, and then some. They already had an informal agreement about custody and access to the children, but that was no longer the point. White believed that Mary, saw the children as a financial instrument to be traded, and a fierce battle commenced regarding the amount of child support she wanted to receive.

The battle concerned three of the children, as Barry Jnr had already decided on his own that he wanted to live with his father. Lanese, Nina and Darryl spent weekdays with their mother and weekends with their father.

But White wanted to have all the children full time, as he explained: "I wanted all the children to be together and felt I could provide a better home for them." Mary was having none of it and, although she did not really want permanent custody, there was no financial benefit for her in that.

Mary's first step was to hire the best and meanest divorce attorney she could find. Then her husband was forced to hire his own lawyer to negotiate with his wife's. He hired Ned Shankman, a young attorney in an up-and-coming Los Angeles law practice. Unfortunately the young Shankman was no match for the older and more experienced rottweiler lawyer who was working for Mary.

Mary's lawyer had only one tactic and that was to continually say "No". So the divorce settlement looked as though it would end up going to trial. But virtually on the steps of the courthouse, the lawyer finally said "Yes" and won Mary the astonishing sum of $10,000 a month, half for her and half for the children. It was an extraordinary settlement, and the very surprised Judge said so when it was read out. But White wanted the matter settled and wanted his children to have the best. As he said: "To me it wasn't about the law, it was about my children." He also thought that his wife deserved to share in his success: "By now my music was on the radio and in the charts and Mary and I felt her and the children were entitled to a piece of my action."

On top of the settlement, he bought Mary a new house in Encino. "I could afford it and it was a relief to be out of the courtroom."

With the divorce settled, it was time for Barry White to remarry without delay. So in July 1974 he and Glodean James secretly flew to Las Vegas for a quick wedding in a typical small Las Vegas purpose-built chapel, with just the two of them and an unknown witness present. White explained: "We wanted to keep the rhythm of our romance right." They chose Independence Day, 4th July, for the nuptials and told as few people as they could get away with.

But other people had other ideas, particularly Russ Regan, who wanted to celebrate the wedding of two of his biggest stars in what he thought was the correct manner. His true huckster instincts came to the fore and he set about planning a wedding reception to which he invited most of the music industry.

The venue was the Century Plaza Hotel, the crescent-shaped 19-storey building that stood on the Avenue of the Stars in Hollywood on the old 20th Century Fox backlot. Regan booked out the grand ballroom, the scene of so many famous Hollywood parties.

It couldn't have been glitzier and more public, and it was the last thing Barry and Glodean wanted – but there was little they could do about it. As the photographs later showed, the maestro and his leading lady, a storybook couple, stood smiling and greeting their guests, in between subtle ear nibbles, clearly wishing they were someplace else.

Regan was genuinely a world-class huckster and parties were something he did really well, although in truth the party was more about him than Barry and Glodean White. With the honeymoon fire still burning, the happy couple stayed for the minimum time they deemed respectable before fleeing, holding hands, to their waiting limousine for home.

Not that it bothered Regan. He was having the time of his life showing off to his contemporaries how his 20th Century Records, thanks to the success of Barry White, was now one of the hottest labels in town.

The elaborate party must have cost close to $25,000, and White detested the sort of blatant showing-off in which Russ Regan specialised. He much preferred to be at home with his children and was never a party animal, as he explained: "I'm a homebody person by nature. I'm romantic at heart and prefer to stay out of the social mix, remaining close to the ones I love instead."

As a happily married man with six children, White quickly adapted himself to his new life. He gave up touring in the summer months so he was home for the children in their school holidays, and took the family on vacation to Hawaii every year.

Now they were married, the couple stopped using birth control and sure enough Glodean soon got pregnant. In 1975 Shaherah White duly arrived to cement the union and bring the number of children in the combined family to seven. But that was that, they decided seven was enough for any family, and Glodean resumed using birth control.

But despite a household filled with joy and happiness, Barry White found family life in Hollywood difficult, as he confessed: "Trying to have a successful career and a family life are all about endless trade-offs and compromises. Impossible odds stack up against any attempt at being a star, a father, and a husband all at the same time."

To counter it Barry and Glodean imposed a very strict regime on their children. They over-compensated with some heavy discipline, which went down badly with the children, who had previously been used to a looser and much less strict lifestyle. But it gradually started to work as the message got through that pocket money had to be worked for and good behaviour was rewarded with tangible benefits.

Barry White explained the philosophy that he and Glodean had worked out: "How would they know what's right or wrong otherwise? Because they were little gods and goddesses who would one day grow up to be big gods and goddesses imbued with the power and the knowledge that I and their mothers have bestowed on them.

"I always set a good example in my own home because kids know the difference between putting up a front and parents who really care. My children knew that I loved them and would always love them. They were secure in their self-image because I am secure in mine. It was so important because our paths are chosen at such an early age."

Being Barry White the father rather than Barry White the performer became the most important goal in his life and he wanted to demonstrate his love to each of his children all the time. He deplored the attitude of parents who never hugged their children or showed them outward affection: "I know kids who were never hugged by either one of their parents, so every time I saw my children the first thing I did was hug and kiss them. I wanted my kids to know how important they were to me and that I was there for them with love in my heart."

But Barry White's image of his family got a nasty battering in 1975, just 12 months after his divorce, when he had a chance encounter with his ex-wife and their three children outside a shopping mall on Martin Luther King Boulevard in Los Angeles. White had taken an old friend called Blanchard Montgomery to a favourite Taco restaurant for a plate of burritos.

As they left the restaurant, White spotted Mary's distinctive green Cadillac at a distance on the other side of the road. At that moment his children also spotted him and they waved. Mary was with her new boyfriend. The children got out of the car and ran towards their father to say hello and greet him affectionately as Mary and her boyfriend watched from afar.

White was shocked to the core when he saw that the children were dressed in what he regarded as rags. He had never seen them like this before, as they were always immaculately turned out when he arrived to pick them up on Saturday mornings. When he asked them why they were wearing old clothes and shoes, they replied that it was what they always wore. White then glanced over the street to see that Mary and her boyfriend were dressed in expensive clothes and shoes and were well manicured, in sharp contrast to the children.

White suddenly realised that he was being conned, and the $10,000 a month he had so generously agreed to pay his ex-wife was not being spent on his children but on herself and her new boyfriend. He thought back to his own mother and how she had scrimped and saved so that he and his brother Darryl were always well turned out.

A red mist descended as he recalled his feelings: "Oh yes, those two looked good, and I felt that I was being made into a complete jerk."

What happened next was truly frightening. White literally lost control of himself, not out of anger but out of blind cool rage. He had a permit to carry a gun in his car, and his .357 Smith & Wesson Magnum was in the glove compartment. He carried it for self-defence, as he explained: "Like every street-savvy musician, I felt the need to be able to take care of myself at all times, especially when I was out by myself."

But the last thing White had on his mind that day was self-defence. He suddenly wanted to kill his wife for dishonouring his children – and the boyfriend too if he got in the way. Blanchard Montgomery, a wise old gentleman, sensed what was happening and ran across to the open car door. He leaned in and put his hand across White's wrist, temporarily restraining him from taking the gun out of the open glove compartment. He said: "BW, please don't do this. Man, you've got so much to live for and you are going to blow it all away on this woman. She's not worth it, BW." White glared at his friend and said, "Let me go," but did not attempt to prise himself loose. After the longest 10 seconds of Blanchard's life, his friend relaxed his grip on the gun and pushed it back in the compartment and locked it.

He went over the road to where Mary and her boyfriend were standing and looked her straight in the eye, saying nothing. She knew what he was cross about and she knew why – it didn't need saying. She knew she had been found out.

After a few seconds, White wheeled away and told Lanese, Nina and Darryl that he would see them at the weekend.

He seethed all the way home and, after dropping off Blanchard, slumped down on his settee and explained to Glodean what had happened. "I want those children back," he told her, and resolved that evening to get full custody, whatever and however much it took.

The next day White drove down to his lawyer's office to see Larry Thompson. Thompson was on a retainer to handle his business affairs and White thought that he would be best placed to handle the situation rather than bringing in Ned Shankman again. White told Thompson that he wanted full custody of Lanese, Nina and Darryl and he didn't care how much it cost. He told him: "I'm sending her all that money and she dresses them in rags. One way or another she has to be out of their lives."

White and Thompson discussed it and decided that the best way to handle the situation was to simply make Mary a cash offer for full custody of the children. White told him to offer up to $250,000 cash.

Thompson promised his client that a letter would go out that same day offering her just that.

But Thompson was really humouring White, and had no intention of sending out any such letter. For one, he knew that his client didn't have the money –

well he did have it, but he didn't. Theoretically White was on course to earn $2.6 million that year just from his record publishing company, but after tax and other deductions his income would be less than $1 million and his living expenses had ballooned. He had also bought an expensive house in Sherman Oaks and was doing it up, together with another smaller house for his wife. He was a typical man who had got rich very quickly and was unaware of any form of restraint. In fact, he was spending money like water. He had still not learned that to be really rich takes a serious amount of money, and White didn't actually have it.

In fact, at that very moment Thompson knew that Barry White was in the red at the bank. Not that it was a problem, as the bank manager loved Barry White and his music and, more importantly, could see $200,000 coming in and going out every month. So Thompson wrote the letter, sent a draft to his client and neglected to find a stamp for the envelope, an old lawyer's trick.

White was truly bamboozled and wrote in his 1999 memoirs: "Something really weird happened, the kind of karmic event that has stayed with me for the rest of my days. For one reason or another Monday went by and Larry didn't get around to sending out the letter. Tuesday came, again, no letter. Wednesday, same thing. On Thursday I went back to Larry's office to find out what was going on."

Thompson told him: "Barry, I'm sending it today without fail. She'll get it tomorrow or Monday, whichever way her mail runs."

White continued the story: "That sounded good enough for me." He went into the studio the following day, a Friday, to cut a new record that would become *I'm Qualified To Satisfy You*. By four o'clock in the afternoon he and Gene Page, Jack Perry, Frank Kejmar, Ray Parker Jnr and the musicians had finished up and a future hit record was down on tape. They all knew the recording was very good and it been a very satisfying day. White then headed home to Sherman Oaks to Glodean and Barry Jnr, Kevin, Bridget and the new baby, Shaherah.

Going home on a Friday afternoon was always a great pleasure for him. Everything about it pleased him. He loved pulling into his driveway knowing that the weekend was ahead of him and all the joy he knew that would bring. He called it "Our household of hers and mine and ours". That Friday afternoon the greetings and hugs seemed more effusive than normal and all the children were in good spirits, looking forward to the weekend in the sun around the swimming pool. Sadie, their grandmother, was also staying for the weekend.

White was not due to collect Lanese, Nina and Darryl until the following morning for their weekend visit. But just after six o'clock the doorbell rang. Sadie answered the door and suddenly shouted out "Nessie!" Thirteen-year-old Lanese had showed up at the front door unexpected and on her own.

She ran into the house, greeting her excited brothers and sisters. Sadie brought her into the lounge, where her father was resting. He sat her down on his knee and asked her what had happened. She told him she had walked the half mile from her mother's house. White sensed that his daughter was upset: "I could tell she was scared, thinking I was going to be angry that she had run away from home." He asked her if her mother knew she was here and Lanese nodded as she told her father: "I don't want to live with Mummy, I want to live with you." He noted that his daughter was wearing the same rags he had seen her in at the mall.

He told Lanese to go to the room she shared with Bridget at weekends and get washed up ready for supper. He asked Sadie to go up and get the clothes and the old toys she was carrying so they could be thrown in the trash.

White expected a call from Mary within the hour to say that Lanese was missing, but there was no call. The following morning the bell rang at the front gate and woke White. He put on his dressing gown, looked out of the window and saw Nina and Darryl at the foot of the hill outside the gate. He rushed downstairs, pressed the button to open the gate and let them in. White recalled: "Mary had come by and dropped them at the foot of the hill with all their clothes, toys and bikes, everything they owned, and had driven off."

White picked everything up, carried it to the house and closed the door. All his seven children were safe inside, reunited permanently for the first time together – he couldn't help but smile as it seemed that the lyrics to a hundred tunes flooded his brain all at the same time.

By now the whole house was awake and buzzing. White went into his study and closed the door. Despite the hour he dialled Larry Thompson's house and told him the news: "You're not going to believe this, Larry – I've got all my children, man." White thought that Mary had responded to the letter. Thompson replied: "That's great, and by the way I never sent the letter. I'll make proper arrangements to do the right thing and see that everybody's taken care of legally and fairly."

As Thompson replaced the receiver he smiled to himself. He had correctly sensed what was about to happen and had deliberately never sent the letter, thereby saving his client a considerable amount of money. He was in no doubt that if Mary had received that letter she would have demanded $500,000 or even a million, and that his client would probably have told him to pay it. Now he could negotiate a sensible cash lump sum to replace the $10,000 a month that White was paying her and everyone would be happy.

Barry White was certainly happy as he had all his children – Barry Jnr, Lanese, Nina, Darryl, Kevin, Bridget and Shaherah – under his roof that Saturday morning.

All the old clothes were thrown away and it was a delighted troop of children that Glodean piled into the car to take shopping that Saturday morning. White recalled: "From that moment I promised myself their life was going to change."

The union of the White and James families was now complete. As Barry White said: "Glodean was terrific through all of this. She never made any distinctions to who were her kids and who were mine. She treated all of them as if they were one family and so did I. That's the way we wanted it and that's the way the kids felt as well. She never showed the slightest difference to any of them which was so important to their well-being and sense of family."

When they returned from the mall, White brought them all together into the lounge and told them it was a new beginning for the family and they were now together forever. It was a joyous occasion and for the next 10 years that joy continued unabated as they all grew into adulthood, as White remembered much later in an interview with 'Rolling Stone' magazine: "I was strict but we played together, shooting water guns, playing basketball, swimming for nine hours in the pool. But when Daddy said stop, they stopped."

As he took control of the parenting duties for Lanese, Nina and Darryl, he was horrified at what he found. Their school records were terrible from an academic and discipline perspective. They were uniformly bottom of their classes and were guilty of disruptive behaviour and petty theft at school. When White phoned his ex-wife for an explanation, Mary merely said: "Barry, they're difficult kids."

He told her he would "handle it".

And he did.

CHAPTER 31

The Signature Song

The breakthrough single

January to March 1974

As 1974 dawned, Barry White had a big reputation to live up to and knew that his next move had to be something very special. Up to the end of the previous year he had enjoyed just one No 1 record, which had sat at the top of the Billboard singles chart for precisely one week. This was *Love's Theme*, under the guise of the Love Unlimited Orchestra. White had greatly enjoyed his seven days at the top of the charts and wanted to repeat it. He realised that the thrill of being on top of the charts was like no other and was heady stuff indeed, and all the more exciting in that it had come from one of the most unlikely tunes.

But like many things in Barry White's life, that single success was mostly accidental. He wrote his songs for albums although, like all artists, he knew that break-out single records were very important for album sales, and for artists generally. But he could never specifically write a single. He wrote songs for his albums and hoped that hits would emerge from them, which they generally did.

Having tasted the top, White racked his brains searching for something special that would take him back to No 1. He wanted to feel the rush of elation again that he had felt on Friday 9th February 1973, when he first learned that *Love's Theme* had gone to the top of the Billboard singles chart.

The magic came again from the most unlikely of sources.

One afternoon White was sitting around at home, in a makeshift studio, with his friends Sterling Radcliffe and Tony Sepe. For some reason that no one remembers now, Radcliffe, who also acted as White's unofficial road manager, went to the piano and played a tune he had composed 21 years before but had never found anyone interested in recording.

White suddenly sat up, surprised by what he was hearing. He told Radcliffe that he really liked the song. Radcliffe was stunned and said it was called

You're My First, You're My Last, My In-Between, which he had originally imagined as a country and western song.

He told White that he would bring in a cassette of the original recording he had made in 1953 when he was only 23 years old. White realised that it was a complete mouthful of a title and started rolling the words around in his mouth until he came up with: *You're the First, The Last, My Everything*.

The next day Radcliffe was true to his word and, as soon as the cassette went into the machine, White was absolutely enthralled with what he heard. He listened to the song over and over, searching for inspiration. After a few hours he suddenly sat up and told Radcliffe: "Forget country and western – this is disco."

As soon as they arrived at the studio, White and his team got to work on completely revamping the song, refashioning both the melody and the words. The original lyrics that Radcliffe had written were thrown away and a clomping sound in the background was taken out of the melody. Ray Parker Jnr strummed along on his guitar while the ideas poured out of Barry White as he reimagined the whole song. He kept the basic structure, but by the end had completely rewritten the lyrics – only a few of the original words survived. The lyrics White came up with included the extraordinary line that no one thought was possible, but which really resonated when White sang it: "We've definitely got our thing together, didn't we baby? Isn't it nice? I mean, really, when you really sit and think about it, isn't it really, really nice?" White completely recast the song as a disco number and upped the tempo. He called in Gene Page for a second opinion and together they worked on an arrangement, while bassist Wilton Felder added a riff to replace the clomp. When he had finished, Radcliffe and Tony Sepe knew that they had something special on their hands.

Jack Perry witnessed the process first hand: "It was hardly a dance record when it started out. It was brought to Barry as a country and western track where the lyrics were partially spoken. And it had little clomping sounds." Perry believes the real genius was Wilton Felder's bass riff. He said that when that went in the result was a foregone conclusion and "the rest was history".

Greg Williams, a session musician, remembered the magical relationship between White and Gene Page as they worked on the arrangement: "Barry would tell Gene how he wanted the violins on top of the cello. I remember, he'd scream, 'Make the motherfuckers dance, Gene!'"

Although it had been a totally off-the-cuff collaborative effort, White knew there was something very special there and was certain it would become a huge hit.

Writing royalties from an enduring hit song could be very substantial and almost immediately he divided up the writing credits so there was no dispute later. Radcliffe, the original creator, was allocated 30 per cent, Sepe got 20 per cent and White 50 per cent. Sepe and Radcliffe were delighted, although in truth none of them knew at the time that it would become Barry White's greatest hit and signature song. They quickly knocked up an instrumental version for the B-side called *More Than Anything, You're My Everything*.

You're the First, The Last, My Everything exploded into the charts and was an instant hit right out of the box. Only strong competition meant that it got no higher than No 2 in the Billboard US singles chart, but it spent two weeks at No 1 in Britain. It became White's fourth Top 10 hit on the Billboard Hot 100 singles chart.

Jack Perry recalls the euphoria that gripped the world that summer: "I remember walking into a club in Switzerland and the DJ was playing this song. The strings, that voice, the beat were all meshing perfectly."

You're the First, The Last, My Everything, like all singles, quickly left the charts, but it did not fade away in the public consciousness. Far from it – it was played all summer all over America and was the year's most visible record. It was to be the song that would last forever, one that upcoming generations would always identify with Barry White. It would become an evergreen, his most popular song and his signature tune for the next 29 years, even enduring for many years after his death as a party and discotheque staple.

Later it was to feature in innumerable films and television programmes, and got a new lease of life from the 'Ally McBeal' TV series. It became so famous that today more people remember the song than they do the singer, but it will always be inextricably linked to Barry White. It has never been covered by another artist – no one dared.

CHAPTER 32

Can't Get Enough

Third solo album

August 1974

Barry White had become one of the biggest recording and performing stars in the world. He was a global sensation and his unique sound had captivated a generation of music lovers.

Physically imposing, dressed in colourful costumes, he and his supporting acts, the Love Unlimited girl group and the 40-piece Love Unlimited Orchestra, had already toured the United States twice and Europe once, playing to sell-out houses on every occasion.

There was no one bigger than Barry White and journalists clamoured to interview him. They found themselves facing a physically imposing 6 foot 3 inch man weighing more than 350lb. But he was a gentle giant, and interviewer after interviewer wrote that he was "not as monumental in person" as they expected. Many described his "impeccable manners and courteous demeanour" and noted his respectful approach to dealing with the press and the fact that he was "charming company". He told them: "With me, what you see is what you get."

The truth was that he loved the attention of the world's media. He liked talking about himself and his music, and journalists lapped it all up. It seemed that no interview request would be refused and no subject, however intimate, was off limits. When one writer asked him if he was guided by God, he replied that it was an interesting question. The first time he was asked he gave the wrong answer. He said that, despite his mother's convictions, he was never particularly religious and that he had rejected her early attempts to involve him in the church.

But that soundbite, however innocent, did not play well and, as a prominent black singer, it was not a good answer. It caused the first controversy of Barry White's career. So, in later interviews he modified his response: "To me, God is my best friend. I talk to my God and I love him and I have been guided by a voice that has been inside my head ever since I was born. A voice that has guided me with a sureness and I've tried my best to obey. I know it when I hear it and I listen when it talks to me." That went down a lot better.

He also insisted that despite all his success he had remained humble: "To me, a great man is a humble man. I learned about the positives and negatives when I was a boy so I have worked on my positives. Being too critical, for example – I worked on it. And it has helped me through my life. It has helped me stay humble but without putting myself down."

But despite all the talk of humbleness, White eventually became addicted to being interviewed and the attention and the success of his records went to his head. He started to spout what amounted to pretentious nonsense to journalists, who lapped it all up and printed it verbatim, often making him sound arrogant.

Bob Fisher, writing in 'New Musical Express', summed it up when he wrote: "It's sad to see a potentially great artist dragged into a self-induced mire of pretension."

After the Fisher interview, and the article that he realised had more than a grain of truth in it, White stopped talking for a while and focused on his next album, destined to be his greatest. The third solo album, which he would eventually call *Can't Get Enough*, would prove to be the biggest hit of his career.

1974 was the year when Barry White and his team would peak in excellence. Headed by Gene Page, the arranger, it included Jack Perry, Ed Greene on drums, backing singer Tom Brock, engineers Frank Kejmar and Paul Elmore, and the incomparable Ray Parker Jnr.

Parker was typical of the talent White gathered around him in that period. He had come to prominence as a 16-year-old in 1969 as a member of Bohannon's house band at the legendary 20 Grand Detroit nightclub. He then fell in with a group called The Detroit Spinners, whose lead singer, Bobby Smith, was so impressed with Parker's guitar skills that the group asked him to join their touring act.

Through that he came into contact with Marvin Gaye, with whom he recorded and co-wrote some songs. The first No 1 single in which he had a hand was for Honey Cone, an American R&B and soul all-girl group.

In 1972 he went to work for Stevie Wonder on his album *Talking Book*. He was also the lead guitarist for Stevie Wonder as the opening act on The Rolling Stones' American tour of that year.

That led to session work for Holland Dozier & Holland, which is where he first came across Barry White, an association that was to change his life.

Parker was recommended to White by Lamont Dozier. White called him up and he became his life for the next two years. White immediately recognised Parker's supreme talent and couldn't stop talking about him. Word soon got around and he was hired for sessions by most of the greats of the time, including The Carpenters, Aretha Franklin, Bill Withers, The Temptations, Gladys Knight and the Pips, Herbie Hancock, Tina Turner, and Diana Ross. For the next three years his diary was full for every day of the year as his guitar talents were heard on one in every ten hit albums released in America during that period. Eventually word of his talent reached the ears of Clive Davis, and he was signed to the Arista record label as an artist in his own right, and the rest was history. His first single, *Ghostbusters*, went to No 1 all over the world and launched him as a major star.

It was said later that Parker was the man responsible for giving Barry White the extra zest that made him so successful between 1972 and 1975. Certainly he was present on every one of White's biggest successes and White was never as successful again after Parker left to pursue his solo career.

White was extraordinarily lucky to have people like Parker, Page and Kejmar around him in that period, and the tragedy was that he was not able to hang on to Parker for longer, or really to recognise the impact the legendary young guitarist had made on his music.

But that was for later, and in 1974 the team was ready to make history together.

Their confidence was sky high when they all assembled at Whitney Studios in Glendale in early 1974 to record Barry White's seventh album. It was the album that would spawn the biggest-selling single of his life and meant that he would eventually become an everlasting icon.

By then Barry White could afford to hire any studio the team wanted, but he had fallen in love with Whitney's sound and didn't want to record anywhere else, as he explained: "As I told my mother, to know music isn't to write it or read it, it's about feeling it and Whitney was where I felt it."

Greg Williams, one of the session musicians, said that White simply liked the sound that reverberated from the Whitney studio walls: "Barry always started with the drums, that was his foundation, because they held the groove; then the melody, then the lush string arrangements." Like all the musicians at Whitney in that period, Williams was in thrall to Barry White: "I learned a lot from Barry about arranging and I loved the way he would direct Gene on the strings. Not taking anything away from Gene, because he was a genius, but Barry had very definite ideas about what he wanted."

The new album started and finished with an instrumental called *Mellow Mood*, which attempted to harness some of the vibes of *Love's Theme*, but it was a sound-alike composed by White with Tom Brock and Robert Taylor.

The second track was the history-making *You're the First, The Last, My Everything*, followed by the dreamy *I Can't Believe You Love Me*, which White had composed at home at 3 o'clock one morning. Even White's harshest critic, Bob Fisher, liked the song and described it as "an insomniac's daydream" which was high praise from him.

The fourth track was *Can't Get Enough*, regarded by almost everyone in White's team at the time as the album's best track. The song had an unusual gestation, as White revealed: "One beautiful night after I had made love to Glodean I just got out of bed. I'd been married about four months. She went to sleep and I went to the kitchen and wrote me a song called *Can't Get Enough of Your Love*."

In fact, *Can't Get Enough*, with a beautiful string arrangement by Gene Page, was regarded as the song most likely to be a break-out hit and became the first song from the album to be released as a single. It reached the Top 20 in most countries in which it was released and actually topped the Billboard singles chart in America briefly, making it White's second No 1 in America after *Love's Theme*.

It was a sensation, and Jack Perry recalled the effect it had on him when he heard it on the radio for the first time: "I was driving over a bridge in the port of Los Angeles. You're up in the air and you can see the city lights and it's beautiful. I was just coming down the crest of the bridge on the other side when I heard this song on the radio. It was so new and fresh – R&B with pop on top and Latin grooves in between. 'This guy is a genius,' I said to myself."

The fifth and sixth tracks were more dreamy melodies, *Oh Love, Well We Finally Made It* and *I Love You More Than Anything*. These were also White's own compositions and have become enduring White classics.

When the album was finally in the can, the mood was sky-high as White gathered all his men together at his home for a post-production party. Everyone was there, including Larry Nunes, Russ Regan, Gene Page, Jack Perry, Ed Greene, Tom Brock, Frank Kejmar and Ray Parker. It proved to be the last time this crack team would all work together on a White album.

The album sleeve featured five drawings of White by the artist Al Harper in a pastiche of light shining at various angles with added funky graphics. It wasn't one of White's greatest album sleeves, and Bob Fisher called it "Below Barry White's usual standard of kitsch".

Surprisingly the critics didn't particularly like the album when they reviewed it on release. 'Rolling Stone' magazine led the onslaught, even though *Can't Get Enough* was eventually ranked No 281 in its list of the 500 greatest albums of all time. The magazine was faintly dismissive of the Barry White sound and the new album. It said: "White's lush compositions have become dance and make-out standards. Here he has turned out five more in what is now an overly familiar mould. The formula is shimmering pools of violins whipped to a light chop, into which White sinks his leaden vocals, half-spoken, half-sung, always as if from the next pillow. Sometimes it works but the sameness gets oppressive and *I Can't Believe You Love Me*, carried to 10 minutes 23 seconds, is downright numbing. White may be a master of the new black mood music, but he's Xeroxing himself down to a faint, smudgy shadow." 'Rolling Stone' finished the review by calling the album a "boudoir drama".

Barry White wasn't used to his music being described as "downright numbing" and it was not a description his fans recognised. He also didn't like the description "boudoir drama".

He didn't speak to reporters at 'Rolling Stone' for a long time after that. But that publication wasn't alone. Bob Fisher in 'New Musical Express' was very scathing: "On *Can't Get Enough* there's nothing apart from the title track that really stands out – and to make matters worse, the playing time is very short and it's hard to find anything distinguished on the ballad side." Fisher was astonished at the lyrics, called their writer a "one man marriage guidance counsellor" and ridiculed his approach to writing music, although he did admit that the lyricist was "one of the most successful recording artists of the decade, picking up gold discs like other people pick up groceries, who had become prolific to the point of saturation."

Fisher also got personal: "Despite the fact that he looks as though he could stand in for Godzilla, it is as a sex symbol that he seems to score most of his album sales."

Another critic went as far as to say that he thought the release of the new album meant that the Barry White phenomenon was over: "That low sensual growl and those crawling lyrics, the whole concept that he now works in, sounds tired and jaded."

Fortunately other reviewers were a lot kinder. Gene Sculatti wrote: "The songs are written swiftly, arranged deftly and executed with all the dignity and aplomb befitting their intent; aimed like a sweet dagger into the heartland of female radio America, they never fail to connect."

The retrospective 'Allmusic' review called White: "The bedroom alchemist coming up with another solid batch of lush, proto-disco gems." The reviewer also highlighted two other outstanding tracks on the album, *I Can't Believe You Love Me* and *Oh Love, Well We Finally Made It*, which it said "qualify as two of White's most fetching slow burners".

Barbara Salvo, writing in the British music paper 'Melody Maker', said: "His fusion of the traditional orchestra section with a rhythm section playing pop/soul songs shed a new sound on American airwaves. Barry's music has quickly become universal and able to fit into any situation. It is the dinner party music of tomorrow."

The album was unaffected by what the critics had to say and topped the US album charts in all three categories of LP, soul and R&B. Surprisingly it only went to No 4 in Britain, a country where White was arguably more popular than he was in America.

The success of *Can't Get Enough* also revived interest in White's first two albums, *I've Got So Much To Give* and *Stone Gon'*. Both re-entered the charts as people discovered Barry White for the first time. Ed Greene recalled: "When Barry was hot the guys in the band would be so excited to get back into the studio. We were jazzed to be part of that magic. And we fed off the thrill of making great records for Barry. He was a tremendously gifted leader and we wanted him to succeed, so we could keep the magic flowing."

The end of 1974 was one long party and the praise lavished on Barry White from all quarters in those three months he recalled as being "almost embarrassing". As he said: "Lady Music is the one I'm always trying to please. She holds me up, obsesses me and sometimes drives me crazy."

At the end of the year he flew to Japan and when he landed at Narita Airport much to his surprise he was mobbed by waiting fans. On a high throughout the short tour, he was acclaimed wherever he went, so much so that when he landed back in Los Angeles on a Saturday morning his life had changed. In the time he had been away 'Cash Box' magazine and 'Record World' had voted him the No 1 pop and rhythm-and-blues male vocalist of the year. He was mobbed at LAX by huge crowds chanting the lyrics from *You're the First, The Last, My Everything*. At the airport he literally bumped into Stevie Wonder, who was on his way to perform at a concert in New York. White introduced himself and it was quickly obvious that no introduction was necessary and that Stevie Wonder knew all about Barry White. Years later Wonder remembered that meeting at the airport: "I told him I heard his song on the radio and that I really liked the song." The two men got on a like a house on fire immediately and sat on an airport bench chatting, as Wonder recalled: "We talked and laughed and it was a nice meeting. I will always remember that moment and it was very special to me."

And it was not only Stevie Wonder – it seemed that in 1974 the whole world was crazy about Barry White. And it surely was.

This was to lead to trouble as a pirate album emerged containing some Barry White original songs entitled *No Limit On Love*. Its release upset Russ Regan, although it had nothing to do with White or his record company. White consulted his lawyers and racked his brains to try to work out where the songs had come from.

Eventually it emerged that Bob Keane had kept hold of the master tape containing ten unreleased demo songs Barry White had written and recorded at Mustang Bronco Records eight years before, long before he was famous or anyone had heard of him. When White became an international star, Keane recognised that the old tape might have some value and searched through his basement, desperately trying to find it. Eventually he found a dusty old box and there it was. When he played it he realised that the songs were of surprisingly good quality and wondered how he had failed to recognise White's genius all those years before.

Keane sold the master tape to Stan Greenberg's Supremacy label, a subsidiary of Scepter Records, which was run by the legendary Florence Greenberg, Stan's mother. She had founded Scepter in 1957 when, as an ordinary New Jersey housewife, she had inadvertently discovered the Shirelles, four girls who were classmates of her 16-year-old daughter Mary-Jane. She formed her own record label and the rest was history as she launched the careers of Burt Bacharach and Hal David and the likes of Dionne Warwick.

Supremacy decided to release its own Barry White album of 'new' songs. As long as he paid White the standard performer royalty and the publishing royalties, Greenberg was free to do what he liked with the music, much to the chagrin of White and 20th Century Records.

Side one of *No Limit On Love* had six tracks: *I've Got The World To Hold Me Up, Under The Influence Of Love, Your Heart And Soul, Long Black Veil* and *All In The Run Of A Day*. On Side two was *Come On In Love, Fragile – Handle With Care, Out Of The Shadows, Where Can I Turn To* and *I Owe It All To You*.

It was distributed by Bernie Sparago's Springboard International company, which owned an interest in Scepter Records. Stan Greenberg credited himself as the album's overall producer, although Barry White had produced and arranged all the tracks. The backing music was credited to the non-existent Barry White Orchestra, which was really a rag-bag of musicians White had persuaded to come and play for nothing eight years before.

The music was creditable but had none of the finesse of Gene Page and Frank Kejmar. It was pure opportunism but, due to the nature of how the record industry worked, and as long as the proper royalties were paid and recognition given, there was nothing anyone could do about it.

The album sleeve really infuriated Barry White. Dick Smith, a veteran sleeve designer, was hired together with artist Jim O'Connell. Smith hired three lookalikes of Glodean and Linda James and Dede Taylor to pose for a photograph taken by Richard Marx; they held a framed charcoal drawing of White by O'Connell. This drawing and the lookalikes made Barry White doubly furious, and he consulted a lawyer to see if anything could be done to stop it. The lawyer advised him to just ignore it and it would go away. The lawyer was right – White's fans proved very discerning and virtually ignored the album, which predictably went nowhere. It was soon forgotten.

The New York Times capped Barry White's year when an article suggested that he was responsible for the so-called 'baby boom' that was happening. He responded: "Not me personally, but my music."

By this time Barry White was starting to understand the basis for his commercial success – the separate appeals of his music to both men and women. He firmly believed that men and women listened to music differently: "Every man and every woman feels and hears their own thing when they listen to music. Women use the music to get their men to relate to them better, talk to them, tell them what's on their mind."

That separation became the basis for everything he did, as he explained: "Women have special insight that men cannot comprehend. They react sensitively when they hear a chord change or a lyric. They are attracted to pretty things and feel them in a special way. Men on the other hand identify with the delivery of the message. They hear themselves amplified through my voice and my words set to music, music that makes them want to get close to their girls and in the mood to make love."

But he realised that men and women listen together: "My songs deliver the words that lovers may not speak aloud but want to hear themselves say or have said to them. If you love someone you must not be afraid to tell them, to show them and Barry White is the one artist, who actually was in the bedroom with you at your most sacred sensuous moment of your life." Once he understood the blueprint there was no stopping him, and the new *Can't Get Enough* album was about to make him America's biggest-selling singer of 1974.

1974 was a remarkable year for Barry White, the like of which he would never see again. He didn't know it at the time, but *Can't Get Enough* and the two hit singles that came from it represented the very peak of his career.

CHAPTER 33

Two More Orchestrals

Rounding off an extraordinary year

December 1974

Barry White's new fame won him an offer to write the soundtrack for a movie called 'Together Brothers', conceived by 47-year-old director Bill Graham. A well-known television drama director, his TV credits were impressive and included episodes of American dramas such as 'Dr Kildare', 'Ironside' and 'The Fugitive'.

'Together Brothers' was his first proper cinema-release movie; it was a knock-off of 'Shaft', the hit movie of 1971, and sought to cash in on what people called 'black-exploitation' films. 'Shaft' had been a huge success, earning $13 million from a budget of less than a million. But more importantly for White, the soundtrack album had shot to No 1 on the Billboard album chart and the single, *Shaft*, had also gone to No 1 and had won three Grammys for its singer and writer, Isaac Hayes.

Barry White had been most impressed by Bill Graham's 1960 documentary about Leonard Bernstein and the New York Philharmonic Orchestra, based on a concert that Bernstein had performed in Berlin. White worshipped Bernstein, and this convinced him to take the movie assignment when perhaps he should have turned it down. At his first meeting with Graham, White hardly discussed the movie and pumped him for everything he knew about Bernstein.

Despite their vastly different backgrounds and ages, the two men got on well. But the money being offered was very small as the movie's budget was less than $400,000 and the soundtrack represented less than five per cent of that. But the rights to an album were included, and for White that represented another ambition to join the great classical composers who had written film scores. It was also to be filmed at his birthplace in Galveston, Texas, and that resonated heavily with him. So he jumped at the opportunity, especially as the producers paid for the studio time and he saw it as a good vehicle for the newly formed Love Unlimited Orchestra.

In preparation, White and Jack Perry spent a day going around Los Angeles's new and second-hand music stores buying all the film soundtrack albums they could find. Then they shut themselves away in White's house to listen to every one and try to make sense of the project they had taken on. They then wrote the outline score over a period of seven days during the Christmas holiday. However, the project stalled as financing negotiations continued and it almost went into turnaround, but suddenly came alive again and White and Perry were given less than a week's notice to get the music going.

After many late nights they went into a studio for a week with a small orchestra. The movie was projected onto a white wall and they watched the rough cut while putting together the 21 individual tracks of music that would accompany the scenes.

The process created a hotchpot of good and bad music, and many of the tracks are forgettable. Only the grandly titled *People Of Tomorrow Are The Children Of Today* proved to be a classic White orchestral composition that was truly worthy of his name.

Some tracks were sound-alikes of Isaac Hayes's 'Shaft' soundtrack, but not as good. But 'Shaft' was the only reference point White had for the kind of movie that 'Together Brothers' was. Much of the rest of the album is derivative, including recognisable influences from John Williams and Ennio Morricone.

However, Barry White was happy with it at the time: "It was my fastest accomplishment to date but I seemed to work even better under pressure." Stephen Cook's 'Allmusic' review calls it "an appealing and welcome release" benefitting from "solid material throughout". But he also says that the album has "plodding moments", and that it was repetitive.

But overall Cook said the music "reflects White's romantic soul style: ghetto streets flowing with champagne" and "White's spacious and silky arrangements and the Love Unlimited Orchestra's adroit backing are substantial enough to offset the album's weaker moments." The vocal version of *Somebody Is Gonna Off The Man* and the soundtrack's one hit, *Honey, Please Can't You See*, was a 2-minute version that White put on his next album *Stone Gon'* as a 5-minute version; it went to No 44 in the Billboard singles chart 100, and No 6 in the R&B chart.

Some of the tracks, such as *Can't Seem To Find Him*, represent pleasant variations of typical lounge music, an area of music that Barry White visited just this once. There are some excellent arrangements, which Gene Page helped out on, particularly *So Nice To Hear*, which had strong and varied arrangements. Cook called it "an effective three-way collage of funk, noir ambience, and orchestral bombast." He shrewdly concluded that 'Together Brothers' is only for dedicated White fans, and was "respectable" at best.

If White had been given a bigger budget and more time, and could have afforded to use Gene Page, then it could have been a classic, but the combined lack of all three meant that it wasn't. But the album benefitted from the 'Barrymania' that was raging at the time, and went to No 85 in the US album charts and No 15 in the R&B chart.

The movie itself was a turkey, taking a mere $1.1 million at the box office and attracting a lot of criticism. Almost immediately White tried to distance himself from it, saying: "I'm not interested in police chases and guys selling dope on the corner. The only reason I did 'Together Brothers' was because 20th Century led me to believe the movie was important to them, but it really wasn't." But he couldn't resist bigging himself up, adding: "The movie didn't do nothing, but the album went platinum."

In late 1974 another movie project came his way, this time with a starring role and voice-over in a live action/animated film called 'Coonskin'. It was a crime caper and Barry White was approached by director Ralph Bakshi to play two roles, as Sampson in live form and Brother Bear in animated form. His voice featured heavily in the movie, which was about three African-American animal characters, a rabbit, a fox, and a bear, who run an organised crime racket in Harlem.

Why White agreed to appear in what was a very dubious project is uncertain, although it had a serious message that appealed to his sense of justice. The Hollywood Reporter newspaper described it thus: "Ralph Bakshi is against, as this film makes abundantly clear, the cheats, the rip-off artists, the hypocrites, the phonies, the con men, and the organized criminals of this world, regardless of race, colour, or creed."

The movie was damaged when it ran into a barrage of criticism for being racist. The US Congress of Racial Equality (CORE), a radical group, criticised what it called its "racist content", but that didn't stop the New York Times calling it "a masterpiece".

Barry White was lucky to avoid the storm as the characters he played did use words that emphasised "racist references and vulgarity". Eventually he realised that he had been duped and did not realise that he would be playing a cartoon character: "I tried to stop the movie from coming out because of the cartoon parts. I didn't know what the movie was about until I was finished. It's the kind of picture I can't take my kids to, very filthy and vulgar."

CORE was determined not to see the movie succeed and Elaine Parker, chairman of the Harlem division, told Variety magazine that it "depicted us as slaves, hustlers and whores. It's a racist film to me, and very insulting." She then said tellingly: "If it is released, there's no telling what we might do." CORE asked Paramount not to release it, saying that it was "highly objectionable to the black community".

Paramount still wanted to release the movie, but equally it did not want to unleash a racial storm. So it gave the rights back to Bakshi and the producer Albert Ruddy, who got it distributed by Bryanston, which went bust two weeks after its cinematic release. It would be rereleased later, but with White's original words overdubbed with a new script by an actor called Ben Gage. Luckily the controversy did not damage White's street credibility and the movie faded into obscurity and was quickly forgotten.

Incredibly, in the middle of 1974 Barry White and Gene Page got to work on a third Love Unlimited Orchestra album, which they intended to call *White Gold*. The impetus was simply the amount of raw music of a very high standard that White was churning out, with nowhere for it to go. White and Jack Perry spent weeks getting the basics together before calling on the expensive time of Gene Page, who was also very busy. But they realised that Page was the missing ingredient in so much of the music and there was no one like him in the whole of Hollywood.

Interestingly White and Perry conceived the concept for the album cover first. They went to California Jewellers Inc, a store in Beverly Hills, and asked to borrow a selection of very high-value gold items to put together for a photograph for the cover of the album. The highly suspicious jeweller had heard of Barry White but was still not sure that the actual gentleman in his very posh shop was indeed the musician. Eventually White played him an LP in his shop and sang the words, convincing the suspicious jeweller that it was him. But the jeweller was still not very sure about letting White and Perry walk out of his store with $100,000 of gold jewellery. The deal clincher was when White agreed to credit him on the cover of the album, and he was then allowed to leave with the items under his arm.

The jewels were mounted on a set by Glen Ross and Richard Kriegler, who got Ron Slenzak in to do the photography. It was a bit of a lash-up, albeit glitzy, and it worked after a fashion.

Finally, White, Page and Perry, together with engineers Frank Kejmar and Steve Hall, went to Whitney Studios in Glendale together with their 40-piece orchestra to put the album together. They emerged a week later with a master tape.

In truth, *White Gold* was but a shadow of *Rhapsody in White*, which was and is the quintessential orchestral album. But it was still very good, with 11 tracks and more than 40 minutes of music.

Amy Hanson, reviewing it for 'Allmusic', said: "*White Gold* is the band's third 1974 release and, though it cannot eclipse their debut, *Rhapsody in White*, White pulls out the tried-and-true formula across this album, which is loaded with the expected orchestral numbers – heavy on the strings, of course, and interspersed with White's own vocal nuggets. The problem is, however, how many times can this really play out?" Hanson picked out a track called *Satin Soul*, but said the real gem was *Always Thinking Of You*, written by Ray Parker Jnr. She called it "rich, full of life, and a great groove". She also liked *You Make Me Feel Like This (When You Touch Me)*, but called the rest "a throwaway".

White Gold reached No 28 on the US album chart and No 10 on the R&B chart but did not do well internationally, hardly showing up on any of the charts except in Australia, where it got to No 93. Hanson summed up the Love Unlimited Orchestra's contribution to 1974 music very succinctly: "No matter how good or bad, the Love Unlimited Orchestra provided a sound that was integral to the decade and a service to purveyors of shag carpets and crackling fireplaces everywhere."

Ray Parker Jnr, still not 20 when White was having all this success, was amazed: "The Love Unlimited Orchestra was just wonderful for me, this was probably the tightest band I have ever played with before or since because Barry would come in with that attitude and he would already know, he would already have the songs and know how he wanted them to go."

Jack Perry couldn't believe how prolific White was during that period: "The guy used to do three albums at one time. We would be in there for hours. We would start at 10 in the morning and come back out at 2am and come right back the next day at 10am."

White could hardly believe it himself, and was proud of his prodigious output. But some wise heads in the music business were not so sure and thought he was overexposing himself. Bob Fisher, a man who never held back, was heavily critical of White for doing too much during that period, and accused him of continually "rehashing his winning formula". He wrote: "Keeping your name upfront is one thing, but this is ridiculous." He said that White's prolific output in that period had "damaged his artistic credibility … the whole syndrome of sophisticated orchestral soul just can't stand that amount of exposure." He added: "The music has now reached a point where its standing as soul or black music amounts to no more than one of those Joe-Loss-plays-the-hits-of-Motown things."

It was valid criticism, and maybe the albums should have been spread over a wider period. Fisher called it "a suicidal course in market saturation," but did admit that all the albums were "selling like crazy" as indeed they were.

It had all been part of that amazing year called 1974. But perhaps the high point for Barry White was when the great Henry Mancini appeared with his orchestra at the Hollywood Bowl that year. Included in the programme was Mancini's rendition of *Love's Theme*. After it was played, Mancini paid full tribute to White, telling the audience: "Barry's music crosses all barriers of religion and colour and touches the hearts of people everywhere."

When he heard what Mancini had said White was floored – he couldn't quite believe it, but it was also the moment when, as he revealed later, he knew it was "all real".

Up to then it had all seemed like a dream.

But then the dream almost hit the buffers, just as he was working on his fourth solo album to be called *Just Another Way To Say I Love You*. In late 1974 he noticed that he had a sore throat. He often had sore throats, especially after heavy periods of singing, but they quickly went away after a few days of resting his vocal chords. But this one didn't, and after a week he visited a specialist doctor at Cedars-Sinai Hospital. The doctor quickly found the problem: "Mr White, you have polyps growing on your vocal chords. Not a problem, we can remove them, and they probably won't return, but you won't be singing for a couple of months." The specialists told him that there was an 80 per cent chance that they could fix the problem, and if they couldn't his singing career, and possibly his life, would be threatened. The doctors also warned that he would have to change the way he sang and do specific voice exercises for the rest of his life. At the time he had just laid down one of his favourite songs, *Let Me Live My Life Loving You Babe*, and he took it as a sign: "It seemed as if the song had taken on a sacred quality that had to be honoured by my never singing it the way I had recorded it."

It was a scary time, and after the operation White was silent for 30 days, unable to speak. Then, on the 31st day, his voice returned as if it had never gone away. The scare changed his whole approach to life, as he admitted to Marc Eliot in his 1999 memoirs: "Each day that I can sit down and write a song and take to the stage and sing it is one more day I am fortunate to have." He always maintained that his voice was "better than ever" after the operation.

White took all this as a sign and devoted himself to his craft of singing and writing songs. As he said: "I realised there were no guarantees in life of anything."

CHAPTER 34

Just Another Way to Say

Fourth solo album

March 1975

By early 1975 Barry White was at the height of his powers as he began work on his fourth solo album, which would end up being called *Just Another Way To Say I Love You*.

He had become an industry within himself and, between his touring act and his record company, there were 51 full-time people on the Barry White payroll.

Just Another Way to Say was 39 minutes of music that was being eagerly awaited by Barry White fans across America. After originally being promised to fans in time for Christmas, it was finally was released on 25th March 1975, having been delayed because White realised he had set the bar very high.

Can't Get Enough had been so successful that following it up proved much more difficult than he expected. Instead of a month in the recording studio he took three. But the delay did nothing to dampen the ardour of his fans. It was an instant hit and such was his following that devotees were forming queues at some New York record shops on the morning of its release.

White wrote all the songs except track three. It represented a new way of working for him, and the recordings were spread over the three months rather than dedicated sessions. Some of the old crew had departed, particularly Ray Parker Jnr, who was a great loss. But Frank Kejmar and a new young engineer called Steve Hall were on hand, together with Gene Page and Jack Perry.

By now the American public knew what sort of music to expect from Barry White. It was a precise, highly defined formula that was exactly in fashion. And he delivered exactly what they wanted and the album was undeniably strong.

It started off with arguably the weakest track, *Heavenly, That's What You Are To Me*. But its tempo was strong and, despite its perceived weakness at the time, it has endured as a classic White track.

The second track, *I'll Do For You Anything You Want Me To*, at just over five minutes, was immediately recognised as classic Barry White with a strong melody, superb lyrics and a wonderful Gene Page arrangement. It was no surprise that it became the first single to be released from the album, making No 40 on the Billboard singles chart and No 4 on the R&B chart. In the UK it quickly entered the Top 20 at No 20.

All Because Of You was the first slow ballad on the album and it also gradually became a White classic. It was co-written with Frank Wilson and Michael Nunes and had an instrumental introduction that lasted 2½ minutes before it burst into life with somewhat corny lyrics, which was very untypical of Barry White and included the immortal line: "Girl I'm just sitting here and wondering how your love comes down on me like rolling thunder." The lyrical composition was not the greatest of White's career, and some lines made little sense. But in the end the great melody made it all work.

The final track on side one was *Love Serenade*, which completely vanquished the lyrical problems of the previous track and was a homily to lovemaking; it contained the immortal verse: "Baby take it all off, I want you the way you came into the world, I don't wanna feel no clothes, I wanna see no panties and take off that brassiere, my dear." Only Barry White could get away with that.

Side two led off with the second single, *What Am I Gonna Do With You*, a highly commercial track which became White's biggest success of 1975, peaking at No 8 on the Billboard singles chart and No 1 on the R&B specialist chart. In the UK it quickly made the Top 10 and climbed slowly to No 5. One critic wrote: "*What Am I Gonna Do With You* has a simple melodic groove, pounding rhythm section, elaborate arrangement, growling singing, all done in imaginative close harmony and the usual soft-core sex lyrics."

It was followed by one of Barry White's longest-ever tracks, *Let Me Live My Life Loving You Babe*, which one critic called "unbearably pretentious" and "sleep inducing", but perhaps that was the point. Whether that was meant as praise or criticism is uncertain, but the track became an absolute Barry White classic. Another critic said: "Barry White and his band are even more sure of themselves than usual and the music flows endlessly, pushed along by his unlimited confidence."

The title of the song was suggested by Abby Schroeder when she heard White play it at his home during a visit with her husband Aaron. It was also arguably Barry White's favourite song of all, as he said: "It touched me in a very special place. I first heard it in my head all at once in an explosion of violins and rhythm that came together and evoked for me a beautiful woman and a handsome man making love. It had deep chord progressions that gave it a wonderfully elegant sound behind its various melodies."

White also believed that the song reflected his lifelong love for the person he always called 'Lady Music'. As he said in his memoirs many years later: "To me that was the real message of the song, because I did indeed want to spend my life loving Lady Music. To continue to write and perform so that I could see the great melody we call life reflected in the eyes of the people who hear it."

The album closed with a bass-heavy instrumental that was leaden and self-indulgent and bore little relation to Part 1, but at least it was only just over two minutes long. One critic described it as "silly", and they were right.

The album itself topped the R&B albums chart, the fourth in a row to do so, and peaked at No 17 on the Billboard albums chart. It reached No 12 in the UK.

It also proved beyond doubt that long, slow instrumental-dominated tunes would be played on American radio stations, as White pushed that theory to the limit with *Let Me Live My Life Loving You Babe*. One fan, calling into a radio station after a DJ had criticised the album, said it was like an "abstract painting and that it was necessary to step away and absorb the work in its totality to 'get it'." There was something in that, and certainly hundreds of thousands of record buyers did "get it".

Rolling Stone magazine, whose reviews had up to now been very cutting, suddenly turned around. Reviewer John Landau wrote: "Barry White seemed so filled with self-parody at first that it was easy to dismiss him. But it is becoming increasingly obvious with every additional release that he is a very talented man."

Rolling Stone didn't hand out such praise easily, and it was clear that the magazine had been completely won over and was as good as admitting that it had got it wrong in the past, as Landau wrote: "His music feels like the beat of the universe, the perfect tempo." He continued: "His distinction rests with the fact that he is currently one of rock's great bandleaders. At his best, he can perform any song." But White didn't get away scot-free, as the magazine added at the end of its review: "White's talent is limited but undeniable and I find it worth wading through his sillier efforts to get to the more convincing ones."

By mid-1975 the album had once again caught the mood of America. Senator Edward Kennedy had discovered Barry White, and said so when he was interviewed. He revealed that White's music had been on a loop over the speakers on his yacht that summer. Oscar de la Renta told readers of 'People' magazine that he had White's music playing in his shops continually. The contemporary artist of the moment, 29-year-old Jamie Wyeth, revealed that he played nothing else in his studio while he worked and that his wife, Phyllis, a member of the du Pont family who was confined to a wheelchair, also loved it.

To promote the album White, who could not really believe what was happening to him, was interviewed by 'People' magazine and, in a very reflective mood, he called his career a "snowball that just started rolling". He believed his music was unique and said: "I never dreamed I would revolutionise the business." At that time he had every reason to believe that the statement was true, and when the writer from 'People' asked him, "Have you any other unachieved ambitions?" he replied, "I have to be honest and say no."

Deep down inside White was humbled and deeply appreciative of his success. Barely two and a half years before he had been struggling to get by day to day and now every time he received his personal bank statement it showed six zeroes after the number.

Strangely, he found that being rich made him feel uncomfortable and he resolved to put something back into the world.

Right from the start of his success White had been trying to help the black underclass of Los Angeles from which he himself had come just three years before. He chose to go back to his own roots in South Central Los Angeles, where he knew there was still extreme poverty, and resolved to try and help the youth in the ghettos.

More than anyone, White realised that the youth of today are the future of the world tomorrow, as he said in early 1975 in an interview with 'Jet' magazine: "It has been said that if the future generation cannot surpass the current generation then there is no progress."

He also believed that the power of love was motivating him: "You can express love through an understanding of youth that will motivate you to help them." He added: "I just couldn't sit still as a man, as a human being, and not do something to help these young people."

His first move was to stage a special benefit concert at the Shubert Theatre in Los Angeles to raise money for the West Coast National Youth Movement (WCNYM). He had observed the WCNYM doing great work in inner Los Angeles and he was keen to do anything he could do to help: "I look back on my early life in the south-east section of Los Angeles, as compared to where I am now, and see a dedicated group of people such as the West Coast National Youth Movement working hard to overcome and to improve the same type of situation I was faced with growing up and needing help to get their program over."

But his actions were not entirely altruistic. In 1974 White had hired a market research firm to try and find out where and why his music was selling, and was surprised to see a very high percentage of black people buying it. So he hired Warren Lanier Enterprises, a PR firm that specialised in reaching black communities, to find out what percentage of music in Los Angeles was being sold to the black community. The numbers were astounding. He said: "I found a whopping share of record sales are made to these communities."

He urged every record industry executive he met to actively help the ghettos, telling them this was where so much of their music was sold and it was in their interests to help: "I was simply saying to the record company, put some money into the ghetto to show gratefulness to the people who really need it."

He really believed that sales of music in central Los Angeles were ready to explode, as he explained: "We're the only race on this planet that knows how to sing a happy song at bad times and we're the ones buying records. Now take the ghetto people who can't even pay the rent. But they can go out and rip off a record player or a cassette player and buy what they like. It's what they feel inside."

CHAPTER 35

Prolific Producer

Protégés fail to break through

1974

After his first few solo successes, Barry White couldn't wait to get back to what he enjoyed most – producing and recording music for other artists. He realised that he needed to establish his own production company and turned to Russ Regan to finance it. Regan wasn't too delighted to be taking on the financial burden, but White's star was shining so brightly that he had no real choice but to agree to whatever his artist wanted.

So after a bit of argy-bargy, White got Russ Regan's lukewarm backing for his own production company, which he called Soul Unlimited Records (SUR) and which was the fulfilment of all his dreams. It enabled him to do what he liked doing best – promoting and developing the careers of young artists and those of his friends.

It was something that White thought he was very good at it – but in truth he wasn't. In the whole of his career none of the new third party acts he developed and produced ever achieved any real success. There were sporadic achievements but they were only very sporadic and certainly not worth the huge effort he put into it.

Russ Regan was dead against it from the start and wanted him to focus totally on his own career and the Love Unlimited girl group and orchestra, where he was consistently successful. As Regan was always reminding him: "Don't fool with success." But White couldn't help "fooling with success" – it was in his blood. In fact, the more Regan said it, the more White doubled down, determined to prove him wrong.

Barry White was an intensely ambitious man. He was also a generous man and a bountiful man. As soon as he achieved one thing he wanted to move on to the next, and for it to be bigger and better – that was his nature. He wanted to help others achieve success but in the end, almost inevitably, he spread himself too thinly trying to achieve it. He never saw it that way and believed his prodigious output of albums and intense work ethic was a virtue. But in reality it was a burden, and one can only speculate on what he might have achieved personally if he had concentrated just on his own career. But he couldn't help it and he always saw producing, not performing, as his first love.

Years later White admitted that he had tried to do too much in 1975: "Look at my discography and look at the dates of all my releases and you'll say it's impossible for any one human being to write, arrange, produce and sometimes sing all that music so fast."

And in between all this activity in the studio he was also touring. In 1975 alone he visited Europe twice to sell-out crowds.

The biggest problem he faced was finding enough talented artists to develop, as competition for the next big thing was intense. In the end he decided to focus mostly on personal recommendations and the standout people from his own retinue of support artists and musicians.

His first stand-alone artist was a 28-year-old singer from Texas called Gloria Scott. Born in Port Arthur, her mother was a singer and she came from a musical family. She had a great pedigree and in her childhood had sung gospel songs alongside Sam Cooke in their local church. Later she performed as a backing singer for Sly Stone, Johnny Otis, and Ike & Tina Turner. Sly Stone was the first person to spot her potential and she only narrowly missed being selected as a member of Family Stone, his backing group.

Having missed out on that, Scott got together with a group of friends and formed a band called Gloria Scott and the Tonettes. They were good enough for Warner Brothers Music to take an option, pay for studio time to record a single and release it. But it didn't sell and Warners didn't take up its option on the band.

After her two near-misses, Scott was introduced to Barry White by a mutual friend, Sunny Chaney. After listening to her sing, White was impressed and rashly signed her to a seven-year contract that called for her to record two albums a year.

Everyone was optimistic about Gloria Scott's future except Russ Regan. He turned down the chance to release her first album and wouldn't change his mind – and this time he was right.

Scott was bitterly disappointed, but White explained his own experiences with Regan and told her it was a "badge of honour to be turned down by Russ". He took the tapes to Neil Bogart's newly formed label Casablanca Records, which was more desperate for material, and Bogart didn't hesitate.

The first album was called *What Am I Gonna Do*, and White worked on it in the studio with his young protégé Tom Brock. Brock wrote most of the songs and Gene Page and Frank Kejmar arranged and engineered the album.

But there was no standout song and the album was just not good enough. No one could deny Gloria Scott's talent as a singer, but she lacked something indefinable, something that no one could quite put their finger on.

When he listened to the tapes, in his heart Barry White knew that Russ Regan had been right in his assessment. But he passed the final cuts for production, feeling powerless to do anything about it. He just wasn't experienced enough as a producer to see how to fix it.

There was another problem. Unlike his other artists, White never 'connected' with Scott, so they never really communicated in the studio, a vital ingredient in musical success. The best producers really connect with their artists and look for certain things in a song – the intonation, the pocket and the climax. In the studio, making a hit record is all about creating harmonies, stacking vocals, and creating thirds and fifths to match the chords of a song. But White didn't have the breadth of technical knowledge required to bring out the best in Gloria Scott. He knew instinctively how to bring out the best in himself, Glodean, Linda and Dede, and his orchestra, but was lost with Scott. A good producer knows to look for it and how to ask for it, as Gene Page said: "It's all about enunciation and rhythm patterns." It just wasn't there with Scott.

Two singles were released from the album, the title track, *What Am I Gonna Do*, and a second track called *Help Me Get Off This Merry-Go-Round*, a melodic ballad written by Tom Brock and Robert Relf. Both were competent recordings but in truth they were too formulaic, which was also the case with the remaining seven tracks. Unsurprisingly sales were poor.

Scott recorded a second album, but after the poor sales of the first there was no enthusiasm at Casablanca to release it. But there was one standout song that Neil Bogart agreed to release as a single, *Just As Long As We're Together (In My Life There Will Never Be Another)*, which had been written by Barry White with Frank and Vance Wilson specifically for Scott. Bogart's instincts were good and it was a Top 20 hit in early 1975. But despite that success he still wouldn't release the album and it was put on the shelf.

And that was that as far as Gloria Scott's mainstream career was concerned, and she sat out the remaining six years of her seven-year recording contract, drawing a salary from Soul Unlimited Records and waiting for another break.

Barry White was just too busy during those years to put in the sort of effort he knew would be necessary to turn Scott into a star. She became bitter and inevitably blamed him for her lack of success. She became the 'nearly girl' of pop music and wherever she went, whatever she did, she was never quite good enough. She was also desperate to record the songs she had written herself, but none of them were thought good enough and, as Gene Page recalled, "She never got that."

Page was adamant that Gloria Scott was very lucky to have worked with Barry White: "Barry added a very great deal to whatever he did personally. He was the driving force and it's just the combination of him with the string arrangements, which I come up with, that makes for the hits."

It just didn't work for Gloria Scott.

Recalling her predicament years later, Scott said of her association with the maestro: "I don't even think he listened to my music. All the songs were written by other writers in the Soul Unlimited company. They were good songs and I just sat around for six years." She was unable to hide the bitterness: "It was horrible and very frustrating. It was supposed to be two albums a year and we did record another album that wasn't released. He did not live up to the contract. I got kind of angry. I got bitter but it didn't do any good."

Jack Perry was very disappointed when Scott's career stalled, and he didn't know why. He said, "She was simply a great singer."

Subsequently Scott softened her attitude, admitting that her music had benefitted greatly from the magic touch of Barry White. But ultimately she was another singer who believed that the music she wrote was superior – and nobody agreed. She said: "I think I had a lot of good songs of my own at that time but I just went with what he chose."

The ultimate destiny of the second album was always something of a mystery and the master tape was lost to history. "All the tracks were cut," she said, "but never saw the light of day. I'll never know why."

Many years later one of the tracks surfaced as *I've Got To Have All Of You* on a posthumous Barry White multi-CD album called *Unlimited*, put together by Jack Perry. It was arguably the best work Scott ever did.

Ultimately Scott enjoyed success in Germany, which took her music to heart, and now she regularly performs in Europe. Her one and only album now sells for well over $100 in second-hand record shops and on eBay.

Undaunted by Gloria Scott's failure to break out, White's next artist was 32-year-old Tom Brock, an American soul singer also from Texas. His real name was Tom Brocker, but White got him to shorten it to make it "more friendly". The two men had met when White was just a struggling hopeful and he had bonded with Brock, who became a permanent member of his studio production team, a role that would later be described as a 'hanger-on' in the music industry. But Brock 'hung-on' long enough to prove his worth and was a key member of the team that worked hard to turn Gloria Scott into a star. Then it was his turn.

Like Scott, he also only released one album, *I Love You More And More*, which was produced by White and Gene Page. And like Scott he only got one shot at fame, but ultimately proved to be not quite good enough.

The title track, *I Love You More And More*, was arguably the best piece of music on the album, but Brock didn't have the musical range to be a successful solo artist, as Jack Perry recalled: "*I Love You More And More* was a Barry White groove without Barry White singing. Brock was an awesome talent who made classy records with Barry and he became part of our Soul Unlimited production team after years of working his way around California."

The album produced two singles, the title track and *If We Don't Make It Nobody Can*. But neither could break through into the charts. The truth was that the Brock album suffered, like the Scott album, from being sound-alike and formulaic.

A few years later one of the other tracks on the album, *Have a Nice Weekend Baby*, became something of a cult classic and a popular disco hit in Jamaica, as Jack Perry recalled: "The song was a sleeper from Tom's album and DJs played it every night in Jamaica."

It was also covered by another Soul Unlimited band called West Wing. They were another Barry White failure, and their first attempt, a single called *Falling*

In Love Is A No-No, went nowhere. West Wing then recorded an album called simply *West Wing* and surprisingly Russ Regan liked it and agreed to release it on the 20th Century label. *Falling In Love Is A No-No* wasn't deemed good enough to be included, the album sold very few copies, and the group drifted into obscurity to make it three failures in a row for White's new production company.

Ever since they had met, Barry White had urged Gene Page to do an album of instrumentals under his own name. But, like White, Page was a reluctant performer, preferring to remain behind the scenes. Finally, however, once he had enough songs, Page was persuaded to release an album called *Hot City*, which was quickly picked up by the Atlantic label, as Jack Perry recalled: "Gene got known outside the musicians' world because of Barry's hits and when he was signed for his own album on Atlantic, Barry produced it."

Gene Page remembered: "It was actually the suggestion of Barry and my brother Billy that I do an album. Barry just said he wanted to do an album with me. Naturally, I was very excited and after we'd signed with Atlantic, we began working on material that he'd written and that I'd written."

It was a success, and a single taken from it, *Satin Soul*, entered the Top 10 of the most played disco records of 1974. Barry White loved it and recalled: "I could do anything on this album with Gene that my imagination allowed." Page returned the compliment: "Barry is the most generous person I've ever worked with and when we work it's just like a party." The *Hot City* album became White's most successful third party project.

There was also a lot of activity with Barry White's old friend Earl Nelson, who became a constant figure in his world in the 1970s. Nelson was a talented performer and songwriter with a long history in the record business. In 1974 the two got together to produce an album called *Come On In Love*, which found a home at Warner Brothers Music. Nelson performed under the pseudonym Jay Dee, and the album enjoyed some sales success. Five of the nine tracks were written by Barry White with help from his friends, and Nelson and White had a great time in the studio putting it all altogether. Their combined talents gelled to produce some generally great but inconsistent music.

The best piece on the album was called *You've Changed*. This haunting song, originally written by Bill Carey and Carl Fischer, was sung beautifully by Nelson after White had completely rearranged it and almost recomposed the beautiful melody. It showed off White's talent in a way that no one thought possible and exposed a side of him previously unseen. In different times it might have been a huge hit, but it got lost in the moment.

Years later, Jack Perry chose to include it in the posthumous Barry White multiple CD *Unlimited*. Perry explained: "Like he did with Billy Joel, Barry reinvented this standard tune. The anticipation from the intro is classic and Earl's singing is monumental. The ending is typical of Barry's musical intelligence; you expect a big finish, but instead the fade goes on forever. It's like a dream."

Track three on side two was called *Your Sweetness Is My Weakness*. Later White rearranged the track and turned it into a White classic that sounded entirely different from Earl Nelson's version.

Come On In Love was probably the best third party album Barry White produced, and Earl Nelson was probably the most talented third party artist that White ever worked with.

But it was to prove Soul Unlimited Records' swansong. White knocked the company on the head in late 1975 when he finally realised how much it was costing him. A few million dollars had flowed out of the door to achieve very little.

Russ Regan and Barry White split the cost between them. White could easily afford it, but he blamed his two joint managers, George Greiff and Sid Garris, for the losses. As a result he parted company with them at the end of that year, although Garris continued to conduct the Love Unlimited Orchestra at live performances.

Four years later White would forget all his troubles and try again to recreate Soul Unlimited in the guise of Unlimited Gold.

It was to prove no more successful.

CHAPTER 36

Larry Nunes Retires

Barry's mentor is ruined

December 1974

It is no exaggeration to say that without Larry Nunes there would have been no Barry White. Nunes rescued him from obscurity in 1972 and nurtured his career until he could stand on his own two feet and no longer needed his support.

The two men had first got to know each other nine years before in 1965. Over the following years they built a relationship that would eventually lead to the creation of Barry White as a singing superstar.

Larry Nunes had started out in the music industry in 1950 when he was 20 years old. From nothing he built a fortune, thought to be as much as $20 million, from a retail system he invented called 'rack jobbing'. It was an integrated service that extended music retailing into outlets that didn't usually handle it.

The company he founded was called Tip-Top Record Services Inc and eventually it grew to account for half of all the unit sales of music sold across America. Massive volumes of records and tapes went through Tip-Top's 16 warehouses and at the company's peak 200 warehousemen were employed despatching thousands of parcels to shops across America every day. It was a huge operation.

Nunes was ahead of his time as a businessman and he was the first to introduce mass-marketing techniques to retailers. Tip-Top was also one of the first warehouse distributors to fully computerise its operations.

Outside business, Larry Nunes was a devoted family man who had married young and had five children who in 1973 were aged between 11 and 19. His wealth allowed him to live in grand style in a huge mansion in Sherman Oaks.

Nunes was regarded as one of the top salesmen in the music business and one of its hardest-working executives, but he always operated in the shadows and was never the public face of any of his companies. This led to plenty of rumours inside the industry that he was connected to the Mafia. But the truth was less interesting. He was just media-shy and hated his photo being taken or seeing himself written about. It is said that he employed a public relations man to keep his name out of the press and he told friends that he neither craved public attention nor sought it. He owned lots of record companies, including Mustang Bronco, but no one had any idea that he was the ultimate boss.

That all changed when he merged his companies with Transcontinental Investing Corporation (TIC), which bought Tip-Top Record Services and all his other businesses for a rumoured $15 million in shares at the very end of 1967. Transcontinental, known in the business as Transcon, was one of the first music conglomerates that thrived in the sixties and seventies. The original business had been started by Bob Lifton in 1961, and he had gradually merged his business with those of the other co-founders under the Transcon banner. All the founders had swapped their shares for TIC shares and Transcon ended up as a very powerful organisation quoted on the American Stock Exchange.

The merger effectively brought all of Larry Nunes's music interests under one banner together with those of the co-founders, Bob Lifton, Howard Weingrow, the Freedman brothers and Charles Schlang.

After Nunes came aboard, Transcon, run day-to-day by Bob Lifton, went on an acquisition spree, buying other related businesses for cash or shares or a combination of both. It grew very quickly as it integrated the companies it bought into its various divisions. It also fully computerised the newly acquired businesses, creating huge efficiencies, cost savings and synergies.

But Transcon was more than racking and distribution. It had subsidiaries in recording, promotions, events and publishing. Among the industry veterans who had sold their businesses to Transcon and had gone to work for it were Mike Curb, Jim Guercio, Joe Levine and Art Resnick.

Officially Larry Nunes was just a senior vice-president of Transcon and that was the way he liked it. But beneath all the success, Larry Nunes nursed a very dark secret. He was a compulsive high-stakes gambler, and thought nothing of dropping a million dollars over a weekend in his favourite haunts in Las Vegas or Atlantic City.

Eventually this gambling habit, which he could not shake off, left him very poor indeed. Virtually the whole of his $20 million fortune was frittered away on the gambling tables of Las Vegas. In one terrible period in the early 1970s he lost a staggering $4.5 million over a single weekend. And the problem was worse than it looked. Not only had Nunes gambled away his own money, but he had also gambled away the money he owed to the US Internal Revenue.

He quickly realised it was over for him at TIC when he went to his co-directors and asked for help, and was refused. By then every share he owned in the company had been sold or pledged. He was aware that possible bankruptcy beckoned and his position would be untenable once he was made bankrupt. Things came to a head when he sold his last share in TIC, and his partners, realising that his problems were terminal, showed him the door in 1974. At 44 the great Larry Nunes was broken by a gambling addiction.

Barry White had no idea that there was a problem until Nunes paid a surprise visit to his house one weekend. After a few pleasantries, Nunes opened the conversation saying: "I've got to talk to you Barry – I want to retire."

When he heard that, White almost had to pick himself up off the floor. After all, Nunes was only in his mid-forties. He replied: "Why, man, we're on top of the world. We've got it all, Larry – why would you want to walk away from that?"

Nunes answered: "Because I am ashamed." Nunes confessed to White that he had been a secret gambler for 22 years and now everything was gone and he owed millions more to the American taxman that he couldn't pay. He told White that his gambling habit had "eaten him alive".

Apparently Nunes hadn't paid a tax bill for all of that time, and now the day of judgement had come. Eventually Nunes got to the point and asked White for a gift of $100,000 so he could retire. The tax problem would be solved by a personal bankruptcy, but this was his day of reckoning.

White was as shocked as he had ever been in his life. He thought to himself: "This is Larry Nunes, the man who gave me my big break in music and is now sitting in my house asking me for one hundred thousand dollars so that he could afford to retire."

It was a difficult moment as the master-pupil relationship was suddenly and brutally disrupted. After a few moments' thought, White told Nunes not to worry as he would make it happen. As Nunes got up to leave, an emotional Barry White grabbed him and bear-hugged him. In a flood of tears he told

Nunes: "Larry, everything I have I owe to you and everything I have is yours – I will make this right."

The following morning White asked Russ Regan to attend a meeting at the offices of Nunes's private company, Mo Soul Productions. Regan arrived with his team of executives, expecting a difficult negotiation on a contract extension. Instead they were met by White on his own with the news of Nunes's retirement. Without revealing the sordid details, he told Regan and his team that he wanted 20th to pay Nunes $100,000 as a retirement gift.

The request was greeted by silence, then White noticed a distinct shuffling of feet under the table. He had expected an immediate resolution and the $100,000 to be offered straight away, so was surprised and somewhat disgusted when it wasn't. He didn't like this reaction and after a few seconds he apologised and said he had misspoken and Nunes would like $1 million as his retirement package.

Eventually Regan agreed to pay Nunes $1 million, albeit at the cost of extending White's contract out into the future. Effectively White had paid the $1 million to Nunes himself from his future advances.

But Nunes's tax problems meant that the money was in danger of being seized by his creditors, namely the IRS. So he asked White to buy the mansion in Sherman Oaks, which he did for $280,000, the sum being paid to Nunes's wife, which solved most of the family's problems. The house was much too big for Nunes and his wife now that their children were grown up and had flown the nest. White bought another smaller house for the couple to live in next door.

The purchase of Nunes's house was not entirely altruistic as White had long admired the Sherman Oaks mansion and decided to make it his new family home. He also separately bought all the land that stood between the mansion and Nunes's new house so that they were effectively joined. Nunes lived quietly on top of the hill and the two men played backgammon every afternoon.

Nunes later came clean to his wife and told her what had happened. He handed responsibility for his financial affairs to her as they moved to their new home.

Nunes was true to his world and did retire with his modest nest-egg, enjoying his time with his now grown-up family. He ceased to be Barry White's manager and the business duties were transferred to Abby Schroeder, while his personal management was taken over by Ned Shankman.

These enforced changes rocked Barry White to his core. It was the end of an era. The events of the last few months of 1974 were very difficult for him to bear and hit him very hard. Nunes was his closest friend, his creator and his manager, and his forced retirement left White shocked at the suddenness and unexpectedness of his friend's change in fortune. One minute he was there, a larger-than-life figure in Barry White's world, and the next he was gone. It caused White to do some very deep soul-searching, questioning his own success and whether it could be sustained.

At the end of the process he concluded that it could, and vowed not to let it change his life.

CHAPTER 37

Barry Builds Barryland

Move to dream house in Sherman Oaks

1975

As soon as Barry White bought Larry Nunes's Hollywood mansion in 1974, he called in the builders. Even though Nunes's house was a proper Hollywood mansion and in great condition, White envisaged something even grander for himself and his family.

White had fallen in love with the house when he had stayed there in the early seventies and Nunes had lent him his guesthouse, situated in the grounds, when he was down on his luck. It was there that he had received the infamous 'changed-my-mind' phone call from Russ Regan and where he had first made love to his wife, Glodean.

Sherman Oaks, situated in the San Fernando Valley, was exactly the sort of neighbourhood where Barry White wanted to live. It was private but accessible and very handy for his children's schools. The area had come into being in 1927, named after its founder, General Moses Sherman. He was a director and shareholder of the Los Angeles Suburban Homes Company (LASHC), which bought up the land and built the first houses and shops. Sherman was also a partner in the Los Angeles Pacific Railroad and made a fortune by having an early 'heads up' on where the railroad was headed for next. He bought up land first, then watched its price skyrocket in value when an announcement was made about the new railway line.

Sherman's LASHC bought 1,000 acres of land and divided it up into one acre plots. In 1927 it sold off each plot it did not want for $780 and built spec houses on the rest.

Sherman Oaks grew to be one of the most prosperous areas of greater Los Angeles, covering nine square miles, and by 1974 it had a population of around 38,000 people living in 17,000 homes.

The neighbourhood included a portion of the Santa Monica Mountains, which gave Sherman Oaks a lower population density than other regions in

Greater Los Angeles. There were only 3,300 people per square mile and the average household size of two was amongst the lowest. It became popular with divorcees, although no one really knew why.

The neighbourhood was 82 per cent white, and contained a surprisingly high number of people born in Iran. They had moved there in great numbers in the early seventies before the Shah of Iran was deposed in 1979. Altogether more than 3,500 Iranians lived happily there and it was constantly rumoured that Ayatollah Khomeini's hitmen were roaming the streets looking for exiles on their 'marked lists'. No one knows how long they stayed and whether they found any.

Barry White's new house occupied two of those original acres and had been much modified since it was built in the early 1930s. Larry Nunes had bought it in 1965 for $80,000 after he had sold his record business to the giant Transcontinental Investment Corporation for a rumoured $15 million. Flush with cash, Nunes spent twice as much as he paid for it doing up the house. Ten years later White paid Nunes $280,000 for the whole plot, which included three other smaller houses.

White's first move was to commission a huge extension, which increased the number of rooms in the main house from 21 to 28. When the extension was finished, the Whites moved into it while the builders refurbished the rest of the house. He also commissioned a big extension to the original guesthouse, and expanded it to be able to accommodate ten guests at a time, as well as a second swimming pool for the exclusive use of his guests.

He had taken over Larry Nunes's staff when he bought the house and recruited more, as he explained: "I have a big home and eight people working for me. I have two cleaners, two cooks, a butler and a waiter and so on." He made sure his family and any guests who were staying at the time never wanted for anything.

While this was going on Barry White worked with landscapers and another building firm to create his dream garden. And what a garden it turned out to be! Jack Perry described it as a "huge complex" rather than a backyard.

The grounds were transformed into a mini-wonderland for his children. The centrepiece was a huge circular swimming pool with a pool house that was said to be one of the most luxurious in the whole of Los Angeles. The

Olympic-sized pool was specially lit, with a rock waterfall above it. It was heated to 35 degrees and cost more than $100 a week in electricity to keep it at that temperature.

The waterfall was surrounded by its own intimate tropical garden, which he designed himself. He loved his garden, which was lush with grass and exotic plants that thrived in the climate. "I love just sitting outside quietly with nobody around. Nobody but me and nature."

Jack Perry remembered: "The garden was unbelievable. He'd landscaped it himself to be a tropical Garden of Eden, with a pool and even a waterfall." Perry remembers many a happy day sitting by the pool with White's other great friend and collaborator Frank Wilson, writing songs and lyrics for presentation to the maestro, most of which were rejected as not being good enough. Perry says: "At that time I practically lived in the house. I had my own office there and did marketing and odd jobs, as well as writing songs with Barry."

In 1979 White built a proper tennis court and a separate badminton court.

Outside was a small compound filled with bird cages where the Whites indulged a hobby of collecting rare birds of South American origin. White told a reporter from 'Ebony' magazine that the fish and birds he kept at home represented two parts of a "trilogy of life" that fascinated him and his wife, representing water, air and earth, which the world was made up of; the birds represented the air, the fish the sea and horses the earth. He said: "You see so much of the very essence of life in those three things."

The existing interiors of the original house were all changed to suit Glodean's taste. White called his new house "blue heaven", and inside there was a 'blue' theme running throughout. He told reporters who visited that blue was the colour of "his moment". The house had three hues of blue: a navy shade he called "deep", a royal shade he called "passionate", and a soft blue he called "baby blue". Drapes, wallpaper, sofas, carpets and furnishings were all co-ordinated in the various blues.

A white grand piano sat in the main living room and over it was a huge glass chandelier. The top of the piano and every other flat surface were lined with family photos, all with chrome frames.

Many people might have viewed the master bedroom as gaudy, but it was perfectly coordinated in the three blues down to a silver hue to the blue tinted wallpaper. The bedroom also contained a rare bird in a gilded cage and a very sophisticated electronic box by the bedside that controlled every function of the room from the curtains to the lighting. The bedroom opened up through French windows into the garden

But White's pride and joy was his saltwater fish tank. Built into the walls, it contained 500 gallons of water. "I love that," he said. "I love watching my fish. I can sit and do that for eight hours straight."

It was a short walk from the pool to the stand-alone recording studio in the garden, which was equipped with all the latest equipment including the latest multi-track mixing board, which Jack Perry swooned over.

White named the recording studio R.I.S.E. Laboratories ('Recording In Sound Excellence'), and it became a profit centre in its own right, being hired out to record companies whenever possible.

White said only half-jokingly to a reporter from 'Ebony': "This is my kingdom and this is where I reign. I often sit in here for nine or ten hours straight." When asked if all the material things wealth and success had given him had made him happy, he answered: "Money will just buy you a little more happiness, a few more fish, a few more birds and another horse or two."

It summed up his life at the time.

But as much as he made it his home, he found that it was as if his great friend Larry Nunes was still there, as he admitted: "As much as we made it our own, I always felt in some ways like a fortunate caretaker. It was a good feeling to know that Larry Nunes had raised his kids in this house and now I was going to raise mine there as well."

CHAPTER 38

Money and Horses

All to play for

1975

Midway through 1975, Barry White finally realised that he was doing too much and there was a real danger of burnout. He also noticed that the quality of the music was suffering. His record sales had peaked at the end of 1974 and were now on the decline. His fourth solo album, *Just Another Way To Say I Love You*, had been nowhere near as successful as the previous three, although it was still a big hit.

It was also apparent that success had gone to his head and his ego was growing disproportionately to his falling record sales. Despite his street smarts and personal savvy, he found he was not immune to the flattery and the praise that was spread liberally around him. It was a fate suffered by everyone who was successful in Hollywood. He thought he could resist the 'bullshit', but belatedly found that he was just as vulnerable as everyone else. And even more disturbingly, he found that there was nothing he could do to counter its negative effects.

As a result he lost touch with the realities of the music business and came to the conclusion that the declining sales of his albums were someone else's fault – namely his record company.

Even if in his heart of hearts he knew that wasn't true, deep down he suspected that music fashions might be changing, as he told 'Jet' magazine at the time: "Soul music is going to die out. Black producers and songwriters are not just writing the blues anymore. What's going on is they're incorporating beautiful string arrangements, that's not really soul music." But he reiterated that it was just history repeating itself, as it had in the music business ever since the stylus had been invented: "Take the sounds of the 1960s and the sounds of today – say, The Stylistics – and you can see the music now has a very classy feel." It was certainly true of his own music, which had evolved over the three years since he had first broken through.

White also did the other thing that artists do when faced with decreasing interest in their work – he blamed the marketing. But the truth was that the marketing was good and 20th Century Records was putting a huge effort behind all his album releases.

Disregarding that, White decided to put the pressure on the label to do better. He took a big risk and demanded that a huge marketing effort be put behind his next solo album, *Let The Music Play*, Love Unlimited Orchestra's new release *My Sweet Summer Suite* and Love Unlimited's *He's All I've Got*. He particularly felt that the three girls could achieve a real breakthrough with more money behind them, as he explained: "We'd never been able to cross over Love Unlimited onto the pop charts and I wanted it to happen."

Russ Regan listened as politely as he could as White laid out his plans in the 20th Century boardroom. Then he decided to be frank. He told White bluntly that there was no more they could do. He showed him the figures and how much cash was already being spent. Regan told him: "It's a truism of the music business that more marketing often means less sell-through."

But by now White's arrogance and his opinion of his own ability had reached dizzy heights, and he told Regan that he didn't believe him. He said: "I'll promote the albums myself."

White told Regan that he wanted a person-to-person meeting with Dennis Stanfill, the 49-year-old head of the 20th Century Fox parent organisation. Regan was flabbergasted and said, "Whoa boy, Dennis doesn't do meetings like this with the talent."

White replied, "He'll do one with me."

Regan just let out a long whistle and said: "OK, Barry boy, I'll set it up, but don't say I didn't warn you."

Stanfill was a formidable character. A Rhodes Scholar, he had risen to the top of 20th Century Fox in 1971, just two years after he had joined as head of finance. His two previous jobs had been investment banking at Lehman Brothers and as a vice-president of finance at the giant US publisher Times Mirror.

Fox had been facing bankruptcy when Stanfill arrived to take charge, but he had quickly revived the studio, so much so that he took it from a stock market value of $40 million when he arrived to $800 million when he left ten years later.

A face-to-face meeting with Stanfill was difficult for even Regan to arrange for himself, let alone an artist who Stanfill hardly knew. Regan told White he would get back to him about it.

But White took matters into his own hands, and sent Stanfill a telegram. A month went by and Stanfill didn't respond. White sent a second telegram and still heard nothing.

It was clear that Stanfill did not want to get involved in the creative process at any of the Fox companies. His talent was finance and administration, and he knew it. Unlike many top Hollywood executives, who were starstruck and loved mixing with the talent, he was savvy enough to know it was not for him.

White was riding so high in 1975 that he believed he was a master of the universe and was not going to be ignored by a suit like Dennis Stanfill. So he sent him a third telegram, this time specifically demanding $1 million to promote his next album. He wrote that he wanted Stanfill to hand it to him personally at a meeting in the 20th Century Fox boardroom. This third telegram was an act of extreme arrogance, challenging Stanfill to keep ignoring him at his peril.

While all this was going on, Russ Regan became distressed at a situation that was rapidly in danger of running out of control. So he took matters into his own hands to try and avoid the showdown he could see was coming between Barry White and Dennis Stanfill.

Regan was under pressure. White's output was so prolific that his multi-album deal would soon be exhausted and he would be free to walk away from his contract within a year. Although his sales were declining, every album went gold, earning 20th Century Records enormous profits. Regan knew more than anyone that, without Barry White, 20th Century was an empty shell.

So Regan went directly to Stanfill and the 20th Century Fox board and got White his million dollars. The ease with which the board of directors handed over the cash emboldened White, and he told Regan that he had made a mistake and wanted $2.5 million. He sent Stanfill another telegram to tell him so. Stanfill read this as meaning that White wanted to get out of the contract. So this time Stanfill didn't ignore it. He called him up personally and said: "I'm sorry I took so long to get back to you, Barry, but I've been kind of busy."

White wasn't impressed, as he told Marc Eliot in his 1999 memoirs: "What angered me so much was the sheer arrogance – I was after all the biggest-selling artist on the label." It was true that between Love Unlimited, the Love Unlimited Orchestra and his solo efforts he was generating about $36 million a year in revenue for the label: "Here I was trying to make them even more money by helping to ensure that the new albums crossed over, and yet I was still a nigger to this white man. This wasn't only about money but also respect. It was a war I felt I couldn't afford to lose."

A meeting was quickly arranged. White took the meeting very seriously and prepared for it carefully. He decided to take all his advisers with him, including Larry Thompson, his lawyer, his then managers, Sid Garris and George Greiff, his accountants, Eli Boyer and Laurie Fernandez, and business managers Abby and Aaron Schroeder. All eight of them met at Sherman Oaks beforehand and travelled over to 20th Century's Hollywood offices together in a minibus that White had hired for the day.

Just before they left, White went to his bedroom closet, took his .357 calibre Magnum handgun from the top drawer and put it in his inside coat pocket.

When he came out, only Aaron Schroeder noticed the bulge in his coat and guessed what was causing it. Schroeder said nothing, but wondered to himself what they had let themselves in for that Friday afternoon. He thought to himself: "Maybe Barry's going to hold Stanfill up."

As they chatted on the way over in the bus, they were all confident that they would be returning with a cheque for $2.5 million.

When they got there they were immediately shown to the boardroom where Russ Regan and some executives from the record label were waiting. But there was no sign of Stanfill. A few minutes later he breezed in and immediately greeted Larry Thompson, who he already knew, warmly. But that was it. He sat down and looked at Regan to lead off the meeting.

White was stunned when Stanfill didn't greet them individually and introduce himself, and was immediately seething at this perceived insult.

Suddenly he took his .357 Magnum out of his pocket and laid it on the table in front of him. There was an audible intake of breath from everyone present, including Stanfill, who thought he had seen everything in Hollywood but was certainly not used to guns being drawn at his meetings. But White didn't care.

He was furious and thought to himself: "If you're going to treat me like a nigger I'm going to put on a real 'ghetto gang-banger' show for you."

As everyone else appeared speechless, White decided to speak first: "Well, Mr Stanfill, I feel that we needed to have this meeting because there has been a little disrespect here." As he spoke he ran his fingers up and down the gun resting on the table.

Seeking to remove some of the tension from the room, Stanfill replied softly: "Mr White, please call me Dennis." This only seemed to make White angrier and he said: "Well, all right, Dennis" and repeated what he had said.

By now Stanfill had regained his composure and sought the high ground: "Barry, what's the problem? You've got the million dollars, what's the next thing on your agenda?"

White replied: "Dennis, it's not a million anymore, I thought you knew that."

Looking over at Regan, Stanfill said: "Well, how much is it?"

White said triumphantly: "Its $2.5 million," adding by way of explanation, "because you've been so disrespectful."

By now Stanfill had had enough of Barry White and refused to respond. He turned around and addressed Larry Thompson directly: "Larry, tell Mr White I'm not going to do that. I'm not going to pay $2.5 million. I've already got $1 million approved by the board and I'm not going back to them as it will look like I don't know what I'm doing."

He turned round to face White again, pointing his finger in his face and saying: "That's my positon and it's not going to change."

Russ Regan winced – he couldn't take his eyes away from Barry White's gun laying on the table. Thirty seconds passed and no one said anything.

Then White suddenly exploded, shouting at Stanfill, "Get your finger out of my fucking face!" as he grabbed for his gun.

Russ Regan made to dive under the table, but before he could look up White had stuck the gun in his trouser belt, shouting: "You better worry about your next record, Dennis."

With that he turned to leave.

White walked slowly down the office stairs rather than take the elevator, then walked as slowly as he could through the Fox backlot towards the waiting minibus. He already knew he had overplayed his hand. Either Russ Regan would come running after him to say that he could have the $2.5 million, or Barry White was in big trouble without a record company to release his next three albums.

White was almost back to the bus when he heard hurried footsteps kicking up the dust behind him. To his intense surprise he saw that it was the 20th Century Fox chairman of the board running after him. When he was within earshot, Stanfill shouted, "Barry, come back."

White pretended not to hear him and carried on walking "slowly" as he later described it.

By then White knew he had won: "The whole thing was playing out like a movie but without the cameras running. Only this was for real, no camera running, just the real time clock of my life." He said many years later: "I knew that if I got in my car that was the end of my association with 20th, which was something neither myself nor the label could afford."

Stanfill cried out: "Barry, wait a minute! Let's talk – what is it you want?"

White turned over his shoulder and said: "I told you – I want $2.5 million to spend on new promotion and sales staff so I can make sure my records get the exposure your people haven't been able to provide."

Stanfill stood still and simply said: "I'll get you everything you want, now come back and have a cup of coffee. My secretary has bought some cakes."

The mention of coffee and cakes caused White to smile. Stanfill had hit his first correct note. He put his arm round Stanfill and whispered in his ear: "Thank you, Dennis."

The two walked back arm-in-arm through the backlot. A relieved Stanfill told him: "Believe me, Barry, everything is going to be fine."

When they got back to the office, the coffee and cakes were all laid out but no one had dared touch them. When they sat down Stanfill announced to the room: "Gentlemen, we have come to an agreement and everything is going to be fine – Barry is going to get his $2.5 million." White, pushing his luck, leaned over and whispered, "Oh, and I'd like it by Thanksgiving eve," which was less than a week away. Stanfill smiled and said, "as good as done, Barry."

Stanfill told him to return the following Wednesday. When Wednesday came Stanfill invited a few journalists in to witness the agreement, thinking the resulting publicity would do no one any harm. It was not every day a record company handed an artist a cheque for $2.5 million and Stanfill doubted it had ever been done before.

But White said he'd prefer to do it privately, and they retired to a side room, leaving 20 reporters feasting on the caviar, blinis and sour cream and swilling down the Dom Perignon that had been laid out.

Stanfill, Regan and White sat round the table and White once again laid his .357 Magnum on the table in front of him. This time Stanfill ignored the gun and turned on the charm. He had brought his wife, Terry, a big-time fan, to meet Barry White. When he saw the gun he looked at her nervously, but Terry joked to White that she always brought a gun whenever she had something serious to say to her husband. It broke the ice and when the business was concluded White went next door to mingle with the reporters and even taste some champagne, his first glass in seven years.

As he was leaving, White turned to Stanfill and said: "Thank you, Dennis. I'm glad we got this sorted." Terry Stanfill stood on tiptoe to kiss the maestro on the cheek, and White responded with a bear hug. Russ Regan looked on and thought to himself: "Even by the standards of the music business this has been an interesting week."

When White left, Stanfill and Regan breathed a sigh of relief, as Regan remembered many years later: "When Barry came to pick up a $2.5 million check and laid his .38 calibre gun, still in its holder, on the desk, I guess he thought he couldn't play too safe on the streets with a check that large."

As soon as he got in the limousine, White told the driver to put his foot down. He was anxious to get the check to the bank before it closed for Thanksgiving. But after they had gone a mile he changed his mind and decided to keep the check over the weekend. On the way back to Sherman Oaks, the past week gave him plenty to reflect on.

There was much anticipation at home, as his family awaited his return. Everyone knew what he had gone for and wanted to know the outcome. At the door he was greeted with warmer hugs and kisses than normal. White said nothing until he got into the lounge, then he declared as he waved the envelope around: "Here it is!" But he had something more profound to say to his family: "I want everyone in this room to know that this money is not just dollars. To me it represents in equal parts my musical talent, self-determination, self-respect and self-esteem."

White took the check out of the envelope – everyone wanted to see it and touch it, and it got passed around. Glodean asked if she could take it over to Sadie Mae's house so she could see it. He replied: "Sure, but be certain Sadie doesn't smudge the ink." White recalled that it turned into a wonderful family Thanksgiving celebration: "We all had a lot to be thankful for in the White household."

The following Monday White deposited the check, then went for a meeting with his accountants. He had an idea and he wanted to share it with them. As the family was growing up, the oldest children were starting to get interested in horses, and so were Mum and Dad. He told Eli Boyer and Laurie Fernandez to "pull a little taste" out of the $2.5 million so he could buy a horse.

Eli Boyer went berserk and shouted: "No, no, no, you're not getting into horses – that's how artists always lose everything."

White explained to Boyer that he was not planning a racing stable but had an idea to become a breeder. Breeding was usually a profitable occupation and Boyer calmed down a little as White said: "I never planned to race my horses, just to breed them."

It started when Barry bought Glodean a brown and white American paint horse called Mandingo for a whopping $5,000. Then he bought an Appaloosa for himself called Apollo Blue, which cost $20,000. Horses for the whole family quickly followed. Then he bought some mares. Soon he had half a dozen horses, which had cost more than $150,000.

The fascination with the American paint horse breed was interesting. It is a breed that combines the characteristics of a western stock horse with a pinto's spotted pattern of white and dark coat colours. The breed was developed from a base of spotted horses with quarter horses and thoroughbred bloodlines, and grew to become one of the largest in North America.

The purchases led to a meeting with famed horse-breeder Tom Ulmer. After a few conversations, White realised that he really liked Ulmer and got talked into becoming a serious horse-breeder. The two men formed a partnership, with Ulmer supplying the expertise and White the money.

It proved to be an expensive hobby and soon half a million dollars had disappeared into the new business and White became a leading light in the

American Paint Horse Association. After nine months he owned 59 horses and leased a 250-acre hill ranch at Hidden Valley in southern California – owned by the actor Richard Widmark – in which to keep them.

The ranch was idyllic and he and Glodean visited it as often as they could. There were no post-purchase regrets and both of them thought it was the best thing they had ever done.

Ulmer proved to be a talented breeder and had a wonderful way with horses. He quickly bred three prize-winners called Jay Bar, Fifth Wheel and Hi-Fidelity. He also turned Mandingo and Apollo Blue into prize-winning horses. White's timing proved to be good and the value of paint horses soared to around $30,000 each. After a year his stable was valued at nearly $2 million and at its peak comprised 159 horses.

So successful was Ulmer that other owners tried to lure him away to work for them, but he stayed loyal to Barry and Glodean. Other owners started bidding for White's stallions and every day offers of between $40,000 and $80,000 were coming in. The trouble was that neither Barry nor Glodean wanted to sell, as they had fallen in love with all their horses and knew them all by name. Two years later their value had risen to nearly $3 million.

These were very happy times indeed, and there was nothing that Barry and Glodean enjoyed more than being chauffeured up to Hidden Valley with their young daughter Shaherah for a day with the horses. In March 1979 'Ebony' magazine featured them doing just that and they appeared blissfully happy as they walked up a hillside completely filled with horses. White said: "I loved to drive out and see the horses. I'd get out of the car as soon as we got there and walk amongst them."

Late that year they took their first Christmas vacation as a family and headed for Hawaii. It became a ritual and for the following ten years they flew to Honolulu for the holidays. But there was only one condition. All the children had to have made their grades at school. Needless to say, they all did. As White said: "We are a very close family, we all hang together all the time, all nine of us."

It was an idyllic time and Barry White could not have been happier.

CHAPTER 39

The Music Bursts Out

So many melodies

1975

By late 1975 Barry White was a global superstar. He had put out 11 albums, four for himself as a solo artist, three for the three girls of Love Unlimited, and four for his Love Unlimited Orchestra. All of them had been hits except for the disastrous 'Together Brothers' movie soundtrack album, which everyone now agreed had been misconceived.

He had scored two gigantic worldwide single hits with *Love's Theme* and *You're the First, The Last, My Everything*, and had enjoyed more than a dozen Top 20 singles. He had also found time to produce seven albums for third party artists and his distinctive sound dominated American radio stations for the period.

In the process he had created his own highly original musical presence, described by one critic as "Barry White's own version of the California-soul style". Another described it thus: "Barry White's music is the aural equivalent of wine and roses, jacuzzis and satin slippers, combining simplistic soul grooves with lush arrangements. His unique blend of pop, soul, and disco has lit up the decade and his unique distinctive voice purrs seductively and has captured the moment." Natalie Cole, the Grammy-winning female artist, said: "Barry's rich orchestrations with that pounding soulful drive and those sweeping violins have given new meaning to getting in the mood for love. You know it is him with the first chord and the first word."

Don Cornelius of 'Soul Train', arguably the biggest influence on soul music in America, said: "He wasn't just singing for your mate and your bedroom, he was singing and writing for his own bedroom." White said of his own music at the time: "My music is sacred always. Music is the most powerful element to human peace, tranquillity, heartaches, and heartbreaks. Music has something in it that if you're up, it can take you higher, and if you're down, it can take you lower."

He told Cornelius that he regarded it as truly ironic that his first No 1 had been the first song he had ever written, *Love's Theme*, in 1964. The tune had stayed, unrecognised, on the back burner until White, out of desperation, had taken it off the shelf to fill one of the many gaps in Love Unlimited's *Under The Influence of Love* album. The only reason that it remained an instrumental was, he said, that he never had time to write the lyrics: "Such is the way great music is born and becomes a hit." Equally amazing was the way that *Love's Theme* became a discotheque hit, the first instrumental to do so.

As a result Barry White was credited with kicking off the era of the discotheque in America, which culminated in the opening of Studio 54 in New York. Whether he deserved that credit or not was debatable, but certainly from 1974 to the end of the decade his music dominated the disco scene in the United States. On the streets his music was called 'hustle music', and what made it so was the tempo – it wasn't too fast.

White admitted that he owed much of his success to the early believers, the DJs in Los Angeles discotheques. He had acknowledged before that, "The discos helped me 100 per cent... When you get a smash out of there you usually get a big one."

Music industry insiders believed it was the magic of Gene Page that gave Barry White his distinctive musical sound. Ned Shankman, his lawyer, explained: "Producers had used strings in soul music before, but not the way Barry did. He played these big string sections like it was an individual artist. He had a brand-new sound that was so intoxicating."

And every song Barry White wrote contained a story, just as every album had a strong theme. Daryl Easlea of 'The Record Collector' magazine said: "There were always strong morals behind his love raps, often espousing the joys of monogamy and doing right by your woman. The fact that a man was prepared to spend such time pleasuring a lady acted as a role model to a generation of males, content to be chauvinistic with their peers but happy to love under White's tutelage. The notion of being taken care of and being looked after was central to his message. It comes as no surprise that it has been said that more children have been conceived to White's music than that of any other artist. The simple truth was that all of his records were ruminations on the same topic." In response to Easlea's comments, much reported at the time,

White simply said: "Love had become a very neglected word in our society. I'd like to see it back with the class and meaning it used to have."

Joe Nick Patoski, the well-known music critic of the time, said of Barry White's music: "It's pretty, almost syrupy and easy to grasp, with soaring strings that reach a crescendo as predictable as the sunrise. The words are simple and sweet, a one-on-one clichéd romanticism, babe, love as the common denominator of every song. It is Stravinsky with snap, Mantovani you can move to. The clincher is of course the half rap, half baritone soul shout that has too often triggered the perfunctory 'son of Isaac' comparisons."

The mention of Isaac Hayes by any reviewer was sure to spark a reaction from Barry White. He was compared with Hayes at every opportunity, the implication being that he was a 'rip-off' of Hayes. At first he was annoyed, but as his record sales climbed so his attitude to the non-stop comparisons mellowed. As he said: "People have started to say Isaac is copying Barry White, but he doesn't really sound like me, he still doesn't. He's into his own thing and I'm into mine. I just feel I'm better in mine than he is in his."

Privately White thought Hayes was ripping off his music. As he said: "After *I've Got So Much To Give* Hayes came up with *Joy*. He did three songs on there that sounded like my first album. I love the production because I believe it sounds like a Barry White production. I listened to it and it sounds a lot like *Love's Theme*."

Although he has never intellectualised in the manner of his peers, White's legacy was already established by the end of 1975 – whatever followed would just be a bonus. Don Cornelius of 'Soul Train' summed up White's impact best: "There was no match for Barry White. His music is just going to live forever."

CHAPTER 40

Family Bliss

10 years together in harmony

1975 to 1985

Once they had got all their children, Barry Jnr, Lanese, Nina, Darryl, Kevin, Bridget and Shaherah together, Barry and Glodean set about creating the perfect family environment at Sherman Oaks. The birth of Shaherah in 1975 was the final piece of the jigsaw.

The union of the White and the James families was seamless and it seemed that it had always been so. Barry White called his new family 'the Brady Bunch' after the television sitcom that was topping the ratings on the ABC network at the time.

The family environment was very important to Barry White. He said: "I don't think I could live in this world, rich or poor, without a family, because a family represents something to a man." He added: "I just love kids."

And that meant spending as much time as he could with his children, something he struggled to do with all the demands on his time, as Glodean remembered: "He wasn't a typical artist that liked to be out on the road all the time with all the glamour and all that stuff. He wasn't about all that – he was about family."

Jack Perry was around at White's house throughout that period: "Barry was a family man and he looked at not only his family but he really respected family people, a husband and wife that were together for years and had children – he loved that."

While the house was filled with joy there was some sadness. As a housewarming present for his wife, he bought a baby tiger, which they kept caged in the garden. Three months later it caught pneumonia and shortly afterwards died. The death caused tumult in the family and he vowed never to keep an animal caged, at home, again.

But the gesture reflected the intense joy he felt in being married to Glodean: "My wife is one of the greatest, most beautiful flowers from the garden of woman. She is very strong and she's a Libra. She is very attentive to me, she's very loving to me and she is a wonderful mother to our children. Even more than being a perfect wife, she is a great friend to me. We really hang together. And what I have found with her, I could probably never find again in life. Because that kind of relationship is very rare."

The sentiment was mutual and both Barry and Glodean were determined that their united families would feel secure in their home environment. But they were also equally determined that the children would do well at school, and that meant imposing a disciplined environment from the outset. Lanese, Nina and Darryl needed the most attention, as Barry and Glodean believed, whether true or not, that their childhoods had been disrupted by their mother, and they were determined to reverse the damage.

White instinctively knew what he had to do: "I am a man bright enough to know which side of the road is the right side. I have to have an image of myself for my children."

They started by enrolling all the children at the same schools. It took a huge effort, but they were helped by the fact that they were all of similar age, and Barry Jnr, Kevin and Bridget effectively became mentors to the other three. White remembered: "Eventually they all began to improve their grades and had no more behavioural problems. I made sure they knew how to be polite and be nice to people. I taught them what my mother had taught me – that it was nice to be nice. Everything came from the way my mother raised me. She always demonstrated love around the home. She gave me my understanding of humanity and it was important, and I was determined to be the spiritual power and moral leader of my family."

It didn't hurt that their grandmother was constantly around to reinforce the message.

When the youngsters protested that they had not been subject to the same disciplines as their father, he told them: "It's a different day and a different time." He was determined that they would learn: "I'm a strict person, I am a person who believes in discipline, I believe that when it's time to work, it's time to work, and when it's time to play, it's time to play, and never confused the two."

White remembered the discipline he imposed as being very important to how his children turned out, as he explained: "Our paths are chosen at such an early age. Parents today do not know how to raise their kids because they weren't raised properly themselves. They don't know how to make a real commitment to each other by getting married and taking responsibility for the lives they bring into the world. They don't know how to commit to their jobs; they don't know how to commit to their own welfare and security."

He was constantly able to call on Sadie to help with the parenting duties. He wanted her to recreate the environment for his own children that she had for him: "She let me know what was possible in life. She taught me that when a child is raised and never sees any disasters, they'll have the illusion that everything is fine in the world, when the reality is that often it's not. That experience from my mother gave me my wisdom."

White firmly believed that the ability to make a proper commitment remained paramount in life – no matter what the commitment might be. He explained: "Once I commit to someone or something, be it to my lady or raising our children, I see it as a spiritual contract that must not and cannot be broken. In that sense I will always have the last word in what happens to me." He believed in "practise what you preach and practise what you teach" as an inviolable mantra.

Sometimes it got difficult to keep things on an even keel and White strived to keep the household normal despite the fact that Michael Jackson was a regular, often daily, visitor to Sherman Oaks. Dionne Warwick and Elton John were regular visitors, and Muhammad Ali also became a very close friend of the family and called round every few days. Jackson and Ali were just two of many famous people who liked to come and hang out with Barry White. People valued his counsel, as they knew it came from the heart.

But the constant celebrity visits became a problem to the children, especially Darryl, who was always the most easily led of the White clan. Darryl began to live in a fantasy world and became particularly close to Muhammad Ali. White strived hard to teach Darryl what was reality and what was unreality, and that the illusion of fame was just that – an illusion. He explained: "One should never get hung up on people being famous. A person's character means more than anything. I don't care what they tell me about themselves – the way they act tells me more."

Darryl's sweet nature ultimately made the distinction, guided by his father, and the danger passed.

But White also had his own difficulties when Muhammad Ali came calling and found it very hard not to be star-struck by the incredibly charismatic boxer. They had first met by accident, and White told Ali how much he had meant to him in his youth, both as a black man and a citizen of the world. White's honesty impressed Ali immediately, and it helped that he also liked his music.

The two men instantly clicked and became very good friends. White found Ali a combination of childlike innocence and a man of great knowledge and good judgement. White said of him: "There are men and there are gods and he was truly one of the rarest of living legends – he was both."

White was intrigued by Ali's dual personality. Outside the boxing ring he found him a caring and compassionate individual of rare quality. But he saw a different person when he was about to get into the boxing ring, as he described: "He'd be talking about something all light and funny and then suddenly, without warning, he got into his warrior head. His eyes shifted and took on the look of a very sleek and dangerous cat. I saw that same look on his face after he destroyed an opponent. He was awesome when he left the dressing room and went into the ring, as he was for every fight."

The White family regularly used to travel to Las Vegas to watch Muhammad Ali fight and White found similarities in his own character: "I get a similar kind of intensity when I am working at my art in the studio or alone by myself working deep into the night."

After they met, White attended most of Ali's fights as an unofficial member of his support team, and Ali reciprocated by attending many of White's American concerts.

But it was Ali's penchant for dropping into the White family home at all hours of the day and night that caused havoc with the family. He fancied himself as an amateur magician and thought nothing of waking the children early in the morning so he could show them the latest magic tricks he had mastered. The children loved it, but White worried that they would think it was normal for Ali to come into their bedrooms at all hours and perform magic tricks exclusively for them.

During the course of many long conversations, White found that Ali longed to be a successful entrepreneur, but he also learned that he did not have a very good head for business and most of his ideas were not good. White dissuaded him from most of them. But he couldn't dissuade him from continually dropping by at unlikely hours and waking the children when he couldn't sleep and craved attention, which Barry and Glodean's seven children were only too pleased to give him.

Barry White loved boxers and Muhammad Ali introduced him to most of the greats who were still alive, including the greatest of all, Joe Louis. When White came across him, Louis was down on his luck, greeting visitors at a Las Vegas casino. White remembered: "I was honoured to shake Mr Louis's hand. In spite of some of the bad things he fell victim to in his life, I hoped he knew how much he was loved and appreciated by so many people of all colours and races in America and around the world."

White was also introduced to Marvin Hagler. They had something in common in that they had both been to jail and had had to fight extra hard to make their lives a success as a result.

Ali also introduced White to Mike Tyson. When Tyson realised it was Barry White he was talking to, he dragged him off to where his limousine was parked and opened the back door. Spread over the back bench was virtually every Barry White CD that had ever been released. Tyson told him, "I love you man," and he meant it.

Although he couldn't avoid celebrity relationships, generally White preferred not to socialise with other famous people and always avoided social activity with record industry executives, as he explained: "I don't socialise with record industry people. I have a few friends in the business and that's it. It's an insane world out there and I don't want any part of it. My friends are everyday working people. Record people get too locked up in themselves. The people who are my friends I've known for years. The few friends I had then I have now."

Through all of this White maintained a cordial relationship with his ex-wife Mary. By now he was all too aware of her shortcomings, but he took the same attitude to her as he did to his father. He continued to support her and pay her an allowance despite the fact that she had received a large lump sum when he got custody of the children.

One other problem White found vexing as a family man was going away for long periods on tour, especially when it took him outside the United States. It meant leaving the children at home, except for the baby Shaherah, who travelled around with them. When Barry and Glodean went to Europe they could be away for six weeks at a time, as Glodean recalled: "When he had to go out and be on the road it was a job, and when the job was over we came home. It was very hard on Shaherah with her being the baby and travelling with us since she was born. I still performed up until the day she was born." White dismissed this as being all part of his job, and said of his wife and young baby: "We work together, we live together and we go everywhere together."

But the time away was crucial to his family in one very important way – money. He desperately wanted to give his family financial security: "I wanna make damn sure my wife and my children don't have to suffer, or want for anything in life. So I'm all about the business of being successful in business because it's the bottom line that counts in everything you do." That search for financial security kept him on the road for large parts of the year and in the studio for the rest.

Aside from those demands, Barry White found parenthood a huge joy. He had the money and time to enjoy it and appreciate it. And there was a lot of joy in the White household, as Shaherah later confirmed: "Seven of us children were there living in the house and there was never a dull moment. My father loved joking around and pranking and we used to run around the house and my brothers and sister and my mother and father we would scare each other. It sounds kind of crazy. We got scared one night and my father would be standing there – he was 6ft 3in and he would scare the crap out of us."

As a reference point he continually went back to his own relationship with his own parents at the same age: "I got a deeper appreciation of my own parents and a more profound understanding of how difficult it must have been for them, and I was so happy they both lived long enough to see me succeed. I took care of my mother in every way I could, providing her with whatever she wanted, which wasn't much. I gave her an abundance of the love that she had instilled in me as a little boy."

Dealing with his father was rather more difficult, as he explained: "Having long ago made my peace with what I knew to be the physical and emotional limitations my father had to deal with in his youth, I wanted to provide as beautiful a twilight for him as I could. Despite whatever anger I may have felt as a boy, when I grew into manhood I felt a great pride to have been born of his seed."

White was proud that his father was his own man and never asked his son for anything, even turning down his offer of a new house. But he did buy him a brand-new pick-up truck without telling him. He had it delivered to his home and left it on the drive so he couldn't refuse it.

In July 1980 it suddenly didn't matter any more when Melvin White suddenly succumbed to lung cancer at only 69 years of age. From diagnosis to his death was just a matter of weeks and the cancer was undoubtedly caused by heavy smoking throughout his life. He telephoned his son from hospital just before he died and the last words he said to him were, "I am very fortunate to be the father of Barry White." After a difficult relationship, spanning four decades, Barry White loved to hear those words.

White had always built his life based on loyalty and that came to the fore once he was successful. He began to realise that there was something in his psyche that bred intense loyalty to others, which extended all the way down to Russ Regan. White could have left 20th Century Records many times for better and more lucrative deals, but he chose to be loyal for as long as the relationship ran its course.

Even with his new-found fame, he basically still saw the world as he had when he was the Barry White who had stolen car tyres and gone to jail. That was the essential person that remained within him. But he was also equally conscious that the world now saw a wholly different version of him – a man who made and performed the music they loved. As he described himself: "I was several Barry Whites, part public figure, part private man and lyrical riffer, and part philosophical spiritualist. But when I was writing a song I became Barry White the songwriter. When I needed someone to put it all together in synch – the voices, the orchestra, the chorus and so on – I became Barry White the producer. When I needed someone whose voice carried my combined efforts I was Barry White, the singer."

He never really came to terms with the fact that he combined all these skills in one person. It was so unusual he just accepted it and rarely thought it through. In time he came to recognise it as much as a burden as a benefit. He explained: "Each of these skills is an art form in itself and each requires an individual artist to do it justice. Each has to work with all the others to help assist and develop who he is and what he has. Each has to bring something new and different to the table. And each is a part of me"

White believed they all added up to 'Barry White, the man'.

And he often quoted an expression: "Out of many there is one."

That was Barry White.

CHAPTER 41

Let the Music Play

Fifth and sixth solo albums

1975 and 1976

Afrer enjoying his horses and a very relaxing summer, Barry White was anxious to get back into the recording studio. He found he had been relaxing too much and it was difficult to change his routine back to work.

But a new album, which he was to call *Let The Music Play*, beckoned, and the lure could not be resisted. In reality, the long vacation had done him the power of good and for many *Let The Music Play* was the best half-hour of music of his career.

This outcome was a surprise, as the recordings were beset with problems. White had managed to fall out with his greatest ally, Gene Page. It was a friendly fall-out, but a fall-out nevertheless. It meant that *Let The Music Play* was the first of White's albums that did not include Page's immense talents. Likewise, Page decided not to ask White's assistance for his second solo album, *Lovelock*. Both albums were to suffer badly from the respective absences, but Gene Page was to miss Barry White more than Barry White missed Gene Page.

Page tried to explain it away: "Our schedules just didn't coincide and Barry needed to go ahead with his work. He felt that it was necessary to try for something different, which can always be achieved by changing the formula somewhat."

Page replaced White with his brother, Billy Page. But he admitted that the album was the poorer for it: "It was successful, although it could have done better. But it's a problem with an artist like myself who doesn't really perform." In truth, Page's album failed, as he admitted: "I was satisfied with the album but for some reason things always sound better to me when they're successful."

But Barry White was so busy he hardly noticed the problems that Gene Page was having – he had plenty of his own. It proved immensely difficult for him to write without Page at his side. He knew what the concept was but had to learn a new way of working without his friend's help. On his own for the first time, White constructed his theme for the new album very carefully. In the past he had always added the lyrics at the end, when both men had sorted out the melody, as Gene Page revealed: "Many times, Barry wouldn't even write the lyrics till then."

For the new album White wanted to reflect on the ups and downs of love and the hurdles that had to be overcome in almost every relationship. This time the lyrical content did not speak of endless nights of making love and developing relationships, which had featured in earlier tunes, but focused on what love really meant and the consequences of true love.

The opening track was *I Don't Know Where Love Has Gone*, at nearly five minutes, followed by the bouncy *If You Know, Won't You Tell Me*, both written by White on his own.

I'm So Blue and You Are Too was the third track and a classic Barry White ballad at seven minutes long.

Opening side two was *Baby, We'd Better Try To Get It Together*, with a striking introduction and a four-minute upbeat tempo. Surprisingly it was also released as a single, but predictably failed to make an impact, reaching No 92 on the singles charts and 29 on the R&B chart; it performed most strongly in the British charts, reaching No 15.

You See The Trouble With Me was the most promising song on the album, and White wrote it together with Ray Parker Jnr, although surprisingly he did not give Parker a writing credit. It was released as a single in February 1976 and reached No 14 on Billboard's Black Singles chart; it was also a bit hit in the UK, climbing to No 2 and just failing to reach the top slot by a couple of dozen sales.

The album closed with the title track, *Let The Music Play*, which was also the third single release. It remains one of Barry White's better-known songs, and got to No 21 on the Billboard singles chart, No 4 on the R&B chart, and No 9 in the British chart. It was an unusual track because the lyrics spoke about a break-up, a rarity for White.

The album itself reached No 8 on the R&B albums chart, peaked at No 42 on the main Billboard albums chart, and reached No 22 on the British chart.

Considering the effort and money that had been put into it, sales were very disappointing. Russ Regan wasn't surprised, as he knew that his promotional people were the best in the business and if they couldn't make a record sell, no one could.

One problem was thought to be the length. It was only 31 minutes and six tracks, and this was poor value in an era when much more music was being offered on albums. The standard was now 40 minutes, but White stuck to the standard 30-minute format – either he hadn't noticed the change or he ignored it. But no one will ever know how many casual purchasers looked at *Let The Music Play* and Bruce Springsteen's *Born To Run* and decided that Springsteen was offering 30 per cent better value. Similarly, Isaac Hayes's *Groove-a-thon* also had 40 minutes of music.

Aside from that, it was also clear that the Barry White sensation had peaked and was now coming down the other aside. He was still enjoying high sales and more or less everything went gold, but the fact remained that sales were declining and the excitement was fading.

Much of this was due to the rise of rap music and the advent of hip-hop. White watched the new phenomenon take over the discotheques but didn't recognise the danger to his own career. But he recognised how important rap music was to the youth of America: "The greatest thing that ever happened to young people is rap music. It gave them an outlet to express their frustrations and get it out of them."

White believed he could survive the new rap era by pouring huge resources into the marketing of his new album, and he hired legions of promotion staff to hawk a record that he knew was some of his best work ever.

But it wasn't enough.

Barry White's golden era was over and, no matter how good the music, he would never again reach the sales heights of the past. But for year upon year into the future he failed to recognise the trend and tried everything he could to reverse it – but as Russ Regan had predicted, that just made things worse.

White may not have won over record buyers, but he had finally won over all the reviewers. The critics, who without exception had come round to Barry White's musical style, loved it. One said: "The arrangements are of the highest order here, full of sophisticated orchestrations and silky but solid rhythm tracks." Another said: "The album was something of an overlooked gem." White focused on the word 'overlooked' and couldn't help but agree, but what else could he do to make it sell better?

Penny Valentine, arguably the top music journalist of the time, touched on the fact that White's musical style alienated some would-be buyers: "Barry White has harnessed a sensual, very direct, very intimate approach, and wrapped it up in a way that's become generally acceptable. Some people don't find it acceptable. They find it embarrassing because they think strong manufactured emotion like this is considered tasteless and embarrassing."

She added: "*Let The Music Play* is really White at his best. His appeal is bisexual, not as someone once said asexual, that would be an impossibility – the music relying as it does on a strong feeling of romantic sexuality. It's romantic in a world where romance has had little part to play for so long. I'd guess, aside from all the sociological factors, that's its main appeal."

White's music also affected Penny Valentine, who wrote mainly for 'Street Life' magazine, in other ways, as she readily admitted: "I heard Barry White's first album under strange circumstances – feeling low and blue in Los Angeles, late at night, through a hotel bedroom wall. What it did to me emotionally is a little odd to relate so I won't, but that traumatic introduction to his then unknown, unheard approach has stuck with me right through."

Barry White quickly put the disappointment of *Let The Music Play* behind him and consoled himself by following it up with two more Love Unlimited Orchestra album releases. He loved going into a studio with an orchestra to record an album more than anything else. The two new albums were called *Music Maestro Please* and *My Sweet Summer Suite*. The first turned out to be one of the most disappointing efforts of White's whole career, and quickly faded into obscurity with no memorable enduring (or endearing) songs.

My Sweet Summer Suite, released shortly afterwards, was rather better and an attempt to make amends. The title track was also released as a single after it took off in discotheques. It was a surprise success, jumping to No 1 for three weeks on Billboard's dance/disco chart and crossing over to the soul chart, peaking at No 28 on the R&B chart and 49 on the Billboard main singles chart. It became known as the Los Angeles disco anthem, played endlessly on local radio stations and in clubs.

But White was running out of creativity. What had burst out of him two years before had dried up, and his instrumental melodies were developing a sameness that he found hard to shed.

The truth appeared to be that Barry White had been so successful for a run of 36 months that there was bound to be a comedown and a musical hiatus. When it happened, he was not sure how to handle it.

The obvious solution was to manage the decline. But no one really believed there was a decline, and a lack of marketing and sales promotion was continually blamed for the fact that the records were failing to sell as well as in the past.

And then another bombshell was dropped

Dennis Stanfill was gradually forcing out Russ Regan as head of the label. No one knew why – as far as the world was concerned Regan had done an excellent job in reviving the label since 1973. But once it was known he was going, things would never be the same again at 20th.

The second album of 1976, a solo effort called *Is This Whatcha Wont*, followed at the very end of the year, released just after Thanksgiving in time for Christmas. After their falling out, White and Gene Page had made up their differences to their mutual benefit. White took his now regular team into the studio, consisting of Page, Frank Kejmar and Barney Perkins, together with Tony Sepe and Frank Wilson.

Despite its wonky title, musically it was another of the great Barry White albums with some magical strings arranged by Gene Page. All five songs were written by White on his own, the only album on which he wrote everything. It opened with *Don't Make Me Wait Too Long*, which was released as a single and peaked at No 20 on the Billboard R&B chart.

The second track was extraordinary. Called *Your Love So Good I Can Taste It*, it was the quintessential Barry White sound and opened with six minutes of pure instrumental. Then as the violins swelled, leading to the opening crescendo, White launched into the lyrics: "There's nothing like it in the world, baby, believe me, you've got it all," followed by "sexy lady, let me love you baby". The track was "awash", as one commentator described it, "with distant horns and strings." Jack Perry said: "It's the kind of music you listen to when you're driving and cruising around." *Your Love So Good I Can Taste*

It was also one of Barry White's personal favourites, as Perry recalled: "Barry never played his records after they were finished and released. He'd say, 'They got it, I'm on to the next.' Yet he did play this one." The sound on *Your Love So Good I Can Taste It* owed a lot to the guitar skills of Ray Parker Jnr, but again for some reason White failed to credit his contribution.

The third track, *I'm Qualified To Satisfy You*, was the second single and went to No 25 on the Billboard R&B chart. But neither of the tracks issued as singles was able to breach the Top 10. In Britain it was a different story, and both were bona fide hits, reaching Nos 17 and 37 respectively.

The penultimate track on the album was *I Wanna Lay Down With You Baby*, at 8½ minutes; by most accounts it was the weakest track and was never heard of again. Aside from a few seconds, it was 8½ minutes of musical nonsense that White had created to make the album up to 30 minutes. But some reviewers liked the pointlessness of it – one called it a "sensual slow burner", whatever that meant. In truth it sounded as though White had made up the lyrics at the piano and put it together in a few minutes as a joke.

The album closed with a song called *Now I'm Gonna Make Love To You*, which became another standard White classic and was everything the previous track wasn't.

White hired his favourite designer of the moment, Len Freas, to design the album sleeve. Freas had made his name designing distinctive sleeves for The Carpenters. He used a photograph Gene Brownell had taken for a Love Unlimited Orchestra sleeve the year before, and created a Red Indian headdress image in a cacophony of colours as background. It wasn't particularly memorable and Freas was not used again.

Is This Whatcha Wont marked the start of a sales decline that would now greet every new Barry White record. Nevertheless it was well received and reached No 25 on the R&B chart, but was the first album that did not make the R&B Top 10. It peaked at a disappointing No 125 on the main Billboard chart.

The album's low sales caused considerable concern in White's close circle and at 20th Century Records. One problem was, again, the 30 minutes of music. Subtracting the worthless eight minutes of *I Wanna Lay Down With You Baby*, there was only 22 minutes of serviceable music on the album and fans reacted badly to it. It started the angst that was to dominate the next 25 years of Barry White's life. Sales of his albums would never again reach the heights they had in 1973 and 1974 and would generally disappoint as each album was released. It was just the way of things.

Glodean White, Linda James and Dede Taylor fell early victims of the downturn. In light of his big cash advances and the $1 million the company would be asked to give to Larry Nunes, the new men in charge at 20th Century Records took a much harder line than in the past. When White wanted to release Love Unlimited's fourth album in late 1976, after hearing it the label's new executives refused. There was no blaming Russ Regan this time. They simply refused point blank to release it, saying that it was 'not commercial'. In the end White had to offer to pay for the new album personally and front up the manufacturing and marketing costs to get it released.

He called the album *He's All I've Got*, putting it out under a new label he called Unlimited Gold, but the album sleeve notes stated that it was manufactured and distributed by 20th Century Records. But there were no singles and very little marketing as White fought a running battle with his own record company.

Fortunately there was nothing wrong with the music; it was a stellar Love Unlimited album heavily influenced by the Motown sound. Love Unlimited, as a group, had inevitably always been compared to the sound of The Supremes, and White sought to exploit that connection with this crossover album.

All but the first song of the seven tracks was written by him alone. The first track, *I Did It For Love* was composed by Linda Laurie and Terri Ettinger, and had originally been written for The Supremes, who turned it down for a variety of reasons, one being that the tempo was too slow. So Ettinger, who had written a lot of material for Diana Ross, including the famous *The Last Time I Saw Him*, took it to Barry White for Love Unlimited. White snapped it up and included it as the new album's opening track. It was the only single from the album and clearly the best track.

The second track was *Never, Never Say Goodbye*, which had a very serviceable melody and lyrics and was heavily influenced by the Motown sound. The third track, *Whisper You Love Me*, was another upbeat track with a heavy Supremes influence. *He's Mine* was a more traditional Barry White song at just over 5 minutes. *I Can't Let Him Down* was probably the weakest track on the album and was a sound-alike of no particular distinction.

The album finished with a real flourish with two outstanding tracks. The first, *I Guess I'm Just Another Girl In Love*, was a classic White sound, and the second was the ballad and title track *He's All I've Got*. It was nearly 7½ minutes long and a favourite of all Barry White fans to this day. Both songs were to appear on 'best of' albums in later years.

Because of the situation at 20th Century Records, the album was eventually lost and failed to breach the charts, despite the quality of the music.

White was furious with 20th and believed that it was all about Dennis Stanfill getting revenge for his humiliation of two years before. White was doubly angry because of the debilitating affect it had on the three girls, and their confidence in him.

But to him it was more than that. He had started his career with Love Unlimited and the album was significant because it was the first on Unlimited Gold. Afterwards he said that the title track was a message to the three girls: "I wrote about reaffirmation and meant it as a clear message to Love Unlimited that I was still their Uncle Barry. And would be for as long as they wanted. I knew they were hurt and afraid at what had gone down at the label and I wanted to show them that no matter what I was behind them."

Glodean White played down the drama and said: "We had no reason to feel in the shadow. We knew who daddy was. We were the babies and he's the daddy." White recalled Dede Taylor saying to him: "Uncle Barry, you're the baddest and we're still your babies, right?" White replied: "That's right, all three of you, no matter what."

All through 1977 Barry White seethed with anger at his treatment by 20th as he searched for a new record label. But despite the animosity leaving would not be easy, as he revealed: "It had not been an easy decision. There were a lot of things I had liked about being on the label." But whatever his innate sense of loyalty, there was no way that Barry White would be staying now that Russ Regan had been put on 'gardening leave' and rarely came into the offices.

All the goodwill had gone.

CHAPTER 42

On Tour in the Seventies

A joyful time for all

The 1970s

One thing Barry White had learned early in his life was the value, for an artist, of touring and playing live performances. So immediately after his very first hit record with Love Unlimited he had taken to the road, first across America playing smaller venues and later to the biggest concert venues in the world.

The lust to tour was always unexplained, as White had always told people that he hated performing and that all he ever wanted to be was a producer and arranger of music.

He also hated flying and would never fly when he didn't absolutely have to, which meant that there were a lot of long coach trips across America and Europe. And he never flew in a plane where he could see the propeller, always maintaining that he felt better in a jet because he said he understood the propulsion system. But his entourage did not share his fears and they hated the long coach journeys that resulted from their boss's flying phobia.

Aside from that, the tours were very happy affairs. One sound technician, who worked with White in New York and was on his bus continuously through the seventies, said: "Not only was he a great singer but he was also a great performer. There were all kinds of people in the orchestra travelling around together on the bus. It was a microcosm of America – old people, young people, blacks, whites. And they all got on fine. This man, Barry White, brought black music to whites and white music to blacks. It didn't matter what colour you were, he crossed the colour lines. He was for real and I digged him for it."

The Barry White concerts were not simple affairs, and on tour he was backed up by more than 50 people, including the three girls of Love Unlimited, the 30-piece Love Unlimited Orchestra, three female backing singers, and the maestro himself. The orchestra was conducted by the irrepressible Sid Garris, who, in his flamboyant white topcoat, was fast becoming a star in his own right. It was a class act in those days, featuring many prominent musicians including ace guitarists Ray Parker Jnr and Melvin 'Rah-Wah' Watson. Sid Garris said: "The collection of people Barry gathered together was remarkable even by his standards."

There were also different rules on tour. Glodean was no longer Barry's wife but a member of Love Unlimited. It was all business, even to the extent that she would call him 'Mr White'. The show may have been complex, but the format was simple. The orchestra were ranged at the back of the stage and on stage for the whole time. Above it was draped a huge banner that read: 'Barry White – Love Unlimited'.

All the shows were preceded by an afternoon of rehearsals, although everyone knew the routine backwards, as Sid Garris remembered: "We didn't talk down to audiences like a classical symphony, but played what they related to. A lot of the young people at the concerts had never heard or seen a French horn and they cheered when they heard it."

Generally it was a three-act concert. The first scene was called 'The Grand', which was the Love Unlimited Orchestra playing 25 minutes of various arrangements from its albums, vigorously conducted by Garris. The second was called 'The Intimate', which was Glodean, Linda and Dede in a 45-minute set, again backed by Garris and the orchestra. Finally the third scene was called 'The Maestro', which featured an hour of the man himself.

Barry White almost always entered the stage from below. He was clad in a silk suit, in one of a variety of very loud colours from his wardrobe, with a lighted cigarette in one hand, wireless microphone in the other. He shook hands with the boys in the audience and exchanged kisses with the girls in the front row. As critic Joe Patoski observed: "First comes the whispering words, then the strings and the croon follows. The message is love, sweet love and the crowd's hysteria subdues to attentiveness."

In fact, White spent as much time off stage with the audience, singing into his wireless microphone, as he did on stage. He always seemed to have a cigarette in his hand and was constantly shaking hands and hugging girls.

The closing climax of the show consisted of all three acts coming together for a final extravaganza as violins tuned up and horns blasted out. But there was no precise formula and every show was different – each had its own special atmosphere, which led to some variable performances. For example, the 1975 concert in Frankfurt, which was broadcast as a live television special in Germany, was a magical three hours. But almost exactly the same show at the Albert Hall in London, in May 1975, was much less so. No one knew why – that was just the way it was. But everywhere they went, they played to packed-out houses.

The tours also gave Barry White a chance to indulge his favourite passion – chatting with journalists. They loved him and couldn't get enough   and he seemed to love them back.

On tour, White was accessible to any journalist who asked. After the show he was quite a sight, and more often than not greeted them backstage in his favourite velvet and silk purple dressing gown with a glass of Chivas Regal scotch whisky in one hand and a Benson & Hedges menthol cigarette in the other. One journalist described him as "greeting his media disciples with the avuncular dignity of a minor African despot."

After his concerts there was always a lavish buffet supper for the press, and even his fiercest critics were welcome to eat and drink at his expense. In fact, the criticism rarely troubled him and he always seemed to have time for everyone, even Bob Fisher of 'New Musical Express'.

After watching him perform at London's Albert Hall for the first time, Fisher had compared him to a mental patient in an asylum: "This huge character still tugs at a million heart strings all around the world as he growls and incants his tomes of love and lust like a refugee from Broadmoor. There has never been a more unlikely sex symbol in any of the media. Yet as a sex symbol he certainly gains most of his enormous popularity."

Whatever that really meant, and one could never tell with Bob Fisher, it reflected the mood of journalists who couldn't really understand the phenomenon of Barry White. He was something they hadn't seen before and they were not at all sure if they liked it, although they had to acknowledge that the audience did.

Fisher repaid White's hospitality when he witnessed a fiasco at a concert at Villa Park, a British soccer ground in Birmingham, in May 1975. The rain poured down and the concert had to be virtually abandoned after the first five minutes as water got into the sound equipment. Fisher wrote as if it had never happened and ignored the reaction of the rain-sodden fans, who had paid a considerable amount to get soaked to the skin.

As demand for interviews grew, more praise was lavished on him, and White began to forget his previous vows of humbleness. One interviewer described him as "egotistic and cocky", but acknowledged that these qualities were "all necessary prerequisites for survival in the world of pop."

Philip Norman, the famous 'Sunday Times' writer, who saw White perform for the first time at London's Albert Hall, wrote: "From Manila to Macclesfield his voice can be heard, grunting and gasping in a register of emotions from A to B flat, invariably expressing agitation at the prospect of imminent sexual intercourse and yet sounding as if someone is throttling the vocalist with a pillow. He has become one of the most successful black American solo performers, with 50 gold discs celebrating the sales, and perhaps the uniformity, of his material. He is in England again, playing to rapturous concert audiences of whom few, significantly, are black. With tickets at £7.50 each, the tour represents a major triumph of opportunism over content."

Norman, like all the music critics, just didn't know what to make of Barry White, and a frequently quoted description was "unlikely pop star". Another reviewer wrote: "The paunchy frame somehow doesn't fit the husky bedroom voice of record. His dress tonight was a crushed velvet multi-hued jacket, burgundy pants and white shoes. It is slicker Vegas styled than pimp flash."

White was unmoved by the criticism of his dress sense and defended his all-silk wardrobe: "I sweat when I work, and I need light clothes so I always wear silk. Silk is the sexiest material to me. It just feels good next to the skin."

Once the concert was over, he would change into a favourite cream-coloured tracksuit and a grey woolly hat. He never liked being photographed in his post-concert outfit. He knew photographers would shy away from the hat, and refused to take it off. If they asked why, he told them, "It's Barry White's trademark," inevitably referring to himself as he always did in the third person, which was a trait critics called "magisterial".

Barry White didn't shirk from playing difficult venues. The most difficult was at Detroit in the mid-seventies, at the height of the car manufacturing depression. By then his entourage was getting used to the better things in life and in Detroit they complained bitterly after being billeted in a run-down hotel.

A few thousand fans had been expected and everyone was unprepared for the 14,000 people who bought a ticket and packed into the Detroit Olympia hockey arena on Grand River Avenue, leaving only a thousand seats unsold. There was no security as it had been deemed unnecessary. Local Detroit police were forced to intervene to hold off the thousands of enthusiastic fans who couldn't believe a big star like Barry White had come to Detroit.

This concert was particularly difficult as the makeshift stage, in the middle of the arena, was too small for the 30-piece orchestra, as Ray Parker Jnr remembered: "This stage was a joke and with all the problems the show didn't get started until well after 10.30. Barry didn't get on stage until after midnight."

But the atmosphere in the dressing room as the huge crowd gathered outside was electric. By show time the girls of Love Unlimited were in very high spirits and oozing sex appeal in their glittery evening gowns. They couldn't wait to get on as Sid Garris's orchestra warmed up the audience, eventually stoking them up into a frenzy.

In the clamour a fight broke out in the second row. For a while it looked dangerous as people climbed up on to the stage and tried to force their way backstage into the dressing rooms. White had to come out on stage early and appeal to the crowd for calm: "Hey, hey, hey, cool it now. We didn't come here to fight."

And immediately the fighting ceased.

The Detroit concert was national news, but White himself was unmoved: "Some folks say I'm carrying the wrong message, bringing white people and black people together, but I want to see the world in a better condition for all people."

But despite the brave talk, later he wouldn't go to venues like Detroit. As he explained: "For me to jeopardise my safety, it has to be something special. If I die, that's the end of it, right? Not the audience but me, right? So I only go where I enjoy going."

New York was his favourite American city outside Los Angeles and he loved the sophistication of the people and the quiet appreciation of the fans he received in the Big Apple: "They are my special friends and I'll cherish them until the day I die."

And he was not afraid to experiment with the New York crowd. In 1978 he took an 80-piece orchestra to Radio City for a series of performances. Interestingly almost the entire orchestra was made up of women. It was an experiment to see if he could hear a difference. He explained: "All of the strings, French horns, horns were all women. The only men on the stage were my rhythm section. It was very beautiful, very exciting for ten nights." In the event there was no difference between an all-male and a mixed orchestra. But although it may not have sounded any different, the audience loved it, as White said: "I broke the Radio City record for sell-outs for that many nights."

He also particularly enjoyed performing in England: "England has been good to me and I have been good to it. There's no place that I love more on this planet than England."

It was only the tax situation with Britain's Inland Revenue that stopped him going to London more often, as he said: "I know that when I go to England I'm going to have a good time. And I tell other singers who don't want to go that they had better go and make friends with the real people." He was also a big fan of Britain's first woman Prime Minister, Margaret Thatcher: "I sent a message to Mrs Thatcher, to congratulate her. You see, I believe in women, I really do. I think England has got now what history will report as one of the best states-people of all time in Mrs Thatcher."

Sometimes in Europe he performed two separate shows a night, which was something he would never do in the United States. He explained: "In Europe, we did 28 shows in 14 days and everyone enjoyed it. Especially in London."

In the fall of 1974 he went on a short tour of Japan, not expecting much. But the Japanese promoters had done lots of advanced work and issued promotional copies of all his albums to generate interest, and he found rapturous crowds waiting for him at venues. White, who never learned to speak any foreign languages, marvelled at people who could not speak a word of English but enjoyed his music nonetheless: "They're people no different than I am and I'm no different than they are, when you keep it on that level it is very easy to respond to them."

All through the seventies he spent a quarter of his time on the road performing every night. And everyone had the time of their lives.

CHAPTER 43

Sings For Someone You Love

Seventh solo album

1977

1 977 was the year in which the Barry White bandwagon started to falter. The signs had been there for months as White's ambition and ego finally got ahead of his abilities. His attempts at producing independent acts had gone badly wrong as none of them had sold many albums, despite showing lots of promise. It was a huge disappointment for him as acts like Tom Brock, Gloria Scott, West Wing and Danny Pearson failed to break though.

His own previous album, *Is This Whatcha Wont*, had sold poorly and had not produced a hit single – it had quickly disappeared from record stores, leaving barely a trace.

The biggest problem proved to be the problem itself. White had no idea why *Is This Whatcha Wont* had sold so badly. The music was as good as ever and some of it was as good as it got.

Despite having received backing from Dennis Stanfill, White couldn't have chosen a worst time for a dip in sales. Although it was in reality just a sales blip, which all artists suffer from time to time, White saw it differently and effectively panicked in an attempt to stop the rot. For the new album he handed over the songwriting duties to others so he could focus on his performance. He also decided to break with the past and include more than 40 minutes of music on the album instead of 30.

There seemed to be a myriad of other problems surrounding the album. There had been big changes at his record company and most of the people he had worked with since 1973 had left. Russ Regan was still president, but his power was much reduced, and Dennis Stanfill was taking a personal interest in the label, which he had never done before. The new managers at 20th were not impressed with Barry White and resented giving him the $2.5 million he had demanded. So they kept the pressure on.

The new album was called *Barry White Sings For Someone You Love*. It was a tribute to Ray Charles and the recording was finally finished in July 1977.

However, when the new executives at 20th first heard it they were apoplectic. Collectively they came to the conclusion that it did not have the 'usual Barry White sound' and was therefore in breach of their contract with White. Dennis Stanfill was delighted and saw an opportunity to get at White and show him who was boss – he gave the go-ahead for the company's lawyers to write to White seeking financial redress.

It was an extraordinary letter and when White opened it at his home he was as angry as he had ever been. He got into his car and drove straight round to 20th's office without stopping to think. When he got there he pushed the security guard aside, ignored the receptionist and went straight up to the executive floor. He stormed past Russ Regan's secretary and ran into Regan's office, waving the letter above his head and threatening mayhem.

Regan, who had been expecting this response, was not at all surprised. He held his hands up and said, "Nothing to do with me." When White calmed down, Regan quietly told him that Dennis Stanfill was taking his revenge for having been humiliated over the $2.5 million check.

White quickly realised that Regan had nothing to do with the letter and appreciated the heads-up from an old friend. He remembered: "I'd put a lot of work into the album and I knew the label's attitude was just one more salvo in what was now a seemingly never-ending power and control game between Stanfill and me."

White was genuinely surprised by Stanfill's attitude, as elsewhere the 20th Century Fox film division was enjoying its best ever year, off the back of the Star Wars franchise. Its share price had quadrupled from $6 to $27 in a few months.

After some quiet consideration, White was minded to ignore the letter, but was advised by his lawyers to reply formally, in writing. He wrote: "20th executives wouldn't know the sound of an explosion if it went off in the next room." He told them the reason it sounded different was that he had "turned the lights down and brought the music up in that now familiar, idealised haven of romance into which I always took my listeners." He wrote that he didn't expect them to understand that either, and he was right – they didn't.

There was some truth in 20th's concerns, but not the negative comments it drew. Jason Elias, a reviewer, noted that there had been a "slight change to the musical formula." He said that White's "over-the-top musical extravagance" was gone and had been replaced by a "sleeker more relaxed style". Elias explained: "Barry White is so laid back on this album, he's almost reclining."

The new album had a poor start and sales were slow. White once again blamed the marketing: "All my fears about leaving the promotion of the album to the label had come true."

The slow start inspired White to work even harder to make the album a success; he took a large part of the $2.5 million and devised a promotional campaign. He then went out on the road promoting the album and the singles. This move was a success and three singles from the album entered the charts; *It's Ecstasy When You Lay Down Next To Me* eventually sold three million copies. The album yielded three R&B Top 10 singles, two of which entered the Billboard main singles chart. As a result of White's efforts the album was one of his most successful ever, as he explained: "I sold the shit out of that album and in spite of all their bitching it became one of my biggest hits yet."

Stanfill was embarrassed when the album topped the R&B chart, and also reached No 8 on the Billboard album chart.

Barry White Sings For Someone You Love became an iconic album, with all the songs now regarded as Barry White classics. Track one was *Playing Your Game, Baby*, written by Austin Johnson and Smead Hudman; it was the first song that Hudman had written, and he went on to become a prolific writer of Barry White songs over the next 18 years. It came in at over seven minutes long, was released as a single and made the R&B Top 10.

The second track was *It's Ecstasy When You Lay Down Next To Me*, written by Nelson Pigford and Ekundayo Paris and running to seven minutes play time. It was also issued as a single and was White's biggest hit since 1975, going to No 4 in the Billboard singles chart and peaking at No 1 on the R&B chart. It was the start of a long association between White and Pigford and his songwriting partner Ekundayo Paris. However, it proved to be the last chart success for Barry White for 18 long years.

Barry White wasn't surprised that it sold so well, and felt a real affinity with the song. He loved the word 'ecstasy' so much; for him it meant much more than the dictionary definition, as he said: "I can define ecstasy in a single word

– 'joy'. What a man feels when he lies with the woman he really wants to be with, that's ecstasy. There are many ways to communicate ecstasy."

He believed ecstasy was at the heart of real love: "It lets the spiritual electricity we call love pass from one heart to another and ecstasy becomes the medium through which that love passes."

The song's lyrics expressed the physical aspect of ecstasy as well as the emotion, as White described it: "When I fall in love with a woman it is always a total experience of a sexual jolt of pure joy, given as well as received."

The song reflected all that.

The third track was *You're So Good You're Bad*, written by White's business manager, Aaron Schroeder, and the famous composer Jerry Ragovoy. It ran to just over six minutes and was Ragovoy's first song for White – he enjoyed it and would do more in the future.

Side two was led off by *I Never Thought I'd Fall In Love With You*, 4½ minutes long and written by Ronald Coleman; he too was working with White for the first time, and would do so again.

Track five was *You Turned My Whole World Around*, written by long-time White collaborators Frank Wilson and Danny Pearson; at seven minutes 49 seconds it was the longest track on the album.

The last two tracks, numbers six and seven, were of a more sensible length at less than four minutes, and in many people's opinion were the best on the album. Track six was *Oh, What A Night For Dancing*, written by White and Vance Wilson, which zoomed into the main Billboard chart at No 24 and peaked at No 13 on the R&B chart. Track seven was *Of All The Guys In The World*, written by White and his new protégé, Danny Pearson; it was a genuine Barry White masterpiece, revered by his real hard-core fans the world over.

White was rightly ecstatic about the success of the album's three singles. It was also vindication for Jack Perry, who had urged White to put more music on the album. But in one sense it didn't work, and it was clear that White had padded out some of the tracks by repeating the lyrics, which did not improve them.

At the end of the process Barry White breathed a huge sigh of relief. It had been a gruelling period of his life but it had worked and had brought his career back on track. But the endless rows with Stanfill and the infamous letter had worn him down. He sensed the beginning of the end for his relationship with 20th Century Records, especially as Russ Regan was seemingly heading for the exit himself.

He began secret negotiations to leave the label.

Part 4

17 years of slow and gradual decline

CHAPTER 44

The Death of Larry Nunes

Only 48 and gone from a heart attack

September 1978

L arry Nunes's life changed completely when he moved to the smaller house in Sherman Oaks with his wife in 1971. Suddenly his was a quiet and sedentary life with no drama or action of any kind. It was a predicament he had brought upon himself, the consequences of being an out-of-control gambler. His gambling had ruined him and his family and had it not been for Barry White, Nunes and his wife would have had to move to a poorhouse. He was saved from that humiliation by White's dramatic intervention.

It was difficult for such an active man to suddenly be doing nothing. Nunes had worked hard as an entrepreneur for 26 years and created a personal fortune in excess of $20 million. Now he knew it was over and accepted his fate as his wife took control of all the family money. They both knew that if Nunes had money he would just gamble it away again.

But Nunes soon found some excitement, and it came from the American Internal Revenue Service (IRS). When the IRS examined Nunes's affairs, it turned out that he had never paid any taxes in his life.

Very belatedly, Nunes discovered that all income was taxable and that his gambling losses were non-deductible. One day an inspector called and told him that "every dollar gambled is a taxed dollar."

So it was a huge shock when a letter from the IRS arrived in mid-1974 demanding $6 million in back taxes, an amount they calculated was owed on back income from as long ago as 1958. Larry Nunes knew that he owed that amount and more, and he could see no way out. Every cent he possessed had been gambled away and his bank account was empty. Personal bankruptcy was inevitable.

Nunes declared bankruptcy in late 1974 as the only way to get the taxman off his back. At that point he relinquished any roles he had in the Barry White organisation, which were taken over by Aaron and Abby Schroeder of A. Schroeder International Inc and Ned Shankman's management company Shankman, De Blasio, Melina Inc.

Then in 1976, refreshed and apparently cured of his gambling addiction, Nunes re-emerged as manager of a rock act called Brent Maglia. He oversaw the production of an album called *Down At The Hardrock Café* and spin-off singles called *Hannah, The Runaway* and *It's Your Love*. There were high hopes for the album, and Nunes walked down the hill to play it to his friend Barry White.

As they sat down in his lounge, in the house where Nunes used to live, White looked at his friend and thought to himself: "Has it come to this?" He realised that during the two years he had been away in retirement, Nunes had completely lost his 'ears', a vital talent for someone in the music industry. At that moment White vowed to himself never to retire, after having seen what it had done to Larry Nunes. The album was not the sort of music that White enjoyed, although he told Nunes it was a "respectable effort".

White knew, in his heart of hearts, that he should tell his friend the truth – that in his opinion the album was not good enough to make a big impact. But he couldn't bring himself to do it.

Larry Nunes found that he still had some clout in the music industry and the album was released by Fantasy Records, which had recorded Dave Brubeck, Creedence Clearwater Revival and Ike and Tina Turner. Fantasy also released the album in Germany and Italy.

It wasn't a hit, but to White's surprise it didn't fall flat either. Sales were respectable enough for there to be talk of a second album for the group in 1978.

So when Larry Nunes went to bed on 16th September 1978 he was full of optimism for the future. But that optimism was sadly misplaced. In the early morning of the following day he had a massive heart attack that killed him almost instantly as he lay asleep.

He never knew anything about it, and when his wife went to wake him with his usual mug of hot steaming black coffee, she found him cold. Her first instinct was to run down the hill to find Barry White and tell him the news. But she found she couldn't do it, and a Los Angeles police officer volunteered to deliver the news.

At around 11 o'clock the officer walked down the hill and up the drive to the White mansion, Nunes's former home. He walked past the guest house where a young Barry White had sent many a night wooing his future wife, Glodean. He walked around the rear of the house into the backyard, as all visitors did, and knocked on the door. Glodean answered and could immediately sense trouble. She didn't like the look on the officer's face when he asked to speak to Mr White.

He was shown into the lounge and declined an offer of coffee as Barry White motioned him to sit down, pain etched all over his face. At this point it was clear that the officer was present to deliver some very bad news indeed. He said as matter-of-factly as he could muster: "I've been asked to tell you, sir, that Mr Larry Nunes died last night. He died in his sleep of natural causes." He added: "I understand you and he were good friends."

Barry White remembered that he actually laughed when the officer had finished speaking and said: "No, not Larry – you must be mistaken. He was as right as rain the other day and he's only 48."

The officer replied: "I am afraid so, sir – there can't be any doubt about it. His wife has identified him."

With that White's expression and whole demeanour changed as he took in the news. Glodean slumped in her chair, unable to believe what she was hearing about their friend, mentor and neighbour.

The officer waited until both had taken in the news and were composed, then said: "I am afraid I have a few questions, all routine of course." He started off: "Can you tell me where you both were between 10 o'clock last night and six o'clock this morning? These are all routine questions I have to ask – you understand."

Barry and Glodean just looked at each other and both burst into tears. Glodean was absolutely distraught and immediately frightened for the future. It was just too much for either of them to take in. The police officer gave up his questioning and beat a hasty retreat, leaving two people absolutely devastated as if part of themselves had been taken away – Larry Nunes had been that important to them.

White spent the next few hours telling Glodean all the stories about Larry Nunes that he had never dared tell her when he was alive – how they had met in 1965 at Mustang Bronco Records, and how over the next eight years they had built a relationship that had resulted in Barry becoming one of the most famous performing artists in the world. He told Glodean: "There were no signs that he was not going to live forever. As far as I can remember Larry never spent a night in hospital and I had never known him visit his doctor."

"Maybe he should have," replied Glodean.

The rest of the day went by in a blur. At two o'clock they climbed the hill to pass on their condolences to Larry's wife and his five children, who had all gathered in the house. Then they walked back, arms round each other, crying their eyes out to wait for the children to arrive home from school, when they told them that their Uncle Larry had died.

White recalled his own reaction in his 1999 memoirs: "When I heard this news I felt as though my whole world had gone with him. To this day nobody has, or ever will, fill the personal and creative void he left in my life."

Larry Nunes's short obituary notice appeared in the Births, Marriages and Deaths column in the 'Billboard' magazine issue of 20th September 1978. It read: "Larry Nunes, long active in the music industry as manager of Barry White and a rack jobber with Monroe Goodman and Tip Top Music in California, died Sept 17 in Berkeley. Nunes recently had been serving as personal manager of fantasy act Brent Maglia."

And that was it. The magazine had given Larry Nunes what it deemed was the appropriate send-off, its cuttings files giving little clue to the power that Nunes had once wielded in the record business in the sixties. It didn't say that Nunes had been responsible for half of all record sales in that 10-year period, that he had invented rack jobbing or, most importantly of all, that he had invented Barry White.

It's no exaggeration to say that without Larry Nunes there would have been no Barry White. Before 1972, after 15 years of trying, White had failed to break through into mainstream music until Nunes rescued him.

But now he was gone.

THE DEATH OF LARRY NUNES

CHAPTER 45

The Man Album

Eighth solo album

1978

A year after the success of *Barry White Sings For Someone You Love* and its multiple single releases, Barry White followed it up with an album simply called *The Man*, released on 22nd September 1978.

The Man was his own nickname with his fans, and it followed Russ Regan's mantra of "not fooling with success". It contained 47 minutes of music and was heavy with songs written by other writers. It was a recipe that had worked with the previous album, and Barry White was not arrogant enough to tinker with it.

It became his sixth solo album to top the R&B album chart and went to No 36 on the Billboard main albums chart. The only disappointment was in the UK, where it struggled to reach No 46 on the chart in a country where Barry White had previously been very popular.

Three singles were released from the album, but none of them sold well. The most successful was *Your Sweetness Is My Weakness*, which went to No 2 on the R&B chart and No 60 on the main LP chart.

But from a legacy point of view, the stand-out was White's cover of Billy Joel's original hit *Just The Way You Are*, from the year before. Taken from his album called *The Stranger*, Joel had written and performed the song, and it had been arranged by Phil Ramone.

Barry White hardly ever covered other artists' work and certainly not so quickly after the original release. But *Just The Way You Are* was a Barry White song and he couldn't resist it. Gene Page rearranged it and most people agreed that his version was much better than the Joel and Ramone version.

The opening track of the album was called *Look At Her*, a combination writing effort from Frank Wilson, Raymond Cooksey and Tommy Payton. In truth it was overlong at seven minutes 40 seconds, but was a typical Barry White song that has endured to this day.

The second track, *Your Sweetness Is My Weakness*, was even longer, at more than eight minutes. But it was easily the most successful track on the album, and was written by White.

Side one closed with the eight-minute *Sha La La Means I Love You*, again written solely by White. It was released as a single and reached No 55 on the UK singles chart, but failed to make an impact in any other market.

Side two of the album opened with the shorter *September When I First Met You*, which White wrote with Frank Wilson, Paul Politi and Ervin Brown. Wilson and Brown got credit, but had done very little – it was mainly the work of White and his old friend Politi. Although virtually unnoticed at the time, over the years it became a Barry White classic. Its origins were far from usual. White and Politi had been friends since they were teenagers and had written many songs together before White became famous. Their first hit together had been *It May Be Winter Outside in* 1973. White had called in Politi to help him write *September When I First Met You* because it was about his wife Glodean and when they had first met. Politi had been present that day and had witnessed their first meeting, as he explained: "The song was about Glodean, as they had met in September and it was about vowing to make every day a new September, to remember how you felt when you first fell in love and not to take each other for granted. Barry put women on a pedestal. He wanted to write songs about love and nothing else. Glodean and Barry had a wonderful relationship."

But the song proved to have a difficult gestation and nothing seemed to work. White and Politi spent all day sitting by the pool in White's garden at Sherman Oaks, but were getting nowhere with the song. White got frustrated and thought to himself: "If I can't write a song about when I first met the love of my life then what good am I as a songwriter?"

Suddenly he decided that they were too comfortable and that was why there was no creative spark. He got up from his sun-lounger and said: "We've got to go to Vegas." A very surprised Politi, who was enjoying the early-afternoon sun, remembered: "Barry thought it wasn't working and said he didn't have any creative juices. I argued against it but he could be very stubborn, so we got in the car and drove to Vegas."

Getting in a car with Barry White was the last thing Politi wanted to do. It was a 4-hour, 280-mile journey in the scorching heat of the desert, and White was a terrible driver. Politi said: "Barry could do everything well except drive, and he used to scare the hell out of me."

The reason for the sudden journey soon became clear. White had written *Can't Get Enough Of Your Love, Babe* in a hotel room in Las Vegas and booked the same room in The Stardust hotel, as Politi remembered: "He called ahead and said he had to have that specific room. They moved the person who was in the room so we could have it."

But it proved to be a wasted effort, as Politi admitted: "We were sitting in this stupid room with a little tape recorder, when we could have been in his garden."

In the end they gave up and the next morning they set out for home. During the journey White started humming away in the car and Politi suddenly interrupted him and said: "Hey, that's good." He got out his tape recorder and by the time they arrived back at Sherman Oaks the song was in the bag: "We wrote most of the song in the car on the way home."

Track five was *It's Only Love Doing Its Thing*, written by Jimmie and Vella Cameron, a young brother and sister team of songwriters at the very start of their careers who had just come into Barry White's orbit. Gene Page's arrangement made it into something it really wasn't, but it launched the Camerons' career.

Track six was *Just The Way You Are* and, just as Gene Page had thought, it proved to be the perfect song for Barry White's sound. It had been a huge hit for Billy Joel, reaching No 3 in the Billboard singles chart and winning him two Grammys for record of the year and song of the year. White extended it from Joel's four minutes 47 seconds to his own version at seven minutes, with a new start and a new middle. Most people, especially in Britain, thought his version better than Joel's original. It was released as a single and, despite being only a year after the original, it reached No 45 on the R&B chart and peaked at an unexpected No 12 on the UK singles chart. Joel's version had only got to No 14 in the UK, so this was a big triumph for White.

In truth, Barry White was a much better singer than Billy Joel, and had it landed in White's hands first it could have been one of the biggest-selling records of all time. White loved the song as much as he loved his own compositions. "I have a lot of respect for Billy Joel," he said, "and this a very sensitive song. It deals with very sensitive words which sometimes we are not always able to say. It's the kind of song I always want to leave with people, the kind of song that deals with how I feel, and I want people to remember it."

Whenever White sang *Just The Way You Are* live on stage it had a big emotional effect on him and his eyes always moistened. The stage act version ran to more than nine minutes with additional commentary on life and love from the singer. If he had ever had to choose one song from his career, even though he didn't write it, it would probably have been *Just The Way You Are*.

The album ended with another similar-sounding classic called *Early Years*, composed by Ronald Coleman. It was simply sublime; the introduction was arguably White's best singing performance ever, and it perfectly complemented *Just The Way You Are*.

The lyrics of *Early Years* were superbly crafted by Coleman and it resonated perfectly with what Barry White's fans, who had grown up with him since 1972, were thinking. The lyrics were arguably the finest Barry White ever sang in an original song.

The Man came straight off the back of the success of *Barry White Sings For Someone You Love* and was considered the sequel. The two albums represented a mini-revival for White and gave him plenty of hope for the future, although it signalled the beginning of the end of his relationship with 20th Century Records and Russ Regan.

CHAPTER 46

A Label of His Own At Last

Ground-breaking but flawed deal with CBS

1976 to 1977

W hen Russ Regan finally left 20th Century Records, after months of so-called 'gardening leave', he used his severance pay of $3 million to set up his own label, which he grandly called Millennium Records. But Regan was primarily a sales and marketing man with little real feel for music, and Millennium was destined to fail. Barry White thought briefly about following Regan out the door of 20th and into Millennium, but decided against it. He wanted a label with financial and marketing muscle.

He found that at CBS Records, which was prepared to give him the money he wanted. The deal was arranged by Bruce Lundvall, who had been promoted to President of CBS's US domestic label in 1976. Lundvall was looking to make his mark on the company and the timing was perfect for Barry White.

Bruce Lundvall had joined CBS in 1959 fresh out of college, and eventually became one of Clive Davis's protégés. His specialist area was jazz, and after Davis was fired his eventual promotion to the top job in North America had been a surprise.

Lundvall heard on the grapevine that White was unhappy and unlikely to renew his contract at 20th, so decided to make a move before other labels. Almost as soon as he heard the news, he called his wife and told her to pack his bags. He sent his chauffeur to collect them, then was driven to the airport to catch the 'red-eye' that same evening.

As soon as his plane landed in Los Angeles he drove straight to Sherman Oaks and began a week of wooing. White remembered: "No sooner had word got out about my unhappiness at 20th, than Bruce Lundvall made a personal call on me at my house to talk things over."

The bearded 42-year-old was an old-school charmer and told White what he wanted to hear. When he uttered the immortal line, "The best deserve to be the best and that's why Barry White should be at CBS," Barry White was smitten.

CBS Records certainly was the best and the biggest record label in America at the time. Part of Bill Paley's CBS Television group, it had been built up into a colossus by former president Clive Davis, and annual profits were in excess of $50 million.

Barry White was deeply flattered by Bruce Lundvall's charm, and admitted: "I took this as a great compliment because everyone knew that CBS was the premier mainstream record label and the class act of American music."

The two men got on well and after a few days of talks thrashed out a deal that gave White a $2 million advance against royalties. White recalled: "CBS offered me a lot of money to sign and I stood to make close to a hundred million dollars if everything had worked out."

But still he hesitated: "In spite of everything on offer I was still reluctant and I said to Bruce, 'CBS doesn't need Barry White. I almost went with Clive once but now I need a label that needs me, that will go crazy to make sure my records will jump off those charts. You have five hundred and something other artists who need you more than you need them or me.'"

So White didn't sign immediately, although he and Lundvall bonded and developed a form of trust. In truth it was hard not to like Bruce Lundvall. He exuded honesty and integrity, as one contemporary said: "When Bruce spoke, the person listening believed every word he said – he was that sort of man."

But White wondered how such a mild-mannered man could have had risen to become head of CBS Records. The record industry was a cutthroat business headed by extroverts who invariably liked a drink or something stronger. Lundvall was not that man, and it made Barry White nervous.

Gradually White realised that he did not want to sign a conventional record deal. Even though it was an unwelcome necessity, he found that he had enjoyed the process of putting out Love Unlimited's *He's All I've Got* album independently and wondered whether the same business model might work with CBS.

Suddenly an idea started to form in White's head.

It was not a new notion. Many years before he had tried to raise money to start his own independent record label to record third-party artists, but potential backers had only been interested in him. He had spent months trying to raise money and had failed miserably to get anybody interested. He recalled: "The problem had been the financing. The music industry was an overwhelmingly white-dominated industry and it was hard to get the money and after having no success lining up investors I re-evaluated my position." He believed that his failure had been down to racism and wrote in his 1999 memoirs: "Oh yes, it was fine for black people to make hit records but it's only when we wanted to keep some of the profits they generated that certain people became very nervous."

Gradually the idea was reborn to start his own label, which he would call Unlimited Gold Records, the name he had used to release *He's All I've Got*. He dusted off his old business plan and decided to pitch the idea to Bruce Lundvall.

When Lundvall returned to Sherman Oaks, White told him he would sign on certain conditions: "I told him I had two conditions. The first was that I had to have my own record company and the second was that I wanted a reversion deal." This meant that if at the end of the contract it was not renewed White would retain ownership of copyrights and the master tapes would be returned to him. The overall arrangement he described was as it had been for the *He's All I've Got* album. Under the deal, CBS would take care of manufacturing and distribution for an agreed fee and built-in profit, and the balance of the money from all sales would be paid to Unlimited Gold Records.

Although the deal was everything White wanted, it was very expensive for him personally. He agreed to forfeit the $2 million upfront that Lundvall had originally offered, and to take no advance royalties. He would only receive any money after the records had been released and CBS got paid. CBS also agreed to contribute towards his overhead, but only after the record had recouped its costs.

Although Lundvall was reluctant to agree to such a deal, he was tempted by Barry White's offer to take no upfront advance. It meant that CBS could effectively sign White for nothing. After a few moments' thought, Lundvall said, "Yes." White smiled and held out his hand.

And it was done.

But in reality it was far from done. Back in New York the lawyers in CBS's contracts department tried to row back everything that Lundvall and White had agreed. Abby Schroeder went to Black Rock, the nickname for CBS's headquarters in New York, to negotiate the deal's finer points.

Aaron and Abby Schroeder strongly advised White not to do the deal. In his heart of hearts Aaron knew that Barry White's best days were behind him. He had noticed how, the better his music got, the lower the sales of his albums were. The 53-year-old Schroeder, very knowledgeable in the ways of the music industry, had seen it happen to other artists time after time as their music had fallen out of fashion. He told White: "Barry, don't do this – there are dangers in every line of this contract." Schroeder implored his friend not to go ahead, but it fell on deaf ears. For Barry White this was his dream deal, and he had an unshakeable belief in himself.

One aspect of the deal that Aaron Schroder did like was Barry White's right to own the master tapes at the end of the contract. To Schroeder's recollection, this concession had never been granted in a contract to any artist before, and CBS lawyers fought tooth and nail against it. Abby Schroeder had strict orders not to back down, even at the risk of walking away, as White recalled: "I have to credit Abby for making it work. She kept insisting that if it was going to be my label then it had to mean that I owned what was on it without qualification." White later admitted that he was very surprised when the CBS lawyers finally conceded the point. White also insisted that the clause was out in the open and not confidential. He wanted other artists to know what was possible.

As soon as he signed the deal, White immediately started looking for new artists to record while he worked off his 20th contract: "My intention was to develop new acts and I immediately set up an A&R division." He was filled with optimism that he could at last fulfil his dream of being a producer for artists that he would discover and make into stars. As he said later in his memoirs: "I was ready to rumba, baby." The following three years proved very exciting as the label went through its long start-up phase.

Once signed, White hoped that his new contract could be kept secret, as he still owed 20th Century Records three more albums, and had considerable advances to pay back on them. But inevitably the news leaked out, and on 2nd October 1976 'Billboard' magazine revealed the new deal and the name of the new joint venture label, Unlimited Gold.

The leak was tricky, with 2½ years still to go on White's and the Love

Unlimited Orchestra's contracts. Only the three girls of Love Unlimited were out of contract at 20th Century Records and, with Russ Regan on the way out, there had been no enthusiasm on either side to renew it. Thus the three girls were the only artists immediately available to record on the new label. They had been particular victims of the changes at 20th Century, when executives had refused to release any more albums after the relatively poor sales of *In Heat* in 1974. Glodean White was particularly scathing of 20th's attitude, believing that they didn't begin to understand the music business. As she said: "The disco era has been a time for solo artists, and female groups have always peaked in and out throughout the history of the business."

When White's new deal and its terms were announced, the whole of the music industry took a sharp intake of breath. Previously contracts had always been skewed in favour of the record company. But the nature of this deal and its terms produced plenty of consternation throughout the industry. Traditionally, artists, writers and producers got 15 per cent of the revenues and the record company got the rest, often as much as 50 per cent after paying its costs. It meant that running a record label was tremendously lucrative.

White's deal had turned the whole business on its head, with the record company getting 15 per cent and the artist 50 per cent. What could possible go wrong?

Everything, as it turned out.

CHAPTER 47

I Love to Sing the Songs I Sing

Ninth solo album and last with 20th Century

1979

After he signed his new deal with CBS to set up Unlimited Gold Records, White saw out his own personal contract at 20th Century Records as quickly as he could, as he said: "I remained very bitter about the label's actions and knew that it was time to leave."

The contract called for one final solo album, and *I Love To Sing The Songs I Sing* was the ninth of Barry White's career. It was released on 10th April 1979, and was his last on the 20th Century label.

20th was now nothing like the company White had first joined in 1973. It had renamed itself 20th Century-Fox Records and the era of Russ Regan had ended as slick-suited executives from the parent company took the helm. Without Regan, the new bosses had very little idea of what they were doing, and had little time for Barry White or his music. They hated him and he hated them – there was no love lost at all.

White put the personal animosity aside as he went into the studio to record *I Love To Sing The Songs I Sing*. He produced yet another album full of enduring classics, despite the fact that Gene Page wasn't around for much of the production. Ronald Coleman and John Roberts, assisted by veteran engineers Frank Kejmar and Paul Elmore, took his place.

White dedicated the new album to the sounds of Motown and the opening title track reflected that spirit, and was almost a homage to his heroes, Brian Holland, Lamont Dozier and Eddie Holland. The album was a collaboration between four writers, White himself and Paul Politi, Frank Wilson and Ronald Coleman.

Frank Wilson was Barry White's childhood friend and they had written songs together since they were 14. Their first job together had been doing studio jobbing work for Motown in the sixties. Wilson also had a group called The Remarkables with his two brothers and a cousin, with occasional appearances by his sister and brother-in-law. Young Ronald Coleman had a host of songwriting credits to his name.

Track one was the title track, *I Love To Sing The Songs I Sing*, co-written by Paul Politi and Frank Wilson. At just under three minutes, it was one of the shortest compositions of Barry White's career, but was a classic White song and would endure. It was released as a single, making No 53 on the Billboard R&B chart, which in no way reflected its quality – five years earlier, there is no doubt it would have been a huge hit.

The second track was *Girl, What's Your Name*, composed with Danny Pearson, White's young protégé, and Frank Wilson. It was a soothing tune regarded as a classic White song by fans. The third track reflected Ronald Coleman's impact on White's music. Called *Once Upon A Time (You Were A Friend of Mine)*, it was a six-minute masterpiece, perfect for the Barry White style. Coleman had been a protégé of Lamont Dozier, and was now firmly established at White's side; he would go on to have a great writing career. The last track on side one was *Oh Me, Oh My (I'm Such A Lucky Guy)*, which was a collaboration between White, Wilson, Politi and Ray Cooksey, and again regarded as a classic by many.

The first track on side two was *I Can't Leave You Alone*, written with Tony Sepe. Arguably the most forgettable track on the album, it was very poor and was never heard of again.

Ronald Coleman composed the sixth and seventh tracks alone. The first was *Call Me Baby*, at just over eight minutes long, and the last was *How Did You Know It Was Me?* at nearly seven minutes. Both were classic White songs and established Coleman as the most talented writer on White's team, and a man who knew exactly what suited his master's voice.

The completion of the *I Love To Sing The Songs I Sing* album should have been the end of Barry White's relationship with 20th Century Records. But not quite. Under his old contract he still owed 20th another album for the Love Unlimited Orchestra. But it was not an album he wanted to put any major effort into as he was keen to move on to his new deal with CBS as quickly as possible. But he realised that he could indulge himself at his record label's expense, as they were contractually obliged to pay for and release whatever Love Unlimited Orchestra album he wanted to record. He also wanted to do an album without the heavy burden of songwriting, to enjoy the freedom of being able to play and arrange someone else's music.

The Barry White sound was massively influenced by old movies and their music, and few realised what a dedicated movie buff White really was. He was continually intrigued by film music, so one morning he woke up with a brainwave of doing a movie themes album with the Love Unlimited Orchestra.

White watched old movies every night in his screening room at Sherman Oaks. He even took his own movie projector with him on tour. Tony Sepe, who travelled on all the tours, recalled: "When we went to Europe and Japan we had to bring our own movie projector because that was all he did. He didn't come out of his hotel room when we toured."

Barry White prided himself on being able to recall any movie, saying: "Let me see a certain scene and I'll tell you the picture. And I'll give you the dialogue word for word. I've seen 'King Kong' 21 times, 'The Maltese Falcon' 32 times. All those old movies were the greatest. Actors like Bogart, Cagney, Tyrone Power, Spencer Tracy and Gable don't come off that way anymore."

So he decided to put his movie knowledge to good use for his last album with 20th Century. He also thought the album could be a commercial success with the right promotion.

Thus *Super Movie Themes* was born. He already had one track in the bag, the adaption of John Barry's 'King Kong' theme that he had reworked for Dino De Laurentiis in 1976. This had been extremely successful and White decided to rework all the pieces for the new album in the same style. It was, however, a serious mistake and he ended up with nine sound-alike tracks that vaguely resembled the themes they were supposed to be.

The opening track was the theme from 'Superman', which the Love Unlimited Orchestra murdered. Track two was the 'King Kong' track, as it had appeared in the 1976 film. Track three was *Night Fever* from 'Saturday Night Fever', which the orchestra murdered again. Track four, *Grease*, was also murdered. Barry White wrote track five, which he called *Intermission*, to replicate the feeling of a visit to the theatre. It was desperately disappointing and not up to his usual standard.

Side two started with Isaac Hayes's *Shaft* theme. Surely Barry White couldn't murder this – but unfortunately he did. Track five was the theme from a 1959 film called 'A Summer Place', made popular by the Percy Faith Orchestra and a hit in 1960. The White treatment of this beautiful theme was an affront to the ears of his fans. Track six featured the theme from 'The Way We Were', originally composed by Marvin Hamlisch with lyrics by Alan and Marilyn Bergman; the White treatment was simply awful and again an affront to Marvin Hamlisch and Barbra Streisand. If either of them had been friends of his before, they wouldn't have been after this.

Track seven was from the film 'As Time Goes By', and was another affront to the original. The final track was an adaption of an original White composition from 1974 that had previously been released as a single by Love Unlimited, grandly titled *People Of Tomorrow Are The Children Of Today*. Stripped of its original lyrics, it was the best track on a very poor album.

A theory that circulated at the time was that *Super Movie Themes* was Barry White's revenge against Dennis Stanfill as part of his ongoing feud with 20th Century Fox. If it was, it backfired, and White did his own reputation as a musician no good at all.

The release of the album marked the first serious criticism that White had received from journalists. Even John Abbey of 'Blues & Soul' magazine, an avid White admirer, was moved to write negatively about *Super Movie Themes*: "The movie themes album didn't knock me out."

When White read the criticism he claimed that he had been made to record the album by 20th Century Records against his will, and proceeded to blame Dennis Stanfill, claiming that it was all the label's idea: "It was their idea," he said. "They wanted an album of movie themes and I gave it to them." When John Abbey suggested that his heart wasn't in it, White agreed with him.

The malaise spread to *I Love To Sing The Songs I Sing*. The new deal with CBS had been announced before the album was released, which meant that 20th put very little effort into promoting it. When it was released White was already working on his new deal with CBS and his next album called *The Message Is Love*.

White also had no time to promote *I Love To Sing The Songs I Sing* and it languished unloved in record stores. Unsurprisingly it was the least successful solo album of Barry White's 20th Century career, reaching No 40 on the R&B albums chart, which six of his eight previous albums had topped. None of the singles released from the album made any impact on the charts.

As for *Super Movie Themes*, it was a disaster creatively and commercially and a stain on Barry White's career. Years later he revealed to close friends that he had started the album with good intentions but deliberately sabotaged it to get back at Stanfill – something he regretted years later.

So Barry White signed off from 20th Century Records with a whimper. Between 1973 and 1979 he had released 20 albums for the company, and almost all of them had achieved gold record status in America – a quite remarkable achievement.

A year after Barry White left the label, 20th Century Fox shuttered its record label for good and closed the company down.

That decision said all that needed to be said.

CHAPTER 48

Unlimited Gold Takes Shape

Barry White's musical revolution

1978

As Barry White ran down his contract at 20th Century Records, he was putting a lot of thought into his new label, Unlimited Gold. He had long admired Island and Chrysalis, two independent record labels. He particularly looked up to Chris Blackwell, who had taken Island Records from unlikely beginnings on the island of Jamaica to huge international success in just a few years. Equally he was in awe of what British entrepreneurs Chris Wright and Terry Ellis had achieved at Chrysalis Records in London in an even shorter time.

They were his models and he fully intended to build Unlimited Gold into a top record label on the same lines, passionately believing that he could do it. But the thinking was flawed, as at the root of his passion was a lack of respect for himself as an artist. He had never been happy being purely a performer and was desperate to fulfil his ambition of running his own record label and having a stable of successful artists under his control.

But as much as Barry White dreamed of being a big-shot producer and a Svengali to the stars, it proved to be a folly and never happened. In the end it was to cost him as much as $10 million, which came straight out of his own pocket and, for a while, would leave him virtually destitute.

It was a dream he had chased before and he seemed to have forgotten what had happened five years earlier, in 1973. Back then White and Larry Nunes had been partners in an independent production company called Mo Soul Productions, and it had failed miserably; they had been unable to launch the careers of any artists. White also seemed to have forgotten that the *He's All I've Got* album, which he produced independently for Love Unlimited, had not worked particularly well either. The failures should have acted as a warning, but they were forgotten and buried in the past.

It was as if they had never happened, and White declared: "We are going to keep a small, selective roster. That's the only way to make it work. If you have nine or ten acts, how do you get them all played? No, I want four or five tight acts. That's all I need, that's it."

The failure to learn from and avoid the lessons of the past would mean five years of relative misery as his roster of artists all failed and his own career went into reverse gear along with them.

There were many reasons for failure, the main one being that he didn't seem to realise that the deal he had signed with CBS gave that company little incentive to see him succeed. In fact, it could be argued that it gave CBS a big incentive to see him not succeed. If it had worked out, every artist would have wanted the same generous deal that White had been granted, and CBS would never have allowed that to happen. So the Unlimited Gold label experiment had to fail, and that is exactly what happened. CBS couldn't afford for it to work, and it didn't.

But Barry White thought he knew it all, and went into the deal with plenty of confidence. He said: "A lot of people make a mistake in investing money because they invest in a lot of other things outside of themselves when they should be investing in themselves, especially if they've really got something going that can keep on making money for them instead of gambling on something they are not sure of."

The sentiments he expressed were very laudable and in many ways sound business judgement, except that what he said had never applied to the music business. There was a golden rule for artists: "Never spend your own money, always spend your record company's money."

Although the economics of the music business were skewed heavily in favour of the record label, that was what had always happened. Record companies took all the risk and consequently took most of the profits. It was a system that had endured for years.

But Barry White was totally convinced that what he was doing was right. He was prepared to take that risk and no one could have dissuaded him, as he said at the time: "I'm sure of myself and my music. And I'm also sure of Glodean, Linda and Dede. That's why I started my record label with them; we've been a winning combination."

Simultaneously Barry White was making enemies on other fronts and, instead of staying under the radar, he was emboldened by his new ground-breaking deal with CBS. He thought he was untouchable and started a very public campaign to get a better deal for songwriters.

Much of his own income came from writing songs and he was in a very fortunate position as he co-owned all of his publishing rights. But writers generally were paid very poorly, typically 1.5 cents on the dollar. White called for that to be increased to 2.5 cents on the dollar. He said: "We feel that writers are entitled to a higher royalty – that's what a hit song comes from. It's all about the music. If you have no writer you have no industry. The life of a copyright is very important, it's the only thing that you've got that is better than real estate. A copyright in a song is better than real estate and will last forever."

Naturally his words upset the record companies and, although they were laudable sentiments, in voicing them publicly he also annoyed the major music publishers. Most of them were linked to the record labels, so the wrath of the whole industry was aroused. It was the wrong time and created hostility just as Barry White needed everyone's goodwill as he struggled to get his new record label off the ground.

Despite the early missteps, at first there was plenty of optimism surrounding the venture. Barry White appointed himself chairman of the board and his wife Glodean was made an executive vice-president. He quickly found offices for his new label at Studio City in the San Fernando Valley, a short drive from his home in Sherman Oaks.

The choice of president of the new Unlimited Gold label was crucial, and White took as much care in the selection as he could. After a long search he appointed Rod McGrew to run the label from day to day, but the reason for his decision was far from clear. McGrew was known as a spiritualist rather than a record executive, and his experience of business was limited to a few years running a radio station.

McGrew had attended the Maharishi International University in Los Angeles, where he had studied transcendental meditation and the seven levels of consciousness in life and existence. He had continued his spiritual studies and development through adulthood, first with Swami Muktananda through the practice and teachings of Siddha Yoga, and later Kundalini Yoga as taught by

Yogi Bhajan of the Sikh community. After that he had set up his own business called Love & Happiness Productions Inc, which had promoted the concept of what he called 'spirit in business'. This went nowhere, but brought him into contact with Stevie Wonder, who was also a spiritualist. Wonder appointed McGrew to run his FM radio station, KJLH, which stood for kindness, joy, love and happiness. Based in Los Angeles, McGrew filled many of the top roles himself, including presenter, program director and general manager.

However, after a few years Stevie Wonder grew tired of the losses and McGrew found himself on the street. It was then that he met Barry White, who was also a big fan of spiritualism. The two men's personalities immediately gelled and White offered McGrew the job as president of Unlimited Gold after hearing his hard-luck story and choosing to believe it.

White also brought in Jack Perry as head of A&R, together with Lauri Fernandez, both reporting to McGrew. Tony Sepe, Elmer Hill and Hosea Wilson were also brought on board, and a host of support staff hired. Glodean White revelled in her new role as a record executive, and believed in her husband and his ability to make it work. As she said: "The first thing an artist would want to have is a well-known and qualified producer, and we have one built in. I think it's a blessing and it's always been like a family affair."

White was determined that his new company would be well managed, and in the beginning it was: "I feel I run the tightest ship in the music industry. I have the greatest executives in the world. People like Tony Sepe, Elmer Hill and Hosea Wilson. We have a very strong organisation. But it only works because the top man stays on top of it all.

"Sure we have business and personal problems, but I stay completely involved in all of it. You see, the industry is a business and I have to stay completely involved always with my people. With a small organisation, it's like a family and every objective has to be focused in the same direction. I feel like I have a small army."

Unlimited Gold was formally announced on Tuesday 25th July 1978 at the week-long CBS Records annual convention in the Royce Hall at the University of California in Los Angeles (UCLA). It was the biggest convention ever held by CBS, and Barry White was the star turn. He made a long speech standing at the giant white podium in front of more than 1,000 people.

The convention was based at the Century Plaza Hotel, spilling out into neighbouring hotels, and over five days was attended by 1,400 delegates from 32 countries. It was presided over by CBS Records' chief executive, Walter Yetnikoff, who revealed that company sales for 1978 would exceed $1 billion for the first time ever. He said: "As a group we have doubled in sales over the last four years and we didn't start off from a tiny base to begin with. The same numbers show a two and a half times growth in profits."

Yetnikoff, who had succeeded the legendary Clive Davis as leader of CBS Records five years before, called for even more efforts in the year ahead. Then he spoiled it. He was an inspiring leader, but hobbled by his own extreme ego. He wanted everyone to now that he and he alone was responsible for all the success, and not Clive Davis, but when he made some snide references regarding his predecessor they were greeted by negative murmurings from delegates in the hall. Years later he took Davis to lunch to apologise for what he had said that day.

Sensing that the mood had changed, Bruce Lundvall, architect of the Barry White deal, took the stage and said: "CBS has always had the vision and it still has the vision as industry leaders." He was clearly referring to the controversial deal with White, but he reeled off a list of achievements where CBS had led innovation in the music business: "We have the most enlightened A&R expertise in the industry."

Despite the problems, it was clear that CBS Records was on a high and, alongside White's new label, it was also announced that CBS had signed up Johnny Rodriguez, Marilyn McCoo, Billy Davies Jnr, David Crosby, Graham Nash and Gladys Knight.

After the official business, the evenings turned into one long party that Barry and Glodean felt obliged to attend. At one of the late-night parties, Bruce Lundvall performed a two-step to the sixties tune *Winchester Cathedral*. The grand finale on Saturday 29th July saw 1,300 beach balls fall onto delegates from the ceiling.

Pumped up by the convention and free to get to work after the official announcement, White unveiled his first act, the brother and sister songwriting duo of Jimmie and Vella Cameron. He said: "I believe they are going to be really big. I have never seen as much genius in a woman in her early stages as I can see in Vella." White said the new label would be built around them.

To celebrate the launch of the new label, White did the unthinkable and shaved his beard off. Later, when no one recognised him, he realised it had been a mistake and quickly grew it back: "I love Barry White with his beard. I grew it back. There's no difference in the man, it's just facial. It grew very even, and I love hair."

Following on from the CBS convention and the publicity surrounding his new label, White was formally recognised for his achievements in the academic world. The University of Waco in Texas awarded him an Honorary Doctorate of Music and he was chuffed that he was now Dr Barry White. Then UCLA followed up and awarded him one of its doctorates.

White was delighted with these two awards, and it brought an amusing aside in his family life. He was a big fan of the British TV sitcom 'Fawlty Towers', which starred John Cleese, and he particularly loved the episode called 'The Psychiatrist', when Basil Fawlty (Cleese) becomes confused with husband and wife guests in the hotel both being doctors, particularly when Basil asks the husband how he has become 'two doctors'. Hearing that, five-year-old Shaherah shouted across the room: "That's you, Daddy – you are two doctors!" Despite the comedy aspect of being 'two doctors', White was delighted to be recognised for his music, recognition that he had failed to achieve so far at the Grammy Awards, which had rankled for years and would continue to do so. Aside from that, family life continued to get better and better. At the end of the year he bought his mother a new house, near his own, in Sherman Oaks.

The children of Barry White

Above: Top row (L to R): Kevin James-White, Darryl White and Barry White Jnr. Bottom row (L to R): Denice Donnell, Bridget James-White, Shaherah White, Lanese White and Nina White.

The millennium tour of Australia 2000

Above: Barry White photographed on stage, at the age of 56, during his millennium tour in Australia on 25th November 2000.

The 1988 Red Cross Ball in Monte Carlo

Above: Barry and Glodean White attend the Monaco Red Cross Ball in 1988. They were on tour in Europe together and performed at the Sporting Club in Monte Carlo during the visit.

Jack Perry: Barry White's best friend and confidant for 32 years

© Eagle Rock Studio 4

Above: There is no denying that the most significant person in Barry White's life after his mother was Jack Perry. Perry first met White in 1971, coincidentally the same day that White was introduced to the three girls of Love Unlimited. From that day onwards he rarely left Barry White's side and was present at virtually every recording session the maestro took part in.

Above: Abby Schroeder was Barry White's business manager after Larry Nunes retired. She had the unenviable task of presiding over his affairs in the last few weeks of his life.

Above: Aaron Schroeder was a famous songwriter and worked closely with Barry White throughout his career, publishing his songs and managing his affairs along with wife, Abby

Above: Ray Parker jnr belived he owed much of his later success to his association with Barry White in the 1970s. He was devastated by his death in July 2003.

Above: Marc Eliot co-wrote Barry White's memoirs published in 1999. Eliot was also Walt Disney's biographer and the author of many show business books.

Barry White could not replicate his own success with others

Barry White seemed to have a jinx on the third party artists for whom he produced albums over the years. None of them achieved any success, aside from Gene Page, but they left a rich legacy of music that was immortalised by Jack Perry in his Barry White 'Unlimited' book and album of records in 2009. His failure with other artists seemed inexplicable to himself and others. It was a source of great frustration to him.

© Imperial Records

© Casablanca Records

No reward for first album
The Kindred Soul of Danny Wagner was Barry White's first ever produced album. Bob Keane financed the album and took all the glory when it was released in 1968; White was not even credited on the paperwork, but it was all his work.

Talent doesn't shine through
Indicative of how tough it is to succeed in the music business as an artist was reflected in the experiences of Gloria Scott. Her first album in 1974, *What Am I Gonna Do*, was produced by Barry White and his Soul Unlimited production company.

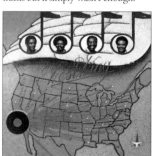

© 20th Century Records

© Atlantic Records

© Warner Bros Records

White protégé falls at the first hurdle
Tom Brock, was a talent who was at Barry White's side for most of his career. His attempt at a solo album in 1974, *I Love You More and More*, produced by White, fell by the wayside. There were some great individual tracks but it simply wasn't enough.

Gene does his thing
Barry White encouraged Gene Page to perform as an artist in his own right. *Hot City*, released in 1974, was a big success and became a disco favourite. Page went on to do more on his own, but his heart was never in being a performer.

JayDee's beautiful singing
Earl Nelson, a long-time Barry White collaborator, was arguably the most talented artist to be produced by Barry White. On this album, *Come On In Love*, he went under the name of Jay Dee and produced some fine songs.

© 20th Century Records

© CBS Records

© CBS Records

Another failure
West Wing was a group discovered by Barry White, and Russ Regan of 20th Century Records took a liking to them. Regan financed this eponymous album and White produced it. Despite a few nice tunes it failed to sell many copies.

Another protégé falls down
Danny Pearson was a talented songwriter. More importantly, he was a Barry White protégé who was the first artist to sign with the Unlimited Gold/CBS label in 1978. His album sold moderately well but, like all the other White artists, he ultimately failed.

The brother and sister duo
Jimmie and Vella Cameron started working with Barry White in the late seventies and were talented artists and songwriters in their own right. White encouraged them to make an album, *Song Painters,* in 1981.

BARRY WHITE

"MAESTRO OF LOVE"

25ᵗʰ ANNIVE[R]

Above: Barry White celebrated his 25th anniversary in music in 1994 and a party was held at the Hard Rock Cafe in Los Angeles, California. It was a muted celebration, as by then the Maestro had parted from his wife Glodean and lost his way musically.

Above: Shaherah White, aged 19, and her father Barry White are seen together in Sydney, Australia, in 1994 during the Asian leg of that year's world tour. Shaherah's was a constant fixture on tour during the 90s.

Above: Barry and Glodean White on stage at the American Bandstand on 15th April 1981 to promote their new album of duets, *Barry & Glodean*. The show aired on the ABC network to huge ratings.

Above: Barry White embraces Luciano Pavarotti at the end of the their epic duet of *You're the First, The Last, My Everything* at the 'Children of Afghanistan concert in Modena, Italy in 2000. It was a *magical moment* in both of their careers.

Above: On Wednesday 20th October 1999 Barry White finally launched his memoirs, called 'Love Unlimited', co-written with the journalist Marc Eliot. Fans queued around the block at Barnes & Noble's New York store to get his signature on a book.

Above: Sadie Mae Carter, Barry White's mother, photographed in 1988 by Gene Page at a recording studio. She was the guiding light of his life and gave him his grounding in music at a very young age. He was very close to his mother his whole life until her death in 1996.

Above: Chaka Khan and Barry White on 'The Tonight Show' with host Jay Leno on 1st November 1999 to promote the new *Staying Power* album. Khan dueted with White on one of the tracks.

The relationship with Katherine Denton

Above: Around 1990 Barry White met Katherine Denton, who became his new girlfriend and was with him until his death in 2003. At the time she had just turned 20 years old but the then 45-year-old singer connected spiritually with the young woman and they became an item. They soon moved in with each other, first in Sherman Oaks, then Las Vegas, and finally back to California.

Above: By the beginning of the 21st century Katherine Denton and Barry White were an item of more than 10 years standing. She accompanied him all over the world on tour in his latter years, effectively becoming his nurse as his health deteriorated. Here they are photographed at an event in Paris in 2001.

© Paul Harris/Getty Images

Above: On 15th November 2001 at his home in Encino, California, Barry White poses with some of his gold and platinum discs awarded for sales of his music over 28 years.

© Vanity Fair

Above: In August 2002 Barry White flew to New York to take part in a 'Vanity Fair' photoshoot for the cover of the November issue. He appeared on the gatefold cover with nine female artists, which the magazine called Barry's Angels. The photoshoot was held in New York's meatpacking district in a blistering August heatwave. From left to right they are Gwen Stefani, Jennifer Lopez, Sheryl Crow, Alicia Keys, Norah Jones, Eve Jihan Jeffers, Nelly Furtado, Shirley Manson, Barry White and Debbie Harry.

Above: A portrait of Barry White taken on 9th September 1986 by the famed paparazzi photographer Ron Galella in Los Angeles, California.

Barry White and Katherine Denton at home in Encino

Above: Barry White's final home was at Encino, California, and marked his return to the city after the Northridge earthquake. On 15th November 2001, two years before his death, he let photographer Paul Harris into his house for a series of photos with his girlfriend, Katherine Denton.

Above: Katherine Denton had a big influence on Barry White in the later stages of his life. Gone were the gaudy colour schemes in his home and out went the outrageously over-the-top furnishings. The house, which White had bought for close to $2 million, was understated compared with his previous homes. But he still enjoyed a huge swimming pool in the backyard.

The death of Barry White – 4th July 2003

Above: On 4th July 2003, as Americans celebrated Independence Day, it was announced that Barry White had passed away. Immediately on hearing the news his fans took to the streets around his house, laid flowers and lit candles as a mark of respect.

Above: On 12th July 2003 around 40 close family and friends gathered at Santa Monica pier and boarded the yacht 'Mojo', which then put out to sea. Half an hour later Barry White's ashes were scattered into the sea. The event was notable by the presence of Michael Jackson, who had chartered the yacht for the service. All the guests got their feet wet as the water came over the rear deck.

Induction into the Hollywood Walk of Fame

© Paul Archuleta / Filmmagic

Above: Glodean White is seen surrounded by the extended White family of children and grand-children when the patriarch was inducted into the Hollywood Walk of Fame on 12th September 2013. The ceremony was timed to coincide with what would have been Barry White's 69th birthday, had he lived. He was the 2,506th person to be inducted into the Walk of Fame and to have his own star.

© Michael Ochs / Getty Images

Above: Glodean White and Linda James speak at the press conference at the unveiling of the Barry White star at the Hollywood Walk of Fame on 12th September 2013.

© Waring Abbott / Getty Images

Above: Berry Gordy, the founder of the Motown record label, and Jack Perry at the Hollywood Walk of Fame. Motown almost signed Barry White when he was a fledgling artist in 1969 and offered him a $1,000-a-week contract. White, although penniless at the time, inexplicably turned down the offer.

One of the last photographs of Barry White

© Alamy

Above: Barry White was photographed at the annual Black Entertainment Awards on 25th June 2002 in one of his last public appearances before his death on 4th July 2003. By then he was very ill and in and out of Cedars-Sinai Hospital for dialysis sessions.

Barry White: 12th September 1944 – 4th July 2003

Above: Barry White as all his fans will remember him, photographed in relaxed mode in his dressing room at the Regal Theatre in Chicago, Illinois, on 1st June 1990 before a concert.

UNLIMITED GOLD TAKES SHAPE

CHAPTER 49

The Message is Love

First album at CBS

August 1979

T he dust had barely settled on his last album at 20th Century before Barry White was back in the recording studio working on his new album, titled *The Message Is Love*. It would be Barry White's tenth solo album and the most important of his career.

As the first album on his new label, Unlimited Gold, it was absolutely vital that it succeeded. The theme of the album was simple enough; it was just about love between two people, and with it came a subtle change of style, as White admitted: "There is a lot more singing; more melodic songs and stronger lyrics." White and Paul Politi closeted themselves together for a month and wrote most of the songs. Unfortunately they struggled from the very beginning to find a groove.

The opening track was called *It Ain't Love, Babe (Until You Give It)*. The lyrics and the melody were confusing, it was not a typical Barry White song, and certainly not single material. The second track, *Hung Up In Your Love*, was catchy but ultimately forgettable.

Track three, *You're The One I Need*, was brought to White by jobbing composer Smead Hudman. It was one of the better tracks on the album, but it too was formulaic and ultimately not good enough. The last track on side one was called *Any Fool Could See (You Were Meant For Me)* and was a typical Barry White song and rather better, with a catchy tune and lyrics.

Love Ain't Easy, the opening track on side two, was a ballad but simply not up to the standard of previous White efforts. Amazingly it was released as a single. The penultimate track, *I'm On Fire*, had been brought to White by amateur writer Robert Jason. It was a surprisingly stylish song and became a fans' favourite over the years. The last track, *I Found Love*, had a clever melody and lyrics and was arguably the best track on the album.

But by then it didn't matter.

Just when Barry White needed to step up to the plate with his tenth album, he failed to find what was needed. Afterwards it was clear that the process had been a gamble and rushed in an effort to get an album out quickly. But the gamble failed and what was arguably the most important album of Barry White's career became a sales disaster.

Three singles were released and all three bombed. The first, *It Ain't Love, Babe (Until You Give It)*, failed miserably, peaking at No 58 on the Billboard R&B chart and not even getting into the Top 100 on the Billboard singles chart. The second single, *Any Fool Could See (You Were Meant For Me)*, did rather better, getting to No 37 on the R&B chart, but again failing to dent the Billboard Top 100 singles chart. *Love Ain't Easy* was released as a third single, in desperation after the failure of the first two. But it was the poorest of the lot and struggled to get to No 75 on the R&B chart. Many believed that the song probably wasn't even good enough to be on the album.

Despite its lack of quality, the album was launched in the summer of 1979 with a big party at the famous Chasen's restaurant in Los Angeles. The venue was chosen carefully and, despite its faded grandeur, was still the place to be seen having lunch in Hollywood.

To celebrate, Glodean White commissioned a special cake with icing in the design of the album's cover. But even the album cover disappointed, with a confusing and forgettable design by Tony Lane and Bobby Holland featuring flowers bursting out of the lid of a grand piano.

The management of CBS Records turned out to launch their new famous artist together with, it seemed, virtually every mainstream reporter in Los Angeles.

Barry White revelled in the occasion and told reporters that he now had 60 gold and 15 platinum discs from his seven-year recording career. That surprised many and the savvier reporters made a mental count and couldn't come close to that number. But White was on a high that night and wasn't going to let the facts get in the way of a good story. His speech didn't make a lot of sense as he told journalists that his music reflected two sides of what manhood ought to be: "The power side means I am very domineering in business and in music, the sensitive side of me are the strings." He also said that his music was his "weapon" in the "war between men and women", which he said was "a conflict that was the longest, bitterest and most destructive in history." He continued: "It's screwing up the whole human condition."

Barry White really did believe that night that his music was part of the solution to the world's problems, and the reporters present dutifully wrote it all down. He also told them about his latest acquisition, a softball team made up of children under four years old. He called them The Maestro Players and had them all kitted out in matching uniforms and caps. He coached the team himself. Barry and Glodean and Linda and Dede posed with the team for photographs, which were published in newspapers across the country.

It was all part of a huge publicity push for the first solo album with CBS, and anticipation was extremely high. That made the disappointment even greater when the first sales figures came in. White was genuinely mystified: "My last two albums were both platinum and now I have come behind them with what is, in my opinion, a better album, with a far wider spread than either of the last two."

In an effort to boost sales White quickly organised a nationwide tour across America with Love Unlimited and the Love Unlimited Orchestra. It started with two dates at the Felt Forum in New York and at Madison Square Garden in front of more than 5,000 fans. He then moved through the United States at breakneck speed, performing 20 times in six weeks, ending at The Coliseum in Oakland, California. He proudly told the assembled crowd that, 16 years before, he had helped build the 20,000-seat venue.

But the tour and the marketing could not disguise the fact that *The Message Is Love* was Barry White's poorest-selling album to date and a big disappointment both critically and commercially. The three singles failed to provide any sales impetus. The album couldn't breach the top 10 of the Billboard R&B chart, getting no higher than No 14, and could only reach No 67 in the main album chart. It was abysmal, and the poor performance set the pattern for the next decade – not one of his albums for the new label would make the Billboard Top 50.

Astonishingly, only a few months after its release White started to blame CBS for the poor sales: "There have been a lot of problems internally at CBS here, domestically, and we are doing things to change the problems at CBS. It is a huge company." Everyone shook their heads, as CBS could not have been doing better.

Soon afterwards he got to work on Love Unlimited's fifth album, called *Love Is Back*. It was to be the final 34 minutes of music from the girl group, who disbanded shortly afterwards, eight years after having been formed.

It was another album written from a woman's point of view and arguably some of Love Unlimited's greatest music. It was certainly much improved from their debut album of eight years before. Back then the quality of the music had been patchy and the songs indifferent. Now it was a whole different ball game and for their farewell White wrote and produced some outstanding music. Most of the seven songs on the album were written by White, Paul Politi and Frank Wilson, sitting in White's garden at Sherman Oaks under the umbrellas that surrounded the swimming pool.

When they got to the studio, a newcomer called Ben Kirk joined Gene Page on the orchestrations and arrangements. However, it didn't work out, and Kirk never worked with White again.

The album started with a track called *I'm So Glad That I'm A Woman*, considered by many a hymn to women. It was certainly popular with many young women who played it time and time again and considered it their anthem. Somehow the lyrics jived with them. The three girls, Glodean, Linda and Dede, sang every word together, opening with: "In the morning when I wake up, as I comb my hair, I can hear my daddy saying, 'it's a big, big world out there' while putting on my make-up, his words linger in the air, just use the love I gave you and you can make it anywhere." The chorus was: "I'm so glad that I'm a woman and know I wouldn't trade, I know I got it made, cos we are the life line of mankind and now is the time for me."

The second verse went: "Life is much a challenge, we live it day by day, you never know what's gonna happen or what might come your way. Just stop and think about it, there's nothing we can do, men can't live without us and we can't live without them too."

The song has endured to this day among women of a certain age, who play it whenever they feel they need a mood lift. *I'm So Glad That I'm A Woman* was issued as a single but sold only moderately as musical tastes had changed. There was no doubt that eight years before it would have been a huge hit.

The second track was *High Steppin', Hip Dressin' Fella (You Got It Together)*, which was just a continuation of the first track in the same upbeat manner. It was also released as a single.

The third track, *When I'm in Your Arms, Everything's Okay*, continued the upbeat theme, but the lyrics and melody were nonsensical and not worthy of White, Politi and Wilson. The song died a death and no one remembers it today.

Side two launched with *If You Want Me, Say It*, which was released as the third single from the album. It was another classic Barry White song. The fifth track was *I'm Givin' You a Love Every Man Is Searchin' For*, and the best that could be said about it was that it was a catchy number. It had little else.

The sixth track was called *Gotta Be Where You Are*, and proved that Barry White, as the sole writer, still had what it took to compose great music and imbue it with passion. *I'm His Woman*, the final track, had been brought to White by a freelance songwriter called Barbara Borde and was refined by White and Paul Politi. It turned out to be the last piece of music recorded by the group, although they didn't know it at the time.

Although Love Unlimited continued to tour with Barry White for a few years and provide backing vocals in the studio for him and his other artists, they never went into the recording studio as a stand-alone group again. Their time had run its course and their mentor had run out of ideas. The sound was also fading away, and even The Supremes were no longer having the success they were used to – that era and that sound were finished.

In 1979 Love Unlimited decided to stop touring, and that was virtually the end.

They left a fine legacy, however, intertwined with the Barry White legend. They had enjoyed their first hit in 1972, their first and only Top 10 album in 1973, and their first and only No 1 single in 1975. In the seventies Love Unlimited, the Three Degrees and The Supremes were the only girl groups that mattered.

White remembered the end of the group in his memoirs: "They decided it was time to go their own individual ways. I didn't blame them. In fact I encouraged the decision. We'd had a great run and the ladies had had a blast travelling all over the world whilst building themselves very substantial nest eggs. Now the day had come, as I knew it would, that even though they were sad, because they loved to sing, they were not only ready but eager to get on with the rest of their lives. Linda had found a man she wanted to marry and Dede returned to college."

Linda James married a Swiss doctor called Dr Hannes Hunziker and went to live in Berne, Switzerland. Glodean carried on being wife to Barry White, and in 1981 they recorded an album of duets together called *Barry & Glodean*.

There was always hope that things might change and the group might be reunited, but the end finally came when Dede Taylor was diagnosed with cancer in 1985 at the age of 38. She declined quickly and died on 29th November of that year signalling the true end of Love Unlimited.

THE MESSAGE IS LOVE

CHAPTER 50

Sheet Music

11th solo album

1980

Aftr the failure of the first album on his new label, Barry White rushed into production a new album called *Sheet Music*, seeking to improve his situation with CBS Records, whose executives were already disappointed with the sales figures.

But *Sheet Music* was not as good as *The Message is Love*, and there were clearly problems developing with the music. Either White had spread himself too thinly among his other artists or the stresses and strains of running his own label had taken their toll on his creativity. It was obvious something was wrong and it is no exaggeration to say that the *Sheet Music* album was arguably the low point of his entire career.

He had fallen into the same trap he had in 1974 and 1975 – trying to do too much too quickly. The quality of the work and the attention to detail suffered badly, and was reflected in the sales of albums. It was strange, as his modus operandi with regard to everything else in life had been the opposite, as he said: "I always believed that if an artist's talent, his gift, is real, he doesn't have to use it up all at once."

Not for the first time he failed to follow his own advice.

Sheet Music opened with the title track, written with Paul Politi; at more than seven minutes long it was simply uninspiring and certainly never destined to get on to any future 'greatest hits' album. In the old days White might have thrown this track away as being simply not good enough, but it seemed that neither White nor Politi could tell what was good and what was indifferent any more. *Sheet Music* wasn't a bad record, it was simply average, and that summed up the problem.

The proof that they had completely lost their way came when, unbelievably, *Sheet Music* was issued as the single from the album, with an instrumental version on the B-side. One reviewer called it "desperate" and unsurprisingly it failed to enter any of the charts.

Track two was *Lady, Sweet Lady*, written by Norman Sallitt. It had a better tempo and was a typical Barry White tune, but it proved to be the only song that Sallitt wrote for the maestro.

The third track, *I Believe In Love*, was written by White, Austin Johnson and Smead Hudman, who were all occasional White songwriters. It was very poor and a mixture of some of his previous songs done very badly. The best review it received described it as "repetitive", which it certainly was.

It seemed that things couldn't really get much worse, but they did with the opening track on side two, *Ghetto Letto*, a true musical mess written by White, Politi and Vella Cameron. This was actually one of Barry White's favourite songs because of its Latin-funk theme, as Jack Perry recalled: "The song was about all of the languages, the slang in the ghettoes."

It was followed by a calypso-themed song called *Rum & Coke*, written by Al Stillman, Jeri Sullivan, Morey Amsterdam and Paul Baron.

It was not until track six that the album got serious and became a recognisably Barry White production with *She's Everything To Me*, written with his friend Bernard Butler. Unfortunately the song was lost in the morass of *Sheet Music*, but it later became a Barry White classic. The last track was called *Love Makin' Music* with lyrics by Aaron Schroeder and the melody by his composing partner, Jerry Ragovoy. This again was classic Barry White-type music that would endure.

For some reason Barry White chose to record the last two tracks of *Sheet Music* in Spanish, and they were issued as a 12-inch single in America called *Ella Es Todo Para Mi (She's Everything To Me)* on the A-side with *Mi Nueva Cancion (Love Makin' Music)* on the B-side. Both versions proved popular, but not enough to get them into the charts.

The album was Barry White's lowest-selling record to date, and it also failed to break through into the charts. The 'Allmusic' review considered that: "*Sheet Music* reveals the downside of the situation with a slew of well-below-the-grade numbers and feeble, redundant grooves, a low point." It certainly was that.

On 12th September 1980 Glodean, seeking to cheer up her husband after the disappointing sales figures for his new album, threw him a surprise 36th birthday party. It was a party with a difference – Glodean transformed the Sherman Oaks mansion into a scene from the 'Arabian Nights', including a real camel roaming the front yard. She had got the idea from a vacation they had spent together in Hawaii the previous summer.

The party had to be kept a secret as Barry White hated any social gathering or party, especially those he deemed to be "without purpose". He also abhorred small talk and it had always been up to Glodean to guide him through social occasions. It was another reason why any parties Glodean organised for her husband were always kept secret until the last minute. If he had known about the birthday party he would not have attended. As it was he had no choice as Glodean and his friends managed to keep it from him.

Glodean arranged for him to be out of the house by sending him to Alhambra to view a property she had told him they ought to buy. White agreed to drive over and look at it, but was mystified when Glodean made numerous excuses as to why she couldn't accompany him.

The first clue he got that anything unusual was going on came as he drove his Rolls-Royce Camargue up to his front door that afternoon. The surprise was total. "What's a camel doing here?" he thought to himself, rather innocently. He did not have to wait long to find out, as more than 200 friends burst out of the front door and surrounded the car, rowdily singing 'Happy birthday'. But White still didn't get the connection with the camel, saying to Glodean: "What's a camel doing at our front door?" But he soon saw the point when he went inside and through the back door. He didn't recognise his own backyard, which had been completely decked out in canvas.

The whole of the grounds had been made into an 'Arabian Nights' scene by a professional props company, complete with actors playing the parts of belly-dancers, fortune-tellers, genies and Persian waiters. There was even a man on a flying carpet suspended over the swimming pool on wires.

Vast tables of food had been laid out for the 200 guests and there at the end of the garden was Gene Page and members of the Love Unlimited Orchestra playing away in front of a huge wooden dance floor set on top of the lawn.

The party had been sent up in only six hours, and White admitted to reporters that he had been taken completely by surprise, calling Glodean "slick and sly". He said: "This is the first time she has ever taken me completely by surprise."

The biggest surprise for White was the arrival of Linda James, with new husband Dr Hannes Hunziker, a Swiss doctor. They had flown all the way from Berne, Switzerland, to attend. Other guests were Los Angeles Mayor Tom Bradley, TV presenters Don Cornelius, Regis Philbin and Dick Clark, DJ Wink Martindale, actress Jaye Kennedy, and Jermaine and Tito Jackson. All of the Temptations were there, together with Nancy Wilson, Marilyn McCoo and Billy Davies.

The party was said to have cost $25,000, but Glodean bridled when asked the cost by reporters: "Talking about how much something costs is kind of tacky." When pushed, she merely said that the cost was "enough".

CHAPTER 51

Barry & Glodean

12th solo album is a duet with his wife

August 1981

At the end of 1980 a somewhat desperate Barry White was casting around in search of an album concept that could restore his flagging fortunes. The good old days were most certainly over, and two years after starting his own label he was haemorrhaging cash. Things were not at all comfortable and his dream of building a big independent record company were fading fast.

It was his wife Glodean who came up with the idea of a duets album. Love Unlimited had broken up and she was searching for a new role for herself, hoping to emerge as a solo performer in her own right. But she was far from sure what she wanted to do next. She had great potential as a solo artist if only she could step out of the shadow of her husband. But that was not easy to do. The very thing that had made her career was now the same thing that was holding her back from making any more progress.

So she thought that a good first step would be a duets album with her husband. By this stage Barry White was so desperate that he would have tried anything, and he accepted his wife's offer for them to perform together.

For the new album White went back to basics in a bid to recapture his lost mojo. He assembled a crack team of engineers, Frank Kejmar, David Hernandez, Howard Wolen and Gary McGachan, to work on the album. Gene Page focused all his efforts and brought in Hidle Barnum and John Roberts to help with the arrangements. A 44-year-old veteran, Barnum had worked with Lou Rawls, Frank Sinatra and Count Basie, and brought a new dimension to the sessions, while John Roberts was a serious technical musician. The huge resources White brought to bear demonstrated his resolve to restore his musical fortunes. He also assembled a young team of songwriters with whom he worked to try and recapture his old sound.

It was in many ways a last throw of the dice.

The album opened with a stunning 3½-minute instrumental called *Our Theme*. It was an effort to recapture the magic of *Love's Theme*, and there were plenty of reasons for wanting to do that; *Love's Theme* was an ongoing success for White and was continually being played at discos and on the radio, bringing him royalties of $8,000 a month on its own.

After the opening, the album burst into immediate life with an "infectious" track called *I Want You*, written with Jimmy Levine and Lowrell Simon. Simon, a 27-year-old soul singer, was a new songwriting partner, and had long wanted to work with Barry White. When he finally got the call he couldn't contain himself or believe that it had finally happened. *I Want You* was a catchy number that reflected its title with the Whites singing alternately, then together.

The third track was *You're The Only One For Me*, written with Vella Cameron, who was emerging as a serious composer, together with her brother Jimmie. It was another catchy tune with constant changes of pace and tempo, and featured the Whites singing together with Glodean alternately on her own.

Track four was called *This Love*, written by Fleming Williams, who was a singer with a group called The Hues Corporation, and another young songwriter who had long admired Barry White and was grateful to get a chance to work with the maestro. It was a typical White song and beautifully arranged by the new team of Page, Barnum and Roberts. One reviewer described it as "almost a four minute musical work of art."

The final track on side one was *The Better Love Is (The Worse It Is When It Is Over)*, written by Adryan Russ, a young Broadway writer. It was a change of pace with a long instrumental lead-in and lyrics led by Barry White with Glodean taking a secondary role. It was a true love song and effectively told the story of the White marriage.

So far so good, and side one of the new album gave every indication that Barry White was back on track. The new young songwriters he had introduced to his team had made a difference.

Side two opened with a track simply called *You*, written with Vella Cameron. It was a strange two-part song, the first part being a 30-second instrumental, then a gap followed by a slow orchestral movement and exchange of lyrical love between Barry and Glodean in real time. It was classic Barry White and would endure into the future. Glodean's voice was at its most silky and most magical on this song.

It was followed by *We Can't Let Go Of Love*, written with Brent Maglia and Vito Giovannelli, a songwriting duo who were also working with Barry White for the first time. It was a fast-tempo duet about life in the bedroom with the Whites. Five years before it would have gone straight to the top of the charts, and at another time would have been a gold-selling record. It was sensational.

The eighth track, co-written by Vella and Jimmie Cameron, was called *You Make My Life Easy Livin'*. It told a story of new love, effectively a narration of the process set to a smooth Vella Cameron melody. The ninth track was *Didn't We Make It Happen, Baby*, written by Barry White with his young protégé Danny Pearson. It was a classic Barry White story of the problems of falling in love and succeeding in love, again effectively a narration spoken over a pleasing melody made better by an exceptional arrangement by Gene Page. The album closed with *Our Theme – Part II*.

Michael Jackson recommended that White use his photographer, Todd Gray, to take the album's cover photo, which turned out to be a great move. Gray was a top photographer and the go-to guy for Jackson. He proved his worth that day in the studio, albeit at a huge cost. Hairdressers, make-up teams and stylists were summoned, and the outcome was arguably the best and most memorable album cover of Barry White's career. He had his hair styled by Adolpho, one of the top hairdressers in Beverly Hills, and a stylist called Sibongile Bradley braided Glodean's hair into a memorable arrangement. Tara Posey supervised the make-up for both of them.

They were dressed in white sable coats with nothing underneath against a starry black background with beautiful gold typography picking out *Barry & Glodean* in all their glory. It was a wonderful cover, and kicked off a new hair-braiding craze across America.

Creatively, if not commercially, the album succeeded, and *Barry & Glodean* saw White back to almost his very best. Andrew Hamilton of 'Allmusic' called the album "delightful" and it was. *Barry & Glodean* was certainly Glodean White's finest ever performance, and her silky delivery showed what an excellent singer she really was.

All the effort and expense paid off; *Barry & Glodean* was seriously better than anything White had produced in the past three years and got him back on track. But inevitably the album was overlooked when it was released. Barry White had gone off the boil, CBS had lost confidence in him and little effort was put into the marketing, meaning that sales were disappointing. CBS did not press enough copies to meet what demand there was and many fans found they couldn't buy it.

Although Glodean White was delighted with the album, she chose to leave her career there and not capitalise on her own individual success. She was happy as a housewife and settled back into running the White household at Sherman Oaks, content to let her husband carry on his day-to-day struggle with the music industry.

Meanwhile Jack Perry was trying to find artists to record on the Unlimited Gold label and was having only limited success. He was finding it very different from six years before when he had last been on the lookout for new artists. Now it was a very competitive landscape. Dozens of A&R men were out every night in the clubs of New York and Los Angeles looking for talent, and any artist that showed the first sign of having any was quickly signed up.

But White was determined to continue trying, as he believed that his future was as a producer first and an artist second, as he said: "I'm a record producer. And when every record producer finds an artist, they have to set out to find the artist's platform. What is he going to speak about? What is going to be his image, what is going to be his style?"

Perry also knew that there were big risks. The upfront investment in a new album by a new artist could easily run to $250,000, and there was no guarantee of success, or even covering the manufacturing and distribution costs, as White explained: "You have to be honest with yourself because you don't know if it's right or wrong until it comes out."

In the end it proved so difficult that just two artists were signed to Unlimited Gold, managing an album each, neither of which managed to recoup its costs.

The first was 25-year-old Danny Pearson, whom White had first met as a teenager and had nurtured, encouraging him to write music and using him as a backing singer on his solo albums. Pearson had a good falsetto voice that matched well with White's bass baritone. White co-wrote a couple of songs with him and found him a useful foil to his own skills. Jack Perry remembered:

"Danny became the first new artist released on the Unlimited Gold label and just like that his record was a top 20 R&B hit."

But, as far as the album was concerned, it was wishful thinking. Perry had slightly misremembered and *Barry White Presents Mr Danny Pearson*, reached only No 108 on the Billboard R&B album chart, while the single taken from the album, *What's Your Sign, Girl*, reached No 16 on the R&B singles chart. It was a creditable performance and Pearson showed undoubted promise, but he got lost in the White/CBS fallout and was never really heard from again.

The second act was the brother and sister songwriting team Jimmie and Vella Cameron. They could both sing and write their own songs, and Vella had written some superb melodies for Barry White's lyrics that had found their way onto three of his solo albums.

Before they met White, Vella and Jimmie had recorded albums in the late sixties and early seventies. The first, in 1968 for the Imperial label, was called *Heartbeat*, and the second, four years later for Atlantic, was called *Jimmie & Vella*. Nether had been successful.

But Barry White was taken with Vella Cameron and encouraged her and her brother to write new material. In 1981 Unlimited Gold released an album called *Song Painters*, but it bombed and thereafter Jimmie and Vella faded from view and failed to live up to their potential. They were just another couple of artists who failed to break out after being given every chance. The lack of success also took the edge off their songwriting talents.

Between the Camerons and Danny Pearson, Barry White had to write off more than $500,000; CBS made him pay back every dollar that had been spent on the two artists from his own pocket. He didn't regret it, but it hurt as it was money he didn't really have.

After ten years of trying, the reality was that Barry White had not been able to break out any artists aside from himself and Love Unlimited. These latest failures caused him to give up, and in the end he had no idea whether it was bad luck or bad judgement that had cost him success. He put it down to both and cut his losses. He never released another third-party album again.

What he didn't give up on was his Love Unlimited Orchestra, which absorbed all the unused material he generated. The orchestra's albums sold surprisingly well, having established a cult following among fans who loved playing the music in their private basement discos and at their louche dinner parties. It proved a surprisingly large audience.

Using the orchestra as a vehicle, White had also pioneered the concept of the 'instrumental with lyrics' (IWL). These were instrumentals to which he added seemingly random lyrics to part of the track, dreamed up by the team in the studio, some of whom were given writing credits and some not, according to Barry White's whims.

In 1981 Barry White formed a brief relationship with Webster Lewis, a 38-year-old bandleader from Baltimore, Maryland. Primarily a jazz musician, he had released his first record in 1971 and had signed with the Columbia-CBS-owned Epic label in 1976. He mixed jazz with disco and had some success with two singles. He met Barry White when he was moonlighting as a session musician and the two men got along well. The relationship eventually led to his recording an album of IWLs called *The Love Unlimited Orchestra Presents Mr. Webster Lewis' – Welcome Aboard*.

Jack Perry, David Hernandez, Gary McGachan and Howard Wolen, under the direction of Frank Kejmar, all went to the Whitney recording studios in Glendale with a 40-piece orchestra for a few days of expensive recording. The album was released in 1981, during the CBS era, and consequently had limited promotion. It was, however, a fine production with a lot of good music on it. Opening the album was the title track, *Welcome Aboard*, which was a catchy instrumental co-written by Elwin Rutledge and Jack Perry. *Dreams* was the second track, written by Webster Lewis himself with lyrics sung by Glodean White. Track three was called *Night Life in the City*, co-written by Carl Taylor. Lewis and White co-wrote track four, *Lift Your Voice And Say (United We Can Live In Peace Today)*, which had a catchy melody that went down well in discos.

The first track on side two was called *Easin'*, a delightful instrumental with lyrics, which, if released in a different time, could have been a big hit. Co-written with Nathan East, a soul singer, it was adored by those of White's fans who managed to buy the LP. It was followed by track six, an instrumental called *Antigua Blue*; written by legendary songwriter Rudy Clark. *Antigua Blue* went on to become a White instrumental classic. Following on was a track written by Jimmie Cameron called *Wind*. The last two tracks, *Strange* and *My Fantasies*, were co-written with Darnell White.

The stylish album cover seemed to get almost as much attention as the LP itself, with Todd Gray doing the photography and Ben Cziller and Helaine Bruck the design. However, sales proved disappointing and there were no more albums with Webster Lewis, who went back to his band career.

CHAPTER 52

Beware of Change

13th solo album

November 1981

After the abject commercial failure of three successive albums on his new label, it was time for Barry White to take stock of the situation he found himself in. His music was no longer popular and new technology was forcing him to re-evaluate everything he thought he knew about making music.

The truth is that he appeared to be very confused. He wasn't sure if there was any future for traditional musicians at all with the advent of computer programs and hardware that could replicate any musical instrument and reproduce it flawlessly.

His first instinct was to ignore the changes taking place, as he didn't know any different, thinking that musicality could overcome the machines. As he said: "They have machines for this sound and machines for that sound, but one thing remains the same. The song is the most important thing. That hasn't changed. As long as I can still write a song, there'll be a place for me in music."

Consequently he went into the MCA Studios in Whitney to record his 13th solo album with a full retinue of musicians.

The album, called *Beware*, kicked off with the title track, which was by far the best song on the LP. It was an old song with a considerable history behind it before Barry White made it his own. It had been written in the fifties by Jo Ann Belvin for her husband, Jesse Belvin, to perform, but their careers were cut short when they were killed in a motor accident in 1960. The song was later covered by a group called Toni and the Showmen in 1965. Barry White had always liked it and had long wanted to cover it; it would not be the first Jesse Belvin number he would record.

The song opened with lyrics that could easily have been written by White: "I love your style and baby I love your smile, I dig the way you talk, so exciting the way you walk, beauty is in the eye of the beholder baby and I want you to know that all I see is you and what I see is what I like – you are what is missing in my life, so beware." *Beware* is now regarded as a Barry White classic track and forever associated with him.

Track two, *Relax To The Max*, carried on in the same vein, and was co-written by Lowrell Simon, who was now regularly on the Barry White team. It was a typical White slow number about seducing a lady.

The third track, *Let Me In And Let's Begin With Love*, upped the tempo with a brilliant melody written by Vella Cameron and lyrics written by White, then the fourth was *Your Love, Your Love*, a catchy up-tempo number written with Lowrell Simon. The last track on side one was *Tell Me Who Do You Love*, co-written with a new member of the White retinue, Darnell White. It was a classic Barry White solo dance number with White talking first hand to a lady who has intrigued him.

Side two kicked off with an upbeat track simply called *Rio De Janeiro*, written by White and co-writers Carol and Marlon Jackson specifically to mark his upcoming tour to Brazil, where it would be released as a single prior to his visit. Marlon was Michael Jackson's youngest brother, and Carol was his wife; both had long wanted to work with Barry White, and their dream was fulfilled.

The next track was a slow, haunting number called *You're My High*, co-written with 26-year-old Nathan East, who had been a member of White's band since the earliest days when he was a teenager.

The strangely named *Oooo...Ahhh* was a gospel-type song penned by White with Fleming Williams and Jakki Milligan. Probably the weakest track on the album, it was never destined for a future 'greatest hits' album selection.

The penultimate track was *I Won't Settle For Less Than The Best (For You Baby)* from the White/Cameron writing team, but it didn't inspire any reaction from White's fans.

The last track was called *Louie Louie*, which had been written by Richard Berry in 1955 and had achieved cult status in the 26 years before White covered it. White's extended version ran to just over seven minutes, but it was poor and the song did not suit his style. It was included on the album with one eye on the upcoming tour of South America.

Beware was destined to fail just like the three previous albums, even though it contained some good music. It was clear that Barry White was falling out of fashion, which, coupled with CBS's lack of action to promote the album, spelled disaster for sales.

Something was drastically wrong and Barry White had lost his mojo. But even worse, it was clear that his music was no longer hip. After much soul-searching, he realised that hip-hop, rap and swing beat were the new flavour, as he said: "In my mid-forties I had to shift my mind without losing my soul."

But he should have seen it coming and only had himself to blame. As early as 1979 Jack Perry had been perpetually warning him about the technological changes that were coming. But while he continued to be successful, White ignored him. Perry was keeping abreast of developments, but against his advice White continued to bring 40-piece orchestras into the studio, at huge cost. Because he chose to ignore what was happening he lost his chance to introduce the new technology gradually, and consequently was at first totally unprepared for the changes it would bring.

The failure of the three albums concentrated his mind and eventually, as he said himself, "Barry White got it." He explained: "I saw change was inevitable. People were tired of the ordinary bass sound, the live drum sound and the piano. They wanted to hear something else. They wanted to hear a piano but they didn't want it to sound like a piano. They wanted to hear drums but they didn't want it to sound like drums."

It could easily been game over, as White freely admitted: "I was locked into a style of recording and I knew I had to unlock and relock without losing the lock I already had. In the middle of my forties I had to sort my mind without losing my soul."

Although he eventually "got it", White admitted that he didn't know how to handle the change and deal with it. His solution was to take a backwards step and virtually retire from active service.

He wasn't the only high-profile artist to be having problems. Stevie Wonder was going through the same agonies as he sought to adapt. The two got together to compare notes and found they were suffering the same frustrations, as White said: "Stevie Wonder and I were probably the first to deal with technology on a very fluent basis."

While he was starting work on his next album at his Sherman Oaks studio,

Jack Perry introduced White to what was then called the 'Midi Protocol'. Midi was a completely new way of creating music, and was an acronym of Musical Instrument Digital Interface. It allowed a wide variety of electronic instruments, computers and other devices to connect and communicate with one another musically. A synthesiser call the Prophet-600 was the first to include Midi as standard equipment in 1982.

David Smith of Sequential Circuits is credited as the father of Midi. It was a genuine revolution and allowed a musician to take a simple melody, play it through a keyboard, feed it into a mixer and hear a completely orchestrated version of it without having any musicians present in the studio. Although synthesisers already allowed musicians to create different sounds in a similar way, Midi allowed them to keep all recorded tracks in synch with one another and for all the music produced to be set down digitally. The signal could be of various types, from a musical note or sound to how a note or sound was played.

The Midi protocol supported a total of 128 notes (from C five octaves below middle C through to G ten octaves higher), 16 channels (which meant that 16 separate devices could be be controlled per signal chain, or multiple devices assigned the same channel so they responded to the same input), and 128 programs (corresponding to patches or voice/effect setting changes). Midi also included built-in clock pulses, which defined the tempo of the track and allowed basic timing synchronisation within the equipment.

The Midi signal could also be recorded by a computer, then altered through software programs. With the use of a sampler, parts of other songs and sounds could be incorporated and manipulated through a computer keyboard.

Thus, rather than having a band with a drummer, keyboard, guitar and bass in the studio, Jack Perry had the ability to use either a drum machine or sampled loops for a drum pattern, sample a keyboard sound, or use a digital keyboard sound for the keyboard parts; he could even play a guitar part through a sampled guitar sound using the keyboard.

In essence, Midi was the final piece of software that enabled an artist to dispense with musicians, and finally enabled Barry White to break with the past and embrace the new technology.

He took full advantage of it straight away.

After that, things would never be the same again, as White recalled vividly in his 1999 memoirs: "The introducing of this new way of working helped free me to get more into myself rather than having to deal with a roomful of people. In that sense the electronics of the technology elevated the emotions of my songs because it allowed me not only to maintain a contemporary sound but to get further into myself. What many criticised as the death of man-made music actually helped bring new life into mine. Similarly when I decided to get rid of my regular stable of musicians everyone predicted it would be the end of the sound of distinction that had come to define Barry White. Again they were wrong. It was really just the beginning of a whole new era of personal expression, a fresh contemporary way of using the evolving language of music to say what it was I had to say in a song."

The technological revolution meant that White had to part company with musicians he had worked with for 10 years or more – they were no longer required. But White was always at his best when he was alone in a studio composing, as he admitted: "I do my best work in the studio, most of the time by myself or with Jack. I've been able to refine my music to the point where just two of us can and have made entire Barry White albums with me singing and each of us playing various instruments utilising the latest technology. This freed me to take the ultimate creative journey, the inner one, to continue to learn who I am – to recognise my own creatively spiritual voice."

He spent the next three years trying to make new technology work for him, burying himself in the recording studio at Sherman Oaks. He updated it with hardware that recreated the sound of every possible musical instrument without any musicians being present. All the time he was accompanied by his technical guru and musical protégé Jack Perry, trying to make sense of it. Instead of musicians he was suddenly surrounded by computers. Perry totally immersed himself in it and gradually they worked it out. The process effectively saved White's career.

As White said: "I was so used to going into the studio with 10 guys. Now I had to learn how to go in there with one machine." He added: "The fire in my soul was nearly extinguished."

The first album to be made using the new Midi software would appropriately be called *Change*, his 14th solo album. The choice of name was no accident.

CHAPTER 53

Darryl Dies

The end of a brother

December 1982

In 1978 Barry White's brother Darryl left prison after serving a 13-year sentence for murder. His return home was something neither his mother nor his brother had never expected to see. At his original trial the Judge had sentenced him to 50 years and further ordered that the then 20-year-old should never be released back into society. In the state of California it was automatically an indefinite sentence, with no hope of release.

But later the sentence was ruled unconstitutional by higher courts and Darryl, by then 33, finally got his freedom after 13 years inside.

Darryl White had been in and out of prison all his life. But when he was released he resolved never to go inside again, attempting to reform and go straight, or at least as straight as he knew how.

The truth was that Darryl enjoyed his life of petty crime and showed little signs of reform, although admittedly after a total of 17 years of incarceration, more than half his life, he would have preferred not to have to go back to prison.

A lot had happened during Darryl White's time inside, not least the fact that his brother had become a household name in America and a global singing star. But Darryl was unimpressed and when he got out all he wanted to do was lead his own life, firmly rejecting all offers of help and support from his elder brother.

Barry White asked him after his release: "What do you want to do?" The inference was that he could do anything he wanted and his brother would help him with whatever was required. Turning down the offer of a house in Malibu with a swimming pool, Darryl told his brother that he just wanted to go back to his old neighbourhood and lead a normal life. He rejected all offers of help, and looking at Barry's life he didn't like what he saw – it was not for him. As long as he had enough vodka to drink and enough cigarettes to smoke he was happy.

As Barry White recalled to Marc Eliot in his 1999 memoirs: "I knew how difficult it was going to be for him to try and get a job when the first thing anybody was sure to ask about was the thirteen years missing from his record."

White offered to set up his brother in any business he cared to name, but back came the same response: "All I want is a shoe shine stand. But of course I ain't really into polishing shoes – the back room is where the action will be." The clear inference was that the shoe shine stand would be a front for criminal activities, albeit low-level petty crime.

White recalled: "I sighed and thought, always the criminal shite, and realised my brother was irredeemable. I told him I couldn't be associated with any criminal activity."

Darryl replied: "Well, you asked and that is all I could think of."

White gave up trying to help his brother, and instead gave him $100 a week as an allowance, as he told his old friend, Jack Perry: "I gave it to him to do as he liked with until the end of his days."

In his memoirs White recalled that his accountant phoned him and told him that it was too much. He told her: "This is my brother and I'll give him all of my money if I want to – you have no idea what we went through as a family."

White said they never spoke of it again.

So Darryl White went back to his life of petty crime and surprisingly managed to stay out of jail. No one knows what he did with his $100 a week, and he always seemed to be short of money. Doubtless the bookmakers, liquor stores and numerous local drug-dealers benefited the most.

Once again Barry White witnessed his brother's life deteriorate with a sinking feeling of despair. Darryl had been in and out of juvenile hall since the age of only eight, and his biggest problem remained the same – it was the huge chip he carried on his shoulder, genuinely believing that everyone he met was trying to do him down. Sometimes it seemed that he craved violence. Countless times everyday harmless encounters turned into explosive confrontations that only good fortune stopped from becoming catastrophes.

The situation was not helped by the fact that everything came too easily to Darryl White. He was extremely good looking and had inherited his father's hunky physique. Women, usually of the wrong kind, fell easily into his arms.

But amazingly, for 3½ years between 1978 and 1982 Darryl stayed out of serious trouble. He seemed to spend his days quietly in a haze of alcohol, cigarettes and cannabis.

Following his release from prison he hung around with a neighbour in South Central Los Angeles called Ernest Little. Little was 59 years old and enjoyed drinking and smoking, hobbies that Darryl shared and admired. They lodged together in a cheap boarding house that had a very liberal attitude to its residents' lifestyles.

One fateful morning, on Sunday 5th December 1982, Ernest Little declared to his friend that he would fund the day's purchases of liquor and cigarettes if Darryl would go out to the shop. Little handed him a $20 bill to pay for it.

What happened next Barry White later described as "a silly incident that meant absolutely nothing," although he admitted that his brother was most likely "trying to take petty advantage of another man."

Apparently Darryl returned with only the liquor and no cigarettes, and said he had spent the whole $20 on drink. Little didn't believe him and asked him for his change. Darryl told him there was no change. Little was enraged that his friend should try and do him down for a few dollars, so much so that, according to police reports, he went to get his gun. When he returned he pointed it at Darryl and shouted: "You're going to give me my money, motherfucker!"

When Darryl repeated that there was no change, Little pulled the trigger. Darryl somehow dodged the first bullet, but Little fired again and hit him straight in the chest.

Fatefully Ernest Little had managed to take the perfect shot. The bullet travelled straight through Darryl's body, missing all vital organs but his heart, and came out the other side, killing him instantly. Just to make sure, he fired a third shot as Darryl went down, but that missed altogether.

The wound was clean and there was very little blood, so at first it seemed that Darryl had merely been knocked out. Little tried to shake him awake. When he didn't respond he just stood over his body and cried, barely aware of what he had done to his friend. By then police cars were pulling up outside, alerted by neighbours.

The police officers found Little standing over Darryl's body, gun in hand, making no attempt to deny what had happened just a few minutes before.

He was briefly interviewed by homicide detective Steve Morgan, who was quickly on the scene. Morgan read him his rights and arrested him. He was handcuffed and taken away, and a police forensic team was brought in. They went through the motions although Morgan knew, with a confession already in the bag, that this was an open-and-shut case.

With Little arrested and the forensic team having done its work, Darryl's body was removed from the scene. Morgan searched his rooms to find details of his next of kin, and was very surprised when it dawned on him that the murdered man was Barry White's brother. Eventually he found details of his mother Sadie, and went over to Sherman Oaks to tell her that her son was dead.

Sadie Carter was at home enjoying the afternoon sun, but knew there was trouble when she looked out and saw Morgan and a uniformed policewoman at her door. She instinctively knew the news could not be good, and guessed it must be about Darryl.

Her first thought was that he had been arrested again. But she was not prepared for what she was about to hear, as Morgan asked if they could come inside. The three of them sat down in the spacious living room and she shook her head as the detective gently told her what had happened. Sadie had barely seen her son for almost the whole of his twenties and, although she was inwardly prepared for him to return to jail, she never envisioned him dying. She shouted out, "No, not my boy" and couldn't stop crying. When she finally composed herself, she told Morgan that she must go and see her eldest son and tell him the news. Morgan offered to go with her, but she waved him away.

With tears streaming down her face, Sadie walked down the hill and into the house where Barry White was packing his bags prior to catching a flight to New York. The next day he was due to make a speech at the United Nations, having been asked to speak about apartheid by the African National Congress (ANC). White had always refused to perform in South Africa while apartheid existed and his refusal had cost him millions of dollars in lost fees. The ANC party had been mightily impressed.

His mother quietly told him the news and he was not surprised. All he could think about was his forthcoming speech – he had no time to be upset. He

422

was immediately faced with a dilemma: he could not cancel his appearance at the United Nations and knew that he had to take his flight as scheduled. The ANC regarded him as a hero and it was impossible to let them down and cancel the trip.

He put his emotions to one side and was forced to leave his mother alone at home to grieve.

In the meantime the news of Darryl's death had become confused and, when the LAPD released it to the media, somehow the impression given was that it was Barry White, not Darryl, who had been shot and killed.

When White's flight touched down at Kennedy Airport five hours later, he was picked up by a limousine driver. As they were driving into New York the radio was on and the newscaster announced that Barry White was dead, saying: "Barry White died earlier today ... from a gunshot wound to the heart." White was horrified and at that moment realised that he must return home and try and take control of the situation. He realised he had been stupid to prioritise the speech and leave his mother alone at home. He immediately ordered the limousine driver to return to JFK, where he booked on the next flight home.

From a payphone at the airport he called Aaron Schroeder and asked him to issue a press release denying his death. Schroeder mobilised his office and his staff faxed a press release, correcting the situation. Radio stations, realising their mistake, quickly retracted the story, thankfully in time for the network news broadcasts that evening, which ignored it. He also told Schroeder that he could not go ahead with the UN speech and asked him to cancel it.

Meanwhile Sadie, back at Sherman Oaks, heard the news and initially thought she had lost both of her sons. It was a devastating day for the family, and for the rest of his life White regretted having left his mother alone while he flew to New York, realising that he should have immediately cancelled the speech. He later claimed that she never recovered from the shock of that day.

Once back home, the death of his brother suddenly hit him hard. As he described it himself: "For nine days and nine nights, I didn't move, I didn't speak. I struggled to understand the forces that drove his soul in one direction and mine in another. That struggle continued for the rest of my life."

The death of Darryl White at the age of 37 was to be one of the most futile events of Barry White's life. He described it to Marc Eliot in his own memoirs as the "saddest of all my memories." He said: "He was my best friend and my life till he died. He was night, and I was day. He loved the criminal world the way I loved the music world. We both had the same knowledge. One took it and went this way, one took it and went that way. So I tell young people the truth, and a lot of them listen."

It was a very painful time in his life: "It still rips me up inside to think that Darryl has gone. He was so young and so strong. And so full of life. His death took a hard piece out of me."

DARRYL DIES

CHAPTER 54

Dedicated to Change

14th and 15th solo albums

1982 and 1983

In the early 1980s Barry White was trying hard to reconcile the old world he knew with the new world that he knew he couldn't resist. It was to be the toughest three years of his life, when everything that could go wrong did so.

Moreover, in tandem with all the technological change in recording music, the digital compact disc (CD) began to emerge to threaten the very existence of the analogue stylus record, which had thus far been the principal medium of music reproduction.

White had lived through the emergence of the cassette tape, which had existed happily alongside vinyl for 10 years. But CDs were something else, and they threatened everything. The music industry as a whole resisted the change as long as it could until the argument for CDs became too compelling. The jukebox sector was the last to make the change, continuing to favour the stylus until the end of the decade.

But there was no getting away from it, and the future called for music to be produced digitally and played digitally in consumers' homes. It also spelled the end of 'side one and side two' as a concept – a CD had only one side. It was all too much for traditionalists like White. For him the vinyl LP was the ultimate expression of an art form. He found the compact disc completely souless in its small plastic box. It was a physical medium where he could no longer express his creativity.

Barry White was not the only artist having trouble adapting to a changing musical environment. His old rival, Isaac Hayes, was in an even worse funk. His music had also stopped selling and, like White, he placed the blame in the wrong places as he failed to adapt. Hayes blamed imitators who, he said, were "stealing his lunch". He explained: "I looked around and all I was hearing was me and people trying to be me." While White held things together, Hayes disappeared into a black hole amidst reports of wild spending and bankruptcy, drugs, women troubles and conspiracies. White saw what was happening to Hayes and swore he would not follow him down the same path. But when he looked for the positives, but couldn't find many.

Despite his claim to have "got it", this technological change spelled disaster for Barry White, and the appropriately named *Change* was his first album recorded using it. It was made under Jack Perry's supervision, at the grandly named R.I.S.E. Laboratories studio in the garden of White's home in Sherman Oaks. It used all the latest modern digital trickery and the new Midi magic. Some traditional instruments were later added to the music, including some French horns and various strings.

White got all his familiar colleagues together to try and unlock the future. Gene Page, Frank Kejmar and George Bohanon crowded into his small studio to try and work some magic. Bohanon, a noted trombonist, agreed to arrange some of the tracks to give them a different sound. *Change* was also White's first album he worked on with the talented singer/songwriter Vella Cameron, who was to be his bridge between the old and the new.

Change consisted of three tracks overseen by Barry White, the rest being written and arranged by younger, hipper writers, designed to propel White's music into the present day. But his 14th solo album was not to be a happy event and in retrospect would mark a further downward shift in his career from which he would never really recover.

The three tracks he produced, *Don't Tell Me About Heartaches, I Like You, You Like Me* and *It's All About Love*, consisted of 16 minutes and 41 seconds of music. The other 28 minutes and 44 seconds were arranged by Cameron and other people and performed by White.

Consequently the *Change* album was a collision of two different sounds. White's three tracks were traditional Barry White music, which his fans loved, while they hated the five modernist hip tracks.

The attempt to make Barry White hip failed disastrously; the truth was that he was not a hip artist in the traditional sense, and the attempts to update him came close to wrecking his career. Hence the three traditional White tracks were all overshadowed, and *Change* was the worst-selling album of his career to date.

The title track, which opened the album, was arguably the worst of White's career. Co-written with Carl Taylor and John Lopez, it was desperately overlong at more than six minutes. The lyrics were unimaginative and repetitive and the melody was uninspiring. The song could feasibly have caused damage to a listener's ears if listened to for too long and at too high a volume.

The second track, *Turnin' On, Tunin' In (To Your Love)*, was equally diabolical and Barry White's voice was barely recognisable. This five-minute song was the sole effort of Vella Cameron, and was arguably the worst musical track that Barry White ever recorded on an album.

Likewise track three was another five minutes of dire music, called *Let's Make Tonight (An Evening To Remember)*, written by Vella Cameron and her brother Jimmie.

The first recognisable piece of White music was track four, called *Don't Tell Me About Heartaches*, written by John Vallins and famous songwriter Nat Kipner. When Kipner wrote it, apparently his first thought had been to offer it to Barry White, who snapped it up. It was classic White material, sung beautifully by the maestro.

Side two opened with a track called *Passion*, written with Carl Taylor and John Lopez and arranged by George Bohanon. It was seven minutes of ridiculous music and an affront to Barry White's loyal fans – it was not the sort of music they wanted to hear on one of his albums.

The sixth track, also arranged by Bohanon, was arguably worse. Called *I've Got That Love Fever* and co-written with Jack Perry and Vella Cameron, it was repetitive rubbish consisting of more than five minutes of a terrible melody and even worse lyrics.

The experiment with George Bohanon had failed miserably, but it was not his fault. He did what he had been brought into to do, but it was not White music, or anything close to it. It would be the first and last time the two men would work together.

Track seven was co-written with Jack Perry and called *I Like You, You Like Me*. It was pure Barry White and a delight for the ears after all the punishment suffered earlier in the album.

Change closed with *It's All About Love*, written by Vella Cameron and was a sensational piece of music virtually guaranteed to delight Barry White fans all over the world.

The album had been a calculated risk, gambling on the fact that new White fans would be attracted and old ones retained, making it a commercial success. But it did not work and the end result was not pleasing – there were far more haters than lovers.

To promote *Change*, a slimline Barry White, sporting a new, much shorter haircut, appeared at the 'Soul Train' awards show, hosted live by Don Cornelius. No one recognised the figure that took to the stage. White told Cornelius that the new album was devoted to the condition of young people in America, which he did not believe was good. But his responses to the questions were rambling and made little sense, and Cornelius cut him short. His stage performance of the title track was also very poor, and although his new image had been designed to promote the new album, it had the opposite effect, and fans decided that this was one Barry White album to avoid.

One of White's mottos was to push ahead in the face of adversity and never be diverted from the mission in hand. The mission in hand was most certainly the modernisation of the Barry White sound and, seemingly undaunted by the *Change* fiasco, he pushed on straight away with his 15th solo album, called *Dedicated*.

This was the first album where all the tracks were recorded at White's R.I.S.E. studio in the grounds of Sherman Oaks. There was minimal use of musicians, and it was the first album where Gene Page wasn't used, as he was no longer considered hip enough, although he later recorded some additional material at Whitney Studios that was subsequently added to the album.

Dedicated was toned-down modernism, which in effect spelled mediocrity. Interestingly there was no title track and no song called *Dedicated*. The nearest equivalent was the opening track, called *America* written by Barry White. It was a hybrid between the old and new and it worked well, although it was not the Barry White beloved by his fans. In truth it was repetitive and overlong – the kiss of death for any piece of music.

The second track, *Free*, which also ran to five minutes, was a sound-alike written with Carl White, who was a disciple of the new Barry White sound, together with Ricky Roberson, who was along for the ride. It was terrible.

Track three was called *Don't Forget, Remember*, written solely by White with a delightfully catchy melody and brilliant lyrics with a gentle anti-racist theme that every Barry White fan remembers with affection.

Side one ended with *Life*, written with Jack Perry. White dedicated it to his seven children, and the dedication was included in the opening lyrics. The song was about children and a hybrid composition appealing to old and new fans.

Side two opened with *Love Song* by a 40-year-old English writer called Lesley Duncan. She had written it and brought it to White on spec, as she thought it would suit his style. She was right, and it became one of his classic love songs, with what White called the lyrics of love: "The words I have to say may well be simple but they are true. Until you give your love there's nothing more that we can do."

The sixth track, called *All In The Run Of A Day*, was an old recording that White had written with Bob Staunton at Mustang Bronco Records in 1967, and had lain on the shelf after being released unsuccessfully as a single. White laid on a new lyrical introduction, talking about his mother and her impact on his life. He called it "his mother's song", and at its new length of nearly seven minutes it was a pleasant musical ramble and in many ways the essence of what Barry White was all about.

The penultimate track was *Don't Let 'Em Blow Your Mind*, written with Jack Perry. It was another hybrid, bridging the old and new Barry White, and was very satisfying.

The final track was called *Dreams*, co-written with bandleader Webster Lewis, and was a version of an instrumental on the 'Mr Webster Lewis' album with added lyrics. It was bland music, and reflected sales of the album, which proved equally unremarkable.

The album sleeve of was one of the plainest White covers ever produced, featuring a picture of the new slimline Barry with short hair. He chose the photograph with Rod McGrew, and just added his name and the name of the album – a far cry from the effort that had gone into past sleeves. On the back, White gave full credit to everyone who had been involved in the process and dedicated the album to his mother, Sadie, writing: "She dedicated her life to her children with the knowledge of peace, harmony, and goodwill toward man. With my deepest love and love forever."

Having failed to find a new formula to suit the eighties, *Dedicated* was to be the last Barry White album for four years. He virtually stopped recording and went on tour to make his living. His relationship with CBS Records also ground to a sudden halt. As Daryl Easlea of 'Record Collector' magazine succinctly put it: "The wheels fell off Barry White's love wagon."

The touring became a necessity as White had effectively run out of money after a disastrous period between 1979 and 1983, when nothing had gone right and everything that could go wrong had done so.

It was not all bad news, however. Although sales of his new albums were a far cry from those of the past, the advent of the digital compact disc saw many of his old albums re-released in the new format, and sales of his back catalogue were very strong.

Critics who had detested him ten years before were suddenly coming round to what he had achieved, with more a dozen albums under his belt. One persistent detractor, Paolo Hewitt of 'New Musical Express', was just one who changed his mind, as he explained in a dramatic mea culpa: "There was a man that I loathed. At the height of his success, I used to watch his videos in mounting disbelief as he, dripping in extravagance, lumbered around grunting his trite love songs to skimpily dressed women lying around a massive swimming pool. To me, Barry White personified crass with a capital 'C'. Ten years later I now know what some of my friends at the time were trying to persuade me: Barry White created some brilliant records. Devoid of all those clichéd images, which I found so obnoxious, he now stands on his music, and his music alone, as a great songwriter."

There were other compensations during the enforced hiatus. The four years between 1983 and 1987 became a period of deep reflection. Barry White spent as much time as he could with his family and explored some traditional family activities and hobbies he had never had time for in the past. A favourite pastime was camping, and every three or four months the family, all nine of them, headed to the countryside with their tents.

David Letterman, who hosted 'The Late Show' on CBS, heard about the camping trips, and the notion of White camping in the outdoors tickled him. So he invited the maestro to New York to make a camping sketch for the show. Letterman was a big Barry White fan and the respect was mutual. Letterman called his short film 'Camping with Barry White'. When the sketch had played, White was interviewed on the couch to the amusement of the audience. He admitted that his wife Glodean had introduced the family to camping and at first he had only reluctantly gone along with it. He told Letterman: "Where I come from we camped on your chest or your doorstep."

It was a moment of humour at a time when there was little humour in his life.

CHAPTER 55

Harmony of Purpose

A lifelong obession with astrology

1982

An obsession with astrological predictions gradually took over Barry White's life after he first became acquainted with the subject in the 1960s. He was born a Virgo, while Glodean was a Libran; but when he had married her in 1974, according to him, he had failed to see the significance.

In 1978 his interest was really piqued when he was given a new book by Linda Goodman called 'Love Signs'. He said it changed his life. In 1982, when he was at the height of his struggle to recover his musical identity, he discovered an astrologer called Chakrapani Ullal. Ullal was an official adviser to the then Prime Minister of India, Indira Gandhi. He was from a Hindu family of astrologers and a follower of American-based Swami Muktananda.

Muktananda recognised Ullal's talents and invited him to come to America, and after much persuasion he eventually accepted. After a few weeks Ullal was so taken with California life that he moved permanently to Santa Monica where he set up a private practice – which is how he came across Barry White.

Ullal follows the Vedic method of astrology, as he explained: "A good astrologer should have not only astrological knowledge but also a good understanding of the philosophy of life. A Vedic astrologer is expected to lead a spiritually conscious life, and to meditate, do japa, or perform pujas daily. When an astrologer lives his life aspiring to be of service to others the Grace of God may flow through him allowing for intuitive insights, which elevates the practice to another level. The true Vedic astrologer has a yogic mind which is steady and unbiased, judging the influences of the planets but not judging the individual. Vedic astrology is viewed as a divine subject; the astrologer should approach it with true reverence and humility."

The philosophy chimed exactly with Barry White's own. He first went to see Ullal at his Santa Monica offices in 1982, initially just to have his chart done. White recalled that first meeting to Marc Eliot in his memoirs. Ullal told him that he was a realist and a very gifted man. He also told him about his relationship with his father and the impact on his character. Ullal told him: "Your father was never there for you as a child. He was forbidden to have anything to do with raising you. Only a woman with the right knowledge could have made you into the person that you are."

White was mightily impressed. But what he heard next sent chills through his body, as he recalled in his memoirs: "One day towards the end of next year you're going to lose somebody you love very much, but it will pass. You will handle it the way you've handled everything else in your life."

At first White thought that Ullal was talking about his ageing mother, and it caused him to keep a close eye on her for the next 12 months. Towards the end of 1983, when nothing had happened, White admits that he began to doubt Chakrapani Ullal's skills, especially as the year drew to a close. Then on 5th December Darryl White was murdered.

White never doubted Ullal again, and in 1986, when he was trying to get his career back on track, he visited him frequently, as he explained: "Chakrapani's awareness of the astrological motion of our lives affects me deeply. The more I get into it, the more I realise how important, how crucial it is for our understanding of one another. I'm a Virgo and there are some signs that I know I can't deal with. Once I know someone's sign, I begin to know what to look for in him or her as a human being. I still have to get to know the person, but at least I have a pathway to follow that knowledge. Every sign has it weaknesses and its strengths. Take Aries, for instance – they're always good business people, meticulous about work." Naturally when he learned that he much preferred to do business with Arians.

White believed that most people preferred not to know their future, but he wasn't one of them: "Most people do not want to know their whole story but my philosophy is just the opposite and [I take the view] that what you don't know will kill you." He continued: "The more you know, the more you grow. And the astrological charts are an excellent way to get to know yourself better."

He claims to have understood himself much better from Ullal's readings for his chart: "It helped me understand that I am a servant by nature. I want to allow people to pass through my hallway of knowledge and experience, whether for the sake of their career or in the pursuit of the one they love. When I'm in concert I tell the audience I'm their servant that night. My style is to serve up musical and spiritual knowledge, hot, fat and with a lot of excitement."

But just as big an influence as Chakrapani Ullal was Linda Goodman's book called 'Love Signs'. Running to 1,186 pages, it took Goodman eight years to write between 1970 and 1978. White admitted that, from the moment he was given the book, he carried it around with him permanently for the next few years, virtually memorising it from cover to cover: "I couldn't believe how much there was in there about me. Here was a book I could relate to, that talked to me about me, not ancient men and women whom I was somehow supposed to relate to via the ancestral essence of my soul."

Between Linda Goodman and Chakrapani Ullal White believed he learned so much that when he met someone he could, within a few minutes, tell what their star sign was. He explained: "More often than not I was right on the money."

But it was his own relationship with his wife Glodean that inspired him. She was a Libran born on 16th October 1947, three years younger than him. Linda Goodman wrote that both signs are born optimists and White immediately recognised this in himself and Glodean. They both enjoyed huge smiles, typical of their signs, especially when fused together. He also recognised Glodean's reaction to any criticism, which tended to deflate her completely, and was careful not to fall into that trap.

He also recognised his wife's undue influence over his thinking – it was, as Linda Goodman said, "A neat and tidy harmony of purpose."

Barry White could act very arrogantly when he gave others advice. He always trusted his own judgement and was so sure of himself that he felt it was his duty to give the best advice he could to his friends and his inner circle. Sometimes it caused huge rifts such as the time in 1980 when he advised his close friend Sterling Radcliffe not to marry his 21-year-old fiancée Mindy Ross. Ross would be Radcliffe's third wife and he was madly in love with the singer, as she was with him.

Radcliffe had co-written *You're the First, The Last, My Everything* with

White in 1974 and was his unofficial road manager. But the first time Barry White met Mindy Ross at the Frontier Hotel he seemed to take against her. When he consulted Linda Goodman's book, 'Love Signs', he deemed that Radcliffe and Ross would ultimately not be compatible. He told Radcliffe: "She's a young girl and only after you for your money."

By then 50-year-old Radcliffe, who had been married twice before, was a relatively wealthy man from co-writing *You're the First, The Last, My Everything*. Ross herself came from a wealthy banking family and was not short of money. Radcliffe chose to ignore Barry White's advice and the two went ahead and got married, although it did not last.

Mindy Ross always remembered White's antipathy to her, based on what she thought was nothing other than an astrology reading. She said years later: "He really pissed me off back in 1980 and I can still recall the hard look Barry gave me when we met. You would have thought I had 'out for cash' stamped on my forehead. He thought I wasn't good enough for Sterling."

And White was proved wrong as when they divorced Ross left the relationship asking for nothing. She even gave Radcliffe her very expensive engagement ring back.

Mindy Ross was angry for years afterwards, cross with herself because she didn't challenge him at the time: "It makes me angry all these years later, not because he was suspicious of me, but because I let him get away with it. I was too shy to stand up for myself." She cites White's own record with women and his relationships: "When it came to sizing up women I would say the maestro was a bit off-key."

It is just one of many similar stories people tell about White's obsession with astrology, which they often compare to the Vikings' reliance on witch doctors to make key battle decisions hundreds of years in the past.

But for better or worse, from the beginning of the eighties, Barry White's life was dominated by astrology and he based all his decisions on it. From the outside at least, it doesn't appear to have done him a lot of good.

But he would never have admitted that.

CHAPTER 56

Death of a Friend

Marvin Gaye is murdered by his father

April 1984

During all of Barry White's troubled years during the 1980s he received constant offers to produce and arrange records for his famous contemporaries. But he always refused. While he wanted to develop new acts, he had little interest in being a freelance producer, even though he knew he possessed all the skills to do it well. The offers came thick and fast and were often very difficult to turn down, but he always did, and this was the reason why he never worked with Marvin Gaye, an artist he respected above all.

White admired Gaye more than any other performer of the time: "I knew every song in his catalogue from the time he started. I was proud of what he accomplished. He was a truly great musician and could do it all." The two men had lots in common, including many fans outside America. They both shared a love of Belgium and performed there every time they went to Europe.

Marvin Gaye also deeply admired Barry White and said so in his own biography, written by David Ritz: "Barry's sounds have long haunted me. He is both street and sincere."

But despite the mutual respect, they didn't really know each other that well. White put that down to what he called "Marvin's significant dark side". Gaye reminded White of his brother Darryl, who also had a dark side, as he said: "I knew Marvin had some demons and was fighting them. I couldn't get close to him because of his lifestyle."

So White deliberately kept his distance, despite constant overtures from Gaye for them to work together. White admitted that he brushed Gaye off: "Marvin was a troubled man and that is why he and I were not close to one another. If it doesn't agree with me, I keep my distance and let others do their thing."

But in 1984 something very strange happened that changed the situation. It was a Friday morning, 30th March 1984, and White had just returned from a week-long trip to Israel. He was catching up with the news in 'Billboard', the music industry's trade paper, when he came across an article announcing that he would be producing Marvin Gaye's new album, something he knew nothing about. He had certainly not agreed to anything or even discussed it. Apparently Gaye had told a 'Billboard' reporter that Barry White would be producing his new album, but had neglected to tell White himself.

Then he remembered that Don Cornelius had left him several messages on his answering machine while he had been away, pleading with him to return his call. He also remembered an incident that morning at the airport. He had been approached at LAX by some fans, who recognised him; there was nothing unusual about that, and he had enjoyed the banter, signing a few autographs. Then one of them had asked him about Marvin Gaye's new album, and he had been puzzled. Now he knew why.

Before he could collect his thoughts the phone rang, and when he picked up the receiver it was Cornelius at the other end. "Barry, you're a difficult man to get hold of." After the usual pleasantries, Cornelius said: "There's someone here who wants to speak to you." The next thing White knew, Marvin Gaye was on the other end of the phone saying that he had been trying to get in touch. White replied, laughing as he spoke: "Yeah, I just read about it in 'Billboard'."

Gaye came to the point: "BW, you've got to produce my next album."

White feigned disinterest and said he was "not good enough to produce the great Marvin Gaye." He said: "Marvin Gaye doesn't need no producer. I could never produce Marvin Gaye – Marvin is the only one who can produce Marvin." After a brief, but friendly, argument, White offered to help out with some arrangements, and the two men agreed to meet the following Monday to discuss it. Gaye told White that he would drive over to his house at Sherman Oaks at two o'clock in the afternoon.

White gaily said: "I'll be here," to which Gaye replied: "That's fantastic BW," and put the phone down.

Straight away White realised that he was excited. Not much had gone right lately and this was a new challenge he could relish, as he said in his 1999 memoirs: "I looked forward to that meeting so much."

Gaye called up again on Saturday morning and told White: "I'm so excited

– this is going to be the baddest album of my career."

White replied: "I don't know about that, Marvin, but we gonna put out an album they'll never forget."

When he put the phone down, for the first time White realised that Marvin Gaye was serious, and called up Jack Perry. He asked Perry to come to his house on Sunday afternoon to do some preliminary work on a demo song that they could play to Marvin Gaye on the Monday. That evening White started writing a song in his head for Marvin Gaye to record: "By the time I went to bed on Saturday night I was so excited I couldn't think about anything else."

The following day, Sunday, White was woken early by the phone ringing at his bedside. Phone calls like that always worried him, and he picked up the receiver with some trepidation. It was Jack Perry, and White said, half asleep: "Jack, what is it?"

Perry just said: "Marvin's dead."

There was nothing more to be said, and White just replaced the receiver. It was the first of a few calls that morning, including ones from Michael and Jermaine Jackson, to whom Gaye was said to be distantly related. It was a time of incredible sadness and, even though he hardly knew Marvin Gaye, White was bereft.

Later that day details began to emerge about what had happened. Gaye was at his parents' house in West Adams, Los Angeles. It was the day before his 45th birthday and he and his mother, Alberta, were reciting passages from the Bible to each other in her bedroom, early on Saturday afternoon. For some reason Gaye's father, Marvin Snr, who was a church minister, had got it into his head that his son was having an affair with his own mother.

A vicious argument, followed by a physical fight, ended with Marvin Snr going to get his gun, a Smith & Wesson .38, which ironically had been bought for self-defence. He proceeded to shoot his son three times in the chest. One shot went through his left shoulder but the other two penetrated his heart and he died instantly. Alberta dialled 911 and an ambulance was there within six minutes. Within half an hour, Gaye was at the Emergency Room of California Hospital Medical Center and had been officially pronounced dead. There had been nothing the paramedics could do but quickly remove the body from the presence of the distraught parents and leave the Los Angeles Police

Department detectives to work out what had happened.

At Forest Lawn in the Hollywood Hills the following week, Gaye's coffin was left open as visitors filed by. White remembers leaning over the coffin and kissing his would-be friend: "I kissed him on the forehead and rubbed his hands and whispered, 'Sleep, my brother, a peaceful sleep.'" Jermaine Jackson, next in line, did the same.

The funeral was attended by more than 10,000 people, and Stevie Wonder sang the eulogy. Although he had previously bought a burial plot in Forest Lawn, Gaye's body was cremated and his ashes scattered in the nearby Pacific Ocean.

Gaye's father was held in prison as no one came forward to put up the $100,000 bail. He told a Judge that he didn't like his son but hadn't meant to kill him, thinking the gun contained blanks rather than live ammunition. He was let off with a five-year suspended sentence after entering an agreed guilty plea of voluntary manslaughter.

Barry White was very upset and bitterly disappointed, calling his association with the 44-year-old singer "all too brief". Later he said: "His passing hit me hard and broke my heart."

It was yet another blow to Barry White in what was turning out to be a very bad year.

DEATH OF A FRIEND

CHAPTER 57

Down But Not Out

Upheaval, withdrawal and a financial crisis

1984

By the end of 1984 relations between Barry White and CBS Records had completely soured. Bruce Lundvall, White's biggest supporter, had moved on and CBS was considering suing the singer for non-performance of his contract. Sales were so bad that CBS's chief executive, Walter Yetnikoff, told people that he thought it might have been deliberate on White's part. At one point sales of White's back catalogue, now distributed by Polygram, were outselling his new releases at CBS. White was coming down from a hugely successful 12 years during which he had reportedly bagged 103 gold albums, 38 platinum albums, 20 gold singles and 10 platinum singles, and was now unable to replicate, or come close to, the success of his hit-making years.

The original contract, which had started in 1978, had begun with such high hopes. White attempted to explain to Marc Eliot what happened in his 1999 memoirs: "By 1984 the marketplace had changed. My string of hit singles slowed and my album sales stagnated. CBS wasn't interested in any of the acts I had tried to develop." The truth was that none of the third-party acts White had signed to the label had made any impact. As a result CBS had completely lost interest and couldn't wait for the contract to expire. Things were even worse in the UK, where Barry White had always enjoyed big sales. It became a forgotten market and when the London office of CBS refused to release any singles from the *Beware*, *Change* and *Dedicated* albums it was all over.

The last album, under the deal, was from the Love Unlimited Orchestra called *Rise*. The name was well chosen and five of the seven tracks were unadulterated rubbish – probably the worst music Barry White was ever associated with. Some say he did it out of revenge for the way he had been treated by CBS but others thought he couldn't possibly have hated them that much. The orchestra itself had long ceased to exist and, aside from two tracks, called *Goodbye Concerto* and *After Five*, the music was bland, jarring and completely out-of-place. *Goodbye Concerto* and *After Five* are great pieces of modern classical music and the album was worth the price for those alone. They are two of the best classical instrumentals White ever wrote and worthy of a place on any greatest hits album.

After Five was an original composition by White, with a credit for Albert Carter who was in the studio at the time. *Goodbye Concerto* was adapted from an original composition by Tony De Vita, the Italian composer. The strings on both compositions were brilliantly arranged by Gene Page and this is undoubtedly some of his best work.

But both tracks were sadly lost amongst the rubbish and never gained the prominence they deserved. The other five tracks; *Take a Good Look, My Laboratory is Ready For You, Do It To the Music Please, In Brazil and Anna Lisa* were embarrassing to all and were inspired by Unlimited Gold president, Rod McGrew, who rightly got the blame when the album failed to sell.

In essence, *Rise* was just White and his friends playing about in his home recording studio and daring CBS to release it. Under the contract, the label had no choice.

By the end of the contract, Barry White had released 14 albums in total on CBS: six by himself, a duet with Glodean, two albums by Love Unlimited, three by the Love Unlimited Orchestra, and one each by his signings Danny Pearson and Jimmie and Vella Cameron. The only success had been a solo 'greatest hits' compilation.

After CBS's costs had been stripped out and studio time paid for, together with the cost of supporting an executive staff led by President Rod McGrew, Unlimited Gold had lost Barry White a lot of money and had depleted his fortunes considerably. Since 1979, $6.5 million had disappeared. White admitted: "With the overheads I was carrying I was losing barrel loads of money." In all, $10 million slipped through Barry White's fingers during that period, leaving him overdrawn at the bank and in considerable financial trouble. He only survived because of royalty checks for $80,000 that appeared every month.

Unlimited Gold Records had not only failed to live up to its promise, but was also beset by internal wrangling and office politics. Some days it appeared that the 70 people who worked there were at war with each other. Barry White had always considered himself a good judge of people, but his experiences at Unlimited Gold must have given him reason to doubt that. He responded by laying off most of the staff, including Rod McGrew, but sweetened it with redundancy payments that totalled a million dollars. The remaining staff struggled on, never giving up.

Barry White's default position was to blame CBS for a lot of his troubles, arising from the company's lack of marketing support. Jack Perry remembered: "He was very unhappy with CBS because CBS didn't promote his product. They gave him the multimillion-dollar deal and the okay to move forward with the artists but they didn't promote the product."

But the truth was that Barry White had lost his lustre and the overall quality of the 14 albums was very patchy, whereas the 21 albums that had gone before had mostly been exceptional. White said: "I fulfilled all my commitments, I still recorded albums but the world wasn't hearing Barry White like it used to and a lot of people that I had known had fallen out of the business and left."

But the real reason was probably the changeover to new technology and the fact that music was increasingly being created by computer programs rather than musicians. White readily admitted, as he turned 40 years old, that he was having trouble adapting – he was no longer a young man and he knew it. But he was still loath to blame himself.

He claimed that he had reluctantly came to the conclusion that the people in the music business hadn't been looking after his best interests. In an interview with 'Ebony' magazine he called the music business "cut-throat" and accused its executives of lying to him consistently, deceiving him and using unethical tactics that he said damaged his album sales. He told 'Ebony': "They play many games. That's how they earn their living, destroying people and making you see illusions that weren't there." He said that people were not looking out for his best interests and that it was "painful to know".

But some people blamed him, and even the sympathetic interviewer writing in 'Ebony' was inclined to lay blame at his door: "The megastar was like a big dinosaur looking over an unfriendly terrain where love talk was extinct and rap music and computerised songs ruled the land."

In 1984 Barry White was put out of his misery when the original contract finally expired. He went to see CBS executives for the final time for a frank meeting to discuss the future. He told them he wanted out, and unsurprisingly CBS agreed, and it was all over. The company was so relieved to get out of the deal that it let White take possession of all his copyrights, and returned the master tapes to him. He recalled in his memoirs how the delivery driver returning the tapes had told him: "Mr White, I've been picking up CBS masters all my life but this is the first time I've brought them back to where I got them from." White recalled that he laughed nervously and took a deep breath.

The return of the master tapes represented both a finality and the first serious low point in White's career since he had broken through in 1972. He was full of trepidation about what the future held for him, as he later revealed: "I went to bed that night and slept quite peacefully believing that when I awakened things would start to get better. They had to because they couldn't get any worse. Or so I thought."

The next day he went to Studio City to close down the offices and lay off the remaining few staff of Unlimited Gold Records. He gave them generous redundancy checks at the cost of another quarter of a million dollars. It was the last money he had in the bank and he realised that he was facing an immediate cash-flow crisis. Suddenly everything was up for sale.

But even as he pared back his monthly outgoings, his overhead remained high and he found that he needed a short-term loan quickly – the only alternative would be to file for personal bankruptcy. This cash shortage was sure to be only temporary, as he still had more than a million dollars a year coming in from his music publishing and performing. But asking around for money, he soon learned who his friends were.

The ranch at Hidden Valley and all his horses were quickly sold off. But this had a good outcome, as he revealed: "I put feelers out to sell the entire herd and almost immediately I got an offer." The buyer was Berry Gordy, the founder of Motown, who paid him $1 million cash for everything. White recalled: "Berry bought every horse I had and he fell in love with them just like I had before him." But selling them still hurt: "I realised that as much as I loved my horses, they weren't my life – music was, and deep down I knew that I didn't have the resources to continue with what amounted to a very self-indulgent and expensive hobby."

But the money from Gordy was not enough, and he approached his old friend American TV presenter Wink Martindale for a loan. Martindale didn't even ask why he needed it and what he needed it for; he just said, "How much?" and wrote out a check for half a million dollars. White was humbled by his friend's trust and generosity, and very grateful: "He gave it to me without hesitation, no questions asked – that's a friend." Martindale's generosity gave White some breathing space and made him believe in his future again.

After word got round that the CBS deal had ended, there were offers from other labels. But White refused them all, as he wasn't ready to make any new music. He admitted that he had lost interest: "There were people who were screaming but I didn't want a deal and I didn't want to see nobody. I just wanted to take it easy and get into this technology and that's what I did."

But he bridled at any suggestion that he had retired, becoming very angry when he was questioned by journalists, saying: "I never left the business."

But between 1983 and 1987 that's what he effectively did. He stopped making music while he learned all the new techniques needed to create good sound from a computer. The only work he did in that period was touring – he needed the money.

Russ Regan believed that recording didn't really matter at that stage in White's career: "The one thing that Barry White could always do was that he could go to Europe, go to South America and fill stadiums, make money, no problem." His son, Barry White Jnr, agreed: "You can say Barry White in most countries and the eyes and ears still prick up. He just wasn't in the forefront of some things." Glodean said: "He stayed busy just doing stuff."

He also wanted time to think about the future and, after much thought, came up with a plan. Two years after the CBS deal finished, White sought to relaunch Unlimited Gold and make it truly independent with its own distribution, marketing and manufacturing. He developed a business plan to raise $10 million to finance the label and re-establish it as a completely independent studio and record company. He found the money from some oil barons in Texas who wanted to diversify their interests, but then suddenly in 1986 the oil market collapsed and White's deal collapsed with it. He said: "We found the finance money in Texas, but it was tied to oil."

When the deal fell apart White became very depressed for the first time in his life. He was helped through it by Michael ·Jackson; during that period their roles were reversed, and now, with Jackson's career in the stratosphere, almost entirely thanks to the advice White had given him in the late seventies, Jackson returned the favour and helped guide his friend through the new technology. He gave White lots of advice about how he could adapt to the changed conditions and rebuild his career. Jackson's counselling got White off the floor, and by the close of 1986 he was finally ready to re-emerge with all his demons exposed and vanquished.

CHAPTER 58

A New Label

A pseudo rapper emerges for 16th solo album

1987

A s 1987 dawned Barry White was ready to get back to work and record again. His first job was to find a new record label. Going it alone was no longer an option, and he had exhausted every possibility in that direction. Nothing seemed to work out.

Once he had made the decision in his own mind to do it, and put his independent aspirations to one side, it proved relatively easy – there were still plenty of people who believed in Barry White.

One was Jerry Moss, the 53-year-old head of A&M Records and one of the legendary figures in the music industry. He and bandleader Herb Alpert had founded A&M 25 years earlier in 1962. It became hugely successful and by the mid-seventies was the largest independently owned record label in the world, with acts such as Burt Bacharach, The Carpenters, Quincy Jones, Liza Minnelli, Carole King and Joan Baez on its books.

Barry White was introduced to Jerry Moss by Michael Jackson, who told him what great things the label had done for his sister Janet, and how it had launched her to stardom the previous year with her album, *Control*.

Jackson also alerted him to a young executive who worked there called John McClain, who he said was a genius with black artists. Jackson and McClain were very close friends. Jesus Garber, an old colleague from 20th Century Records, also recommended A&M, and confirmed what Jackson had said about McClain. Garber and White had enjoyed a warm relationship stretching back over many years.

Moss and White made an instant connection when they met at A&M's headquarters, which was based in Charlie Chaplin's old studios in Hollywood. Together with A&M President Gil Freisen, the three men soon hammered out a four-album deal, as White recalled: "I made the best record deal I could and got back into production and we came out with the new record in September 1987."

White was very enamoured of the Charlie Chaplin connection, being a huge fan: "He was a people's artist, as I am, and a man whose work I have always responded to on a visceral level and I knew I was someplace special again the first time I planted my feet on the studio lot built by Charlie Chaplin. I could sense Chaplin's strong karma everywhere and felt a real affinity with the man. Like me he was a decent-minded artist whose work found its fullest expression when he was allowed to make it exactly the way he wanted."

White found Moss a refreshing change after his recent experience with record executives, and wished he had signed with A&M at the start of his career. As he said: "Jerry Moss became a real friend. He was honest and says what he means which is very important to me."

But White really benefitted from the extraordinary skills of Michael Jackson's friend, John McClain, the 29-year-old wunderkind who was in charge of developing A&M's roster of black artists. One of the main extollers of rap music, he had joined A&M to rescue its black music division, which had stalled and produced nothing for seven years. McClain had joined in 1984 and took the division from a loss of $5 million to revenues of $50 million by 1987. Moss said of McClain when he introduced him to White: "John's contribution to A&M has been extraordinary. No one has ever made as big an impact in such a short period of time."

McClain's main talent was his uncanny grasp of street smarts and corporate politics, and moved easily between the two. He had got into the music business having been lucky enough to attend the same school as the Jackson brothers, and had formed a close friendship with Jermaine Jackson, which had led to an introduction to Berry Gordy of Motown.

That in turn had led to A&M and Janet Jackson, who was struggling to get out of the shadow of her talented brothers. McClain made it his mission to make her a star in her own right: "All I wanted to do was make her the most exciting female artist out there." And he did just that, by targeting her appeal to the predominantly black, youth-oriented urban market.

McClain was intrigued by the challenge of turning Barry White into a top-selling artist again. He was interested in expanding A&M into contemporary rap and believed that Barry White could make that transition with his music. He told Jerry Moss that he thought he knew what the problem was: "If there is a problem with Barry, it isn't that people have stopped listening to Barry White records, it was that Barry White had stopped making Barry White records."

McClain tried to re-engineer White's music to appeal to that market. He wanted to re-fashion the 43-year-old to give him a much younger image, and dreamed up a whole new look for him. White had put back on all the weight he had lost in 1981. He told White to get a haircut and lose a few pounds, which he did. The new style was, however, less colourful, and for the press conference announcing the new album he wore a baggy black jacket, matching slacks and a lavender-coloured shirt. Fans saw a completely new Barry White, and not many of them liked what they saw.

McClain told White that the new album had to be hip and urban, and White got to work in his home studio. The result was a very different sort of album that was almost unrecognisable as White's work. Called *The Right Night & Barry White*, it was designed as a guidebook to how couples ought to make love, according to Barry White. He said that it "dealt with a cross section of events that happen to everyday people."

He went on: "One thing about my music always remains the same, it's still about love. And it will always be about love until the day I die. I've learned travelling around the world that people don't all eat the same food, drink the same water or like the same wine, but everybody makes love. I don't care what language you say it in, people know what going to bed means, what marriage means, all of it. So I have a common denominator that everybody relates to."

The idea may have been good and the new image may have been right for the times, but musically McClain steered White the wrong way; the resulting album was utter rubbish, and none of the songs have endured. When it was released in 1987 it enjoyed only moderate sales. None of his core fans liked it, and the appeal to his new fans proved to be not enough.

It was a real wake-up call.

White tried to tell people that he had not changed his style, and talked his way out of the failure: "Why change a successful formula? It's not when you come back, it's what you come back with... I'm still doing the Barry White. Few artists know what it's like to sell millions of records internationally and

Barry White is still big around the world. Why tamper with that?" But the truth was that he had tampered with it and produced a poor album. In the pre-release publicity he said that he made albums that made people feel good, but this time he had positively failed.

There were 10 tracks on the album, adding up to a total of nearly 66 minutes of music. The shortest track was five minutes 50 seconds and the longest seven minutes 25 seconds. All were overlong, and Russ Regan, had he still been around, would definitely have dubbed them all 'not commercial'. And this time he would have been right.

White was involved in writing nine of the tracks, and the majority were co-written with friends and engineers who were continually in and out of the studio as he searched for inspiration. He handed out the writing credits like confetti, but it did nothing to improve the music.

The first track was *Good Dancin' Music*, written by White and Jack Perry. It was overlong at seven minutes. The second track was *As Time Goes By*, a remake originally written by Herman Hupfeld in 1931 for a Broadway play and later used as the theme tune for the movie 'Casablanca'. It was urbanised by White and Perry, but many people thought their version was embarrassing and no one understood why it had been included on the album, especially as White had used it once before as an instrumental on a Love Unlimited Orchestra album.

The third track was *Sho' You Right*, which was instigated by Jack Perry, who remembered: "I brought this song to Barry, which I wrote at home. It took me two or three days to get the track together. When I brought it to him he started writing lyrics. I had to go out to a store and it took 20 minutes and when I got back he had the lyrics finished." White said: "The song is about a woman who is guiding the night." Both White and Perry had high hopes for *Sho' You Right*, which was released as a single. White called it "potent" and it enjoyed moderate success, making No 17 on the Billboard R&B chart. It was more successful in Britain, where it sneaked into the Top 20 at 17. It was White's first British hit record since 1978.

The fourth track, *For Your Love*, was co-written with Bryan Loren, who had enjoyed some success with the new computerised music and had also worked with Michael Jackson, but the song was instantly forgettable. For some reason it was issued as a second single and struggled to get to No 27 briefly on the Billboard R&B chart.

The fifth track, called *There's A Place Where Love Never Ends*, co-written with Frieda Brock and Doug Lambert, was music more in tune with the White formula, but it too was forgettable and never made it into a compilation album. The sixth track, *Love Is in Your Eyes*, co-written with Jack Perry and Don Williams, was bland, and the seventh, *I'm Ready for Love*, co-written by Doug Lambert and Ed Martinez, equally so.

The eighth track, *Share*, was written with Charles Fearing, and was the most melodic on the album. It reflected the story of a man asking a woman for a chance to make a relationship work after other men had let her down.

The ninth, called *Who's The Fool*, co-written with Jack Perry and Eugene Booker, was as bland as the rest. It was supposed to be about unrequited love, but the message got lost in the mess of the music and lyrics.

The title track came last. *The Right Night* was written by Barry White, but was terribly misguided and not what his fans wanted to hear.

This was not an album to dance to and the most favourable description that any of the critics came up with was "gritty".

White shrugged off all criticism of the new album, and there was plenty. He said: "You're still dealing with rhythms where you're hearing the drums real loud and Barry White was one of the innovators of that." But ominously he said: "Rap music has emerged and there must be a market for it, otherwise it wouldn't be selling."

He touted the album as a modern sound, implying that it was the music, not him, that had changed so much since he had started out 15 years earlier: "Everybody influences everybody. I was influenced by Jerry Butler, Ray Charles and Sam Cooke. So when I hear a new rapper say they're influenced by Barry White, those are just words to me. I have never considered myself a rapper. I have always considered myself a communicator – one who speaks of substance and things that can help other people better relate to each other. I've always considered myself a person who speaks of positive things. You listen to Barry White's music and you hear a lot of influences. There's jazz and a lot of Latin. To me, Latin music is the closest to black music. It's very rhythmic and it makes a statement. Latin music has fire, just like black music. I've been in

Latin America and I've heard songs that, if they were in America, they would be number one hits."

When questioned as to why the new album was so different from his previous work, he admitted that he had been influenced by the new technology: "The only thing that is different in Barry White's music is the technology I am using. I started in 1979 and was one of the first people to buy a drum machine. From that, I have emerged into the science of technology: computers and X7s."

At the urging of John McClain, White kicked off a huge orgy of publicity and sought out journalists wherever he was in the world. He also hit the road with dates across America. Then he went to Europe with the Love Unlimited Orchestra. At a press conference during the tour there was an embarrassing moment when a journalist asked him: "What *is* love?"

White closed his eyes and, after a few seconds of thought, said: "The thing about love is that it *grows*. Like this plant here. If you came back here in a year this plant will have grown."

The journalist, who appeared to be half asleep, reached out and rubbed a leaf of the pot plant between his thumb and finger. He said: "Um, Barry, this plant…"

"Yes," said White. "It's plastic…"

After a brief pause, White broke down laughing uncontrollably, at his own send-up.

The one market that actually preferred his new sound was Cuba. He was invited to perform in Havana, but declined due to the tense relationship that still existed between that country and the United States.

His music was bootlegged all over Cuba and he was very popular there, but he didn't want to condone the stealing of his copyrights, although that was the only way Cubans could hear Barry White because of the US trade embargo. White said: "Barry White is the only artist in the world that Castro invited to his country, but my attorneys felt it was too political to get involved with. But I remain very respectful to Castro and anyone else who appreciates Barry White's music."

Aside from its success in Cuba, *The Right Night & Barry White* was best forgotten, and largely has been. There was not one memorable White track on it, and that was reflected in the sales. For the first time one of Barry White's albums failed to reach even the lowest echelons of the Billboard albums chart, but it did get to No 28 for one week on the R&B chart.

The critics knew it was wrong. Robin Gibson, writing in 'Sounds' magazine, wanted to like it but couldn't: "Something in the air tells me that the revitalised Barry White is going to be unutterably hip and for the life of me I can't see why." Attempting to understand the change, Gibson suggested: "Perhaps the collective memory of the soul-searchers, hungry for legend, has filtered out all but the voice, the voice."

White went on the Arsenio Hall chat show to promote the album and put the best spin he could on it: "I went through five years of heavy labour and burden with CBS and we got through that five years and now we're with A&M and things are really looking up." He really believed it: "Music is a cyclical business – the seventies was my time, I took a few years off in the eighties, and now I believe my time has come again."

Jack Perry also tried his best to be upbeat: "The first album for A&M did well and it recouped, so A&M was happy with an icon under its wing."

To be truthful, Barry White was grateful for any encouragement. In his heart of hearts he knew that the album was not great, but he was grateful that there even was an album. As he said: "We had started making records again and slowly and surely I got my career back."

John McClain was very surprised at the poor sales, but didn't give up and encouraged White to persevere, reminding him of his earlier career struggles.

But once again it seemed to be very poor advice.

CHAPTER 59

The End of the Affair

Split from Glodean and a secret daughter revealed

1988

At the end of 1988 Barry and Glodean White called a halt to their 14-year marriage and a relationship that had spanned nearly 16 years. It came as a complete surprise, but at 44 and 41 years old respectively they had suddenly decided it was over. White said: "Neither of us wanted to pretend that the spark was still there when it wasn't." He described why he left: "I felt I needed to make some major changes to everything about my life and that included my marriage."

But what was not over was their friendship – that was as strong as it had ever been. As he said in an interview in 'Ebony' magazine: "We had come together as friends which was why we could part the same way."

Neither Barry nor Glodean ever said exactly what happened, but the most vulnerable time for most marriages is when the children leave home and a couple are left on their own. Dubbed the 'empty nest syndrome', it appears to have been what ended the marriage of Barry and Glodean White.

In 1988 most of their children had left the family home to begin their own lives, and the only one left, 16-year-old Shaherah, was hardly ever there. What had once been a bustling nine-strong household was down to two alone in a big sprawling house, with only their domestic staff for company.

Lovemaking, once such a strong part of their relationship, had dwindled, and they realised that they no longer acted as lovers but as close friends, a situation that neither was happy with. There were also financial pressures for the first time in their marriage.

Unlimited Gold had proved a misnomer, and the problems at the record label had absorbed all their spare cash. The horses and the farm had been disposed of, and with them their marriage. Whereas ten years before the White household had been the happiest place on earth, now many days were downright miserable as Barry wrestled with his problems and

Glodean felt powerless to help.

There were no third parties involved, and one day that December the two of them sat down quietly under the glass chandelier in the vast lounge and worked out a separation agreement.

The split was achieved amicably, with White finding a house for Glodean to live in within close walking distance. She kept her own set of keys to the family home and her husband told her that she could come and go as she pleased. He also left her with access to all his bank accounts and everything else. The only thing that really changed was that they no longer shared the same house, as Shaherah White recalled: "My father and Glodean, even though they separated, they still has a very unique relationship."

Glodean White didn't fight it and took it all in her stride. As she said: "He was always accessible to me and I was always accessible to him."

A divorce was never discussed, or even considered.

White said afterwards: "It was simply that our time as lovers, as husband and wife, had run its course, so we kissed and said goodbye and started the journey down the path of the rest of our individual lives."

It was brave talk, but it became clear many years later that White was devastated by the split, not because it wasn't the right thing to do but because he considered it a personal failure. He said: "I vowed that I would rebuild my life and I didn't care what it took or how long it took."

But he never forgot what Glodean had meant to him, and 10 years after the split he said: "Although our marriage didn't last forever, Glodean and I are still great friends. Our relationship had just evolved to a different place in time."

White believed it was an example of how life changed and how it was better to realise that it had and not try to gloss over the fault lines. He always believed that because of the music they made together their relationship would last forever, and that the end of the marriage did nothing to change that. In his memoirs he called his relationship with Glodean a "beautiful and inspirational thing" and said: "I will always love Glodean not in spite of who she is, but because of it. My feelings were just growing and changing, that is the way it was."

Three years after the split, that feeling was to manifest itself in the most beautiful way when Barry White sang Glodean a very public goodbye letter. He wrote what many consider to be the greatest of his ballads, *Whatever We Had, We Had*, which was the last track on his 1994 album *The Icon is Love*.

It was effectively an ode to his wife and started with words that seemed to express his great regret that the marriage had ended: "As the world turns from day to day. As we live, we have to make decisions. And when we make those decisions things don't always turn out the way we'd like them to or want them to."

The song was full of words of regret such as: "We don't have a crystal ball to look into to know what our future is going to be. You meet someone, you care for that someone, you love that one." And it made clear what the future should hold: "We should always remember that we started as friends and there's no reason why we shouldn't end as friends."

The song made absolutely clear that his relationship with Glodean would endure forever, even if they were no longer together, and he believed that time would and had played its part: "You know time has played a very important role on our relationship. It was time that first brought us together and it's time that we separate and leave each other."

The lyrics also expressed the pain and suffering they had been through together as, particularly after 1978, things had not always gone as they had planned: "You know we did a lot of things in those years. We felt a lot of pain through tears, but there's something that we did that I'll always, always be thankful for, as together we created a very special life." And it ends with the haunting words of real regret: "We could have worked harder but who knows we went as far as we could go."

The failure of his marriage, however, exposed him to accusations of hypocrisy. A lot of the things he had said on stage at concerts and to journalists over the years, words of so-called wisdom, became meaningless. He had virtually proclaimed himself as the guru of love, and now he had failed on the biggest stage of all – his own marriage. But he brushed all those accusations aside. In his 1999 memoirs, written with Marc Eliot 10 years later, he expounded on the break-up at length: "Failing in a relationship is nothing to be ashamed of. It simply means you gave it a try and it didn't work. Not be able to pick yourself up and move on with your life is the only real tragedy. How can you ever say to someone I love you today and mean it as I will love you forever? Sometimes a couple's time together just runs out, as one or both change and things don't feel like they used to." The words were true of life, yet stood for everything he was against and contradicted all the advice he had willingly handed out.

But he wasn't finished: "Sometimes people just change their perspective, and their needs and desires change. And a lot of the time the other person resists this change. Some people can flow and adapt and some can't."

There was a hint at the time of the break-up that White had been unfaithful to Glodean, but certainly it was nothing that either of them would admit to. But White did leave the door open to the possibility when he said: "A lot of the time, couples will break up because of a third party, another woman or another man. Maybe the thrill of sex is over or they discover that living together doesn't work for them or they're just not ready or suited to devote the rest of their lives to this one other person. It is no sin and no crime, moral or otherwise, unless the other person takes it as a violation of a specific pledge of faith, which would be unfair since nobody has a crystal ball to predict the future."

The reasons for the break-up were never spoken about by Glodean, and if she ever did, even to close friends, the secret has been kept and probably always will be. It is something she will take to her grave. There was never any question of her being less than 100 per cent supportive of her husband's wishes in public. And he repaid that discretion when he said: "I'm not saying that it's all right to cheat on your partner. I do not think anybody goes into a relationship with that desire. It's just when two people get together, they are taking a chance on the other person and themselves. I believe it is better to enjoy the good times while you have them and then to try preserve happiness like it was deposited in the bank for some future use. People who don't see this waste so much time chasing a dream they can never live out in real life. The only solution is to love as hard as you can for as long as it lasts. And to allow the natural time span about love to flow completely. It may last a day, it may very well last a lifetime but, for however long it runs, enjoy it to the fullest capacity, and you will have few regrets for having done so, no matter what the outcome."

Whatever We Had, We Had was a beautiful melody with beautiful lyrics, and whenever journalists questioned him about his split from his wife he told them: "Go listen to that song. It explains everything. It will tell you everything you need to know and the rest ain't nobody's business."

And as Glodean moved out of the house at Sherman Oaks, another woman moved into Barry White's life. But it was not what it seemed.

Denice, his long-lost and secret daughter, now grown up, re-entered his life. He said: "I felt I had to correct the situation once and for all and I made up my mind to bring Denice into my family."

Denice Donnell was now 26 years old and her natural mother, Gurtha Allen, felt that it was time she knew the truth. White also felt that it was time to regularise the position with his own family, as he explained: "I introduced her to Glodean and my children."

He gathered them all together at Sherman Oaks one day and told them that he had an announcement to make. He told them that in 1962, when he was only 18, he had fathered a daughter, called Denice, with a woman he had never named up to now. He explained: "It happened when I had first come out of jail and I thought Mary and I were finished. I went with another woman. It wasn't anything to do with love, it was really just a sex thing. However she'd become pregnant, and then Mary did too. This other woman and I went our separate ways." After he made his announcement his children, now eight in number, embraced Denice. White remembered: "I must say it was a beautiful thing to see – the way everybody accepted her – as she did them. From that moment we all treated each other as if we were one big family."

There's no question that 1988 was the most difficult year of Barry White's life. He had achieved almost unattainable levels of success and earned tens of millions of dollars from recording, writing and performing. He had suffered a financial and a career crisis and had come through it. But for a man who had many times stated that he valued consistency more than anything, his parting from Glodean was difficult to reconcile. In the end he reconciled it as "being consistent with myself", as he tried to explain in his memoirs: "I never changed my feelings about one person – myself. Consistency in my life was and would always be the ultimate rhythm. It's for that reason that everyone knew the same Barry White. After all, if I'm true to myself, who else that matters could ever lie to me?"

It was a peculiar type of logic coming in the year when his marriage had failed and he had finally recognised the daughter he had expunged from his life a quarter of a century before.

CHAPTER 60

The Man is Back

Avoiding a career-ending crisis

1987

After the disastrous *The Right Night & Barry White* album, John McClain went back to the drawing board to try and find out what had gone wrong. He decided that they had tried to make the transition from old Barry White to new Barry White too quickly and too brutally. For the next album, *The Man is Back*, McClain decided it would be half the new Barry White, to please his new fans, and half the old Barry White, so as not to alienate his old fans. The deal decided between the two men over lunch was that half of the album would be traditional White and the other half the new sound that McClain had dreamed up for him. They eventually came to an understanding as to how the new album would be produced, as McClain explained: "Barry was to have creative control of one half of *The Man Is Back* and the other half of the album was supposed to be filled with other producers' input."

But that was not how it worked out, as McClain ruefully recalled: "When Barry got into the studio he took control of everything." So the plan went out of the window and the result was a high-tech, urban-contemporary-influenced production that was a massive departure from the full orchestral theme of just a few years before. But unfortunately the maestro had thrown out the baby with the bathwater and the result was another pretty disastrous album that predictably only achieved moderate sales.

There was much more hype than quality music in the finished product, and the 17th solo album of Barry White's professional career was talked up by A&M's public relations team as the first of his comeback phase. They said it incorporated "a more contemporary production style while retaining the essential elements of his trademark sound."

That it was actually the second comeback album seemed to have been lost on the PR people, although journalists tamely went along with it. The truth was that the first comeback hadn't worked and great effort was expended by A&M to completely forget about that. *The Right Night & Barry White*, the commercial disaster of 18 months before, was quietly forgotten and not mentioned.

But not by Barry White. He knew that there were only so many comebacks an artist could pull off, and he realised that he had almost used up all of his. The album's name reflected the circumstances, and *The Man Is Back* was White's first album to be primarily released on compact disc. A vinyl release was not planned, so for the first time there would be no side one and side two for White to hide behind – the nine tracks played straight one after the other. The new format was certainly not friendly to the Barry White sound.

The first two tracks, *Responsible* and *Super Lover*, were modern hip-hop-type music with poor melodies and lyrics – instantly forgettable and a real turn-off to traditional Barry White fans. They were written by Jack Perry and rap hotshots Julian Jackson and William Jones.

The next two tracks were written by White on his own. Called *L.A. My Kinda Place* and *Follow That and See*, they were a mixture of both styles to produce two bland songs described by critics as "uninspiring", which was, in actuality, a compliment, as they were a lot worse than that.

When Will I See You Again was more traditional Barry White music, written by White and one of his backing musicians, Terrence Thomas. But it was muddled and confused.

The sixth track was written by veteran songwriter Rusty Hamilton III, called *I Wanna Do It Good To Ya*. It was six minutes of nonsense and featured heavy breathing and all sorts of other gimmicks that were well beneath the talent of Barry White.

It was not until track seven that fans got any recognisable Barry White music. Called *It's Getting Harder All the Time*, it was a rather beautiful piece of typical White music with a nice melody and decent lyrics. Reassuringly it was written by Aaron Schroeder and David Grover, and effectively rescued the album.

The penultimate track, *Don't Let Go*, followed a traditional White theme, and the writing was attributed to Terrence Thomas and White's godson, Chuckii Booker, although Barry White's fingerprints were all over it.

The album ended with a single-track double-header called *Loves Interlude/ Good Night My Love*; at nearly eight minutes long, it was written by Barry White in his traditional style.

There was no obvious single for release, but three were tried out: *Super Lover*, which got to No 34 on the Billboard R&B chart, *I Wanna Do It Good To Ya*, which got to No 26, and *When Will I See You Again*, which made it to No 32. But there was no chance of any of them getting to the main Billboard singles chart – they simply weren't anywhere near good enough for that.

The album itself peaked at No 22 on the R&B chart, only slightly higher than the disappointing showing of *The Right Night & Barry White*. Nonetheless, critical reaction was surprisingly positive, although, having said that, the greatest words of praise used by journalists were "worthwhile" and "enjoyable".

One reviewer called Barry White an "influential soul veteran", but noted that the album wasn't in the same class as his previous work. However, the review said that the album "demonstrated that he hadn't lost his touch as a vocalist, composer or producer."

Once again Barry White took to the Arsenio Hall show to promote *The Man Is Back*. He told Hall that the title came from his absence from recording, which he blamed on his association with CBS, even though six years had passed since the split. Since moving to A&M he considered that things had finally started to look up. It was a giant fib, but he was ever hopeful that it might turn out to be true.

Some of the lyrics on the new album were far more specific than in the past, and White had to defend them, running straight into a row about explicit lyrics, which were becoming more common on pop records. His problem was the track *It's Getting Harder All the Time*. White didn't mean it the way it was taken, and he was challenged about it by Hall. He dismissed the concerns and defended explicit lyrics as long as they were "honest".

But his lyrics would come back to haunt him later in the year.

After the album's release, White went to Europe for a short tour in the fall of 1989. He was booked to play in Monaco at the Salle des Etoiles, at the Monte Carlo Sporting Club where he ran up against the notorious Steven Wells of 'New Musical Express'. The 29-year-old Wells was the music industry's preeminent writer and known for being highly provocative and unapologetic in his writing. A former bus conductor and punk rocker, known by everyone as 'Swells', he frequently took aim at the rich and powerful of the music industry and was known to have a brilliant turn of phrase and a sharp wit. He also did not suffer fools at all and had devastated the careers of many budding artists because he did not believe they had the talent to succeed.

White should never have agreed to be interviewed by Wells, as it could only mean trouble. Ned Shankman assigned his PA, Vicki, to sit in on the interview with strict instructions to end it if White said anything inappropriate. Before White went in Shankman warned him that, with Wells, there was "no such thing as off the record." White smiled and, seemingly unaware of Wells's reputation, believed he could easily handle anything the young British writer would throw at him.

Wells was no fool and sensed that there was a lot wrong in the world of Barry White. He didn't understand the new album and knew that White's fans wouldn't either.

At first White attempted to bluff and bully his way through the interview. When that didn't work, he unwisely suggested that they delay their conversation until the following day so that Wells could see his show at the Salle des Etoiles first.

It proved to be a colossal mistake.

The evening started badly when the lack of a jacket and tie meant that Wells had trouble even getting past the doorman into the venue. He was able to borrow a jacket but took a dislike to the doorman and called him a "ponce". The doorman responded with "peasant", casting a disdainful look at Wells's footwear. Wells in turn took one look at the dinner jacket the doorman was wearing and called him a "professional chimp impersonator". With that the doorman called over a friend and Wells was thrown out of the club straight onto the pavement. Furious, Wells tore off the borrowed jacket, threw it back at the doorman, and hailed a taxi. But when he got to his hotel he realised that he had left all his money in the inside pocket of the jacket. The taxi driver, realising that his passenger couldn't pay, kicked him into the street for the second time that evening, shouting, *Cochon anglais!* Wells knew enough French to know that it meant "English pig". He was humiliated and went to his room seething, and blaming Barry White for all his troubles.

This set the tone for Wells's interview with White the following day. Ned Shankman decided to sit in on it himself and, sensing real danger, twice tried to bring it to a halt – but White just waved him away.

Wells turned the interview into a discussion about women, which spurred White to launch an attack on the filth and corruption he said he saw around him. He talked about the need for new moral values, about how sex and love had been dirtied and cheapened. He blamed Madonna and Cher for what was happening, and said that their stage acts were partly responsible for the cheapening of women.

Wells then goaded White into one of the biggest mistakes of his career when he got the singer to say into his tape recorder that men were not entirely to blame when they committed rape, and that women who "walk around with their short skirts and their breasts exposed" were partially to blame for any harm that came to them.

It was a career-threatening remark. Whether White actually said it or it was taken wildly out of context, no one knows. But Wells himself was in no doubt, and it did White no favours at all when it was published a month later in 'New Musical Express'. In an article entitled 'King Shag Is Back' published in September 1989, Wells printed the quote verbatim, together with everything else White had said in a very misjudged interview.

At the end of the article Wells tore into White, especially his comments about rape. He wrote: "This is, of course, total and utter crap. Rape has to do with power, not sexuality, and it's always dumb to blame the victims."

He also called White a hypocrite and recalled his explicit lyrics from his 1975 album, *Just Another Way To Say I Love You*. He quoted lyrics from the song *Love Serenade*, which started off with: "Take it all off... I don't want to feel no panties, take off your brassiere my dear... Baby, you and me, huh, tonight we're going to get it on... Lick your lips, tempt me, tempt me, tempt me. Make me want you..."

Wells was now completely off the leash and virtually accused White of singlehandedly being responsible for the permissive society of the seventies. He ended the article by ridiculing White's manager, Ned Shankman.

It was not Barry White's finest hour.

White was devastated when he read the article, and realised that he had been a fool. He sat out the next few months hoping it wouldn't be noticed. And he got lucky – his remarks were not picked up by the mainstream media in England or America, probably because it was a Steven Wells article and no one completely trusted what was written.

If they had, Barry White's career may well have been over.

Things could only get better, and they did when later that year White was roped in by his old friend Quincy Jones to be part of a quartet that included El DeBarge, James Ingram and Al B to sing a song called *The Secret Garden (Sweet Seduction Suite)*. The song went on Jones's 1989 album *Back on the Block*, and was quickly released as a single. It was a hit and reached No 31 on the Billboard singles chart, No 67 in the UK chart, and No 1 on the Billboard Black Singles chart for a week.

It was the only bit of good news Barry White had that year. When the sales figures came in for *The Man Is Back* they were miserable, and it was clear the album had failed to make an impact.

So it was back to the drawing board yet again, but not before White got together for the first time with young British singing sensation Lisa Stansfield. Manchester-born, Stansfield had come to prominence by winning a singing competition called 'Search For A Star' in 1980, held at the famous Talk of the Town nightclub in London. Her musical idols were Marvin Gaye and Barry White, and she was born just in time for Barry White's music. The 23-year-old had taken the album charts by storm with her first solo album, *Affection*, selling five million copies throughout the world. It had taken her nine years to break out and she made no secret of the fact that *Affection* had been inspired by Barry White, to whom she dedicated it. That led to the two of them meeting, and they recorded a duet of her biggest hit, *All Around The World*. A DVD and a single were made, and all the proceeds went to a charity that Stansfield supported called Trading Places. It was the beginning of a 14-year musical relationship between them and a growing mutual respect that never wavered.

THE MAN IS BACK

CHAPTER 61

Extra-Curricular Music

Put Me In Your Mix - 18th solo album

1991

At the age of 47, in 1991, Barry White was suddenly starting to really feel his age. Throughout his life he realised that he had never stopped learning about himself, but at the same time he couldn't understand why, after all these years, he understood so little about himself.

His 30-year career in the music business had been such a mixture of fortunes – an abject failure for 15 years, then seven years of a stunning success, followed by seven years of gradual and seemingly unarrestable decline.

As the nineties dawned everything was declining. He was still touring but his act was nothing like a vibrant as it had been in the seventies and eighties. He was still writing music, but the consistency had gone and deep in his heart he knew that half of his compositions were now not so great. And as a singer he was all at sea – he no longer knew whether he was a rap artist or a soul singer.

But Barry White was a determined man and didn't easily throw in the towel. He resolved that his third album on the A&M label, and 18th solo album, *Put Me In Your Mix*, would turn his fortunes around.

And in many ways it did, as he said: "Sometimes you have to speak up for yourself, to let people know what you've done. People forget. I know a lot of them forgot about me."

But there was a price to pay. To get the album made at all, White had to agree to do things John McClain's way. Once again they agreed that the first half of the album would be controlled by McClain and the second half by White. And this time McClain was determined that White would stick to their bargain.

The John McClain section was designed to appeal to the hip-hop generation with no compromises. But, once again, it was a serious affront to the ears of Barry White fans. As a consequence, the second half was not Barry White at his best, but was still better than what had gone before.

Billed as the second album of his comeback phase, it was actually the third under the A&M label – the disastrous *The Right Night & Barry White* had now been completely expunged from history.

The new album was contemporary R&B, with Jack Perry's electronic instrumentation dominant, combined with White's traditional symphonic arrangements. It was a truly family affair, with White gathering everyone around him to help, including his two sons Barry Jnr and Darryl, together with daughter Bridget. Glodean White sang backing vocals.

The whole family, acutely aware of the situation, was trying to help Barry White get through the creative wilderness he had entered. The whole crew assembled at White's house at Sherman Oaks to begin a week of recording. They were crammed into the building in his garden that housed the R.I.S.E. Laboratories recording studio – but crucially there were no instrumental musicians present, as this was an album of the machine age.

The highlights were undoubtedly a duet with his old rival Isaac Hayes called *Dark And Lovely (You Over There)*, and White's adaption of the old Italian song *Volare*.

It opened with a tuneful number co-written with Albert Lucero, Carl Taylor and John Lopez, called *Let's Get Busy*, which was as far away from the traditional Barry White sound as you could get. The second track was *Love Is Good With You*, a six-minute rap that was another new-age Barry White tune, co-written with Jack Perry and W. T. Jones. No one really liked it and the song was arguably White's worst ever composition to date.

Track three, written by White and Perry, was called *For Real Chill*, and was marginally better in so far as it had a recognisable melody. That could also be said for *Breaking Down With You,* co-written by the late Marvin Gaye's brother-in-law, Gordon Banks, and ace guitarist Wah-Wah Watson, under his real name of Melvin Ragan.

Then suddenly the album came alive as White covered the old 1958 hit *Volare*, written by the great Italian songwriters Domenico Modugno and Franco Migliacci. It was arguably the best cover ever of the song, although White had some strong competition from Frank Sinatra, Louis Armstrong, Ella Fitzgerald, Luciano Pavarotti and Dean Martin, among others. It was included in the album only because White was about to tour Italy and play some big venues. Ned Shankman wanted a song around which he could build the visit and that had a chance of getting into the Italian charts. Jack Perry suggested *Volare* and White seized upon it. In many ways its original composer, Domenico Modugno, was an Italian Barry White of the 1950s.

It started with the lyrics written by Franco Migliacci in June 1957. They were inspired by two portraits painted by Marc Chagall. The story went that the two men was vacationing together and there were two prints hanging on the wall of their seaside villa. The first, called 'Le coq rouge', featured a yellow man suspended in mid-air, and the second, 'Le peintre et la modelle', was of a man whose face was coloured blue.

Modugno was due to arrive at the villa but was late, so Migliacci polished off a bottle of wine while he waited, and fell asleep. He started to dream about a man who dreams of painting himself blue, and being able to fly. When he woke up he wrote down what he could remember. When Modugno arrived they worked on a song based on the idea, which they initially called *Sogno in blu (Dream in Blue)*. Then a storm blew up and Modugno, unable to sleep, changed the name to *Volare*, which both of them preferred.

Jack Perry knocked up the music on his electronic machine and White sang the song half in Italian and half in English, mostly the latter written by Mitch Parish, adding a few of his own for good measure.

The song saved the album and one can only wonder why White didn't cover more well-known songs, adapting them to his own style. The famous songs he did cover, *Volare* and Billy Joel's *Just the Way You Are,* were both huge successes.

The title track, *Put Me In Your Mix,* followed. It was co-written with Howard Johnson, a successful soul singer on the A&M label whom John McClain loaned out to Barry White. Johnson had creative control and White had to take a back seat. It was a pleasant rap song but repetitive and overlong at seven minutes, and not good enough to be the title track.

It was followed by *Who You Giving Your Love To*, which was more traditional Barry White fare, although far from his best work.

White and Perry followed it up with a much better effort called *Love Will Find Us*, a seven-minute tune written by them that had a strong central melody and has endured as a hardcore fans' favourite.

Next came an Aaron Schroeder/David Grover production called *We're Gonna Have it All*. It was well below par and was never heard of again.

Finally came the duet with Isaac Hayes, *Dark And Lovely (You Over There)*, which had the potential to become an all-time classic as the two pop baritone giants of the American music industry finally got together. The White composition was good, but not good enough for such a meeting of talents. What the duet did prove for all time was that Hayes's voice, as good as it was, was eclipsed by the maestro's.

The album ended with a remix of the song *Sho' You Right*, which was pure indulgence by the people in the studio that day. And at eight minutes long it was a crazy indulgence.

Reflecting the fact that there was some serious Barry White music in the second half of the album, it was his most successful for ten years, scraping into the Billboard album charts Top 100 at No 98 and reaching the giddy heights of No 8 on the Billboard R&B chart.

To capitalise on the success of the album, Barry White threw himself into a gruelling touring schedule around the world in early 1992. It was to continue for 12 months.

The highlight was his visit to Britain in March 1992 when Kennedy Street Enterprises, Britain's biggest promoter, organised eight shows at six venues over a period of 14 days in Nottingham, Birmingham, Manchester, Newcastle and Edinburgh, with three dates in London at the Hammersmith Odeon. It was a rather more modest tour than in the past, with only 28 in the orchestra, mostly Hungarians. But White was in nostalgic mood and told his audience: "For 20 years I've been making music to dance to, music to listen to, music to make love to."

In London he performed with Lisa Stansfield, who was at the height of her powers. She told the audience: "One of my biggest heroes is Barry White." Her No 1 single *All Around The World* had been directly inspired by White, who said: "She's one of the students in the Barry White school of music. Lisa used my formula for phrasing, my chord progressions, my melody structure, my style of doubling of the harmony."

Great things continued to develop from that relationship, and five years later she successfully covered *Never, Never Gonna Give You Up* as well as duetting on *Staying Power* for the song *The Longer We Make Love*.

Caroline Sullivan, writing in 'The Guardian' newspaper, best summed up the tour: "He has not changed a bit since his 1970s heyday. The polished hair and goatee were intact, as was the black satin suit apparently constructed from a couple of his bedsheets. He carried a hankie, which he delicately dabbed at his forehead when his lurve-talk got emotional.

"His voice, too, remains unaltered by time. Actually, whether it can be described as a 'voice' at all is debatable; it is more a low-register reverberation that is sensed rather than heard. His comments to the crowd were so deep-pitched as to be often unintelligible. It was pretty certain, though, that he was discussing his favourite subject, 'the most sacred act between a man and a woman', that's sex by any other name, and the entire show was built on it. From the boudoir curtain that hid the orchestra to the way the maestro quavered the notes on *It's Ecstasy When You Lay Down Next To Me*, was steamy going. He rumbled through the hits and some new songs that sounded like the hits. He accepted flowers from lust-struck lady fans – it was business as usual."

The success of these tours kicked off ten years of touring America and the world. He may no longer be recording hit albums, but he was a huge star, especially to the 40-somethings who had grown up with his music. As one critic said: "The hip-hop generation of Don Juans recycled his old songs, and he has revived himself in the 1990s."

That he had.

CHAPTER 62

Disaster at Sherman Oaks

Northridge Earthquake shatters dream house

January 1994

In the early morning of Monday 17th January 1994, at a few seconds after half past four, the Northridge earthquake struck Los Angeles. The exact epicentre was in Reseda, a small neighbourhood in the north-central San Fernando Valley, eight miles from Barry White's house and 20 miles from downtown Los Angeles.

Barry White was used to earthquakes; he had lived through hundreds of minor quakes in the 50 years he had lived in Los Angeles. Usually they rocked the ground but did little else, as he said: "They usually rolled in a certain way, creating a kind of swinging action."

He vividly described what happened on that Monday morning in his 1999 memoirs. He had spent the evening of Sunday 16th working in his recording studio at the bottom of his garden. The studio was a stand-alone building on a small hill overlooking the main house.

He finished in the studio and turned everything off at around 3:30am. He strolled back to the house and went into the kitchen to eat a snack and drink some milk before going to bed. At four o'clock he walked into his bedroom suite, sat on the end of the bed and read a few of the headlines in the Los Angeles Times. Then he went into his bathroom. "I brushed my teeth and then walked into the bedroom." The recording session had left him a little heady and he was still wide awake. So he sat down on the end of the bed to do some thinking and plan his routine for the following morning.

Then it happened, as he vividly remembered: "All of a sudden I heard a low groaning whoomp. I glanced around as I felt a jolt that rattled the entire house from the ceiling down to the basement." He rushed outside through the bedroom's open French windows. The high waterfall over his pool had crumbled and the water was coming from the swimming pool and cascading towards the house: "It was like a tidal wave pouring out of my pool." Then he realised he was experiencing an earthquake like no other he had ever seen.

Because of seismic activity in California, building codes dictated that house-owners design their structures to be able to withstand the worst earthquake, but this one produced ground acceleration that was the highest ever instrumentally recorded in an urban area in North America, measuring 1.8 g-force, being felt as far away as 220 miles, as Las Vegas rumbled. The worst damage was in the west San Fernando Valley, affecting the regions of Santa Monica, Simi Valley and Santa Clarita. At 6.7 on the Richter scale, it lasted for no more than 20 seconds, but in those seconds enormous damage was done to property in Sherman Oaks.

There were two aftershocks at six on the Richter scale, the first a minute later and the second 11 hours later. Several thousand minor aftershocks were felt in the area.

Barry White's house at Sherman Oaks was particularly vulnerable because it had a basement, which naturally weakened its support and ground floor rootings. During the few seconds of the quake the house was lifted six inches and dumped back down again on its foundations, completely wrecking the integrity of the structure.

The recording studio, where he had been an hour before, was completely wrecked, together with the guest houses and swimming pool complex. He remembered: "It felt like somebody had literally picked up my house and slammed it down back hard into the concrete. The entire house had moved off its concrete foundations. The sensation was something like standing in the centre of a series of bomb blasts."

Houses on slopes, like White's, were particularly vulnerable. When he had bought the house, Larry Nunes had told him he had built it to withstand the worst earthquake. White reflected on those words as he surveyed his wrecked home. Of course, Nunes had never expected his house to have to live up to that promise, and when it was built corners had been cut everywhere to save money. The White House at Sherman Oaks had not performed as intended when the day of reckoning came, and Larry Nunes was no longer around to take the blame.

But White had been relatively lucky. The overall death toll was 57, and more than 8,700 people were injured, 1,600 of whom were hospitalised for more than one night. As well as White's house, many other homes were completely destroyed and property damage was extensive.

It proved to be one of the costliest natural disasters in US history, coming in at around $20 billion worth of damage, all caused in just a few seconds. As soon as word of the quake was received in New York, insurance company shares plummeted on Wall Street. But the stock market panic that had occurred after the last great California earthquake on Wednesday 18th April 1906, failed to materialise.

The Northridge earthquake had occurred on a previously undiscovered fault and was the first serious one in California for 50 years, the last having been in Long Beach in 1933. But as bad as it was, it was nothing like as serious as the 1906 event in San Francisco, which had measured 7.8 on the Richter scale and had virtually destroyed the whole of the great city.

But it was bad enough for anyone living within 10 miles of Reseda; Barry White was made homeless, and his family home, with so many of his memories, completely destroyed.

Nonetheless his plight was nowhere near as bad as that of the residents of the Northridge Meadows apartment complex, where 16 people, who lay asleep, were killed when the building completely collapsed.

The collapse of multi-storey parking structures was extensive and the Santa Monica Freeway, the busiest road in the United States, was closed for three months. The interchange of the Golden State Freeway collapsed and was closed for a year. The Anaheim stadium, 50 miles away, was also damaged, but the loss of life was regarded as light as it occurred early in the morning of a federal holiday.

As with the 1906 San Francisco quake, most of the damage was caused not by the quake itself, but by subsequent fires, flooding and landslides. Many fires were caused by broken gas lines from houses shifting off their foundations, and flooding when water lines were severed.

The worst damage was caused to multi-storey wooden-framed buildings, of which there were many in California. Buildings with basements, built on slopes like White's, fared worst.

Water quickly became the biggest problem as pressure dropped to zero and firefighters were unable to get access to mains water. Luckily there was no fire and little flooding in Sherman Oaks.

As darkness turned to light that morning, the full scale of the damage became apparent to White as he stood on his hill surveying the scene: "When the sun came up I could see the extent of the damage all along Ventura Boulevard. It looked like wartime."

A week after the quake 41,000 California homes still had no water and disease started to spread, made worse by the fact that hardly any hospitals in the San Fernando Valley were open. Eleven had suffered structural damage and had been forced to transfer their patients to other sites. There was no capacity left, and Red Cross marquees and tents were set up in the car parks of government offices.

Barry White's house may have been destroyed, but his family had survived. He said: "It was a miracle and I am eternally grateful that none of us was hurt." He decided not to rebuild the house but claimed on the insurance and sold the land, which gave him a welcome financial boost. Spooked by the earthquake and the possibility that it would not be the last, he decided that a move out of California might be wise. He said in his memoirs five years later: "The Northridge earthquake accomplished what nothing and nobody had been able to do before – it drove me out of Los Angeles."

DISASTER AT SHERMAN OAKS

CHAPTER 63

New House, New Album, New Start

Move to Las Vegas and the Icon Album

July to October 1994

The 1994 Northridge earthquake in San Fernando had made Barry White homeless and he desperately needed somewhere new to live – and quickly. The earthquake had also frightened him out of his wits and he no longer wanted to live in Los Angeles. He wanted somewhere as near as possible to the city, but sufficiently far away that there to be no danger of experiencing another earthquake.

He admitted that the choice he made, Las Vegas in Nevada, was made out of fear, fear of another earthquake devastating California. He said he was "fearful" of returning to live on the west coast. The loss of his home had been so traumatic that he didn't want to risk it happening again.

There were other reasons for moving away from Los Angeles. White decided that he had become almost institutionalised in Sherman Oaks and, after nearly 20 years, he needed a totally new start. And he was determined to make that completely new start in a new environment.

A few days after the quake he started searching for a suitable property in Nevada. A month later he found a new-build house in a suburb of Las Vegas, about 11 miles from the famous Strip. He bought the modern 8,000-square-feet mansion straight away, paid the asking price and moved in the next day with his new girlfriend, Katherine Denton, and his mother Sadie. He had plenty of money to play with from the insurance pay-out and the promise of the eventual sale of the land.

Katherine Denton had come into his life seemingly from nowhere. He had met her while touring and they had bonded. No one was sure what the relationship was about, but by this time in his life Barry White needed someone to take care of him, and Denton happily filled the role and would do for the next nine years. White had fallen head over heels in love with her at the age of 49, and she was just 24. Despite the 25-year age difference they were in synch with each other almost from the get-go. She was 21 when they first met and consequently they took time to get to know each other. He told 'Jet' magazine in 1998 that she was one of the "sweetest girls I have ever had the privilege to know". He appreciated the simplicity of the relationship: "Among her best qualities is that she's without games and always willing to listen and learn." After 30 years of relationships with strong independently minded women, Katherine Denton was a refreshing change.

It was a true love affair and the pair would often sit up until the early hours of the morning, as he described: "We talked about nothing at all, but anything and everything." And he admitted that it had taught him some new things about relationships: "I've found that a good relationship is all about sharing your mind as well as your time with another human being. True inspiration comes from when I can teach my lover something and she can teach me. That is the glory of the human side of life. Otherwise it's just passing ships in the night avoiding icebergs."

There was no question of marriage, however, as he told Marc Eliot in his memoirs published in 1999. He told him he was done with that after two failures, and realised the damage that divorce did to his reputation. He explained: "I'll never get married again. I'm with Katherine and she is with me and that's what counts. We each know there are no guarantees. We just love each other and will let time take care of itself."

The modern mansion dictated a new, more minimalist way of living. The old-fashioned blue interior theme of Sherman Oaks was completely dispensed with. White was not the same man at 50 as he had been at 30, and he found that his tastes in everything had changed dramatically during those 20 years. The new Barry White style was hip and modern like his music. The decor of his new home was now white walls, black leather, white carpets and glass-topped tables everywhere. It was a contemporary look overseen by Katherine, and he liked it straight away. Two huge black leather sofas dominated the main lounge with a vast stereo system that pumped out pre-programmed smooth jazz on a 24-hour basis. He had also changed his taste in pets. The birds and the horses were gone, replaced by no fewer than 11 German shepherd dogs. But he soon found that living in Las Vegas was "like living in the desert" and, after the clear blue skies and smell of the sea in Los Angeles, he wasn't too sure he liked it.

But his spirits were boosted when he was asked to appear in an episode of 'The Simpsons' called 'Whacking Day'. By then 'The Simpsons' had become a cult show on American television, and White seized on the opportunity. The producer, Matt Groening, offered him a guest slot. It was considered a major honour among the glitterati of Los Angeles, and he recorded the episode during a break in touring in 1993.

It was the 20th episode of series four, broadcast on 29th April 1993. It revolved around the fictional annual holiday of Whacking Day, in which the citizens of Springfield drive snakes into the town square, then club them to death. The tradition appals Lisa Simpson, who finds she has no support from any of the adults in the town, including Reverend Lovejoy, who lies about Whacking Day being supported by the Bible. Barry White arrives to begin the festivities and sings a new version of *Can't Get Enough Of Your Love, Babe*, he re-arranged especially for the show rather than using the existing recorded version. Later White is disgusted when he discovers what the holiday is about and quickly leaves the town square. The episode's central message is against the mistreatment of snakes.

'The Simpsons' helped take his mind off all the upheavals. He also started work on a new album, which he called *The Icon Is Love*. It would be the 19th solo album of his career and the last under his A&M contract.

His first three albums for the label, *The Right Night & Barry White*, *The Man Is Back* and *Put Me In Your Mix*, had in, truth, been disasters, but by 1994 he thought he finally had a sense of where he had been going wrong. Those albums had attempted to combine the old and the new Barry White and pleased no one in the process. He knew that he had to somehow smooth out the new-style hip-hop rhythms to blend with his trademark style expected by his fans. He realised he needed a combination of old and new, not either one or the other. So he started a search to find collaborators to try and make that happen; by now he had realised that he could not do it himself and he had to start listening to outside producers and writers. But he also realised that he needed to work with people sympathetic to his style and method of recording. Gene Page was ill, and for the first time in Barry White's career he took no part in the production.

White found the ideal sympathetic collaborator in Gerald Levert, a 28-year-old singer/songwriter whose father Eddie was the former lead singer of the O'Jays. It was A&M's John McClain who recommended that White got together with Levert. In turn, Levert brought in his songwriting partner Edwin 'Tony' Nicholas.

It was an entirely unexpected and surprise combination. Levert specialised in songs about love and relationships, so it seemed a natural fit. He was very flattered to be asked and admitted he was a closet Barry White fan: "I used to make love to girls while listening to Marvin Gaye or Barry White in my teenage years." But he also admitted that the association embarrassed him: "You wouldn't believe how many people in the record business dogged me when I said I had written these songs for Barry White. They said, 'Why you gonna give the tracks to Barry – he's old.' But we forget that performers like Barry White have given us real music."

The three men got together and wrote two songs that led off the album, *Practice What You Preach* and *There It Is*. The first saw White, Levert and Nicholas combine together perfectly, and was released as a single, destined to finally bring Barry White a hit record after years outside the charts. Indeed, it was his first hit for almost 15 years and got as high as No 18 on the Billboard singles chart, a position that White had not seen in quite a while. It also topped the R&B singles chart for three weeks, spending almost 30 weeks in the charts. In the UK it got into the Top 20, something White hadn't managed there for almost 10 years.

White said the reason for the song's success was simple: "We're going into winter, and the song's a slow-moving thing. People like to cuddle up in the winter, stay home in the winter."

But whatever the reason, *Practice What You Preach* was White's biggest chart success since 1977's *It's Ecstasy When You Lay Down Next to Me*.

Gerald Levert wasn't at all surprised, as he said: "When we recorded *Practice What You Preach,* just hearing him talk got my girlfriend all excited, which made me a lucky man that night and Barry gave me many happy nights with my girlfriend."

However, they didn't have the same success with *There It Is,* which struggled to get to No 54 on the Billboard R&B chart.

The third track was called *I Only Want To Be With You,* and was a collaboration with 35-year-old James Harris III, better known as Jimmy Jam, and 38-year-old Terry Lewis. They were a long-establishing writing and producing duo who had been hired by John McClain to write for Janet Jackson, and he paired them with White. The song was described by Harris and Lewis as being about "taking your time in the love department". But White himself saw it differently, describing it as being a "commitment" song, as he explained: "It's about a guy saying, 'I know what you had. I know what you been through. I'm not about none of that. I only want to be with you.'"

I Only Want To Be With You was completely under the control of Harris and Lewis and was recorded at their Flyte Tyme studios in Minnesota. That and *Come On* were the only tracks ever recorded by Barry White where he had no hand in the producing. It was released as a single but was hardly single material and did not make an impact on the American charts, although it got to No 36 in the British charts.

Track four was called *The Time Is Right*, with White collaborating with Chuckii Booker, whom he had first employed ten years before. After that Booker had gone off on his own to make a successful solo career as a writer and performer.

Track five was called *Baby's Home*, written by White with three collaborators – Barry Eastmond, Gary Brown and Jolyon Skinner. Track six, called *Come On*, was the second production on the album from James Harris III and Terry Lewis. It too was released as a single and got into the Billboard Top 100, reaching as high as No 12 on the R&B singles chart.

The title track, *Love Is The Icon*, was a White/Perry production and a typical modern-style Barry White ballad, which had some very nice and subtle touches and was the fourth single from the album, reaching No 43 on the R&B singles chart – it proved that Barry White had not lost his touch.

Sexy Undercover was the second Chuckii Booker production, co-written with White, then *Don't You Want To Know* was co-written with songwriter Michael Lovesmith, whom White was trying out. It was a competent song.

The last song, *Whatever We Had, We Had*, was also co-written with Lovesmith, and has belatedly become an iconic White ballad. Effectively a love letter to his estranged wife Glodean, it said all there needed to be said about their relationship and how White still felt about his marriage.

Whatever We Had, We Had was as good a song as Barry White had ever written in his career, as well as being one of the longest, at 10 minutes 40 seconds.

The album also contained a remix of *Super Lover* from the 1989 album *The Man Is Back* as a bonus track.

The Icon Is Love astonished observers with its sure-footed blend of modern and traditional White music. That was reflected in the sales, which reportedly reached an astonishing four million copies. It proved that the thirst for Barry White music was still there. As he himself said: "Every song on this album is great, baby. *The Icon Is Love* is blowing up because everything is in alignment. People are tired of clones – artists who all sound like each other."

The album represented a major comeback for Barry White, both critically and commercially, and went on to become easily his most successful album since his heyday. It topped the R&B album chart, and peaked at No 20 on the main album chart, staying there for a very long time.

It also garnered critical acclaim for the quality of the material and its contemporary production. It won the 1995 Soul Train Music Award for best R&B/Soul album and was nominated for a Grammy Award.

'Allmusic' said: "White showcased his seductive, bassy baritone with romantic rap introductions on most of the selections. There is a balance of up-tempo and balladic songs, reminiscent of his days as the king of disco-swing, and the latter is a contemporary funky ballad."

Jack Perry said: "*The Icon Is Love* took off and eventually sold six million units worldwide, and was one of the biggest albums of his career." Whether it did sell that many is debatable but it was certainly well over two million.

Gerald Levert was delighted to have delivered his friend a hit album, and said: "Barry was one of the greatest songwriters/arrangers of all and he was way before his time."

It was the first good news for a very long time, and for the first time in many years Barry White sensed a revival for his music. It eventually proved to be a false dawn, but he rode the success as hard as he could, kicking off another world tour, 'The Icon World Tour', his biggest and most ambitious yet, covering more than 30 countries with more than 50 concerts over a period of 18 months.

It started off in Belgium, a country that had always loved Barry White; some of his best concerts outside America had taken place in Brussels. In the autumn of 1995 he and his entourage, together with around 30 Hungarian musicians, booked into the Stanhope Hotel. If there was a place for a comeback, then Brussels was it. And so it proved on that magical night. The confidence he received from Europe was immeasurable and it sparked an American revival tour, including a memorable few nights at the Paramount in New York. White recalled that he had made his New York debut there as a solo artist 23 years before, when it was known as the Felt Forum. It was an emotional few nights and Jon Pareles of The New York Times described the concert as "the soothing, virile sound of an endlessly renewed seduction."

He had got that right.

Part 5

Four years of physical decline and death

CHAPTER 64

Life and Death Setbacks

Health fails then Sadie and Gene die

1995 to 1998

On 4th April 1996, Sadie Mae Carter died in her bedroom at Barry White's house in Clark County, Las Vegas. As he knelt by her bedside, she took her last breaths and he whispered in her ear how much he loved her as she faded away. It was not a normal mother-and-son departure scene – it was much more than that. Sadie had been such a huge part of his life and he in hers. There is no doubting that she was one of those very special women who come along only once in a while. She was a woman who had touched the lives of everyone she had known in a very positive way – and the life she had touched the most was that of her eldest son. And he was only too aware that without his mother's influence at the very start of his life there would have been no Barry White. Of all the people he had rubbed shoulders with in his career, there had been no one greater than his mother.

Now she was no longer there, Barry White knew that there would be a void that no amount of time could ever heal. In his heart of hearts he knew that his own life was also effectively over. He found it a time for deep reflection. It was the third death of someone whom he had held very close in his life: first his brother had been murdered in 1982, then in 1988 Dede Taylor had died from cancer, but his mother's death hit him in the hardest possible way. A year later he found he still missed her as desperately as he had the day she died: "There's no one I miss more than my mother – she was the greatest person I ever met."

When he read her will a few days later he was surprised to see that she wished her body to be returned to the place of her birth and buried alongside that of her own parents, whom he had never known. So a week later White took his mother's body to Tennessee and, with her eight grandchildren present, she was buried next to her own mother and father at Bethpage Cemetery in Sumner County.

Her passing at the age of 83 was not a surprise. For the previous three years she had suffered from advancing Alzheimer's disease and her death was a relief both to her and those closest to her. The first signs of mild Alzheimer's had started to show eight years before, and White had blamed it on the shock of the murder of her son Darryl. He also blamed himself for not paying his mother more attention in the period following her youngest son's death.

He also believed that his brother's death, his mother's death and the collapse of his marriage were subliminal messages about wealth and fame, as he said in his memoirs: "They were all reminders of why it is not smart to get hung up on false infatuations and other forms of self-adulation, of self-love, like stardom."

All three losses were the cause for some real soul-searching as he tried desperately to find himself. As he tried to explain: "The ultimate definition and reconciliation of one's self is a fiercely private affair and has to come from within. All the fame and money I had in the world couldn't prevent my brother from being murdered, or help me save my mother from dying of her broken heart."

White believed that all of these negative events caused a realignment in his life that made him finally realise what was valuable and what wasn't. He concluded: "It's one of the reasons that I've always made sure that every day my children know how much I love them."

But little did he know that even worse shocks were to come.

In August 1998 he was hit hard again when Gene Page died after a long illness. The illness had taken him out of circulation since the early nineties, and he died at his Westwood home in Los Angeles on the 24th, aged just 58.

Page had enjoyed an unbelievable career, comparable to people like Marvin Hamlisch and Phil Spector, and he was undoubtedly one of the most prolific arrangers/producers of popular music in the seventies and eighties.

His death was very hard for Barry White, but not in the same way as the deaths of Dede Taylor, his mother and his brother. White had a different sort of relationship with Gene Page. They were never close socially, as Page moved into different circles. And they were never that close at work because they had an overlap of skills and there was some professional jealously in the relationship – it never manifested itself, remaining beneath the surface, but it was still there.

Page never thought much of himself as a writer or performer, but he was a genius as a producer and arranger. Truth be told, Barry White was always secretly envious of Page's skills in those areas, but recognised that they added to his music so allowed Page full sway, especially over his earlier recordings. He never allowed that real jealously to get in the way, and was very grateful for his relationship with Gene Page, only fully realising after his death how much of his career he had devoted to his music.

The two men had collaborated for nearly 25 years through 31 albums – 16 for White as a solo artist, five for the Love Unlimited girl band, and 10 for the Love Unlimited Orchestra. It had been an extraordinary partnership, the most successful of both of their careers. No one before, then or since could put together cellos, French horns and violins like Gene Page, and White echoed Ray Parker Jnr's words, describing Page as "session call number one" for any soul producer in Los Angeles. Aside from his success with Barry White, he had arranged the music on more than 100 gold- and platinum-selling records for other artists – White had only been a third of Page's total output. In his 38-year-career Page had arranged music for Michael Jackson, Aretha Franklin, Marvin Gaye, Johnny Mathis, Barbra Streisand, Lionel Richie, Kenny Rogers and Whitney Houston. He arranged Elton John's *Philadelphia Freedom*, which was regarded as one of the greatest musical arrangements of all time.

Gene Page's funeral on Wednesday 2nd September was attended by most of the great and good of Hollywood's music industry. Two of his arrangements, *Always* and *The Greatest Love of All*, were sung by Carl Anderson at his burial. Many of the musicians who worked with him played along in what was an extraordinarily moving graveside ceremony, presided over by Father Minson, who called Page a "man who always cared and shared".

Barry White's grief at the loss of his closest collaborator was absolute, and it took six weeks for him to emerge from his house and finish work on the album. It also caused him to suddenly started thinking of his own mortality. He and Page were of similar age and White spent the two weeks after the latter's death reflecting on the life of his friend. He was heartened by the fact that he had never been in hospital and had hardly ever needed to see a doctor throughout his life. He had never seen any reason to have a full medical check-up. But suddenly Barry White started to fear death, and realised for the first time that he was not invincible.

That had originally manifested itself the year before during his 'Icon World Tour', promoting The *Icon Is Love*, the album that had revitalised his career. He had turned 50 years of age and was starting to feel it. His performances had evolved over the years. When he started touring in 1973, he appeared on stage for less than 45 minutes and split the work with Love Unlimited and the Love Unlimited Orchestra. But the three girls and the orchestra were long gone and now he was having to go on stage and perform for nearly two hours. And the show was much more energetic, with extremely elaborate sets. There were more than 50 people in his travelling entourage, appearing in front of and behind the stage at each concert. No longer could he wing it like he used to – it didn't work like that any more.

The Icon tour was debilitating and almost from the start he had not felt himself. He was becoming overtired, going to bed early and getting up increasingly later. His girlfriend Katherine Denton, who accompanied him on the tour, found herself playing nurse, and did her best to soothe him. She desperately pleaded with him to see a doctor and get a check-up. But he brushed her off with comments like, "Honey, I'm the healthiest man you could ever meet. I don't need no doctors."

And that as she watched him puff on 60 cigarettes a day.

But even he started to worry that something might be wrong when he started nodding off in public and found that he couldn't make it back to his hotel after a concert without falling asleep in the limousine or coach. Worse still, three concerts had to be postponed because of exhaustion. That had never happened to him before and he hated it. But still he would not see a doctor, telling Katherine that all he needed to do was rest.

In October 1995 he finally took her advice and, as a precaution, flew back to the United States for a two-week break and a brief respite from the pressures of the tour. That decision saved his life.

During the evening of Monday 30th October 1995 White was at his home in Las Vegas with Denton. Out of nowhere and with absolutely no warning, he was suddenly struck down by a deep pain in his abdomen, as he remembered in his 1999 memoirs: "One minute I was fine, walking around the house, and the next I was kind of delirious."

White decided to go to his bedroom to lie down. But he immediately passed out and fell down on the floor unconscious. A panicked Denton called an ambulance, which took him to Mountain View Hospital. When he didn't wake up, she telephoned Jack Perry, who got to Las Vegas as quickly as he could. His children followed and took it in turns to stay by his bedside. Suddenly he was fighting for his life. They suffered three agonising days wondering whether he would wake up and what state he would be in.

Throughout those few days Jack Perry refused to go home and held on to his friend's hand for 72 hours. White recalled: "Jack was trying to keep me from slipping out of this world." He wrote in his memoirs that Perry was responsible for not letting him die: "I remember trying to pull Jack along with me into the vast unknown that kept calling. His hand, like the other side of a tug-of-war, fighting to keep me on the side of the living."

Barry White was in a coma for nearly four days and it was touch-and-go whether he would live. A series of tests showed up serious problems with his kidneys, while the causes of other problems he faced were easy to identify. His personal habits were dreadful. He ate what he liked, when he liked and in whatever quantities he liked. Away from home, his life involved staying in the best hotel suites round the world, and he indulged his taste for the richest foods at every opportunity. Added to that was his 60-a-day cigarette habit.

Doctors also found that he had unusually high blood pressure, which incredibly had gone undiagnosed for virtually the whole of his life. As he said: "I had suffered from hypertension, one of the deadliest of diseases, for a long time without knowing it." The high blood pressure had severely affected his kidneys until they had started to fail.

Unusually his eyes were open all the time he was in the coma, but there was nothing there. The hospital's doctors had no idea how to wake him and prepared the family for the worst. They fully expected him to stop breathing at any time and just slip away quietly; they could see no other outcome as his body gradually closed down its functions. He was beyond any form of resuscitation. White remembered later: "I thought this was the end. I'd faced death before in my gang-banging days when I didn't have much to lose. Now here I was with everything on the line, about to lose it all."

But on the fourth day some sort of miracle occurred. Against all the odds Barry White suddenly regained consciousness, with Jack Perry, Lanese and Kevin at his bedside. They pressed the alarm and doctors came running, amazed at this sudden recovery. As White remembered: "I could tell from the look on their faces that they were grateful for my survival and amazed all at the same time." He later described it as a "pure miracle".

If he hadn't been in hospital when the stroke felled him, the outcome would have been very different. As it was, within minutes he was given the latest drugs, which all but negated the long-term effects. The medication brought his blood pressure down to manageable levels and he felt a lot better for it. He was discharged from hospital and went home to Las Vegas.

The speed of his recovery was incredible, so much so that after a few months he was ready to go back on the road and finish the tour. It was an amazing comeback and no one really understood how he had made it and returned from the dead.

Shaherah White remembers it being a very difficult period for all the family: "My father became ill in 1995 and he had to go into the hospital. They didn't know what was wrong with him at first but he was in a coma for about three days after he had a minor stroke and it was pretty scary for me. He had to take some time off although he did eventually go back and finish his last album."

Musically, White felt reinvigorated. From then onwards, until the end of his life eight years later, he took a self-admittedly more philosophical view of the world: "The chance to once more entertain my fans had taken on a new and far more profound meaning for me."

But going back on the road and resuming his career was a terrible decision. The illness had been a warning that, at 50 years of age, it was time to retire and lead a more restful life. But it was a warning he did not heed, for which he would ultimately pay a very heavy price. His quick and seemingly full recovery made him feel invincible. He started a new healthy regime, but quickly fell back into his old ways.

As soon as he left hospital he was anxious to get back to work. The enforced rest had given him lots of ideas for a new album, and the title was obvious after what he had been through – he decided to call it *Staying Power*.

It was to be his 20th and last album, although he didn't know it at the time.

CHAPTER 65

Staying Power

20th and final solo album

1999

After a couple of years in the desert, Barry White soon began to tire of living in Las Vegas. He found it held nothing for him and cut him off from the creativity of mainstream Los Angeles, so much so that he decided that a move back closer to Los Angeles would be best for his career.

But he had no intention of moving to an earthquake zone again. What had happened that night in Sherman Oaks had scarred him for ever and he decided that the safest place, within the Los Angeles area, was San Diego. After taking advice from geological experts, he concluded that the risk of an earthquake in San Diego was minimal.

He found a nice pink stucco house on the waterfront up for rental, and a few days after viewing it he agreed a lease and moved in with his 30-year-old girlfriend, Katherine Denton, and his dogs. The house was situated past the marina and just a few minutes from the Pacific base of the United States Navy's nuclear submarine fleet. He concluded that the US Navy would not have built an important base in an area that was vulnerable to earthquakes.

The new house followed the same interior style of the Las Vegas mansion he had just sold. One visitor called the décor "overpoweringly kitsch" and an "evocative haze of ghetto-fabulousness". White told a bemused journalist, Edward Helmore, who visited the house and commented unfavourably on the décor: "I am, you are, and it is." But Helmore did say that the kitsch was "impressive".

As in all his houses huge black leather sofas dominated the living areas, with a vast stereo system playing smooth jazz on a loop. There was also the return of the obligatory giant fish tank, which was set beneath a glass table in the kitchen. A portrait of Malcolm X hung above the fireplace, just as it had at Sherman Oaks and Las Vegas.

But as soon as he got settled into the San Diego house he found that it was too far away; he couldn't resist the allure of Los Angeles and was soon ready to move again. He said at the time: "I love San Diego, but I'm ready to move back to LA. It has action no other city has. I miss it. That's where my business is, my record business. I need to be near where I'm working."

After the deaths of so many people close to him and his own near-death experience, White was suffering from an identity crisis and all these factors contributed to the five-year gap between his 19th and 20th solo albums. But the simple fact was that after the unexpected success of the album *The Icon Is Love* and the gruelling world tour, White had no energy left to make a new album and no studio on hand in which to record it. Living in Vegas had meant that a day in the recording studio involved a 300-mile round trip. The only real work White had done in the intervening years was some small-scale tours and work on commercials and network TV guest parts.

But the move to San Diego solved that problem and he soon went back into the studio to record his 20th solo album, appropriately called *Staying Power*.

Despite the success of *The Icon Is Love*, in the intervening four years A&M had lost interest in Barry White and had changed out of all recognition. The label had been sold to PolyGram, which in turn had been purchased by Seagram, which had then merged it with Universal and eventually merged it again with Geffen and Interscope – all in the space of five years.

The resulting merged label was run by accountants, not A&R men, and it meant that the old way of working no longer applied. The record industry was also emerging slowly from the vicious recession of the early nineties and was much more risk-averse. Now it was all about the numbers.

The final sales of *The Icon Is Love* were said to be in the millions and it went triple-platinum, but none of the three other albums had exceeded 300,000. His health scare had also frightened the executives at A&M, who were reluctant to fork out the huge advance for a new album deal that White demanded but may not be able to fulfil. There were also people at the label who believed that, even if his health recovered fully, his best work was behind him. Even before the stroke it had been clear that he was not the artist he had been, and the execs at A&M did not want to take the chance. The company was also concerned about the unavailability of Gene Page, White's long-term musical arranger, as well as the five-year gap between *The Icon Is Love* and

Staying Power, which was not positive for his career. White was also not too keen about staying with A&M either, with Jerry Moss and John McClain no longer at the helm.

Normally finding a new record label would not have been a problem but, after such a long absence from recording, no one was rushing to sign Barry White. They thought that it was all over for him at 54 years of age, and in reality it probably was. None of the majors really wanted to know and White was too proud to go back to the hustling he had done at the start of his career. He finally struck a deal with Peter Baumann's Private Music label. Now owned by Bertelsmann Music Group (BMG), it had been founded by Baumann in 1984 as what he described as a "home for instrumental music". Before White was signed, Baumann's biggest artist was Ringo Starr.

Michael Dornemann and Strauss Zelnick, who ran BMG together, were Barry White fans and they approved a one-album deal with a sizeable advance. Both men believed that he still had what it took.

But producing *Staying Power* was a different proposition without Gene Page. The album featured duets with Chaka Khan, Puff Daddy and Lisa Stansfield, and a collection of songs written by White and other songwriters. It seriously challenged White and he found it as difficult as it had been in 1972, when he had struggled for material for his first album for Love Unlimited. White realised that a lot of his skills, which he had previously taken for granted, had deserted him, but he pushed on, hoping that it would come good in the end.

The album featured 11 tracks and 66 minutes of music. Eight of the tracks were written by Barry White, and he and Jack Perry handled all the arrangements. But as gifted as they both undoubtedly were, no one could replace Gene Page, who had been responsible for the Barry White sound. So White fell back into his previous mode of desperately embracing a younger audience and ignoring his traditional fans, so it was a very different and not altogether pleasing sound that emerged.

There was a distinct lack of quality on the album and nothing that resembled a hit single, although publicly Barry White claimed that he was not bothered: "I have never been on that gotta-have-a-hit kick, I love music too much for that."

Staying Power, the title track, opened the album and was the only single released from it. The song was brought to White by amateur writers, Joey Paschal and Rory Holmes – it was the only song they ever sold. A competent effort, the single version peaked at No 45 on the Billboard R&B chart. But it was not good enough to be the title track on a Barry White album.

The second track, called *Don't Play Games*, was also from an amateur writer called Steve Guillory, and had some inspiring elements. It was not far away from being a great Barry White song, but the influence of Gene Page was sorely missed. Without Page's input, *Don't Play Games* failed to make an impact.

Chaka Khan duetted with Barry White on track three, called *The Longer We Make Love*, written specially by Aaron Schroeder and Marlon Saunders. But it was nothing special, even though White and Khan got on well and had a good time recording it. A native of Chicago, Chaka Khan was then 46 years old, and really gelled with White musically. It was a shame that the song was not better put together.

Track four was called *I Get Off On You*, written by White and Perry together with Kashif Saleem. It featured the brilliant guitar playing of Wah-Wah Watson and Chris Clermont, who were clearly having a good time on their instruments. But it was memorable for no other reason than that. It was another effort to capture the traditional Barry White sound, but failed, despite having many of the key ingredients. It seemed that no one knew how to mix the ingredients together any more now Gene Page was no longer around.

Which Way Is Up was written by hip-hop producer Doug Rasheed together with White and Perry. It was yet another desperate attempt to recapture the old sound, but failed again and was another musical embarrassment. The lyrics were generally poor.

The sixth track, *Get Up,* written by White and Perry, was more of the same – one reviewer called it "an affront to Barry White's fans".

Track seven was called *Sometimes*. Written by White and arranged by Hidle (HB) Barnum, it started promisingly but turned into ill-thought musical nonsense. White's fans were horrified that he could include such music, vastly inferior to his work of 20 years before, on an album with his name on the album sleeve.

The eighth track was a cover version of a song called *Low Rider*, written by a collection of people including Morris Dickerson, Charles Miller, Harold Brown, Howard Scott, Jerry Goldstein, Lee Oscar, Leroy Jordan and Sylvester Allen, who were connected to a group called War, a funk group from the seventies. War had a moderate hit with *Low Rider* first time around, but it was unclear why Barry White had chosen to cover it as it did not suit his voice or his style. It was also out of synch with the rest of the album, which was designed to be listened to with the lights turned off. There were literally thousands of songs out there that White could have covered, but for some reason he chose *Low Rider*.

Track nine was called *Thank You,* a simple melody with simple lyrics written by Sly Stone, who had performed it in the eighties. It was re-mixed in the studio by a young Sean Combs, better known as Puff Daddy. It was arguably the best tune on the whole album, and as pleasant to listen to as anything written by Sly Stone – which is more than could be said for track ten, *Slow Your Roll.* Written by White, Perry and Joey Paschal, fans generally regarded it as "dreadful".

The final track was Barry White's famous duet with Lisa Stansfield called *The Longer We Make Love*, written by Aaron Schroeder and Marlon Saunders. It was pleasant listening but a waste of a great opportunity for two great and compatible artists.

The duets with Chaka Khan and Lisa Stansfield added variety to the album but little else. Interestingly, they were the only White tracks on any of his albums with a shared vocal credit.

Although it was widely regarded by his fans as the worst album of his career, astonishingly it won two Grammy Awards in 2000: 'Best Male R&B Vocal Performance' and 'Best Traditional R&B Vocal Performance'. Whether they were deserved or not is another matter, but it had always been a mystery why Barry White had never won a Grammy and had been ignored over the years by the members of the National Academy of Recording Arts and Sciences (NARAS).

Staying Power was the first time White had been recognised; in the past he had been scathing of NARAS for ignoring his contribution to contemporary pop music. In 1973 he had been favourite for the Academy's award for best newcomer, but instead it went to Bette Midler, even though White had burst onto the scene with multiple albums and singles roaring up the charts. White never forgave the Academy for what he regarded as a 'major slight' and was continually critical as he failed to be honoured in any category for the following 26 years, despite NARAS handing out more than 100 Grammys every year. He had undoubtedly deserved to be recognised in previous years for some outstanding work, especially in the mid-seventies. However, the two awards in 2000 were not generally thought to be 'deserved', and many saw them as a belated reward for having been ignored in the past. Jack Perry said: "Barry's two Grammys for *Staying Power* were long overdue for the last album of his career."

Although the awards may have been a sop to the maestro, whom the Academy's voters realised was coming to the end of his career, they were nevertheless a very welcome sop. White was ecstatic when they were announced. His reaction to finally getting his hands on a Grammy was: "Sometimes it takes the Grammy folks a long time to wake up and smell the coffee. I can't believe how long I've lasted."

It wasn't the only piece of good luck for *Staying Power*. Sales of the album got a huge boost when he was invited to sing a special version of *You're the First, The Last, My Everything* for a scene in the popular drama series 'Ally McBeal'. In the late nineties 'Ally McBeal' was a sensational new comedy, created by David E. Kelley, who had been jointly responsible with Steven Boccho for the ground-breaking series 'LA Law'. Kelley had pitched his new show to the Fox channel, which greenlighted it straight away. It became an overnight sensation, starring a new actress called Calista Flockhart who played a young lawyer working in a fictional Boston law firm. It quickly won an Emmy and a Golden Globe.

Barry White sang the new arrangement of the song in episode 18 of the second season, called 'Those Lips, That Hand'. He was in a surreal bathroom setting and the effect of the song on the character, John Cage, played by Peter MacNicol, was a major plot line. Many of the male characters joined him in the bathroom and for 3½ minutes they danced to the song, which caused a minor sensation in America. They were eventually joined by the whole cast. The episode was broadcast on 19th April 1999 and suddenly everyone in America was talking about Barry White again.

The immensely popular series was viewed by 13.8 million households on the Fox network. White's cameo singing role had an impact beyond its initial scope and revived interest in his music, causing a spike in his album sales just as his new album *Staying Power* was released.

Shortly afterwards White got an offer from Trey Parker and Matt Stone, the creators of the 'South Park' animated series, to provide the voice for a character they had called Jerome 'Chef' McElroy. The character was an overweight African-American with a beard, who usually wore blue pants and a red shirt. In most scenes he wore a white apron and chef's hat with the word 'Chef' printed on it. But after much consideration Barry White publicly refused the role because he believed the character disrespected the black community and was a stereotype. Lou Rawls also turned it down, and Isaac Hayes finally took on the role. But the drama surrounding the offer and White's rejection brought him right back to public attention and further boosted sales of his new album.

As a result of all the free publicity, *Staying Power* peaked at No 13 on the Billboard R&B album chart and reached No 43 on the main Billboard albums chart. It made a profit for Bertelsmann, even though the album proved to be eminently forgettable, and no tracks subsequently appeared on any 'greatest hits' albums.

The critical reception was mixed, the overall opinion being that the album was "average". 'Allmusic' reviewer Stephen Erlewine described it as "classy and entertaining", but said that it "doesn't add to the legacy", which it surely didn't, and was a fair assessment.

Shaherah White admits that on *Staying Power* her father was not the man he had once been and said: "When he started work on *Staying Power* the thought of starting and getting into it excited him. He always had the force and passion, it didn't go away, but physically he could only do so much."

The album was released on 27th July 1999, and throughout August and the fall Barry White took to the road for a series of sell-out concerts across America. It was a heavy schedule, and health problems struck him down again; no fewer than seven of the American concerts had to be cancelled and rescheduled because of various personal difficulties. White hated letting his fans down but he kept having to return to Los Angeles to recuperate and rest. The dates were eventually all kept and he returned home again to rest for a few weeks before he was due to leave for Europe in November.

Before that, in October 1999, Barry White finally published his long-anticipated autobiography, which he called 'Love Unlimited – Insights on Life and Love'. He had secured a sizeable advance from the Random House publishing company and the book was published by one of its subsidiaries, Broadway Books. In the UK it was licensed to Virgin Books.

He chose Marc Eliot as his co-writer. Eliot was an accomplished biographer who had written books about Bruce Springsteen, Phil Ochs and The Eagles. His most acclaimed work was a biography of Walt Disney. He had a nice style of writing, but had difficulty getting White to sit down and talk about his life; he was left to his own devices for much of the time.

Consequently, Barry White's biography was nearly eight years in the writing, and when it was finally published it consisted of 11 chapters over 200 pages of text and 36 pages of appendices. Disappointingly there was no index.

The new book was dedicated to his mother Sadie Mae, and there was a photo of them together at the front taken by Gene Page at a studio session. The book comprehensively chronicled the first 30 years of White's life, when he was breaking through and becoming a success, but after that it lost its way and its chronological direction. It had huge gaps and was a less than perfect biography, although of great interest to his legion of fans.

None of this was the fault of Marc Eliot who had tremendous problems in getting it right; it became apparent that Barry White had forgotten some of the key points of his life and Eliot was forced to exhaustively recreate them. Where he relied on White's memory, some chronological mistakes also became apparent.

When it was published, White did a book signing at the Barnes & Noble store on Fifth Avenue, New York, on Wednesday 20th October 1999. He spent two hours at the store and signed more than 300 copies of the autobiography, selling at $23 each. It was a surreal scene, with White sitting on a beautiful yellow leather armchair while Marc Eliot was conspicuously given a hard wooden chair and looked as uncomfortable as he must have felt.

The heavy-duty roster of security guards kept fans away and told them, "Mr White will only sign autographs for people who buy a book." One fan said: "I don't want a book, I want Barry."

The long line of fans was mildly out of control, especially when they got to the head of the line and finally met their hero face to face. A few got carried away and fainted. An unfazed Barry White just carried on signing, saying to each one as he gave them back their book: "You're welcome." Many just said to him, "I love you," and he smiled back at them. Unsurprisingly no one seemed bothered about getting Marc Eliot's signature. He signed and smiled as the fans fawned over the maestro.

When a fan asked for a greeting it was duly delivered, together with whatever personal message White thought appropriate. When one asked for it to be made out to his 72-year-old mother called Dorothy, White wrote on the book, "To Dottie, the miracle girl, love Barry." It was why they loved him.

Years later his son Darryl claimed in an interview that the book had sold over 15 million copies, but in truth sales were disappointing and amounted to only a fraction of that. But Barry White was happy when it was finished and published. He had found recalling his life a more painful experience than he had expected, and was just glad it was all over.

In November he left the United States for the European leg of his 1999 world tour. One memorable moment came in Modena, Italy, where he sung *You're the First, The Last, My Everything* with Luciano Pavarotti at one of the latter's 'Children of Afghanistan' fund-raising concerts, which was broadcast live around the world. White sang in English and Pavarotti sang his lines from a teleprompter in Italian. It was magical.

But in early December White's health failed again just as he was about to fly to London. He was forced to return to California for more rest and 12 concerts were cancelled in Britain and Ireland, including two huge shows at the London Arena. He maintained that there was nothing seriously wrong and that it was merely precautionary: "I'm taking my doctor's advice and taking it easy for a few weeks." He was soon back in the groove and all the dates were eventually fulfilled. By the end of 2000 he was back on the road again in Asia and Australia performing in a run of sold-out concerts in some huge stadium venues.

Barry White was as popular as ever and earning millions of dollars a year from his live appearances across America and the world. But he had recorded his last album and seemed to realise it himself, when he told Edward Helmore: "I don't dwell. When I've finished with an album it's on to the next. I haven't listened to the album *Can't Get Enough Of Your Love* since I finished it in 1975."

Maybe he should have done.

CHAPTER 66

Near the End

The final years

2000 to 2002

After *Staying Power*, Barry White's life began to wind down. He moved out of the rental in San Diego and bought a house in Encino, in the San Fernando valley of Los Angeles. It was not far from his old house in Sherman Oaks and he had finally overcome his fear of another earthquake.

He had quickly tired of San Diego, and although his new Encino home was a much more modest affair than in the past it still had a giant swimming pool in the backyard. He just spent time there, quietly living life with his girlfriend, Katherine Denton.

But it was certainly not all sweetness and light. Denton, after ten years with the maestro, was getting restless and wanted him to make the relationship more permanent. But every time she brought up the question of marriage he deflected. She tried desperately to conceive a baby with him – but it was not destined to happen, his continuing ill health getting in the way of their sex life, which had dwindled to almost nothing. At first she resigned herself to the situation, then threw caution to the wind and openly pressured him to marry her. But he told her outright that he didn't want to marry again and resisted making his divorce from Glodean final in an effort to put off another wedding.

By some accounts, White gave her permission to take other lovers and to try and conceive that way on the basis that they could legally bring up any child that resulted from another union, as their own and no one else would question it. It is said, they agreed they would treat the child as their own. They even agreed a name, Barriana.

At some point Denton took another lover, but it didn't affect their relationship and for the most part they continued to live happily together. It is likely that White probably knew about her plan to get pregnant which eventually came good.

His final years were spent quietly writing music in his own studio at home, but producing nothing of substance that was good enough to record. He was a very good judge of his own work and he knew that the creative spark had left him and he did not fight it. It seemed that he knew his active career had come to a conclusion and he much preferred playing video games and watching ESPN. American football (NFL), baseball and golf were his favourite sports, as he explained to a journalist from 'Rolling Stone' magazine: "What does Barry White do when he relaxes? I stay home and I play video games. I deal with my dogs. I spend time with my children." He added: "People are always looking for me to be a freak and weird but I'm not a party animal."

Despite his illness he could still put on a good show in front of journalists, and to all intents and purposes it was business as usual – no outsider could tell that he faced his final days.

His continuing obsession were his fish and his huge 500-gallon salt-water aquarium that was installed in every house he owned. He really enjoyed watching his fish swim round, and claimed that sometimes he spent all day gazing at his giant aquarium.

But his favourite time was sitting out in the backyard. He just loved sitting by the swimming pool in the garden when there was just him alone in the house. As he said: "I love just sitting outside quietly with nobody around."

He was still visible in Los Angeles and occasionally became involved in local issues. In 2002 he joined community activists who were fighting plans to knock down 70 houses in his old neighbourhood to build a new high school. Part of the playing fields where White used to brawl with rival gags would also become part of the new campus.

He drove down in the back of his limousine to join 300 other protestors led by Congresswoman Maxine Waters. He said: "I have beautiful memories here. I used to live two blocks away. I just don't want it destroyed."

But mainly when he wasn't touring he was a recluse, and just chilled out in the wonderful all-year-round climate of California, preferring not to travel.

One exception came in 2002 when the new editor of 'Vanity Fair', Graydon Carter, invited him to appear on the cover of the November issue of the magazine. It was to be an unusual shoot for the magazine's annual music issue – just him and a dozen or so of the top female artists in America.

In August of that year White flew to New York for the shoot, which was to take place in a studio and on the streets of New York's old meatpacking district. White turned up at the studio on a very hot day together with Jennifer Lopez, Sheryl Crow, Alicia Keys, Norah Jones, Nelly Furtado, Eve Jihan Jeffers, Shirley Manson and Debbie Harry. But one girl was missing: Gwen Stefani was stuck at London's Heathrow Airport when the Concorde flight she was on had been forced to turn round with technical troubles. The shoot was postponed until the following day.

White finally appeared alongside Debbie Harry and a host of other female stars on the gatefold cover. As Graydon Carter had promised, he was the only male singer in the line-up. He wore a black overcoat, dark glasses and a purple tie for the shoot by world famous photographer, Annie Leibovitz.

It was a typical August day in New York with suffocating humidity, which made it very uncomfortable, and the shoot became a serious ordeal. Debbie Harry recalled: "Barry was suffering badly in the heat that day but stoically pretended everything was fine." The resulting feature saw him posing with the girls on an inside flap of the special cover.

He did make one final attempt to go back into the studio when Kevin Liles, the President of Def Soul Records, persuaded him to record a duets album. Def Soul was the newly created R&B spin-off label from Def Jam, which had been founded by Rick Rubin and Russell Simmons and eventually sold to PolyGram; it was now owned by Seagram's Universal Group. Liles believed that White duetting with other top male and female singers would be a big winner, and was very surprised that he had not done a solely duets album before.

White had made a lot of progress and lined up Luciano Pavarotti, the Italian tenor, to sing *You're the First, The Last, My Everything* with him. Music insiders believed that White duetting with Pavarotti would have meant an instant No 1 around the world. White also had James Brown, Luther Vandross and Earth, Wind & Fire signed up to appear on the duets album.

But it was not to be.

CHAPTER 67

The Last

The end of Barry White

2003

Barry White had just started work and done two days in the studio in October 2002 when he was suddenly taken ill. All the good living had finally caught up with him and this time there was no way out, as his son Barry White Jnr recalled: "The illness came in phases and the second time around was emotionally traumatic for him and our family, believe me."

This time there would be no recovery and doctors told him he needed a kidney transplant if he was to survive. He refused outright to accept any of his own family's kidneys and said he would take his place on the list for a transplant.

He was in and out of Cedars-Sinai, and every evening nurses hooked him up to a dialysis machine for a few hours as he waited for a kidney to become available. He performed a handful of concerts during this period, but his activities were severely restricted by his physical condition.

In May 2003 he suffered the stroke that finally felled him, and after that he never left Cedars-Sinai. Three scheduled concerts had to be cancelled.

Shaherah White remembers the day like it was yesterday: "I had just gotten home from work with my daughter home from school. I dropped everything I was doing and I had my girlfriend come and watch her for me and I rushed over to the hospital and there my mother was holding my father's hand."

This time he remained conscious throughout and was in good spirits. But his speech was severely affected and the right side of his body didn't work. It was clear he would never walk unaided again.

The stroke was a severe blow, as White had been moving to the top of the list for a kidney transplant. But he was now in too weak a state for the operation. Shaherah bravely described the stroke to 'Rolling Stone' magazine as a "minor setback" and claimed that the cancelled concerts would be rescheduled and her father would perform again.

Congresswoman Maxine Waters had started a campaign to have a park in South Los Angeles named after the singer. But White couldn't attend a press conference, organised by Waters, as he was so ill. Shaherah White was forced to comment and she lied to reporters when she said that her father's condition was not serious. She said: "He's had a minor setback, but have no fear he'll be fine. He will definitely be performing again."

In her heart of hearts she knew that was not true. Without new kidneys he could not survive. Glodean White was more realistic: "To have him in this serious situation and not knowing which way it was going to turn out was very scary. I was very concerned and it wasn't in my hands."

Shaherah described what happened immediately after the stroke: "He looked at me and started crying and I started to cry. The doctors said it had attacked the right-hand side of his brain so part of him was shutting down. That first week was really rough when everybody got here. We saw the rapid progression and he went down pretty quickly."

When his girlfriend Katherine Denton arrived at Cedars-Sinai, she didn't like what she saw. She surveyed the situation and decided to act. She knew he was dying and wanted to take charge of his care. White's children were furious and believed that she was trying to position herself for after his death so she could take charge of his estate. There was no love lost. They resisted and Denton called up Abby Schroeder, White's business manager, asking her to take charge of the situation at the hospital and be the conduit for her wishes. Schroeder held the power of attorney, which included control of Barry White's medical care. Of course she answered to a member of the family, but she had to decide which one.

Barry Jnr recalled: "The trouble started as soon as my father's business manager, Abby Schroeder, came to town from New York. She had power of attorney and was calling the shots."

It was a highly unusual situation.

Denton was afraid that the presence of the family could influence her boyfriend, and she demanded that he was isolated from outside influences. Barry Jnr recalled: "My father liked his friends and his family around him because it could take his mind off his fears and the trauma. But we were deliberately and directly pushed to the side and out of it."

Shaherah confirmed the situation: "They posted signs on the door and it said 'no friends or family members'. And it said we were only allowed to come in for 15 minutes at a time. We couldn't come in before five o'clock."

Barry Jnr, speaking five years after his father's death, was still very upset, and described the scene as he saw it: "The evil winds they were blowing all around us."

Schroeder, at Denton's behest, hired an outside agency to provide a staff of nurses around the clock to be in White's room at Cedars-Sinai, as Shaherah White described: "When I came to visit with him they would write down the time I came, what we would talk about and what I would say every single time."

His eight children made the best of it; the last thing they wanted was a confrontation or any trouble that might upset their father, who was now powerless to control the situation. Unlike the children, Glodean herself had no problem with Denton and, although she didn't like the restrictions, she acknowledged that Denton had the right to impose them. But it was clear that her husband was upset, although physically unable to challenge Denton's wishes for his wellbeing. By granting the power of attorney many years before, he had effectively lost control of his own life.

Shaherah remembered one particular evening when she was asked to leave after 15 minutes: "My father was just looking back and forth and between us and he couldn't say anything. I said to Katherine, can you give me a few minutes with my father, please? I wanted her to leave the room and she left the room and I started crying and I was very upset and I said to him, 'You need to get better because I know what they are trying to do and you have to get better because they are controlling everything. I'm going to leave right now because Katherine doesn't want me here and Abby doesn't want me here.' And he's grabbing my hand but he couldn't say anything."

This difficult situation continued for a few weeks, then one day Shaherah arrived at his room and he wasn't there. She got the shock of her life, and her first thought was that he had died. But then she thought someone would have told her and went looking for him. Finally she found a nurse who knew something, as she remembered: "He wasn't in his room and I asked the nurse where he was and she said, 'He left today.' I said, 'What – he left?' She said, 'I think he has gone to a rehabilitation centre.' So I call around and I tried to find where he was. I was not told he was leaving – none of us were told."

Shaherah was furious and she wondered what Katherine Denton and Abby Schroeder had done with him, admitting that she had very dark thoughts about their motives: "You don't just pick someone's father up when he is in that condition without saying anything. I was totally frustrated and I finally found him at this rehabilitation centre and when I called there the gentlemen who answered the phone gave me the run-around so I asked to speak to the director. I told the director I was his daughter and I was around the corner and I would like to come and see him and what time are the visiting hours? He replied, 'Oh my, visiting hours are totally open but it doesn't really matter because you are not coming to visit him because you are not going to be let in.' I said, 'What are you talking about?' He said, 'No, I am under strict orders from the power of attorney not to let you in.'"

And that was that.

During that period Shaherah and Barry Jnr visited Denton to plead with her to let them see their father. Denton was adamant that he was not well enough for visitors, but then she dropped a bombshell and any facade of pleasantness was blown away, as Barry Jnr recalled: "His girlfriend Katherine comes out and she tells us she's pregnant, three months pregnant with his baby." Barry Jnr told her: "I don't believe it – it's not possible. That's nice speaking but I just don't believe it."

With that they both left, scarcely believing what they had heard. They knew that it was almost impossible that their father had had any kind of sexual activity in the past year. He had been too ill for the whole time.

None of his children saw their father for a whole month until an emergency meant that he left rehab and was readmitted to Cedars-Sinai. Shaherah White takes up the story: "When we get to the hospital, Abby was standing outside and she tells me, 'Yeah, he was rushed in but you can't go and see him – only I can see him.' I looked at her and all I said was, 'I am going to see him.' And I went in there and I looked at him and they were running tests to find out why he wasn't responding."

Barry Jnr said: "It was very sad – it was more than sad."

White's condition deteriorated every day and it was obvious that he did not have long to live, especially when the seizures became regular occurrences.

One day was particularly bad, as Shaherah recalled: "The hospital staff told me that my father had a 'Code Blue' the previous night. A 'Code Blue' means you are gone. And no one called anyone to tell us."

Barry Jnr said: "Abby and Katherine didn't tell family members, they didn't tell no one that this had happened."

On the evening of 3rd July Barry White's heart stopped three times, and each time he was revived by doctors. By the morning of the 4th the end was near. Some reports say he was already dead and being kept alive artificially by a heart-lung machine. Shaherah says: "I got a phone call and I saw it was the doctor calling me. He said, 'Shaherah, something's going on with your father and I think you should come. His heart stopped this morning and we have been trying to bring him back.' I got hold of my mother and I got my sister on the phone and as I was driving I was calling everyone."

When Shaherah arrived at Cedars-Sinai, she couldn't get immediate access to her father's room and picked up the internal phone by the elevator to call his doctor: "I got upstairs and he tells me on the phone, 'I am sorry, Shaherah, we just lost him.' And I just walked into his room and my father was there and he was gone."

Barry White Jnr arrived a few moments later: "When my father died that was a terrible 4th July."

They sat with their father for most of the day as fireworks celebrating Independence Day started to go off outside, as Shaherah vividly remembers: "Those fireworks, those are for me. That party you have on the 4th July, that's for me, and you will always remember that he had a wonderful life and no matter what they did to him for 10 months he still went out with a bang."

Barry Jnr added: "My father during his career was about love and made love for the world through his music, but at the end he was denied love for himself."

Making Love with Barry White

The bedroom growler

B arry White believed passionately in the principle of love. He called it his 'grand theme', and in the 1970s his music was played by bachelors over candlelit dinners before they beckoned their ladies to the bedroom. Literally millions of twenty-something men and women went to their bedrooms together to the sound of Barry White. His melodies and his lyrics really did things to people that can not easily be explained in words.

An excitable Russ Regan, the former head of 20th Century Records, remembers how it was: "One of the happiest moments of our lives was in 1976 when Barry and I were in New York. The New York Times came out with an article which said that in the last three years the birth rate in America had gone up five per cent thanks to Barry White's music and Barry and I just cracked up. I told him it was the greatest endorsement of his music that he would ever have."

Shaherah White, Barry's youngest daughter, agreed: "My father stands up and he sings to you and he seduces you all night so you can go home with your mate and do the rest of it."

At that time it seemed as though Barry White had tapped into the sexual psyche of the whole world, as he said: "If there is one thing we can all tune into, it is making love. Everybody does it. I have had guys walk up to me on the street and say, 'Barry, I feel like you've been watching me get off.'"

Not only did he increase the birth rate, but he also made the name Barry popular again in America, as he admitted: "A lot of babies have been named Barry. If there was a Barry boom in 1974 and 1975, I was the one responsible for it."

Never a modest man, Barry White was a self-proclaimed love guru for all of his life. At concerts and in interviews with journalists he preached what he saw as the 'language of love', and he had plenty to say on the subject. The first principle was 'loving oneself'. He believed that nothing in the bedroom could be achieved until that was sorted out. He passionately believed that people in love looked at themselves in a very different way and that there was no value to life unless someone had a partner to share it with.

Behind this philosophy was the understanding there was always a monogamous one-to-one relationship going on. He said emotional understanding came from listening to what a loved one had to say, as he explained: "Love brings many fortunes. It brings emotional understanding you never had before as it overlays meaning with feeling."

He believed that true love made people more flexible and bred true compassion in human beings – the main benefit being allowing people to "talk things over rather than fight them out".

Despite continually extolling the benefits of love and loyalty, he was also aware of the dangers. He warned that once the ideal state of living between two people had been achieved, what followed were the ultimate freedoms – but such freedoms were themselves dangerous, as he explained: "That's when all the temptations of living without limits begin. Freedom means the choice to live better not worse. Freedom also means the ability to choose lust not love. You have to know when beautiful sex is a pathway to deep love, not the tawdry cheapest and greatest threat to it. Men and women will succumb to temptation and turn the intensity of feelings that have been awakened by life into a different kind of energy, something to catch new sexual partners."

He warned that such betrayal was cheap and at that point any relationship was effectively over and done with: "Even if no one else knows what you've been up to, you will, and if you cheat on your lover you are cheating on yourself, so what's the point? You have to believe in the sanctity of love and trust it. Remember with love if you abuse it you will surely lose it. It's a high mountain to climb, the summit of love, and there are no free rides, no free passes in love."

Barry White always loved to quote his mother Sadie, and credited her with all his understanding of human relationships. When he was very young she said to him: "You have a choice in life – be happy or be angry. Please be happy as a gift to yourself."

He always said she was his greatest teacher and readily admitted that his first love was his mother, then his music, then the lady he was with. And strictly in that order.

White fervently believed that happiness was a gift, and a gift that could easily be given to oneself with very little effort. But despite that, he also warned that falling in love may not be for ever and that the "capacity to keep on loving never fails".

And he warned about lost loves and unrequited love. He said that when a love had been lost it was too easy to love another for the wrong reasons: "Once we love and we lose we always feel we can never love again. When that happens we make poor choices or throw our love away foolishly believing it makes no difference anyway. This is a clear sign that you have temporarily at least lost the ability to love yourself."

White also had some practical advice to men and women. For men he told them not to promise what they couldn't deliver, or even promise at all: "Don't say in the heat of the moment that you will buy them a washer-dryer, a big house, a new car, furs, jewellery – all of that which you think will make you a better man in their eyes. Don't try to put a price tag on your love. Don't diminish your emotions in that way. You will have done nothing more than helped to achieve the opposite. You will have taken your eye off the love ball. Offer who you are, not what you might or might not have one day further down the line. You will both be better off for it, I guarantee. Don't try and fool yourself because that's the only person you will be fooling. If you aren't true to yourself you will end up exposing yourself in so many ways before the eyes of the one you want most to impress."

For women he told them that initial judgement was crucial: "Be cautious in your selection of men – don't get into a relationship first and then complain that there is nothing you can do that is going to change your man. Know who he is going in and make sure you like what you know."

White always believed that women had the advantage over men in a relationship because they were better listeners. He told men always to talk to a woman as if she was something special: "My mother taught me to listen to what they're saying and what they're not saying. Every woman has multiple powers of knowledge and the only way you get to that knowledge is to listen. You have got to communicate with women, be passionate with women, understand their tears, why they cry so deeply. Those are things that you must embrace to truly deal with women." And he asked the question: "Why do they put up with us then? Because they have to."

Barry White always bridled when anyone suggested that his brand of love was shallow and merely based on human lust: "It was never, ever about mere sexual fulfilment. You will find no lust on any album I've ever made or anything about orgies or sex parties. I do not do that. My songs have been about love because that is a positive way of thinking about life."

He was actually against the sexual revolution that started in the 1960s and was in full swing by the mid-seventies when his music became popular, as he explained: "I think we suffer from too much freedom. Sex and love are different words. Sex goes with lust, which goes with greed. With love comes commitment and communications."

White hated all his nicknames, such as 'The Bedroom Growler' and 'The Walrus Of Love'. He didn't relate to them at all, and said: "They are stupid and come from people who are either envious or jealous." He rejected them all; the only nickname he enjoyed hearing was 'maestro'.

Despite his reputation, he denied that he had any particular seduction routine: "It's whatever works at the time. Just treat women with respect always. Whatever else comes with it comes with it."

And sometimes White was too honest for his own good. He thought it ridiculous that couples listened to his music when they made love: "I don't need no music to make love. When I'm in the mood music would just distract me. I'd start listening to the guitar lines and the bass grooves. Most men like to rush and get off and don't give a shit if they get the lady off or not. I am not that human being."

In the 21st century Barry White's attitudes to sex and women would probably be described as 'prudish'. He was in essence a man of morals, an old-fashioned man, who loved his mother dearly above all. He admitted he was old-fashioned when it came to women: "I'm the kind of guy that it took a year and a half just to get a kiss. I was together with my wife Glodean for five years before we got married. You should know something about the people you're involved with."

Unfortunately he did not always practise what he preached, but that did not stop him preaching it all the same. One of his mantras was that "Love will renew itself if you give it the chance." He believed that love between two people was the "greatest state of being for both the individuals and created a perfect enduring permanent state of happiness." But twice in his life that principle failed him, and there is no better example of that than his split from Glodean, his second wife, in the late 1980s. He always gave the impression that he was the dependable man, the man who was here to stay. Yet with both his first and second wives he proved that was not the case. He said: "That is the message behind my music – it is about a love that endures, that is loyal and true, that is full of passion." Amazingly, those words were said after the collapse of his second marriage and when he was in residence with the third significant woman in his life, Katherine Denton. And he sought to leave no doubt of his sincerity even as Denton moved into his life: "My love is an all-consuming love, it is about a pure world every person wishes he or she could live in – the finest world I know."

Inevitably he modified his views over the years. He said he had meant his views to relate only to the woman he was with at the time. And to his credit, throughout his 58 years there were only three significant women in his life – Mary Smith, Glodean James and Katherine Denton – despite all the endless opportunities that were presented to him.

Most women deemed Barry White, at a weight that often ballooned to more than 400lbs, not to be particularly attractive, and even some of his devoted fans weren't keen on his physical appearance. But they still loved him, and that lack of attraction, so to speak, would never have stopped them taking things further given the opportunity. As he admitted in his own memoir, the number of approaches he received from women were many: "I've gotten car, hotel, and front door keys sent to me in the mail from women with explicit invitations. One even went so far as to contact me by phone willingly offering me her four or five daughters at the same time. She wanted me to teach her and her offspring how to relate to men."

The writer later revealed herself to be a lady called Marjorie Cooke, and White actually took the request seriously and wrote to her with some clear advice. It was evident from his reply that loyalty was a key part of his make-up. He gave it out and he expected it back. "I told her to tell her daughters what I tell everybody. Listen to yourself, your own heart, find your own voice of supreme guidance and you will learn all you will ever need to know. Hear it, trust it. I alone don't know anything you don't already know about yourself. Don't be anything but proud of yourself and your deeds and loyal to the one you love and you will find the reflection of that pride, love and loyalty in your heart."

By the late seventies White, in common with many rock stars of the period, had built up a retinue of followers, mainly musicians, who spent much of their time hanging out with him – men like Tony Sepe, Sterling Radcliffe and Jack Perry, to name a few. He expected total loyalty from them and he also expected them to listen to his advice about women and sex.

With all his self-proclaimed expertise on women and love, Barry White was of necessity very protective of his daughters and their love lives. Shaherah White remembers the hard time her father used to give her boyfriends and those of her sisters. He was certainly not afraid to talk to his daughters in the starkest of terms and certainly not in a way most fathers would have chosen, as he readily admitted: "I taught my five daughters that when they lay down with a man and give them the shit between their legs, they are giving up the only fucking power they've got in the world."

In more than one interview he was quoted as using those exact words, although he reserved his true venom for prospective boyfriends. As he said: "I would look at them and they would always have a problem looking back at me. I used to say it to them straight out, 'So what do you want with my daughter, man – do you want to fuck my daughter? What's your objective, what are your plans? Do you want to get my daughter pregnant? If you do then you will find that my daughter's got a funny father, an ex-gang banger, and he'll kick your motherfucking ass, or have your ass kicked if you're messing with my women.'"

And just in case they hadn't got the message he told them: "Just don't come round here with no bullshit because you are dealing with a very wise man here."

After that tirade prospective suitors usually didn't bother with a second date. If they did survive, more questions would follow: "You don't misuse women do you, boy? You don't beat them up, do you?" White always justified himself by claiming that his words had the right effect and none of his daughters had any problems with men.

He firmly believed that men were the problem, as he told the writer Edward Helmore in 1999: "Men corrupt more easy than women. Men come with a game. Lying, deceiving, telling you to go left when you should go right. It is part of being a man."

And he really believed that.

CLOSE FAMILY CHRONOLOGY
Births, marriages and deaths

Event	Date	Status
Barry White birth	12th September 1944	Eldest son of Sadie Carter
Darryl White birth	11th October 1945	Second son of Sadie Carter
Barry White Jnr birth	29th June 1961	Eldest son of Barry White
Mary Smith marriage	18th November 1962	First wife of Barry White
Lanese White birth	12th December 1962	Eldest daughter of Barry White
Nina White birth	19th May 1964	Second daughter of Barry White
Darryl White birth	20th June 1965	Second son of Barry White
Glodean James marriage	4th July 1974	Second wife of Barry White
Shaherah White birth	6th November 1975	Third daughter of Barry White
Melvin White death	July 1980	Father of Barry White (aged 69)
Darryl White death	5th December 1982	Brother of Barry White (aged 37)
Sadie Carter death	4th April 1996	Mother of Barry White (aged 82)
Barry White death	4th July 2003	Barry White (aged 58)

LIFE CHRONOLOGY

Date	Event	Chapter covered
January 1929	Sadie Mae Carter (mother) moves from Galveston, Texas to Los Angeles	2
July 1931	Woodbridge Van Dyke casts Sadie in a Hollywood movie called Trader Horn	2
August 1943	Melvin White meets Sadie by chance and she falls in love. He is a married man	2
December 1943	Sadie falls pregnant for the first time at the age of 28	2
April 1944	Melvin White admits to Sadie he is already married to someone else	2
August 1944	Sadie travels to Texas to visit relatives whilst she is eight months pregnant	2
September 1944	Barry Eugene Carter is born in Galveston, Texas on 12th September	2
December 1944	Barry Carter takes his father's surname and becomes Barry White	2
January 1946	Sadie Mae gives birth in Los Angeles to a second child she names Darryl	2
August 1946	Sadie Mae discovers Melvin White has two children of his own	2
December 1946	Melvin White and Sadie Mae split up for good	2
October 1947	Glodean James is born in Los Angeles on 16th October	20
January 1948	Sadie Mae buys a second hand piano and teaches her son Barry to play	3
December 1951	Barry White learns to play the piano like a maestro	3
November 1953	Darryl White enters Juvenile Hall for the first time at age of eight	10
July 1954	Barry White joins a local gang called 'The Businessmen'	4
June 1956	Barry plays the piano for Jesse Belvin at his first ever recording session	4
August 1956	The Carter White family moves to a new home at South Hoover Street	4
November 1956	Barry and Darryl form their own eponymous gang called the White Brothers	4
November 1957	13-year-old Barry White meets 12-year-old Mary Smith and they start dating	9
October 1958	Barry White's voice breaks at the age of 14	5
April 1958	Discovers the merits of astrology after chance meeting with a stranger	6
October 1959	Consummates relationship with Mary Smith aged 15. She is 14	9
February 1960	Arrested by LAPD for theft of car wheels from Cadillac dealership	7
August 1960	Released form juvenile prison by sympathetic judge after six months inside	8
September 1960	Joins The Upfronts as group's new bass singer	12
September 1960	Performs in first studio session for The Upfronts	12
October 1960	Mary Smith becomes pregnant by Barry White	9
November 1960	Darryl White is sentenced to 50 years in jail for murder	10
December 1960	The Upfronts release first single called Little Girl. Barry White is not credited.	12
June 1961	Barry White Jnr is born on 29th June	9
December 1961	Barry White arrested on suspicion of murder but cleared and released	11
March 1962	Mary Smith is pregnant for second time	15
April 1962	Gene Page is introduced to Barry White for the first time	14
September 1962	Barry White quits high school and goes to Hollywood seeking work	12
October 1962	Gets first paid job clapping hands for producer Leon Rene and is paid $100	13
November 1962	Mary Smith and Barry White are married on 18th November	15
December 1962	Mary and Barry's daughter, Lanese Melva White is born on 12th December	15

APPENDICES

Date	Event	Chapter covered
December 1970	Records his second song, a single called Little Girl. Once again, it flops	20
March 1970	Writes Your Sweetness Is My Weakness for Earl Nelson to record	20
July 1970	Creates Love Unlimited as a group with Glodean, Linda and Dede	21
September 1970	Larry Nunes becomes equal partner in Mo Soul Productions	21
September 1970	Leaves the family home for the final time	18
October 1970	First record on Mo Soul label recorded called Oh Love Well We Finally Made It	21
March 1971	Larry Nunes agrees to finance Love Unlimited's first album for $32,500	21
April 1971	Gene Page agrees to arrange the music for Love Unlimited's debut album	21
May 1971	Oh Love Well We Finally Made It is released as a single. It flops	21
August 1971	Glodean James falls in love with Barry White	22
September 1971	Love Unlimited go into the Glendale studio to record first album	23
October 1971	Melvin and Barry White reconcile when Melvin visits Glendale studio	23
November 1971	Barry White writes Walking in the Rain With the One I Love	23
December 1971	Russ Regan signs Love Unlimited to the Uni Records label	23
March 1972	Love Unlimited's first album From a Girl's Point of View is released	23
April 1972	Walking in the Rain With the One I Love is released as a single	23
May 1972	Walking in the Rain With the One I Love reaches No 14 on Billboard 100	23
June 1972	Walking in the Rain With the One I Love is a smash hit all over the world	23
June 1972	Love Unlimited embark on their first tour of the United States	23
August 1972	Walking in the Rain With the One I Love reaches No 14 in British hit parade	23
September 1972	Walking in the Rain With the One I Love passes sales of one million singles	23
October 1972	Uni Records is absorbed by MCA Records under new boss, Mike Maitland	26
October 1972	Russ Regan leaves Uni Records and joins 20th Century Records	25
November 1972	Barry White signs solo contract with 20th Century Records	24
December 1972	Barry White records first solo album called I've Got So Much to Give	24
January 1973	Larry Nunes and White play I've Got So Much to Give album to Russ Regan	25
January 1973	Russ Regan hates album, releases Barry White from his contract at 20th Century	25
February 1973	Clive Davis signs White to Columbia after hearing I've Got So Much To Give	25
February 1973	Russ Regan changes his mind and re-asserts rights to I've Got So Much To Give	25
February 1973	Clive Davis reluctantly releases Barry White from his Columbia contract	25
March 1973	I've Got So Much To Give is released on 27th March and goes to No 14 on charts	25
April 1973	I'm Going To Love You Just a Little Bit More Baby is released as first single	25
April 1973	First single I'm Going To Love You... peaks at No 3 in Billboard singles chart	25
April 1973	Mike Maitland releases Love Unlimited from their Uni Records contract	26
May 1973	Russ Regan signs Love Unlimited to 20th Century Records in $90,000 deal	26
May 1973	I've Got So Much To Give is released as Barry White's second single	25
May 1973	I've Got So Much To Give climbs to No 32 on Billboard singles chart	25
June 1973	Blues & Soul magazine calls White's voice "unforgettably melodious"	25
July 1973	Love Unlimited's second album called Under the Influence of Love is released	26
July 1973	Under the Influence of Love is smash hit, peaks at No 3 in the album charts	26
July 1973	Barry White becomes 20th Century Records' biggest selling artist	25

APPENDICES

APPENDICES

APPENDICES

Date	Event	Chapter covered
August 2002	Attends a photo shoot in New York for Vanity Fair magazine	66
November 2002	Barry White is only male on the cover of Vanity Fair with female line-up of stars	66
October 2002	Barry White falls ill and needs regular sessions on a dialysis machine	1/67
October 2003	Abby Schroeder, business manager, issued with a Power of Attorney	1
November 2002	Barry White is put on the list for a kidney transplant	1/67
May 2003	Barry White suffers devastating stroke and goes into Cedars-Sinai Hospital	1/67
June 2003	Stroke ends all hope of a kidney transplant as he is too weak for an operation	1/67
June 2003	Katherine Denton and Abby Schroder deny close family hospital access	1/67
July 2003	On 3rd July Barry White's heart stops beating three times but he is revived	1/67
July 2003	Barry White dies in the morning of 4th July after his heart stops for the final time	1/67
July 2003	The New York Times is first to report the maestro's death at the age of 58	1
July 2003	Glodean White calls Michael Jackson to tell him her husband is dead	1
July 2003	Ned Shankman, his personal manager, issues press release confirming death	1
July 2003	Barry White's body is cremated prior to his funeral ceremony	1
July 2003	Barry White's ashes are spread on the Pacific Ocean at his funeral on 12th July	1

BARRY WHITE PRODUCED ALBUMS

Chron	Year	Title	Chronology	Artist
1.	1972	From a Girl's Point of View	1st group	Love Unlimited
2.	1973	I've Got So Much to Give	1st solo	Barry White
3.	1973	Under the Influence of Love	2nd group	Love Unlimited
4.	1973	Stone Gon'	2nd solo	Barry White
5.	1974	Rhapsody in White	1st orchestra	LU Orchestra
6.	1974	In Heat	3rd group	Love Unlimited
7.	1974	Can't Get Enough	3rd solo	Barry White
8.	1974	Together Brothers	2nd orchestra	LU Orchestra
9.	1974	White Gold	3rd orchestra	LU Orchestra
10.	1974	What Am I Gonna Do	1st third party	Gloria Scott
11.	1974	I Love You More and More	2nd third party	Tom Brock
12.	1974	Hot City	3rd third party	Gene Page
13.	1974	Come On In Love	4th third party	Dee/Nelson
14.	1975	West Wing	5th third party	West Wing
15.	1975	Just Another Way to Say I Love You	4th solo	Barry White
16.	1975	Music Maestro Please	4th orchestra	LU Orchestra
17.	1976	Let the Music Play	5th solo	Barry White
18.	1976	My Sweet Summer Suite	5th orchestra	LU Orchestra
19.	1976	Is This Whatcha Wont?	6th solo	Barry White
20.	1977	He's All I've Got	4th group	Love Unlimited
21.	1977	Sings for Someone You Love	7th solo	Barry White
22.	1978	My Musical Bouquet	6th orchestra	LU Orchestra
23.	1978	The Man	8th solo	Barry White
24.	1978	Barry White Presents Mr Danny Pearson	6th third party	Danny Pearson
25.	1979	I Love to Sing the Songs I Sing	9th solo	Barry White
26.	1979	Love Is Back	5th group	Love Unlimited
27.	1979	The Message Is Love	10th solo	Barry White
28.	1979	Super Movie Themes	7th orchestra	LU Orchestra
29.	1980	Sheet Music	11th solo	Barry White
30.	1981	Barry & Glodean	12th solo (duet)	Barry White
31.	1981	Let 'Em Dance	8th orchestra	LU Orchestra
32.	1981	Beware!	13th solo	Barry White
33.	1981	Welcome Aboard	9th orchestra	LU Orchestra
34.	1981	Song Painters	7th third party	J&V Cameron
35.	1982	Change	14th solo	Barry White
36.	1983	Dedicated	15th solo	Barry White
37.	1983	Rise	10th orchestra	LU Orchestra
38.	1987	The Right Night & Barry White	16th solo	Barry White
39.	1989	The Man Is Back	17th solo	Barry White
40.	1991	Put Me in Your Mix	18th solo	Barry White
41.	1994	The Icon Is Love	19th solo	Barry White
42.	1999	Staying Power	20th solo	Barry White

APPENDIX IV

BARRY WHITE'S SOLO ALBUMS

I've Got So Much to Give (1973) 20th CENTURY RECORDS
Track 1. Standing In The Shadows Of Love, written by Holland, Dozier and Holland, 8m
Track 2. Bring Back My Yesterday written by Barry White and Robert Relf, 6m 40 secs
Track 3. I've Found Someone written by Barry White, 5m 55 secs
Track 4. I've Got So Much To Give written by Barry White, 8m 11 secs
Track 5. I'm Gonna Love You Just A Little More Baby written by Barry White, 7m 20 secs.

Stone Gon' (1973) 20th CENTURY RECORDS
Track 1. Girl It's True, Yes I'll Always Love You written by Barry White 8m 29 secs
Track 2. Honey Please, Can't Ya See written by Barry White 5m 5 secs
Track 3. You're My Baby written by Barry White, 8m 58secs
Track 4. Hard To Believe That I Found You written by Barry White, 6m 49 secs
Track 5. Never, Never Gonna Give Ya Up written by Barry White, 7m 59 secs

Can't Get Enough (1974) 20th CENTURY RECORDS
Track 1. Mellow Mood (Pt I) written by White, Taylor and Brock, 1m 53 secs
Track 2. You're The First, The Last, My Everything written by White, Radcliffe and Sepe, 4m 37secs
Track 3. I Can't Believe You Love Me written by Barry White, 10m 23secs
Track 4. Can't Get Enough Of Your Love, Babe written by Barry White, 4m 31 secs
Track 5. Oh Love, Well We Finally Made It written by Barry White, 3m 54 secs
Track 6. I Love You More Than Anything (In This World Girl) written by White, 5m 2 secs
Track 7. Mellow Mood (Pt. II) written by Barry White, Taylor and Brock, 1m 23 secs

Just Another Way to Say I Love You (1975) 20th CENTURY RECORDS
Track 1. Heavenly, That's What You Are To Me written by Barry White, 5m 3 secs
Track 2. I'll Do For You Anything You Want Me To written by Barry White, 6m 13 secs
Track 3. All Because Of You written by White, Wilson and Nunes, 6m 40 secs
Track 4. Love Serenade (Part I) written by Barry White, 4m 49 secs
Track 5. What Am I Gonna Do With You written by Barry White, 3m 30 secs
Track 6. Let Me Live My Life Lovin' You Babe written by Barry White, 10m 20 secs
Track 7. Love Serenade (Part II) written by Barry White, 3m 13 secs

Let the Music Play (1976) 20th CENTURY RECORDS
Track 1. I Don't Know Where Love Has Gone written by Barry White, 4m 57 secs
Track 2. If You Know, Won't You Tell Me written by Barry White, 5m 4 secs
Track 3. I'm So Blue And You Are Too written by Barry White, 7m 5 secs
Track 4. Baby, We Better Try To Get It Together written by Barry White, 4m 26 secs
Track 5. You See The Trouble With Me written by Barry White and Ray Parker Jnr, 3m 30 secs
Track 6. Let The Music Play written by Barry White, 6m 16 secs

543

Is This Whatcha Wont? (1976) 20th CENTURY RECORDS
Track 1. Don't Make Me Wait Too Long written by Barry White, 4m 39 secs
Track 2. Your Love - So Good I Can Taste It written by Barry White, 12m 29 secs
Track 3. I'm Qualified To Satisfy You written by Barry White, 4m 20 secs
Track 4. I Wanna Lay Down With You Baby written by Barry White, 8m 54 secs
Track 5. Now I'm Gonna Make Love To You written by Barry White, 4m 56 secs

Barry White Sings for Someone You Love (1977) 20th CENTURY RECORDS
Track 1. Playing Your Game, Baby written by Austin Johnson and Smead Hudman, 7m 12 secs
Track 2. It's Ecstasy When You Lay Down Next To Me written by Paris and Pigford, 7m 0 secs
Track 3. You're So Good, You're Bad written by Schroeder and Ragovoy, 6m 15 secs
Track 4. I Never Thought I'd Fall In Love With You written by Ronald Coleman, 4m 48 secs
Track 5. You Turned My Whole World Around written by Pearson and Wilson, 7m 49 secs
Track 6. Oh, What A Night For Dancing written by Barry White and Vance Wilson, 3m 48 secs
Track 7. Of All The Guys In The World written by Barry White and Danny Pearson, 3m 50 secs

The Man (1978) 20th CENTURY RECORDS
Track 1. Look At Her written by Frank Wilson, Ray Cooksey and Tom Payton, 7m 40 secs
Track 2. Your Sweetness Is My Weakness written by Barry White, 8m 4 secs
Track 3. Sha La La Means I Love You written by Barry White, 8m 0 secs
Track 4. September When I First Met You written by White, Brown, Wilson and Politi, 6m 57 secs
Track 5. It's Only Love Doing Its Thing written by Cameron and Cameron, 4m 4 secs
Track 6. Just The Way You Are written by Billy Joel, 7m 9 secs
Track 7. Early Years written by Ronald Coleman, 6m 50 secs

I Love to Sing the Songs I Sing (1979) 20th CENTURY RECORDS
Track 1. I Love To Sing The Songs I Sing written by White, Wilson, Politi & Wilson, 2m 46 secs
Track 2. Girl, What's Your Name written by White, Pearson and Wilson, 4m 5 secs
Track 3. Once Upon A Time (You Were A Friend Of Mine) written by Coleman, 6m 0 secs
Track 4. Oh Me, Oh My (I'm Such A Lucky Guy) written by White, Wilson, Politi & Cooksey, 5m 0 secs
Track 5. I Can't Leave You written by White, Wilson and Sepe, 3m 25 secs
Track 6. Call Me, Baby written by Ronald Coleman, 8m 0 secs
Track 7. How Did You Know It Was Me? written by Ronald Coleman, 6m 44 secs

The Message Is Love (1979) UNLIMITED GOLD RECORDS
Track 1. It Ain't Love, Babe (Until You Give It) written by Barry White and Paul Politi, 4m 19 secs
Track 2. Hung Up In Your Love written by Barry White and Paul Politi, 4m 9 secs
Track 3. You're The One I Need written by Barry White and Smead Hudman, 4m 22 secs
Track 4. Any Fool Could See (You Were Meant For Me) written by White & Politi, 4m 44 secs
Track 5. Love Ain't Easy written by Barry White and Paul Politi, 5m 37 secs
Track 6. I'm On Fire written by Robert Jason, 5m 40 secs
Track 7. I Found Love written by Barry White and Paul Politi, 6m 57 secs

APPENDICES

Sheet Music (1980) UNLIMITED GOLD RECORDS
Track 1. Sheet Music written by Barry White and Paul Politi, 7m 2 secs
Track 2. Lady, Sweet Lady written by Norman Sallitt, 5m 40 secs
Track 3. I Believe In Love written by Johnson, White and Hudman, 8m 1 sec
Track 4. Ghetto Letto written by Barry White, Paul Politi and Vella Cameron, 5m 53 secs
Track 5. Rum and Coca-Cola written by Stillman, Sullivan, Amsterdam, Baron, 2m 30 secs
Track 6. She's Everything To Me written by Barry White and Bernard Butler, 4m 2 secs
Track 7. Love Makin' Music written by Aaron Schroeder and Jerry Ragovoy, 4m 57 secs

Barry & Glodean (1981) UNLIMITED GOLD RECORDS (CBS)
Track 1. Our Theme - Part I written by Barry White, 3m 18 secs
Track 2. I Want You written by Barry White, Jimmy Levine and Lowrell Simon, 4m 24 secs
Track 3. You're The Only One For Me written by White and Cameron, 5m 5 secs
Track 4. This Love written by Fleming Williams, 4m 2 secs
Track 5. The Better Love Is (The Worse It Is When It's Over) written by Russ, 4m 49 secs
Track 6. You written by Barry White and Vella Cameron, 3m 40 secs
Track 7. We Can't Let Go Of Love written by White, Maglia and Giovannelli, 3m 55 secs
Track 8. You Make My Life Easy Livin' written by Cameron and Cameron, 4m 17 secs
Track 9. Didn't We Make It Happen, Baby written by White and Pearson, 5m 22 secs
Track 10. Our Theme - Part II written by Barry White, 2m 42 secs

Beware (1981) UNLIMITED GOLD RECORDS (CBS)
Track 1. Beware written by Jo Ann Belvin, 5m 50 secs
Track 2. Relax To The Max written by Barry White and Lowrell Simon, 3m 42 secs
Track 3. Let Me In And Let's Begin With Love written by White and Cameron, 6m 2 secs
Track 4. Your Love, Your Love written by Barry White and Lowrell Simon, 4m 22 secs
Track 5. Tell Me Who Do You Love written by Barry White and Darnell White, 2m 6 secs
Track 6. Rio De Janeiro written by Barry White, Carol Jackson and Marlon Jackson, 4m 25 secs
Track 7. You're My High written by Barry White and Nathan East, 2m 14 secs
Track 8. Oooo....Ahhh.... written by White, Williams and Milligan, 3m 58 secs
Track 9. I Won't Settle For Less Than The Best written White and Cameron, 4m 20 secs
Track 10. Louie Louie written by Richard Berry, 7m 14 secs

Change (1982) UNLIMITED GOLD RECORDS (CBS)
Track 1. Change written by Barry White, Carl Taylor and John Lopez, 6m 12 secs
Track 2. Turnin' On, Tunin' In (To Your Love) written by Vella Cameron, 5m 13 secs
Track 3. Let's Make Tonight (An Evening To Remember) written by Cameron & Cameron, 5m 9 secs
Track 4. Don't Tell Me About Heartaches written by Vallins and Kipner, 6m 52 secs
Track 5. Passion written by Barry White, Carl Taylor and John Lopez, 6m 58 secs
Track 6. I've Got That Love Fever written by White, Perry and Cameron, 5m 11 secs
Track 7. I Like You, You Like Me written by Barry White and Jack Perry, 5m 30 secs
Track 8. It's All About Love written by Vella Cameron, 4m 20 secs

Dedicated (1983) UNLIMITED GOLD RECORDS (CBS)
Track 1. America written by Barry White, 5m 47 secs
Track 2. Free written by Barry White, Carl Taylor and Ricky Roberson, 5m 2 secs
Track 3. Don't Forget ... Remember written by Barry White, 5m 45 secs
Track 4. Life written by Barry White and Jack Perry, 3m 40 secs
Track 5. Love Song written by Lesley Duncan, 5m 50 secs
Track 6. All In The Run Of A Day written by Barry White and Robert Staunton, 6m 55 secs
Track 7. Don't Let 'Em Blow Your Mind written by Barry White and Jack Perry, 6m 48 secs
Track 8. Dreams written by Barry White and Webster Lewis, 4m 20 secs

The Right Night & Barry White (1987) A & M RECORDS
Track 1. Sho' You Right written by Barry White and Jack Perry, 7m 42 secs
Track 2. For Your Love I'll Do Most Anything written by White and Loren, 4m 24 secs
Track 3. There's A Place (Where Love Never Ends) written by White, Lambert & Brock, 5m 22 secs
Track 4. Love Is In Your Eyes written by White, Williams and Perry, 5m 55 secs
Track 5. Theme Part I written by Barry White and Doug Lambert, 0m 33 secs
Track 6. The Right Night written by Barry White, 5m 50 secs
Track 7. I'm Ready For Love written by White, Lambert and Martinez, 5m 11 secs
Track 8. Theme (Sign of Love) written by Barry White and Doug Lambert, 0m 32 secs
Track 9. Share written by Barry White and Charles Fearing, 7m 12 secs
Track 10. Who's The Fool? written by White, Booker and Perry, 6m 35 secs

The Man Is Back (1989) A & M RECORDS
Track 1. Responsible written by Barry White, Jack Perry and Julian Jackson, 4m 41 secs
Track 2. Super Lover written by Barry White, Jack Perry and William Jones, 4m 52 secs
Track 3. L.A. My Kinda Place written by Barry White, 4m 50 secs
Track 4. Follow That And See (Where It Leads Y'All) by Barry White, 5m 4 secs
Track 5. When Will I See You Again written by Terrence La Mar Thomas, 5m 51 secs
Track 6. I Wanna Do It Good To Ya written by Frank Hamilton, 6m 0 secs
Track 7. It's Getting Harder All the Time written by Schroeder and Grover, 5m 9 secs
Track 8. Don't Let Go written by Chuckii Booker and Terrence La Mar Thomas, 9m 8 secs
Track 9. Loves Interlude/Good Night My Love written by White, Motola and Marascalco, 7m 46 secs

Put Me in Your Mix (1991) A & M RECORDS
Track 1. Let's Get Busy written by White, Taylor, Lucero and Lopez, 4m 43 secs
Track 2. Love Is Good With You written by White, Jack Perry and Jones, 6m 10 secs
Track 3. For Real Chill written by Barry White and Jack Perry, 5m 49 secs
Track 4. Break It Down With You written by White, Banks and Ragin, 6m 24 secs
Track 5. Volare written by Domenico Modugno and Franco Migliacci, 5m 45 secs
Track 6. Put Me In Your Mix written by Barry White and Howard Johnson, 7m 35secs
Track 7. Who You Giving Your Love To written by Barry White, 5m 26 secs
Track 8. Love Will Find Us written by Barry White and Jack Perry, 7m 7 secs

Track 9. We're Gonna Have It All written by Schroeder and Grover, 5m 55 secs

Track 10. Dark And Lovely (You Over There) with Hayes written by White, 10m 5 secs

The Icon Is Love (1994) A & M RECORDS

Track 1. Practice What You Preach written by White, Nicholas and Levert, 5m 59 secs

Track 2. There It Is written by White, Nicholas and Levert, 7m 3 secs

Track 3. I Only Want To Be With You written by White, Harris and Lewis, 5m 1 sec

Track 4. The Time Is Right written by Barry White and Chuckii Booker, 5m 46 secs

Track 5. Baby's Home written by Eastmond, Brown and Skinner, 8m 17 secs

Track 6. Come On written by Barry White, James Harris and Terry Lewis, 4m 38 secs

Track 7. Love Is The Icon written by Barry White and Jack Perry, 4m 38 secs

Track 8. Sexy Undercover written by Barry White and Chuckii Booker, 4m 51 secs

Track 9. Don't You Want To Know? written by White and Smith, 6m 51 secs

Track 10. Whatever We Had, We Had written by White and Smith, 10m 41 secs

Staying Power (1999) PRIVATE MUSIC (BMG)

Track 1. Staying Power written by Joey Paschal and Rory Holmes, 6m 10 secs

Track 2. Don't Play Games written by White, Perry and Guillory, 7m 24 secs

Track 3. The Longer We Make Love with Chaka Khan written by Schroeder and Saunders, 5m 48 secs

Track 4. I Get Off On You written by Barry White, Jack Perry and Kashif Saleem, 6m 30 secs

Track 5. Which Way Is Up written by Barry White, Jack Perry and Doug Rasheed, 5m 42 secs

Track 6. Get Up written by Barry White and Jack Perry, 6m 11 secs

Track 7. Sometimes written by Barry White, 6m 55 secs

Track 8. Low Ride written by Dickerson/Mille/Brown/Scott/Goldstein/Oscar/Jordan/Allen, 5m 17 secs

Track 9. Thank You written by Sly Stone, 5m 46 secs

Track 10. Slow Your Roll written by Barry White, Jack Perry and Joey Paschal, 5m 46 secs

Track 11. The Longer We Make Love with Lisa Stansfield written by Schroeder & Saunders, 6m 27 secs

LOVE UNLIMITED GROUP ALBUMS

From a Girl's Point of View (1972) UNI RECORDS
Track 1. I Should Have Known written by Barry White and Robert Relf, 4m 54 secs
Track 2. Another Chance written by Barry White and Tom Brocker, 2m 51 secs
Track 3. Are You Sure? written by Diane Taylor, Glodean James and Linda James, 3m 16 secs
Track 4. Fragile - Handle With Care written by Barry White, 4m 2 secs
Track 5. Is It Really True Boy - Is It Really Me written by Barry White, 4m 0 secs
Track 6. I'll Be Yours Forever More written by Barry White, 3m 43 secs
Track 7. If This World Were Mine written by Marvin Gaye, 5m 32 secs
Track 8. Together written by Kenneth Gamble and Leon Huff, 3m 10 secs
Track 9. Walking In The Rain With The One I Love written by Barry White, 4m 50 secs

Under the Influence of Love (1973) 20th CENTURY RECORDS
Track 1. Love's Theme (Instrumental) written by Barry White, 4m 8 secs
Track 2. Under The Influence Of Love written by Barry White and Paul Politi 4m 9 secs
Track 3. Lovin' You, That's All I'm After written by Barry White, 4m 29 secs
Track 4. Oh Love, Well We Finally Made It written by Barry White, 3m 50 secs
Track 5. Say It Again written by Barry White, 3m 19 secs
Track 6. Someone Really Cares For You written by Barry White, 5m 40 secs
Track 7. It May Be Winter Outside (But In My Heart It's Spring) written by White & Politi, 4m 14 secs
Track 8. Yes, We Finally Made It (Instrumental) written by Barry White, 3m 45 secs

In Heat (1974) 20th CENTURY RECORDS
Track 1. Move Me No Mountain written by Aaron Schroeder and Jerry Ragavoy, 3m 50 secs
Track 2. Share A Little Love In Your Heart written by Barry White, 6m 5 secs
Track 3. Oh I Should Say, It's Such A Beautiful Day written by Barry White, 3m 32 secs
Track 4. I Needed Love - You Were There written by Barry White, 3m 39 secs
Track 5. I Belong To You written by Barry White, 5m 6 secs
Track 6. I Love You So, Never Gonna Let You Go written by Barry White, 3m 11 secs
Track 7. Love's Theme written by Barry White and Aaron Schroeder, 3m 44 secs

He's All I've Got (1977) UNLIMITED GOLD RECORDS (20th CENTURY)
Track 1. I Did It For Love written by Linda Laurie and Terri Etlinger, 4m 59 secs
Track 2. Never, Never Say Goodbye written by Barry White, 5m 38 secs
Track 3. Whisper You Love Me written by Barry White, 5m 15 secs
Track 4. He's Mine (No, You Can't Have Him) written by Barry White, 3m 34 secs
Track 5. I Can't Let Him Down written by Barry White, 3m 27 secs
Track 6. I Guess I'm Just Another Girl In Love written by Barry White, 5m 11 secs
Track 7. He's All I've Got written by Barry White, 7m 23 secs

APPENDICES

Love is Back (1979) UNLIMITED GOLD RECORDS (CBS)

Track 1. I'm So Glad That I'm A Woman written by White/Wilson/Politi, 4m 1 sec

Track 2. High Steppin', Hip Dressin' Fella, written by White/Wilson/Politi, 5m 32 secs

Track 3. When I'm In Your Arms, Everything's Okay written by White/Wilson/Politi 4m 33 secs

Track 4. If You Want Me, Say It written by White/Wilson/Politi, 5m 41 secs

Track 5. I'm Givin' You A Love written by White/Wilson/Politi, 4m 30 secs

Track 6. Gotta Be Where You Are written by White/Wilson/Politi, 4m 14 secs

Track 7. I'm His Woman written by White/Wilson/Politi, 5m 38 secs

LOVE UNLIMITED ORCHESTRA ALBUMS

Rhapsody in White (1974) 20th CENTURY RECORDS
Track 1. Barry's Theme written by Barry White, 4m 28 secs
Track 2. Rhapsody In White written by Barry White, 3m 53 secs
Track 3. Midnight And You written by Barry White and Gene Page, 5m 10 secs
Track 4. I Feel Love Coming On written by Barry White and Paul Politi, 6m 23 secs
Track 5. Baby Blues written by Barry White, Marty Brooks and Tony Sepe, 5m 30 secs
Track 6. Don't Take It Away From Me written by Barry White, 4m 25 secs
Track 7. What A Groove written by Barry White, 4m 0 secs
Track 8. Love's Theme written by Barry White, 4m 8 secs

Together Brothers Original Motion Picture (1974) 20th CENTURY RECORDS
Track 1. Somebody Is Gonna Off The Man written by Barry White, 4m 23 secs
Track 2. So Nice To Hear written by Barry White, 2m 37 secs
Track 3. Alive And Well written by Barry White, 1m 12 secs
Track 4. Find The Man Bros written by Barry White, 2m 16 secs
Track 5. You Gotta Case written by Barry White, 1m 25 secs
Track 6. Killer's Lullaby written by Barry White, 2m 22 secs
Track 7. Theme From Together Brothers written by Barry White, 2m 50 secs
Track 8. Getaway written by Barry White, 2m 5 secs
Track 9. People Of Tomorrow Are The Children Of Today written by Barry White, 2m 38 secs
Track 10. Somebody's Gonna Off The Man (Instrumental) written by Barry White, 4m 23 secs
Track 11. The Rip written by Barry White, 1m 41 secs
Track 12. Stick Up written by Barry White, 1m 57 secs
Track 13. Dreamin' written by Barry White, 0m 41 secs
Track 14. Killer's Back written by Barry White, 0m 24 secs
Track 15. Do Drop In written by Barry White, 2m 32 secs
Track 16. Killer Don't Do It written by Barry White, 1m 51 secs
Track 17. Here Comes The Man by Barry White, 1m 16secs
Track 18. Dream On written by Barry White, 1m 31 secs
Track 19. Honey, Please Can't Ya See written by Barry White, 2m 21 secs
Track 20. Can't Seem To Find Him written by Barry White and Gene Page, 4m 22 secs
Track 21. People Of Tomorrow Are The Children Of Today written by Barry White, 2m 38 secs

White Gold (1974) 20th CENTURY RECORDS
Track 1. Barry's Love (Part I) written by Barry White, 4m 59 secs
Track 2. Satin Soul written by Barry White, 4m 15 secs
Track 3. Always Thinking of You written by Ray Parker Jnr, 3m 11 secs
Track 4. Power of Love written by Barry White and Tom Brocker, 3m 56 secs
Track 5. Spanish Lei written by Gene and Billy Page, 4m 52 secs

Track 6. You Make Me Feel Like This written by Barry White, 4m 26 secs

Track 7. Only You Can Make Me Blue written by Barry White, 3m 19 secs

Track 8. Dreaming written by Barry White, 4m 35 secs

Track 9. Just Living It Up written by Barry White, 3m 37 secs

Track 10. Just Like a Baby written by Barry White, 3m 2 secs

Track 11. Barry's Love (Part II) written by Barry White, 4m 42 secs

Music Maestro Please (1975) 20th CENTURY RECORDS

Track 1. Bring It On Up written by White, Kastner and Sopuch, 4m 23 secs

Track 2. Makin' Believe That It's You written by Barry White and Emmett North Jnr, 3m 37 secs

Track 3. I Wanna Stay written by Barry White, 4m 38 secs

Track 4. Give Up Your Love Girl written by Barry White and Delacy White, 4m 10 secs

Track 5. You're All I Want written by Barry White, 4m 42 secs

Track 6. It's Only What I Feel written by Barry White and Vance Wilson, 3m 56 secs

Track 7. Midnight Groove written by Barry White and Willie Seastrunk, 5m 33 secs

Track 8. Forever In Love written by Barry White, 4m 12 secs

My Sweet Summer Suite (1976) 20th CENTURY RECORDS

Track 1. My Sweet Summer Suite written by Barry White, 5m 1 sec

Track 2. Strange Games & Things written by Barry White, 4m 10 secs

Track 3. Blues Concerto written by Barry White, 3m 42 secs

Track 4. You, I Adore written by Barry White and Tony Sepe, 4m 59 secs

Track 5. Brazilian Love Song written by Barry White, 6m 9 secs

Track 6. Are You Sure? written by Diane Taylor, Glodean James and Linda James, 4m 8 secs

Track 7. You've Given Me Something written by Barry White and Frank Wilson, 3m 26 secs

Track 8. I'm Falling In Love With You written by Barry White, 4m 18 secs

My Musical Bouquet (1978) 20th CENTURY RECORDS

Track 1. Don't You Know How Much I Love You written by Jon Mayer, 5m 21 secs

Track 2. Stay Please And Make Love To Me written by Barry White and Tony Sepe, 6m 59 secs

Track 3. Hey Look At Me, I'm In Love written by Barry White and Delacy White, 7m 28 secs

Track 4. Love You, Ooh It's True I Do written by Barry White and Erwin Brown, 4m 0 secs

Track 5. Whisper Softly written by Barry White and Vance Wilson, 7m 32 secs

Track 6. Enter Love's Interlude written by Barry White and Vance Wilson, 2m 20 secs

Track 7. Can't You See written by Barry White and Vance Wilson, 6m 59 secs

Super Movie Themes (1979) 20th CENTURY RECORDS

Track 1. Theme From Superman written by John Williams, 6m 1 sec

Track 2. Theme From King Kong written by John Barry, 6m 6 secs

Track 3. Night Fever written by Robin Gibb, Barry Gibb and Maurice Gibb, 5m 10 secs

Track 4. Grease written by Barry Gibb, 3m 13 secs

Track 5. Intermission written by Barry White, 2m 21 secs

Track 6. Theme From Shaft written by Isaac Hayes, 5m 47 secs
Track 7. Theme From A Summer Place written by Max Steiner, 4m 14 secs
Track 8. The Way We Were written by Marvin Hamlisch and Marilyn Bergman, 5m 9 secs
Track 9. As Time Goes By written by Herman Hupfield, 4m 35 secs
Track 10. People Of Tomorrow Are The Children Of Today written by White, 4m 31 secs

Let 'Em Dance (1981) UNLIMITED GOLD RECORDS
Track 1. Bayou written by Barry White, 5m 10 secs
Track 2. Jamaican Girl written by Barry White, 5m 32 secs
Track 3. I Wanna Boogie And Woogie With You written by Barry White, 6m 39 secs
Track 4. Vieni Qua Bella Mi written by Barry White and Tony Sepe, 4m 49 secs
Track 5. Freeway Flyer written by Barry White and Vance Wilson, 3m 23 secs
Track 6. I'm In The Mood written by Barry White and Vance Wilson, 4m 30 secs
Track 7. Young America written by White, Peake, Rosado and Tony Sepe, 5m 52 secs

Welcome Aboard (1981) UNLIMITED GOLD RECORDS
Track 1. Welcome Aboard written by Barry White, Jack Perry and Elwin Rutledge, 6m 27 secs
Track 2. Dreams written by Barry White and Webster Lewis, 4m 48 secs
Track 3. Night Life In The City written by Barry White and Carl Taylor, 4m 55 secs
Track 4. Lift Your Voice And Say written by White /Lewis, 4m 31 secs
Track 5. Welcome Aboard Reprise written by White, Perry and Rutledge, 0m 42 secs
Track 6. Easin' written by Barry White and Nathan East, 5m 3 secs
Track 7. Antigua Blue written by Barry White and Rudy Clark, 4m 39 secs
Track 8. Wind written by Jimmy Cameron, 4m 7secs
Track 9. Strange written by Barry White and Darnell White, 4m 14 secs
Track 10. My Fantasies written by Barry White and Darnell White, 4m 0 secs

Rise (1983) UNLIMITED GOLD RECORDS
Track 1. Take A Good Look written by Barry White, Carl Taylor and John Lopez, 6m 27 secs
Track 2. My Laboratory written by Barry White, Jack Perry and Vella Cameron, 6m 18 secs
Track 3. After Five written by Barry White and Bert Carter, 7m 32 secs
Track 4. Do It To The Music . . . Please written by White, Perry and Cameron, 5m 44 secs
Track 5. In Brazil written by Barry White and Jack Perry, 5m 34 secs
Track 6. Anna Lisa written by Barry White and Al McKay, 4m 58 secs
Track 7. Goodbye Concerto written by White, Testa and DeVita, 4m 4 secs

BARRY WHITE PRODUCED THIRD PARTY ALBUMS

The Kindred Soul of Danny Wagner (1968) – Danny Wagner IMPERIAL RECORDS
Track 1. Harlem Shuffle written by Earl Nelson and Bobby Relf, 3m 12 secs
Track 2. Unchained Melody written by Alex North, 4m 0 secs
Track 3. Out Of the Shadows of Love written by Barry White, 3m 2 secs
Track 4. My Buddy written by Gus Kahn and Walter Donaldson, 2m 20 secs
Track 5. Little Children written by James Ford, 2m 26 secs
Track 6. When Johnny Comes Marching Home written by William Davenport, 2m 36 secs
Track 7. Big Boy Pete written by Don Harris and Dewey Terry Jnr, 2m 45 secs
Track 8. Bring It On Home To Me written by Sam Cooke, 3m 05 secs
Track 9. This Thing Called Love written by Barry White and Rene Goree, 2m 25 secs
Track 10. I Lost A True Love written by Barry White and Frank and Vance Wilson, 2m 8 secs
Track 11. Claudia written by Ron Holden, 2m 15 secs
Track 12. Sonny Boy written by Al Jolson, 2m 58 secs

What Am I Gonna Do (1974) – Gloria Scott CASABLANCA RECORDS
Track 1. What Am I Gonna Do? written by Thomas Anderson and Vance Wilson 3m 41 secs
Track 2. It's Better To Have No Love written by Tom Brock, 3m 16 secs
Track 3. I Think Of You written by Tom Brock, 4m 40 secs
Track 4. Love Me … or Leave Me… written by Lunie McLeod, Tom Brock, 4m 19 secs
Track 5. I Just Couldn't Take A Goodbye written by Tom Brock, 4m 31 secs
Track 6. That's What You Say written by Anderson & Wilson 3m 18 secs
Track 7. (A Case Of) Too Much Lovemakin' written by Tom Brock, 3m 51 secs
Track 8. Help Me Get Off This Merry-Go-Round written by Relf, Scott & Brock, 3m 45 secs

I Love You More and More (1974) – Tom Brock   20th CENTURY RECORDS
Track 1. Have a Nice Weekend Baby written by Barry White and Tom Brock, 4m 30 secs
Track 2. The Love We Share Is the Greatest Of Them All written by Tom Brock, 3m 57 secs
Track 3. There's Nothing In This World That Can Stop Me From Loving You written by Brock/Relf, 4m 52 secs
Track 4. I Love You More and More written by Tom Brock and Robert Relf, 4m 5 secs
Track 5. Naked As The Day I Was Born written by Gene and Billy Page, 4m 30 secs
Track 6.That's The Reason Why written by Brock and McLeod, 3m 55 secs
Track 7. Shake Me, Wake Me written by Tom Brock and Robert Relf, 2m 23 secs
Track 8. If We Don't Make It, Nobody Can written by White, Brock and Relf, 4m 10 secs

Hot City (1974) – Gene Page ATLANTIC RECORDS
Track 1. All Our Dreams Are Coming True written by Gene Page, 4m 0 secs
Track 2. Jungle Eyes written by Gene Page and Billy Page, 4m 50 secs
Track 3. She's My Main Squeeze written by Gene Page and Billy Page, 3m 58 secs

Track 4. Gene's Theme written by Barry White, 3m 28 secs

Track 5. I'm Living In A World Of Gloom written by White, Harrell & Denny, 3m 33 secs

Track 6. Don't Play That Song written by Barry White, 4m 25 secs

Track 7. Satin Soul written by Barry White, 4m 23 secs

Track 8. Cream Corner (Get What You Want) written by Page and Page, 3m 44 secs

Track 9. To The Bone written by Gene Page and Billy Page, 4m 36 secs

Come On In Love (1974) – Jay Dee (Earl Nelson) WARNER BROS RECORDS

Track 1. Jay's Theme written by Barry White, 2m 30 secs

Track 2. Strange Funky Games and Things written by Barry White, 6m 51 secs

Track 3. You've Changed written by Bill Carey and Carl Fischer, 5m 34 secs

Track 4. I Can Feel Your Love Slipping Away written by Anderson and Wilson, 4m 0 secs

Track 5. Come On In Love written by Barry White, 4m 46 secs

Track 6. I Can't Let You Go written by Tom Brock, 3m 45 secs

Track 7. Your Sweetness Is My Weakness written by Barry White, 3m 29 secs

Track 8. Thinking of You written by Barry White, 2m 35 secs

Track 9. You're All I Need written by Barry White and Jay Dee (Earl Nelson), 3m 10 secs

West Wing (1975) – West Wing 20th CENTURY RECORDS

Track 1. I Got A Love For You written by Coleman/Anderson/Wilson, 3m 34 secs

Track 2. Have A Nice Weekend Baby written by Barry White and Tom Brock, 3m 40 secs

Track 3. She Loves Me written by Coleman/Anderson/Wilson, 4m 5 secs

Track 4. Gave Your Love...To Me written by Coleman/Anderson/Wilson, 3m 17 secs

Track 5. We Got A Perfect Love Together written by Coleman, Anderson and Wilson, 4m 7 secs

Track 6. I'm Gonna Love You Just A Little More Baby written by Barry White, 4m 53 secs

Track 7. Look On The Brighter Side Of Love written by Denny, Anderson & Wilson, 3m 59 secs

Track 8. Wanna Thank You, Love written by Coleman, Anderson and Wilson, 2m 40 secs

Barry White Presents Mr Danny Pearson (1978) – Danny Pearson UNLIMITED GOLD RECORDS

Track 1. What's Your Sign Girl? written by Danny Pearson and Tony Sepe, 4m 29 secs

Track 2. Is It Really True Girl written by Barry White, 5m 56 secs

Track 3. Walking In The Rain With The One I Love written by Barry White, 6m 39 secs

Track 4. Let's Go Dancin' (Let's Go Disco Dancin') written by White and Pearson, 3m 22 secs

Track 5. Honey Please, Can't You See written by Barry White, 7m 12 secs

Track 6. Say It Again written by Barry White, 3m 45 secs

Track 7. I'm So Glad I've Got You Baby written by Pearson, Robertson & Sepe 4m 59 secs

Track 8. There's No One For Me But You written by Pearson and Sepe, 5m 19 secs

Song Painters (1981) – Jimmie and Vella Cameron UNLIMITED GOLD RECORDS

Track 1. Here Is Where You Belong written by Vella Cameron, 4m 56 secs

Track 2. Be Fair To Me written by Jimmie and Vella Cameron, 5m 18 secs

Track 3. You're Gonna Need My Love Someday written by Jimmie Cameron, 5m 15 secs

APPENDICES

Track 4. We Share the Meaning of Love written by Daniel Mineya, J & V Cameron, 5m 23 secs
Track 5. Mornin' Time written by Vella Cameron, 5m 13 secs
Track 6. I've Got To Live For Myself written by Jimmie and Vella Cameron
Track 7. Someone Loves You written by Jimmie and Vella Cameron
Track 8. There's No Other Love written by Jimmie and Vella Cameron

BARRY WHITE'S SOLO SINGLES

1966
Man Ain't Nothing (1966) as Lee Barry DOWNEY RECORDS
US Charts Unranked UK Charts Unranked

1967
All In the Run of a Day (1967) BRONCO RECORDS
US Charts Unranked UK Charts Unranked

1970
Little Girl (1967) as Gene West ORIGINAL SOUND RECORDS
US Charts Unranked UK Charts Unranked

1973
I'm Gonna Love You Just a Little More Baby (1973) 20th CENTURY RECORDS
US Charts No 3 UK Charts No 23
I've Got So Much to Give (1973) 20th CENTURY RECORDS
US Charts No 32 UK Charts Unranked
Never, Never Gonna Give Ya Up (1973) 20th CENTURY RECORDS
US Charts No 7 UK Charts No 14

1974
Honey Please, Can't Ya See (1974) 20th CENTURY RECORDS
US Charts No 44 UK Charts Unranked
Can't Get Enough of Your Love, Babe (1974) 20th CENTURY RECORDS
US Charts No 1 UK Charts No 8
You're the First, the Last, My Everything (1974) 20th CENTURY RECORDS
US Charts No 2 UK Charts No 1

1975
What Am I Gonna Do with You (1975) 20th CENTURY RECORDS
US Charts No 8 UK Charts No 5
I'll Do for You Anything You Want Me To (1975) 20th CENTURY RECORDS
US Charts No 40 UK Charts No 20
Let the Music Play (1975) 20th CENTURY RECORDS
US Charts No 32 UK Charts No 9

1976
You See the Trouble with Me (1976) 20th CENTURY RECORDS
US Charts Unranked UK Charts No 2

Baby, We Better Try to Get It Together (1976) 20th CENTURY RECORDS
US Charts No 92 UK Charts No 15
Don't Make Me Wait Too Long (1976) 20th CENTURY RECORDS
US Charts No 105 UK Charts No 17

1977

I'm Qualified to Satisfy You (1977) 20th CENTURY RECORDS
US Charts Unranked UK Charts No 37
It's Ecstasy When You Lay Down Next to Me (1977) 20th CENTURY RECORDS
US Charts No 4 UK Charts No 40
Playing Your Game, Baby (1977) 20th CENTURY RECORDS
US Charts No 101 UK Charts Unranked

1978

Oh What a Night for Dancing (1978) 20th CENTURY RECORDS
US Charts No 24 UK Charts Unranked
Your Sweetness Is My Weakness (1978) 20th CENTURY RECORDS
US Charts No 60 UK Charts Unranked
Just the Way You Are (1978) 20th CENTURY RECORDS
US Charts No 102 UK Charts No 12

1979

Sha La La Means I Love You (1979) 20th CENTURY RECORDS
US Charts Unranked UK Charts No 55
I Love to Sing the Songs I Sing (1979) 20th CENTURY RECORDS
US Charts Unranked UK Charts Unranked
How Did You Know It Was Me (1979) 20th CENTURY RECORDS
US Charts Unranked UK Charts Unranked
Any Fool Can See (You Were Meant for Me) (1979) UNLIMITED GOLD RECORDS (CBS)
US Charts Unranked UK Charts Unranked
It Ain't Love, Babe (Until You Give It) (1979) UNLIMITED GOLD RECORDS (CBS)
US Charts Unranked UK Charts Unranked

1980

Love Ain't Easy (1980) UNLIMITED GOLD RECORDS (CBS)
US Charts Unranked UK Charts Unranked
Sheet Music (1980) UNLIMITED GOLD RECORDS (CBS)
US Charts Unranked UK Charts Unranked
Love Makin' Music (1980) UNLIMITED GOLD RECORDS (CBS)
US Charts Unranked UK Charts Unranked
I Believe in Love (1980) UNLIMITED GOLD RECORDS (CBS)
US Charts Unranked UK Charts Unranked

1981

Didn't We Make It Happen, Baby (1981) UNLIMITED GOLD RECORDS (CBS)
US Charts Unranked UK Charts Unranked
I Want You (1981) UNLIMITED GOLD RECORDS (CBS)
US Charts Unranked UK Charts Unranked
You're the Only One for Me (1981) UNLIMITED GOLD RECORDS (CBS)
US Charts Unranked UK Charts Unranked
Louie Louie (1981) UNLIMITED GOLD RECORDS (CBS)
US Charts Unranked UK Charts Unranked
Beware (1981) UNLIMITED GOLD RECORDS (CBS)
US Charts Unranked UK Charts Unranked

1982

Change (1982) UNLIMITED GOLD RECORDS (CBS)
US Charts Unranked UK Charts Unranked
Passion (1982) UNLIMITED GOLD RECORDS (CBS)
US Charts Unranked UK Charts Unranked

1983

America (1983) UNLIMITED GOLD RECORDS (CBS)
US Charts Unranked UK Charts Unranked

1984

Don't Let Them Blow Your Mind (1984) UNLIMITED GOLD RECORDS (CBS)
US Charts Unranked UK Charts Unranked

1987

Sho' You Right (1987) A & M RECORDS
US Charts Unranked UK Charts No 14
For Your Love (I'll Do Most Anything) (1987) UNLIMITED GOLD RECORDS (CBS)
US Charts Unranked UK Charts No 94

1989

Super Lover (1989) A & M RECORDS
US Charts Unranked UK Charts Unranked
Follow That and See (Where It Leads Y'All) (1989) A & M RECORDS
US Charts Unranked UK Charts Unranked

1990

I Wanna Do It Good to Ya (1990) A & M RECORDS
US Charts Unranked UK Charts Unranked

When Will I See You Again (1990) A & M RECORDS
US Charts Unranked UK Charts Unranked

1991
Put Me in Your Mix (1991) A & M RECORDS
US Charts Unranked UK Charts Unranked

1992
Dark and Lovely (You Over There) with Isaac Hayes (1992) A & M RECORDS
US Charts Unranked UK Charts Unranked

1994
Practice What You Preach (1994) A & M RECORDS
US Charts No 18 UK Charts No 20

1995
Love Is the Icon (1995) A & M RECORDS
US Charts Unranked UK Charts No 20
Come On (1995) A & M RECORDS
US Charts No 87 UK Charts Unranked
I Only Want to Be with You (1995) A & M RECORDS
US Charts Unranked UK Charts No 36
There It Is (1995) A & M RECORDS
US Charts Unranked UK Charts Unranked

1999
Staying Power (1999) PRIVATE MUSIC (BMG)
US Charts Unranked UK Charts Unranked
The Longer We Make Love (1999) PRIVATE MUSIC (BMG)
US Charts Unranked UK Charts Unranked

APPENDIX IX

LOVE UNLIMITED GROUP SINGLES

1972

Walking in the Rain with the One I Love (1972) UNI RECORDS
US Charts No 14 UK Charts No 14
Is It Really True Boy - Is It Really Me (1972) UNI RECORDS
US Charts No 101 UK Charts Unranked
Are You Sure (1972) UNI RECORDS
US Charts Unranked UK Charts Unranked

1973

Fragile - Handle with Care (1973) 20th CENTURY RECORDS
US Charts Unranked UK Charts Unranked
Oh Love, Well We Finally Made It (1973) 20th CENTURY RECORDS
US Charts Unranked UK Charts Unranked
Yes, We Finally Made It (1973) 20th CENTURY RECORDS
US Charts No 101 UK Charts Unranked
It May Be Winter Outside (But in My Heart It's Spring) (1973) 20th CENTURY RECORDS
US Charts No 83 UK Charts No 11

1974

Under the Influence of Love (1974) 20th CENTURY RECORDS
US Charts No 76 UK Charts Unranked
People of Tomorrow Are the Children of Today (1974) 20th CENTURY RECORDS
US Charts Unranked UK Charts Unranked
I Belong to You (1974) 20th CENTURY RECORDS
US Charts No 27 UK Charts Unranked

1975

Share a Little Love in Your Heart (1975) 20th CENTURY RECORDS
US Charts Unranked UK Charts Unranked

1977

I Did It for Love (1977) UNLIMITED GOLD RECORDS
US Charts Unranked UK Charts Unranked

1979

High Steppin', Hip Dressin' Fella (You Got It Together) (1979) UNLIMITED GOLD RECORDS
US Charts Unranked UK Charts Unranked

1980

I'm So Glad That I'm a Woman (1980) UNLIMITED GOLD RECORDS
US Charts Unranked UK Charts Unranked
If You Want Me, Say It (1980) UNLIMITED GOLD RECORDS
US Charts Unranked UK Charts Unranked

LOVE UNLIMITED ORCHESTRA SINGLES

1973
Love's Theme (1973) 20th CENTURY RECORDS
US Charts No 1 UK Charts No 10

1974
Rhapsody in White (1974) 20th CENTURY RECORDS
US Charts No 63 UK Charts Unranked
Theme from Together Brothers (1974) 20th CENTURY RECORDS
US Charts Unranked UK Charts Unranked
Baby Blues (1974) 20th CENTURY RECORDS
US Charts No 102 UK Charts Unranked

1975
Satin Soul (1975) 20th CENTURY RECORDS
US Charts No 22 UK Charts Unranked
Forever in Love (1975) 20th CENTURY RECORDS
US Charts Unranked UK Charts Unranked
Midnight Groove (1975) 20th CENTURY RECORDS
US Charts No 108 UK Charts Unranked

1976
My Sweet Summer Suite (1976) 20th CENTURY RECORDS
US Charts No 48 UK Charts Unranked
Brazilian Love Song (1976) 20th CENTURY RECORDS
US Charts Unranked UK Charts Unranked

1977
Theme from King Kong (Part 1) (1977) 20th CENTURY RECORDS
US Charts No 68 UK Charts Unranked

1978
Hey Look at Me, I'm in Love (1978) 20th CENTURY RECORDS
US Charts Unranked UK Charts Unranked

1979
Theme from Shaft (1979) 20th CENTURY RECORDS
US Charts Unranked UK Charts Unranked

1980
Young America (1980) UNLIMITED GOLD RECORDS (CBS)
US Charts Unranked UK Charts Unranked
I Wanna Boogie and Woogie with You (1980) UNLIMITED GOLD RECORDS (CBS)
US Charts Unranked UK Charts Unranked

1981

Vieni Qua Bella Mi (1981) UNLIMITED GOLD RECORDS (CBS)
US Charts Unranked UK Charts Unranked
Lift Your Voice and Say (United We Can Live in Peace Today) (1981) UNLIMITED GOLD RECORDS (CBS)
US Charts Unranked UK Charts No 76
Welcome Aboard (1981) UNLIMITED GOLD RECORDS (CBS)
US Charts Unranked UK Charts Unranked

1982

Night Life in the City (1982) UNLIMITED GOLD RECORDS (CBS)
US Charts Unranked UK Charts Unranked

1983

Do It to the Music... Please (1983) UNLIMITED GOLD RECORDS (CBS)
US Charts Unranked UK Charts Unranked
My Laboratory (Is Ready for You) (1983) UNLIMITED GOLD RECORDS (CBS)
US Charts Unranked UK Charts Unranked

BARRY WHITE PRODUCED THIRD PARTY SINGLES

1966
I Got Love performed by Viola Wills BRONCO RECORDS
US Charts Unranked UK Charts Unranked

1967
Don't Kiss Me Hello And Mean Goodbye performed by Viola Wills MUSTANG BRONCO RECORDS
US Charts Unranked UK Charts Unranked
I've Got To Have All Of You performed by Viola Wills MUSTANG BRONCO RECORDS
US Charts Unranked UK Charts Unranked
This Thing Called Love performed by Johnny Wyatt MUSTANG BRONCO RECORDS
US Charts Unranked UK Charts Unranked
I Feel Love Comin' On performed by Felice Taylor MUSTANG BRONCO/PRESIDENT RECORDS
US Charts Unranked UK Charts Unranked
I'm Under The Influence Of Love performed by Felice Taylor MUSTANG BRONCO/PRESIDENT RECORDS
US Charts Unranked UK Charts Unranked
It May Be Winter Outside performed by Felice Taylor MUSTANG BRONCO RECORDS
US Charts Unranked UK Charts Unranked

1970
Your Sweetness is my Weakness performed by Jackie Lee aka Earl Nelson UNI RECORDS
US Charts Unranked UK Charts Unranked

1971
Oh Love (Well We Finally Made It) performed by Smoke (Andrews/Nelson) MO SOUL PRODS
US Charts Unranked UK Charts Unranked

1974
What Am I Gonna Do performed by Gloria Scott CASABLANCA RECORDS
US Charts Unranked UK Charts Unranked
Help Me Get Off This Merry-Go-Round performed by Gloria Scott CASABLANCA RECORDS
US Charts Unranked UK Charts Unranked
Just As Long As We're Together performed by Gloria Scott CASABLANCA RECORDS
US Charts Unranked UK Charts Unranked
If We Don't Make It Nobody Can performed by Tom Brock 20th CENTURY RECORDS
US Charts Unranked UK Charts Unranked
I Love You More and More performed by Tom Brock 20th CENTURY RECORDS
US Charts Unranked UK Charts Unranked

1978
Honey Please Can't You See performed by Danny Pearson UNLIMITED GOLD RECORDS (CBS)
US Charts Unranked UK Charts Unranked
What's Your Sign Girl? performed by Danny Pearson UNLIMITED GOLD RECORDS (CBS)
US Charts Unranked UK Charts Unranked

1980
Be Fair To Me performed by Jimmie and Vella Cameron UNLIMITED GOLD RECORDS (CBS)
US Charts Unranked UK Charts Unranked

1981
Night Life in the City performed by Webster Lewis UNLIMITED GOLD RECORDS (CBS)
US Charts Unranked UK Charts Unranked

APPENDIX XII

PRINCIPAL BIBLIOGRAPHY

The Oracle of Del-Fi – My Life in Music by Bob Keane
ISBN: 0976 8105 1 4 Published by Del-Fi International Books in 2006

Insights on Life and Love – Love Unlimited by Barry White and Marc Eliot
ISBN: 0 7679 0364 1 Published by Broadway Books in 1999

The Soundtrack of My Life by Clive Davis and Anthony DeCurtis
ISBN: 978-1 4767 1478 3 Published by Simon & Schuster in 2013

Howling at the Moon by Walter Yetnikoff and David Ritz
ISBN: 978 0767915366 Published by Broadway Books in 2004

Clive: Inside the Record Business by Clive Davis and James Willwerth
ISBN: 978 06 8802 8725 Published by William Morrow in 1975

Anyone Who Had a Heart: My Life and Music by Burt Bacharach &
Robert Greenfield
ISBN: 978 0857 898 0 12 Published by Allen & Unwin in 2013

Michael Jackson: The Magic and the Madness by J. Randy Taraborrelli
ISBN: 978 0283073793 Published by Sidgwick & Jackson in 2003

You Are Not Alone: Michael, Through a Brother's Eyes by Jermaine Jackson
ISBN: 978 0007435661 Published by HarperCollins in 2011

Michael Jackson: Life of a Legend by Michael Heatley
ISBN: 978 0755360536 Published by Headline in 2009

Moonwalk by Michael Jackson
ISBN: 978 0434020270 Published by William Heinemann in 2009

Shout! The Beatles in Their Generation by Philip Norman
ISBN: 978 1567310870 Published by MJF Books in 1981

Paul McCartney: The Biography by Philip Norman
ISBN: 978 0297870753 Published by Weidenfeld & Nicholson in 2016

Going Platinum: How Neil Bogart Built Casablanca Records by
Brett Ermilio and Josh Levine
ISBN: 978 07 627 9133 0 Published by Lyons Press in 2014

John Barry: The Man with the Midas Touch by John Barry
ISBN: 9781904537779 Published by Redcliffe Press in 2008

John Barry: A Life in Music by Geoff Leonard
ISBN: 978-1900178860 Published by Sansom & Co in 1998

John Barry: A Sixties Theme by Eddi Fiegel
ISBN: 978 0094785304 Published by Faber & Faber in 2012

In All His Glory: The Life of William S. Paley by Sally Bedell Smith
ISBN: 978 0671617356 Published by Simon & Schuster in 1990

Call Her Miss Ross: The Unauthorized Biography by J. Randy Taraborrelli
ISBN: 978 1559720069 Published by Birch Lane in 1989

I Heard It Through The Grapevine - Marvin Gaye by Sharon Davis
ISBN: 978 1851583171 Published by Mainstream Books in 1991

To be Loved: Music, the Magic, the Memories of Motown by Berry Gordy
ISBN: 978 0747214175 Published by Warner Books in 1994

Profiles of Black Success: Thirteen Creative Geniuses by Gene N. Landrum
ISBN: 978 1573921190 Published by Prometheus Books in 1997

After the Dance: My Life with Marvin Gaye by Jan Gaye and David Ritz
ISBN: 978 0062135513 Published by HarperCollins in 2015

Motown - Artist by Artist by Pat Morgan
ISBN: 978 1782812357 Published by G2 Entertainment in 2015

The Rise and Rise of David Geffen by Stephen Singular
ISBN: 978 1559724302 Published by Birch Lane Press in 1997

The Operator: David Geffen by Tom King
ISBN: 978 0679457541 Published by Random House in 2000

BILBLIOGRAPHY

The Colonel: The Story of Colonel Tom Parker and Elvis Presley by Alanna Nash
ISBN: 978 1845130251 Published by Aurum Press Ltd in 2004

Rock Gold: The Music Millionaires by George Tremlett
ISBN: 978 0044405481 Published by Unwin Hyman in 1990

Elton by Philip Norman
ISBN: 978 0091748388 Published by Hutchinson in 1991

Billy Joel: The Life and Times of an Angry Young Man by Hank Bordowitz
ISBN: 978 0823082506 Published by Billboard Books in 2005

Q - The Autobiography of Quincy Jones by Quincy Jones,
ISBN: 978 0385488969 Published by Doubleday in 2001

Linda Goodman's Love Signs by Linda Goodman
ISBN: 0 333 26693 5 Published by Harper & Row in 1978

Rockonomics by Marc Eliot
ISBN: 0 7119 1989 5 Published by Franklin Watts in 1989

Hit Men Power Brokers and Fast Money Inside the Music Business by Frederic Dannen
ISBN: 978 0812916584 Published by Times Books in 1990

Divided Soul – The Life of Marvin Gaye by David Ritz
ISBN: 978 0070529298 Published by McGraw Hill in 1985

Barry White Unlimited by Jack Perry and Harry Weinger
Barcode No: 0252717804 Published by Universal Music Enterprises in 2009

INDEX

INDEX

The Author's Favourite White Music

Favourite Instrumentals

1. **Antigua Blue - Webster Lewis**
From the album Welcome Aboard by the Love Unlimited Orchestra, 1981 - Track 7
2. **Can't You See**
From the album My Musical Bouquet by the Love Unlimited Orchestra, 1978 - Track 7
3. **I Feel Love Coming On**
From the album Rhapsody in White by the Love Unlimited Orchestra, 1974 - Track 4
4. **Don't Take It Away From Me**
From the album Rhapsody in White by the Love Unlimited Orchestra, 1974 - Track 6
5. **Easin' - Webster Lewis**
From the album Welcome Aboard by the Love Unlimited Orchestra, 1981 - Track 6
6. **Baby Blues**
From the album Rhapsody in White by the Love Unlimited Orchestra, 1974 - Track 5
7. **After Five**
From the album Rise by the Love Unlimited Orchestra, 1983 - Track 3
8. **My Sweet Summer Suite**
From the album My Sweet Summer Suite by the Love Unlimited Orchestra, 1976 - Track 1
9. **Goodbye Concerto**
From the album Rise by the Love Unlimited Orchestra, 1983 – Track 7
10. **Whisper Softly**
From the album My Musical Bouquet by the Love Unlimited Orchestra, 1978 - Track 5

Favourite Ballads

1. **Girl It's True Yes I'll Always Love You**
From the album Stone Gon' by Barry White, 1973 – Track 1
2. **Whatever We Had We Had**
From the album The Icon is Love by Barry White, 1994 – Track 10
3. **Bring Back My Yesterday**
From the album I've Got So Much to Give by Barry White, 1973 – Track 2
4. **Standing In The Shadows of Love**
From the album I've Got So Much to Give, 1973 – Track 1
5. **I Can't Believe You Love Me**
From the album Can't Get Enough by Barry White, 1974 – Track 3
6. **Love Will Find Us**
From the album Put Me In Your Mix by Barry White, 1991 – Track 8
7. **Let Me Live My Life Loving You**
From the album Just Another Way To Say I Love You by Barry White, 1975 – Track 6
8. **I'm So Blue You Are Too**
From the album Let The Music Play by Barry White, 1976 – Track 3
9. **You Turned My Whole World Around**
From the album Barry White Sings For Someone You Love by Barry White, 1977 – Track 5
10. **Of All The Guys In The World**
From the album Barry White Sings For Someone You Love by Barry White, 1977 – Track 7

Favourite Pop Songs

1. **Just The Way You Are**
From the album The Man by Barry White, 1978 – Track 6
2. **You're the First, The Last, My Everything**
From the album Can't Get Enough by Barry White, 1974 – Track 1
3. **I Love to Sing the Songs I Sing**
From the album I Love To Sing the Songs I Sing by Barry White, 1979 – Track 1
4. **Sha La La Means I Love You**
From the album The Man by Barry White, 1978 – Track 3
5. **I'll Do Anything You Want Me To**
From the album Just Another Way To Say I Love You by Barry White, 1975 – Track 2
6. **Never Thought I'd Fall In Love With You**
From the album Barry White Sings For Someone You Love by Barry White, 1977 – Track 4
7. **Early Years**
From the album The Man by Barry White, 1978 – Track 7
8. **September When I First Met You**
From the album, The Man, 1978 – Track 4
9. **How Did You Know It Was Me?**
From the album I Love To Sing The Songs I Sing, 1979 – Track 7
10. **Baby We Better Try To Get It Together**
From the album Let The Music Play by Barry White, 1976 – Track 4